WITHDRAWN

THE BIRTH OF THE TALKIES

THE BIRTH OF
THE TALKIES

FROM

EDISON

TO

JOLSON

HARRY M. GEDULD

 INDIANA UNIVERSITY PRESS

Bloomington · London

Published in Canada by Fitzhenry & Whiteside Limited, Don Mills, Ontario
Manufactured in the United States of America

Library of Congress Cataloging in Publication Data

Geduld, Harry M
   The birth of the talkies.

   Includes bibliographical references and index.
   1. Moving-pictures, Talking—History. I. Title.
PN1995.7.G36   1975   791.43'0973   74-11887
ISBN 0-253-10743-1   75 76 77 78 79 1 2 3 4 5

For MARCUS—

who asks all the best questions

and most of the right ones—

with all my love.

The talking motion picture will not supplant the regular silent
motion picture.
THOMAS ALVA EDISON, 1913

 I have just been, for the first time, to see and hear a picture talk. . . .
I saw and heard . . . the latest and most frightful creation-saving
device for the production of standardized amusement. . . .
ALDOUS HUXLEY, 1929

 Wait a minute.
Wait a minute.
You ain't heard nothin' yet!
AL JOLSON, 1927

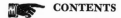

CONTENTS

In many countries 1976–77 will doubtless be celebrated as the fiftieth anniversary of the talkies. Two Warner Bros. feature films, *Don Juan* (1926) and *The Jazz Singer* (1927), led Hollywood and the rest of the world into the sound era, but they were not—as is widely assumed—the first sound movies.

Curiously, although few if any events have had greater impact on the history of film than the coming of the talkies, film historians have paid relatively little attention to how and why the transition from silent to sound cinema came about. It is hoped that the present work will provide the factual groundwork for repairing that neglect. Its emphasis is on the history of American contributions to the evolution of the sound film, but significant foreign achievements have not been overlooked. The book surveys the events that led from the invention of the phonograph in 1877 to that momentous evening in 1927 when an audience at the Warner's Theatre in New York City saw and heard Al Jolson speak from the screen. It also considers the effects of the sound revolution on Hollywood and Hollywood film production during the transitional years 1928–29.

The published sources on which this study was based have all been indicated in the notes, and the reader is advised to consult that original material whenever he requires additional technical or factual information.

It must be emphasized that the present book is not and was not intended to be an analytic study of the films of the transitional period. But, hopefully, it will inspire the preparation of such a work—a project that is both necessary and long overdue.

H. M. G.

Bloomington, Indiana
June 1974

ACKNOWLEDGMENTS

Thanks are due, first and foremost, to Carolyn for her patience, encouragement, and unfailing assistance during a most trying time (involving, among other things, two moves and an oppressively heavy teaching load) while this book was being completed.

A midwestern university library without any special resources for film study was not an ideal place to undertake research into the history of sound movies; therefore I am particularly grateful to Jim Fuhr, Sam Kula, Douglas Moore, and Emily Schenkman for helping me locate or obtain specific source materials.

My indebtedness to several admirable works of scholarship, especially the American Film Institute's catalog of feature films of 1921–30 (1971), James L. Limbacher's *Four Aspects of the Film* (1968), and Raymond Fielding's *A Technological History of Motion Pictures and Television* (1967), will be abundantly obvious. I was also assisted on many occasions by the *New York Times Film Reviews 1913–1931*. Acknowledgments to other specific publications will be found in the notes.

Special thanks are due to Mary Peatman for her assistance in preparing the index.

☞ **THE BIRTH
OF THE TALKIES**

THE INVENTION

OF THE

PHONOGRAPH

The music goes round and round
OO–OO–OO–OO–OO–OO
And it comes out here.
Popular song

Kraahraak! Hellohellohello amawfullyglad kraark
awfullygladaseeragain hellohello amarawf kopthsth. . . .
JAMES JOYCE, *Ulysses*

The story of the marriage of sound and film begins before
cinema—with the invention of the phonograph. Though its
original purposes were in no way associated with cinema, the
talking machine, either Edison's or some variation on it, was to
be used in most of the early attempts to provide sound accompaniments to motion pictures.

As we shall see, the phonograph, invented in 1877, was a by-
product of research directed elsewhere, and its inventor was slow
at first to envisage and develop its application to film. Thereafter, from the 1890s to the 1920s, the history of attempts to link
the phonograph and film is checkered with failures, half-failures,
and abortive successes. Ironically, the combination was to be
perfected and exploited with great commercial success on the

3

very eve of its eclipse by the now virtually standard system of using sound-on-film.

Edison's Tinfoil Phonograph or Speaking Machine received U.S. patent no.200,521, dated December 15, 1877. The U.S. Patent Office could trace no prior claims to any similar inventions, and to this day it is popularly assumed that the talking machine was invented by Edison. However, the priority of Edison's invention was, in fact, challenged in the nineteenth century by the dubious claims of other inventors, notably Léon-Scott, Cros, Koenig, Napoli, and Deprez.*

In 1857, Edouard Léon-Scott, a French amateur scientist, invented a device which he called the Phonautograph. It was capable of making recordings of sound waves but could not play them back. It was, as one historian of the phonograph describes it, "halfway towards a talking machine."[1] The Count du Moncel, a contemporary of Edison and Léon-Scott, commenting on Léon-Scott's charge that Edison's phonograph was a plagiarism of the Phonautograph, noted that Edison's instrument "not only registers the different vibrations produced by speech on a vibrating plate, but reproduces the same words in correspondence with the traces registered." Léon-Scott's machine had certainly anticipated the first function of the phonograph, but, du Moncel noted, "the second function of the Edison instrument was not realized nor even mentioned by Mr. Scott, and we are surprised that this able inventor should have regarded Mr. Edison's invention as an injurious act of spoliation."[2]

In 1863 the German scientist Karl Rudolf Koenig completed an improved version of the Léon-Scott Phonautograph by providing it with a parabolic-shaped horn, thereby extending the ability of the machine to collect and make graphic records of all kinds of sounds. But Koenig, like Léon-Scott before him, did not provide the Phonautograph with any means of playing back the sounds it recorded. The machine was of value only in the laboratory, where it was used by scientists for analyzing sound waves. Nevertheless, as John Cain points out in his book, *Talk-*

* In his *Histoire Comique des Etats et Empires de la Lune* (1656), Savinien Cyrano de Bergerac envisaged a phonograph-like apparatus more than two centuries before it was actually invented. Apparently there were no attempts to construct such a machine until the nineteenth century.

ing Machines, "with the exception of a playing-back diaphragm . . . it [the Phonautograph] incorporated most of the essential features of the Phonograph, namely, a horn or trumpet for concentrating the sound, a diaphragm, a needle, and a revolving cylinder which moved along its axis."[3] In the 1870s, before the invention of the phonograph, a model of the Phonautograph was on exhibition at the Smithsonian Institution in Washington, D.C., where Edison might have seen it. But there is no evidence that he actually did see it or that he was directly influenced by the work of Léon-Scott and Koenig.

A more significant claim to priority of invention was that of the French poet and amateur scientist and inventor, Charles Cros (1842–1888). In 1860, when he was eighteen, Cros envisaged a machine which would record and reproduce the sounds of spoken conversation so that they would be visible and *readable* by deaf-mutes. Nothing came of this idea at the time, although, as we shall see later in this chapter, Cros seems to have anticipated Georges Demeny's Phonoscope of 1891–92. On April 18, 1877, Cros, who was too impecunious to afford a patent, deposited at the Académie des Sciences in Paris a sealed envelope containing a two-page document, dated April 16, 1877, and titled "Procédé d'Enregistrement et de Reproduction des Phénomènes Perçus par l'Ouie." This document, written at least three months before Edison began working on his phonograph, describes the principles of a machine that Cros later called the Paléophone.[4]

As an *idea* the Paléophone was a remarkable anticipation of Edison's machine, but Cros never found the business interests necessary to promote his "invention" nor even the means to build a working model of it. John Cain and others have doubted whether the Paléophone would have worked even if Cros had been able to make it. However, the prior claim of Cros to have invented a talking machine was upheld as early as October 10, 1877 in an article published in *La Semaine du Clergé.* Cros himself, hearing of Edison's work on the phonograph, requested that his sealed document be opened and its contents made public. His request was complied with on December 3, 1877, twelve days before Edison received his U.S. patent for the phonograph. It is not altogether surprising, therefore, that in

France particularly, "there are some whose definition of the term 'inventor' allows them to regard Cros rather than Edison as the inventor of the talking machine."[5]

Other claims to prior invention of the talking machine are not worthy of serious consideration. Napoli and Marcel Deprez were among inventors who, after Léon-Scott and before Edison, attempted without success to make phonograph-like machines. But their work yielded no significant advance on the Phonautograph. Whether or not there is any substance in these dubious challenges to Edison's priority of invention, there can be no doubt that his Tinfoil Phonograph of 1877 was the first talking machine that actually worked. It recorded sounds and reproduced them, and whereas the first of these functions had been accomplished by the Phonautograph, the second had been merely hypothetical until the invention of the phonograph.

Edison's own account of how this invention came about indicates that his phonograph was a by-product of his work in telegraphy and telephony rather than any conscious development of previous attempts to construct talking machines.

> I was experimenting on an automatic method of recording telegraph messages on a disk of paper laid on a revolving platen, exactly the same as the disk talking-machine of today. The platen had a spiral groove on its surface, like the disk. Over this was placed a circular disk of paper; an electromagnet with the embossing point connected to an arm traveled over the disk; and any signals given through the magnets were embossed on the disk of paper. If this disk was removed from the machine and put on a similar machine provided with a contact point, the embossed record would cause the signals to be repeated into another wire. The ordinary speed of telegraphic signals is thirty-five to forty words a minute; but with this machine several hundred words were possible.
>
> From my experiments with the telephone I knew of the power of a diaphragm to take up sound vibrations, as I had made a little toy which, when you recited loudly in the funnel, would work a pawl connected to the diaphragm; and this engaging a ratchet-wheel served to give continuous rotation to a pulley. This pulley was connected by a cord to a little paper toy representing a man sawing wood. Hence, if one shouted: "Mary had a little lamb," etc., the paper man would start sawing wood. I reached the con-

clusion that if I could record the movements imparted to the diaphragm properly, I could cause such record to reproduce the original movements imparted to the diaphragm by the voice, and thus succeed in recording and reproducing the human voice.

Instead of using a disk I designed a little machine using a cylinder with grooves around the surface. Over this was to be placed tinfoil, which easily received and recorded the movements of the diaphragm. A sketch was made, and the piece-work price, $18 was marked on the sketch. I was in the habit of marking the price I would pay on each sketch. . . . The workman who got the sketch . . . asked what it was for. I told him I was going to record talking, and then have the machine talk back. He thought it absurd. However, it was finished, the foil was put on; I then shouted "Mary had a little lamb," etc. I adjusted the reproducer, and the machine reproduced it perfectly. I was never so taken aback in my life.[6]

Edison's account, written years after the event, is actually a simplification of what occurred. The phonograph had a less troublesome birth than most of his inventions, but it did not come about with quite the directness that Edison indicates. There seems to have been at least one intermediate invention, a paper-strip phonograph evolved out of the earlier work on an instrument to be used for recording and reproducing messages in Morse code. While he had been working on the proposed telegraph recorder-repeater, it occurred to Edison that on a similar machine he could "indent on a moving strip of paraffined paper a record of . . . speech, and if the paper were later drawn under a stylus attached to the diaphragm of a telephone receiver, the speech would be reproduced."[7] He constructed such a machine in July 1877, and used it to record and reproduce indistinctly the sound of his own voice shouting, "Hulloo!" The possibilities inherent in this primitive talking machine may seem rather obvious to us now, but they were not immediately discernible to Edison. His mind was at that time preoccupied with the development of telephony and telegraphy, and consequently he thought of the paper-strip phonograph simply as a machine to be used for recording and storing telephone messages for subsequent play-back or transmission. But during November 1877, Edison transferred his attention from the paper-strip phonograph with its limited application in telephony to the invention of a practicable machine for recording and reproducing the human voice.

Early in that November, Edison's associate, E. H. Johnson, had been lecturing in Buffalo, New York, on the subject of Edison's most recent work. Shortly afterwards, Johnson informed Edison that the audiences at his lectures had shown particular interest in the paper-strip phonograph, but they were enthusiastic about the idea of recording and reproducing the human voice rather than any application of the invention to telephony. Now Edison was sometimes influenced by the direction of public interest in his researches, so it is not unlikely, as Johnson was subsequently to assert, that it was this news that persuaded the inventor to concentrate on making the Tinfoil Phonograph.[8]

Whether or not Johnson's statement is correct, there can be no doubt that the transition from paper-strip phonograph to Tinfoil Phonograph occurred during the second half of November. Johnson in a letter to *Scientific American,* November 17, 1877, revealed that Edison was at that time improving the paper-strip phonograph. Less than two weeks later, Edison sketched in his notebooks a design for what was soon to become the Tinfoil Phonograph. It consisted of a brass cylinder, made to move along a hand-cranked metal screw shaft, and a metal stylus affixed to a mica diaphragm connected to the tapered end of a horn. The surface of the cylinder was incised with an unbroken spiral groove. The actual recording surface, known as the Phonogram, was provided by a sheet of tinfoil wrapped around the brass cylinder. To record or play back it was necessary to hand-crank the apparatus by means of a handle that caused the brass cylinder to rotate and move horizontally at regular speed along the screw shaft. In recording, sounds picked up by the horn caused the diaphragm to vibrate and thence to force the stylus up and down as it moved against the rotating tinfoil surface. The action of the stylus dented the tinfoil by forcing it into the incised groove of the cylinder. In order to play back a recording, the machine was again hand-cranked while the stylus was placed on the tinfoil at the point where the indentations began. As the stylus moved along the already indented track, it caused the diaphragm to vibrate and produce sounds (those originally picked up in the recording process) which were, in turn, amplified by the horn attached to the diaphragm. The one apparatus was thus a single, relatively simple device for both recording and reproducing sound.

The machine itself was constructed by the mechanic, John Kreusi, and was tried out to Edison's satisfaction—and surprise— on December 6. The very next day it was demonstrated to the editor of *Scientific American,* and the first published account of the new invention appeared in that journal on December 22, 1877:

> Mr. Thomas A. Edison recently came into this office, placed a little machine on our desk, turned a crank, and the machine inquired as to our health, asked how we like the phonograph, informed us that *it* was well, and bid us a cordial good night. These remarks were not only perfectly audible to ourselves, but to a dozen or more persons gathered around. . . .

This article, which contained a detailed description of the invention and how it worked, also ventured the earliest predictions concerning its future use: it could be employed to send spoken messages through the mail, to preserve the voices of great singers long after they had died, to record testimony offered in court, and to reproduce a last will and testament in such a way that no one could doubt the sanity of the person who had devised it. To these uses was added a prediction of remarkable prescience:

> It is already possible by ingenious optical contrivances to throw stereoscopic photographs of people on screens in full view of an audience. Add the talking phonograph to counterfeit their voices, and it would be difficult to carry the illusion of real presence much further.

Remarkably, Edison himself seems to have been unmoved by this particular prediction. It was conspicuously missing from his own article, "The Phonograph and the Future," *North American Review,* June 1878, though he did enlarge on several of those other prophecies in *Scientific American* and even added several new ones: including the use of the talking machine in providing books for the blind, in aiding teachers of elocution, in making talking dolls and music boxes, and in advertising. At this stage in the history of the phonograph it was not the inventor but the theoretician who envisaged the application of the new invention to the development of talking pictures. True, the prediction in *Scientific American* did not speak of *moving* pictures. The article was, in fact, published some fourteen years before what Gordon Hendricks calls the "achievement of the 'modern' motion picture."[9] However, it predicted the synchronization of photographs and recorded sound and suggested their use before an audience. And in pointing to the phonograph's contribution towards the mechanical reproduction of reality it also provided perhaps the first step towards that "Myth of Total Cinema," as André Bazin described the dream of the pioneers of the motion picture to achieve "an integral realism, a recreation of the world in its own image."[10]

This dream was soon to be expressed in even more vivid detail. On January 3, 1878, the British scientific journal *Nature* reprinted the article on the phonograph from *Scientific American*. It evoked the following letter, published in *Nature* on January 24, 1878:

> The article from the *Scientific American* on the phonograph which is quoted in *Nature*, vol. xvii, p. 190, concludes as follows: —"It is already possible, by ingenious optical contrivances, to throw stereoscopic photographs of people on screens in full view of an audience. Add the talking phonograph to counterfeit their voices and it would be difficult to carry the illusion of real presence much further."
>
> Ingenious as this suggested combination is, I believe I am in a position to cap it. By combining the phonograph with the kinesigraph I will undertake not only to produce a talking picture of Mr. Gladstone which, with motionless lips and unchanged expression shall positively recite his latest anti-Turkish speech in his own voice and tone. Not only this, but the life-size photograph itself shall move and gesticulate precisely as he did when making the speech, the words and gestures corresponding as in real life. Surely this is an advance upon the conception of the *Scientific American!*
>
> The mode in which I effect this is described in the accompanying provisional specification, which may be briefly summed up thus: Instantaneous photographs of bodies or groups of bodies in motion are taken at equal short intervals—say quarter or half

seconds—the exposure of the plate occupying not more than an eighth of a second. After fixing, the prints from these plates are taken one below another on a long strip or ribbon of paper. The strip is wound from one cylinder to another so as to cause the several photographs to pass before the eye successively at the same intervals of time as those at which they were taken.

Each picture as it passes the eye is instantaneously lighted up by an electric spark. Thus the picture is made to appear stationary while the people or things in it appear to move as in nature. I need not enter more into detail beyond saying that if the intervals between the presentation of the successive pictures are found to be too short the gaps can be filled up by duplicates or triplicates of each succeeding print. This will not perceptibly alter the general effect.

I think it will be admitted that by this means a drama acted by daylight or magnesium light may be recorded and reacted on the screen or sheet of a magic lantern, and with the assistance of the phonograph the dialogues may be repeated in the very voices of the actors.

When this is actually accomplished the photography of colors will alone be wanting to render the representation absolutely complete, and for this we shall not, I trust, have long to wait.

WORDSWORTH DONISTHORPE
Prince's Park, Liverpool,
January 12.[11]

A sound feature film in color anticipated as an imminent achievement in 1878! But this proposal was somewhat optimistic. If Wordsworth Donisthorpe had survived until 1935, he would have had the satisfaction of seeing his dream realized in Rouben Mamoulian's Technicolor film, *Becky Sharp*. But in 1878 the phonograph was but a few months old and there were, as yet, no moving pictures. Donisthorpe was a barrister who dabbled in science. His letter was written in blissful ignorance of the problems of synchronization, sound amplification, and motion picture projection. He never mentions the word "film," for it was not until 1889 that celluloid roll film was invented by George Eastman. And when he spoke of the kinesigraph, he was talking of a machine that he had not yet invented, and which was to remain hypothetical until about 1889, when he constructed it with the assistance of W. C. Crofts. Their apparatus has been described as "a machine which operated with a single moving lens and took pictures two and one-half inches in diameter on sensitized paper."[12] Though they patented the machine, there is no evidence that it was satisfactory or that it was ever harnessed to the phonograph.

It is not known whether Edison saw Donisthorpe's letter. If he did, we have no reason to believe that he recognized in it a challenge to accomplish all that had been predicted for the phonograph. In fact, statements by Edison's employee and fellow-inventor, W. K. L. Dickson, indicate that the former's interest in the idea of making talking pictures was not actively aroused until near the end of the 1880s. In the intervening decade, he was preoccupied with the incandescent electric lamp, magnetic ore separators, dynamos, the telephone and the telegraph, and a vast number of other, related inventions, but gave scant attention to the phonograph and its development between 1880 and 1886. However, during 1887, he turned back to the phonograph with the object of improving on his invention.

This resurgence of interest initially had no connection with the idea of making talking pictures, but was an attempt to meet the commercial challenge of an improved talking machine, the Graphophone, produced during 1885–86 by Alexander Graham Bell, Chichester Bell, and Charles Sumner Tainter. The Graphophone worked on more or less the same principles as the phonograph, but it improved upon Edison's machine, as V. K. Chew has explained, by having the sound impressions incised "on the wax-coated surface of a cardboard cylinder which was slipped on to a rotable mandrel; the latter did not move linearly as it rotated, but the recorder was moved along it by means of a feed screw. . . . The performance of the Bell-Tainter Graphophone was such that it showed distinct promise as a business dictation machine. An invitation to Edison to co-operate in its exploitation was understandably rejected."[13] Meanwhile, a challenge to both the phonograph and the Graphophone was looming in the form of the Gramophone, a machine that played disks instead of cylinders. This invention, partly inspired by the Phonautograph of Léon-Scott, was the work of Emile Berliner, who demonstrated it before the Franklin Institute in Philadelphia on May 16, 1888 and began marketing it, together with 7-inch disks made of hard rubber, during 1893.

Edison's feverish activity to improve his own talking machine is reflected in the fact that during 1887–88 he took out no fewer than 33 patents for developments of the phonograph.[14] In June 1888 he had completed an improved machine that he considered competitive with the Graphophone, and this new phonograph was put on the market before the end of the year. A ruthless and complicated business war-of-the-machines followed—at first between the phonograph and the Graphophone; but soon the struggle widened to include the Gramophone.[15]

It was during this period of renewed interest in the phonograph that Edison seems to have turned his attention for the first time to the idea of making talking pictures. Dickson was to recall many years later:

> Edison's idea, as disclosed to me in 1887 at the Newark Laboratory, was to combine the phonograph cylinder or record with a similar or larger drum on the same shaft, which drum was to be covered with pin-point microphotographs which of course must synchronize with the phonograph record. . . .
>
> Before making the drum, which was to fit over the phonograph shaft, I made a small micro camera, using various objectives or lenses taken from one of my microscopes to produce the pin-head photos. In this micro camera I tried Daguerre's process on highly polished bits of silver and developed it in the usual way. The subject I used was a lantern slide of Landseer's stag for all these comparative single still pictures.
>
> The time of exposure was about three-quarters of a minute. Of course, this method was soon abandoned. . . .
>
> I increased the size of the aluminum drum and of the pictures, and coated the drum with a bromide of silver gelatin emulsion; and would have obtained a fairly good result but for some chemical action which took place between the aluminum and the emulsion. That made me try a glass drum and a one-opening rapid shutter. . . .
>
> I just slotted the aluminum drum and wrapped a sheet of Carbutt's stiff sensitized celluloid over it. This proved quite satisfactory and did away with my home-made emulsion coatings. The pictures were sharp and good, and to save time in making prints

or positives, I turned the negative into a positive effect with bichloride of mercury.[16]

The idea of this machine had, actually, been anticipated in 1870 by the British inventor Fox Talbot, though he did not go on to build it. However, the machine Dickson described was not only constructed but also demonstrated with qualified success by the end of 1889. It was little more than a curious toy of peripheral interest in the history of the motion picture. Its microphotographs, on the revolving drum, had to be viewed through a low-power microscope; there was no means of projecting the pictures and evidently no conjunction of the viewing device with the phonograph.

Nevertheless, Edison had begun at last to think seriously about making talking pictures—a subject to which he was to return repeatedly and with many frustrations over the next quarter of a century. An undated letter by the inventor that appears prefatory to the Dicksons' *History of the Kinetograph, Kinetoscope and Kineto-Phonograph,* 1895, states:

> In the year 1887, the idea occurred to me that it was possible to devise an instrument which should do for the eye what the phonograph does for the ear, and that by a combination of the two all motion and sound could be recorded and reproduced simultaneously . . . the germ of [this idea] comes from a little toy called the Zoetrope, and the work of Muybridge, Marie [Marey], and others. . . .[17]

On February 25, 1888, while the phonograph was uppermost in Edison's mind, Eadweard Muybridge, a British-born inventor and pioneer of the motion picture, came to Orange, New Jersey, to give a lecture to the New England Society. In the previous year Edison had established his laboratory in West Orange. We know that the two inventors met, but the influence of this meeting on Edison is open to question. Gordon Hendricks, who has meticulously examined all factual material pertaining to Edison at this period, states: "It is possible that both Edison and Dickson attended this February 25 lecture by Muybridge."[18] Whether or not Edison attended the lecture, it is known that Muybridge visited him two days later at the West Orange laboratory. Muybridge, in the preface to his *Animals in Motion,* 1899, observes,

"It may be here parenthetically remarked that on the 27th of February, 1888, the author . . . consulted with Mr. Thomas A. Edison as to the practicability of using [the Zoöpraxiscope] in association with the phonograph."[19] But Edison contradicts this statement. Gordon Hendricks notes: "In the margin of the [Terry] Ramsaye manuscript [of *A Million and One Nights*] now at Harvard University, opposite the Ramsaye remark that Muybridge wanted to interest Edison in uniting this device with the phonograph" Edison has noted: "No—Muybridge came to Lab to show me picture of a horse in motion—nothing was said about phonogph."[20] However, Hendricks insists that Muybridge's version is the more accurate one. "We can be sure . . . ," Hendricks says, "that the . . . visit [of Muybridge to Edison] was about the idea of joining the phonograph with pictures of motion."[21] And this opinion is supported by the fact that only three months after the Muybridge visit, the *New York World* of June 3, 1888 noted "This scheme [of combining the phonograph and moving pictures] met with the approval of Mr. Edison and he intended to perfect it at his leisure."[22]

At the time of his visit, Muybridge was renowned on both sides of the Atlantic as the first man to succeed in taking "instantaneous photographs." In 1878 he had devised a method for "analyzing motion with a camera and . . . re-synthesizing it in a viewing device."[23] In 1872, Leland Stanford, governor of California, commissioned Muybridge to photograph a trotting horse in order to determine whether at any time the animal had all four feet off the ground. Muybridge's first experiments were unsuccessful, and his work was abruptly and sensationally interrupted when, on discovering that his wife was having an affair, he shot and killed her lover. The bizarre trial that followed would have done credit, half a century later, to the imagination of a Hollywood screenwriter. (It is described briefly in Terry Ramsaye's *A Million and One Nights*.) Muybridge was acquitted by a sympathetic California jury, but he did not resume his work for Leland Stanford until 1877.

When he did return to the challenge, he enlisted the aid of a railroad engineer named John D. Isaacs. Terry Ramsaye rather dubiously credits Isaacs with the inspiration for what followed, although the latter seems for the most part to have been carrying out the instructions of Muybridge. The two men set up a battery of twelve (later twenty-four) still cameras along a race track at 27-inch intervals. "Isaacs worked out a system of electrical contacts with wire stretched at intervals across a measured section of the Stanford race track at the governor's Palo Alto stud farm. As the sulky swept past, the wheels closed the circuits successively and the magnetic releases set off the cameras."[24] The series of photographs taken in this way were, in effect, successive frames of a motion picture.

Muybridge used this technique to take many more photographs of animals in motion,[25] and he went on to produce motion pictures by using these photographs in a viewing toy called a Zoetrope and in a projection machine called the Zoöpraxiscope —neither of which he had invented.[26] In 1886, the year before his lecture in Orange, Muybridge had begun to switch from photographing animals to taking pictures of human beings in motion. If Edison saw any of these later pictures, he may have become further interested in the idea of linking moving pictures of human beings to recordings of the human voice. However, Edison was to claim, rather questionably, that Muybridge showed him only pictures of a horse in motion. At all events, Edison was not inspired to apply Muybridge's actual cumbersome battery-of-cameras technique to the making of talking pictures. Temporarily, he saw more promise in his pinpoint microphotographs.

As we have noted, Muybridge certainly did not originate the idea of linking moving pictures and the phonograph. But neither did Edison—although Edison, the Dicksons, and, later, Terry Ramsaye seem to have gone to some pains to circulate the notion that the idea for this combination was originally Edison's. Thus, the Dicksons, echoing Edison's letter (quoted above) state:

> In the year 1887, Mr. Edison found himself in possession of one of those breathing spells which relieve the tension of inventive thought . . . the phonograph was established upon what seemed to be a solid financial and social basis, and the inventor felt at liberty to indulge in a few secondary flights of fancy. It was then that he was struck by the idea of reproducing to the eye the effect of motion by means of a swift and graded succession of pictures

and of linking these photographic impressions with the phonograph in one combination so as to complete to both senses syn-
chronously the record of a given scene.[27]

There are several things wrong with this statement. First, as
we have seen, the phonograph was not established on a solid
financial basis in 1887: it was being commercially challenged by
the more proficient Graphophone. Secondly, the impression is
given that the combination of motion pictures and the phonograph was first conceived in 1887, by Edison. But this combination had been suggested by others a decade earlier, and in the
intervening years Edison appears to have done nothing to
develop the idea. Thirdly, the notion is conveyed by the Dicksons that it was Edison who first conceived the application of
persistence of vision to the making of motion pictures. To
accept this view is to ignore more than half a century of pioneer
work preceding Edison and Dickson and fundamental to *their*
experiments in making workable motion pictures.

However, their microscopic pinpoint photographs were an
initial step towards the realization of the Kinetophone or
Kinetophonograph—the Dicksons' comprehensive term for the
invention that would achieve the "synchronous attachment of
photography with the phonograph. . . ." The next step has been
obscured by contradictory evidence. In 1889 Edison went to
the Paris Exposition, where he met the motion picture pioneer
Etienne Marey. Marey demonstrated a moving picture projector which used electrical illumination to show a series of
photographs mounted on a revolving disk.[28] According to the
Dicksons, on October 6, 1889, when Edison returned to West
Orange, he entered his laboratory and was confronted with his
first "talkie": "I [W. K. L. Dickson] was seen to advance and
address Mr. Edison from the small 4-foot screen; small because
of the restricted size of the room. I raised my hat, smiled, and
said, 'Good morning, Mr. Edison, glad to see you back. Hope
you like the kinetophone. To show the synchronization I will
lift my hand and count up to ten.' I then raised and lowered my
hands as I counted up to ten. There was no hitch, and a pretty
steady picture."[29] Clearly, Dickson claims here to have rigged
up a movie projection apparatus and synchronized it with the
phonograph.

But this claim is flatly contradicted by a statement of Edison's made eleven years later: "there was no screen as Mr. Dickson says."[30] Gordon Hendricks supports this contradiction by quoting a later comment by Edison: "There was no screen . . ."; but he also mentions a note by Edison in the margin of the manuscript of Terry Ramsaye's *A Million and One Nights* (on file at Harvard University Library) in which the inventor says, "the facts are that Dickson & I had a machine projecting on a screen 5 ft sq at the time we were making peep machines." Hendricks comments: "Since these 'peep machines' [Kinetoscopes] were not manufactured until beginning late in 1893, and were continued until at least 1899, this Edison remark is inconclusive."[31] What Dickson probably exhibited to Edison in October 1889 was not motion picture projection but an apparatus constructed by Dickson for the purpose of viewing the microscopic pinpoint photographs that Dickson had taken on the cylinder machine.[32] We have no means of knowing whether this device was synchronized with the phonograph.

Gordon Hendricks describes Edison's "Motion Picture Caveat IV" (on file at Edison's laboratory in West Orange) dated November 2, 1889, as the first indication that the inventor had "envisioned something else than a cylinder surface for receiving the photographs."[33] In this document Edison refers for the first time to an apparatus he calls the Kinetoscope, and in describing it he states, "The sensitive film is in the form of a long band passing from one reel to another. . . ." The introduction of this idea marks a decisive step away from the cylinder-viewer and in the direction of the projected motion picture.

Between the cylinder-viewer and the projected motion picture was to come the Kinetoscope and its more elaborate sister machine, the Kinetophone. In the form in which it came before the public in 1894, the exterior of the Kinetoscope resembled a closed-in wooden sentry box or casket. It stood about 48 inches high. On top of the box was the eyepiece—not unlike the framework of a pair of opera glasses. By inserting a coin into an appropriate slot, a viewer could peer into the eyepiece and observe a brief motion picture presentation. Inside the machine approximately 56 feet of 35mm film "circulated [at

46 frames per second] in an endless loop under a viewing lens, each frame briefly illuminated by a flash of light through a rotating shutter."[34] Photographs of the exterior and interior of the Kinetoscope may be seen in Gordon Hendricks's monograph, *The Kinetoscope* (1966).

Hendricks assembles a wealth of factual evidence to support his view that this invention should be attributed to Dickson rather than to Edison. Nevertheless, Edison publicized the Kinetoscope as his own invention; he then proceeded to make grandiose claims about it. His "Motion Picture Caveat IV" devotes a paragraph to the combination of Kinetoscope and phonograph (ultimately to become the Kinetophone), asserting that "all the movements of a person photoghd will be exactly coincident with any sound made by him. . . ."[35] In 1899 this development was hypothetical or at best indicated work in progress. Hendricks states, "It appears certain that . . . the only motion picture work at the [Edison] laboratory resulting in practicable apparatus until May, 1891, concerned a cylinder-viewer . . ."[36] This last-mentioned date refers to the completion of the first Kinetoscope. In chapter 15 of *The Edison Motion Picture Myth,* Hendricks quotes various inflated claims for the Kinetoscope. Thus in 1891, Edison maintained that with the Kinetoscope he had achieved or was on the verge of achieving the projection of talking pictures and that it would soon be possible to make films of operas, plays, and the like. Such claims—which were perhaps intended to discourage other inventors from working along the same lines—received widespread publicity in the press and were inflated by journalists into even more fanciful exaggerations or distortions of the truth. Hendricks disposes convincingly of these wild assertions and rumors.

The Kinetoscope was nothing more than a peephole viewing machine, and the pictures it showed were not projected before an audience—only one person at a time could see them. It is possible—though there is no conclusive evidence—that a Kinetoscope harnessed to a phonograph was shown at an exhibition in New York in May 1891.[37] It does appear that such a combination of the two machines was presented publicly two years later at the Columbian Exposition, which opened in Chicago on May 1, 1893. Commenting on the Exposition, *Scientific Amer-*

ican for October 21, 1893, described "Edison's phonograph exhibits and his latest invention, the 'kinetograph' [*sic*]. He photographs the face at the same time one talks into the phonograph. By this method the sound and the motion of the lips in producing it are accurately reproduced." Hendricks considers it

> likely that the motor of the Kinetoscope was attached to the phonograph, and as visitors to the Edison exhibit peered into the eye-piece they heard music. We cannot believe . . . that they heard "the sound and the motion of the lips" as described by the *Scientific American*. Nor can we know whether they heard this music through the ear tubes connected as in the Kinetophone [which was not ready until 1895] . . . or merely through a nearby speaker.[38]

What films would visitors to the exhibit have seen and perhaps heard? We do not know for certain but can surmise that at least one subject shown was that demonstrated when the Kinetoscope was exhibited on May 9, 1893 at the Brooklyn Institute in New York:

> The picture represented a blacksmith and two helpers forging a piece of iron. Before beginning the job a bottle was passed from one to the other, each imbibing his portion. The blacksmith then removed his white hot iron from the forge with a pair of tongs and gave directions to his helpers with the small hand hammer, when they immediately began to pound the hot iron while the sparks flew in all directions, the blacksmith at the same time making intermediate strokes with his hand hammer. At a signal from the smith, the helpers put down their sledge hammers, when the iron was returned to the forge and another piece substituted for it, and the operation was repeated.[39]

Was this action accompanied by sound effects and/or music? Unfortunately, we do not know, but it would not have been inappropriate if Edison had supplied a recording of Dickson playing "The Anvil Chorus" on his violin.

The commercial debut of the Kinetoscope occurred on April 14, 1894 at 1155 Broadway (near Twenty-eighth Street), New York, at what came to be known as a Kinetoscope Parlor. Ten machines were situated in two rows of five in the center of the room, and the charge for viewing each row of five machines was twenty-five cents. The film subjects—each of which ran for less than fifty seconds—were: *Sandow* (the celebrated strong man), *Blacksmiths* (the film formerly shown at the Brooklyn Institute), *Highland Dance, Trapeze, Wrestling, Roosters* (a scene of two fighting cocks), *Horse-shoeing, Barber Shop* scene, and two films of the vaudeville contortionist *Bertholdi*. Most, if not all, of these films had been shot in the first studio constructed exclusively for film production: a wood and tar paper building known as the Black Maria, built in West Orange in 1892 at a total cost of $637.67.[40]

Commercially the Kinetoscope was an unqualified success. One hundred twenty dollars was taken in on opening day, and succeeding days, when news of the novel machines had begun to spread throughout New York, were far more profitable. Crowds flocked to 1155 Broadway, and by the end of May 1894, the Parlor was staying open on Sundays in order to accommodate all who wished to see the show. During May and June additional Kinetoscope Parlors were opened in Chicago and San Francisco, and by October there was a Parlor in Washington, D. C. Before the end of the year, Kinetoscopes were being viewed by the public at 20 Boulevard Poissonière in Paris and at a converted store in Old Broad Street, London.

But what of the Kinetophone? The New York Kinetoscope Parlor showed only silent films at its premiere and probably for several weeks thereafter. However, since 1888, press reports, echoing announcements by Edison himself, had repeatedly forecast the imminent completion of a marketable machine that would combine the phonograph and the motion picture. Agents who leased Kinetoscopes from Edison were led to expect that the Kinetophone would soon replace the more restricted Kinetoscope. As the rumors persisted, Edison became aware that orders for the Kinetoscope were declining. Prospective agents decided to sit tight and wait for the Kinetophone rather than invest in nonsound machines that might quickly become obsolete. In response to this situation, Dickson (and perhaps Edison) set to work during April through perhaps December 1894, to synchronize the Kinetoscope with the phonograph.

There still exists a film made about this time in which we can see, in the background, Dickson playing a violin next to a big phonograph horn which was presumably attached to a recording machine. In the foreground two lab assistants are dancing to the music—whatever it was. Apparently the film was one of Dickson's attempts to achieve synchronization through simultaneously recording sound and picture. A similar effort is to be seen in a contemporary artist's impression of the filming and recording of a boxing bout staged in Edison's new studio in 1894.[41] But these experiments, and any others made during the same period, proved unsuccessful. Probably no later than December 1894, efforts to achieve synchronization were given up, and Edison and Dickson decided to settle for a conjunction of phonograph and Kinetoscope that would provide nonsynchronized accompaniment to the moving pictures.

Edison's lukewarm interest in anything pertaining to moving pictures and the growing demand for a sound version of the Kinetoscope were probably the main motivations for abandoning further experiments and for marketing a machine as unsatisfactory as the Kinetophone. The new machine had a phonograph located in the base of the same box that housed the Kinetoscope. A belt drive connected the two machines and insured that they would begin and stop simultaneously. According to Hendricks, over 1,000 Kinetoscopes were made, but only 45 Kinetophones.[42] This is hardly surprising. The only novelty that the new machine provided was music—seldom appropriate to the scenes it was accompanying—that could be heard through "ear-tubes" while one watched the Kinetoscope pictures. Among the more popular cylinder records for the Kinetophone were "Pomona Waltz," "Jolly Darkies," and "Carnival Dance."

Primitive as the Kinetophone seems today, it was the most advanced step that the nineteenth century was to take toward the realization of talking pictures. Contemporaneous efforts by Georges Demeny in France, William Friese-Greene in England, and Alexander Black in the U. S. A. were even less promising than the Kinetophone.

While a student at the Sorbonne, Georges Demeny (1850–1927) became the pupil of physiologist and motion picture pioneer, Etienne Jules Marey (1830–1904). Marey's special study was animal movement, and he was inspired by Muybridge's trotting horse pictures to turn to photography as a means of furthering his researches. In 1882 he devised two different methods of taking pictures of moving birds and animals. The first was a "photographic gun"—a camera that looked like a wide-bore rifle but which contained, in place of bullets, a revolving dry plate capable of making twelve exposures per second while "shooting" flying birds or swift-running animals. The second was a technique for photographing numerous phases of movement on a single dry plate. In 1893, Marey constructed what "was perhaps the first efficient motion picture projector which could handle more than one scene, using long strips of coated celluloid film instead of pictures set on a disk."[43] Marey's interest in these devices and in the motion picture generally was entirely scientific. Demeny, however, was more enthusiastic about profits than he was about science and invention.

Early in the 1880s, Demeny left the Sorbonne to assist Marey at his studio-laboratory in the Bois de Boulogne. He became responsible for many of the experiments conducted for the purpose of analyzing animal movement, and in due course came to the conclusion that their researches, and in particular Marey's motion picture devices, could be commercially exploited. But Marey would not go along with such an idea. Accordingly, in 1893, the two men parted, Marey to continue his investigations for the sake of science, Demeny to exploit what he had learned during his collaboration with his former teacher. Shortly afterward, Demeny patented a motion picture camera which he called the Bioscope—actually it was nothing more than an adaptation of Marey's latest camera.

Two years earlier, in 1891, Demeny had begun another collaboration—with a speech pathologist, Professor H. Marichelle of the French National Institute for Deaf Mutes. Their idea was to use still pictures of people speaking as a means of teaching the deaf how to speak. For this purpose, Demeny "invented" another version of Marey's "photographic gun" camera. He took large close-up pictures of people talking and used a lantern-slide projector to show them. Demeny claimed that his pictures "conserved the expression of the face as the voice is preserved in the phonograph." But the illustrations in his article, "Les Photographies Parlantes," do not bear him out.[44] Nevertheless, he maintained that he had achieved some conspicuous success in showing his pictures before audiences of deaf people. He also devised a machine suitable for an individual deaf person; it combined features of Marey's revolving disk pictures with the Kinetoscope. Demeny called it the Phonoscope. It was not a new idea, since Charles Cros had proposed it as early as 1860. However, Demeny actually constructed the machine—Cros did not. The Phonoscope consisted of an oblong box about 30 inches tall, perched on a three-legged stand or tripod. The user of the machine peered into the eyepiece on the box and turned a handle, revolving a disk on which were numerous spaced pictures showing a speaker uttering a word. The action of speaking could be watched "frame by frame" or speeded up at the will of the person working the machine. Above a certain speed the effect of motion was achieved through persistence of vision.

Demeny stated that it would be possible to "join the phonograph to the *Phonoscope*" to create the illusion of watching and hearing a real speaker.[45] It is not known whether he ever tried out this interesting combination. It *is* known that he attempted to exploit the Phonoscope through the Société Générale du Phonoscope, established in 1892. But the invention was not a commercial success. Either the deaf and their doctors were not impressed by the machine or else it was not as perfect as Demeny claimed.

More original than Demeny's work was the attempt of William Friese-Greene, the British pioneer of cinematography, to combine a phonograph recording with pictures taken with and projected by apparatus that he had patented. Friese-Greene bought a phonograph in 1887 and in that year filmed a man mouthing the words of a song that was being sung on a cylinder record. He then played back the record while projecting the film. The results were far from satisfactory. His projection method was imperfect, and synchronization was not achieved. However, the experiment led Friese-Greene to speculate on the possibilities inherent in successfully projecting sound pictures. "Why should not moving pictures be combined with records of other sounds—all sounds, speech, traffic, the thud of horses' feet on the turf, the striking of ball on bat at a cricket match, the sounds of human speech? Synchronisation of sound and sight was surely only a matter of improvement in mechanism."[46]

With that in mind, Friese-Greene wrote to Edison in June 1889, providing a careful description of his camera and projector, detailing his experiment in trying to make sound pictures, and suggesting that Edison combine forces with him in order to perfect synchronized movies. The letter was formally acknowledged by an assistant or secretary at the Edison laboratory, and Friese-Greene was asked to forward drawings of his apparatus. Enthusiastically, Friese-Greene sent off copies of the drawings he had prepared when he had applied for patents on his camera and projector. That was the last he was to hear of the matter. Receipt of the drawings was never acknowledged, and in 1910 Edison was to state in an affidavit that he had never seen Friese-Greene's letter or the drawings. That was perhaps true. The correspondence and designs may never have got beyond Edison's secretary. Nevertheless, as Friese-Greene's biographer has commented:

> When Edison patented his . . . Kinetoscope . . . he took out the patent in America, not in England. Was that just an oversight, or did he, knowing of Friese-Greene's patent, realize it would not be possible to get a British patent? The mechanism of the Kinetoscope in 1891 would not have stood the test of novelty in the British Patent Office. It would have infringed part of Friese-Greene's patent.[47]

Alexander Black's anticipation of talking pictures was more spectacular but ultimately no more promising than either Demeny's or Friese-Greene's. Black was a successful novelist and amateur photographer. His enthusiasm for the still camera led him to the lecture platform, and in the early nineties he toured the "lyceum stages" of New England, delivering an address entitled "Ourselves as Others See Us" and illustrating his comments on the wonders of photography with stereopticon slides made from candid camera snapshots. In due course he came to notice real or coincidental relationships in the content of the pictures that he projected, and incipient plot material began to suggest itself. Out of that grew the idea of telling a long and elaborate story in pictures. Thus, early in 1894, Black embarked on his first "picture play."

He prepared a long series of photographic slides showing the adventures of a girl reporter (played by Blanche Bayliss), her boyfriend (William Courtenay), and a villain (Ernest Hastings). The heroine's name, Miss Jerry, became the title of the show. Black selected a wide range of locations in and around New York City. He retained the same viewpoint (camera angle) for each scene, but showed changes in the attitude of the actors. The slides, when projected before an audience were accompanied by a narrator (Black), whose spoken commentary fleshed out the story as it unfolded on the screen. Black "hoped that between the two components of word and picture he would convey the impression of dramatic action."[48] The slides were projected at the rate of four per minute (too slow to achieve the effect of persistence of vision), and transitions between them were accomplished by dissolves made possible by a device within the stereopticon projector. Music, especially composed for the show, was provided by John Hyatt Brewer.

Miss Jerry was a great success. Its premiere, in New York on October 9, 1894, attracted a distinguished audience that included novelists W. D. Howells and Frank R. Stockton, and critics Brander Matthews and Clarence Stedman. Initially the show lasted for two hours, but at the suggestion of Howells, Black reduced it by thirty minutes.

In 1895, following an East Coast tour of *Miss Jerry,* Black prepared his second picture play, *A Capital Courtship,* which was set in Washington. Recognizing the box-office value of celebrities, he persuaded President Cleveland, the future President McKinley, and the British ambassador to pose for some of his scenes.

Black rejected offers to introduce his picture plays into the theater circuits. He sought his audiences among the more "intellectual" or sophisticated upper or middle classes who attended educational lyceum presentations in preference to vaudeville shows. This deliberate restriction of the audience together with Black's waning interest in the picture play and the rise of the motion picture show in 1895–96 insured that *A Capital Court-*

ship, Black's most ambitious and financially most successful picture play, was also the last of its kind.

The premiere of *Miss Jerry* occurred only six months after the Broadway opening of the first Kinetoscope Parlor, so it is not surprising that, as Terry Ramsaye notes, much editorial commentary at that time speculated on or

anticipated an application of the film to the Black idea, when Edison should achieve the screen. This might have influenced Edison. . . . It might just as well have influenced Black, the father of the photoplay. It did neither. . . . Edison was science. Black was art. Between them they held in their separated hands the ingredients of the *aqua regalis,* that universal solvent of expression—the story-telling motion picture. Only time and tedious experience could bring the two elements together into the flowing menstruum of the modern screen.[49]

Time and tedious experience did not help to produce the sound film in the nineteenth century—though, as we have seen, that century made up in variety of methods what it lacked in actual accomplishment. Cylinder microphotographs combined with the phonograph (Edison), projected film combined with the phonograph (Dickson, Friese-Greene), the Phonoscope combined with the phonograph (Demeny), the Kinetophone (Dickson), the stereopticon picture play with spoken live commentary (Black)—all were tried and found wanting.

But if the nineteenth century failed to produce the sound film, it did, nevertheless, see the successful realization of motion picture projection. The commercial debut of the movies dates from the year following the premieres of the Kinetoscope and Black's first pre-film picture play. This debut became possible because of the invention of workable film projectors: in particular, the Bioskop of the brothers Skladanowsky in Germany and the Cinématographe of the brothers Lumière in France. The Bioskop is of less concern to this study than the Cinématographe, a machine that was inspired by the Kinetoscope. In 1894, Louis Lumière visited the Kinetoscope Parlor on the Boulevard Poissonière, Paris. What he saw there suggested the idea of making an apparatus that could project films onto a screen so that many people could view them at the same time.

Within a few months, Louis and his brother Auguste had constructed a practicable machine which combined the functions of a camera and a projector. Their projection method was an adaptation of an earlier projector designed in 1892 by Emile Reynaud and used by him in his Théâtre Optique (established in Paris in 1892) to present moving picture shows of hand-drawn cartoonlike figures.

During March 1895, the Lumière brothers shot their first film, *La Sortie des Usines,* a moving picture of workers leaving the Lumière photographic factory in Lyon-Montplaisir. It was the first film publicly shown at the Paris premiere of the Cinématographe on December 28, 1895. For an admission charge of one franc audiences at the Grand-Café at 14 Boulevard des Capucines, Paris, saw ten single-shot films projected onto a screen. In the temporary absence of Louis and Auguste, the first show was presented by their father, the photographer Auguste Lumière. His commentary, some sort of piano accompaniment, and the astonished gasps of the audience were the only sounds that went along with the pictures.[50]

In the United States, the commercial premiere of the motion picture took place at Koster & Bial's Music Hall, Thirty-fourth Street at Herald Square, New York, on April 23, 1896. On this occasion the show was provided by the Vitascope, a projector designed by Thomas Armat and manufactured and marketed by Edison. Again, as with the Cinématographe, the projected pictures were silent. Nevertheless, the *New York Herald,* reviewing the show, reported

> Mr. Edison is not quite satisfied yet. He wants now to improve the phonograph so that it will record double the amount of sound it does at present, and he hopes then to combine this improved phonograph with the *Vitascope* to make it possible for an audience to witness a photographic reproduction of an opera or a play—to see the movements of the actors and hear their voices as plainly as though they were witnessing the original production itself.[51]

Edison would have a long time to wait before what he told the *New York Herald* was actually realized. However, in view of later attempts to combine the phonograph and the moving picture, the newspaper report is of particular interest. As we have seen with the Kinetophone, Edison had given up on the problem of trying to achieve synchronization. He was now confronted with a second problem: the need for amplification. The comment in the *New York Herald* indicating Edison's desire to "record double the amount of sound" is, presumably, a garbled account of a statement in which he had expressed his awareness of the need to improve the amplifying power of the phonograph if it were to be used before an audience and in conjunction with moving pictures. Subsequently, this same problem was to bedevil many other inventors.

But in the meantime, audiences began to flock to the film shows. For some years they would remain silent, but while they were still a novelty, it was wonder enough—even without sound —that the pictures moved.

CHAPTER TWO

THE APPLICATION
OF THE
PHONOGRAPH

Even in the primitive days sustained efforts were made to
redeem the cinema from its inherent silence. A "narrator" in the
flesh tried to humor the audience; phonograph records were
more or less successfully synchronized with corresponding
images so that the benevolent spectator might nurture the illusion
of listening to a cock crow, an aria, or even bits of conversation;
and of course, musical accompaniment emerged at the outset.
Those premature attempts at sound and speech were abortive; the
narrator yielded to captions, and the phonograph records
disappeared after a while. The time for sound film had
not yet come.
SIEGFRIED KRACAUER, *Theory of Film*, 1960

What is the place of the phono-cinematograph? In the first place,
until the peculiar nasal sound is eliminated from the talking
machine it will not prove popular. . . . Furthermore expression
in tone is practically non-existent. Though the cinematographic
world be flooded with talking and singing pictures, unless they
are of some peculiar interest, the majority of picture-theatre
lovers, after the first wave of excitement and curiosity, will
patronise those establishments where they can see movement
alone.
FREDERICK A. TALBOT, *Moving Pictures*, 1912

The silent film was not silent. Before 1928 movies were customarily accompanied by one or more of the following: sound
effects; music played by live performers; live singers, speakers,
or actors; and phonograph recordings. Only the last of these is

the subject of this chapter and will be dealt with in detail, but a few observations about each of the other forms of sound accompaniment will be in order here.

Sound effects, produced at first by such primitive methods as the clanking of chains and the clacking of coconut shells,* gradually became more sophisticated with the virtuoso-like "performances" of Lyman H. Howe, onetime "itinerant phonograph entertainer" of Wilkes-Barre, Pennsylvania. (Howe is credited with having first used sound effects with movies and also with introducing the technique of having live speakers behind the screen.¹) Eventually, the effects were to be supplied automatically by complex machines designed to be worked by skilled operators.

From about 1908 to 1915 sound effects were frequently used in conjunction with silent films. They were technically known as "traps" and were provided either by drummers in the orchestra pit or by special effects men working behind the screen. At first the range of effects was no more than could be found in most legitimate theaters of the period, but the public appeal of interesting audio-visual effects created a demand for much wider selections of traps than could be managed efficiently by one operator while he was watching the film. In response to this demand, enterprising manufacturers marketed devices with batteries of sound effects that could be played like organs or pianos and in some instances were combined with organs and pianos. Among them were the Allefex and the Kinematophone (each of which could provide up to fifty different sounds), the Dramagraph, the Excelsior Sound Effects Cabinet, and the Deagan Electric Bells (twenty-five bells that covered a range of two octaves.) The August 26, 1911 issue of *Moving Picture World* noted that the Yerkes factory, which produced several lines of special effects machines, was working "day and night" to satisfy the demand for their apparatus. (One such machine was used in the same year to contribute sound to the Kinemacolor film of King George V's coronation, which was screened at the Herald Square Theatre, New York. This showing may

---

* Hale's Tours (1903), a movie entertainment creating the illusion of a train journey, used such primitive sound effects.

have been the very first public presentation in the U.S. of a "sound film" in color.) Public enthusiasm for sound effects declined after 1915, mainly as a result of the increasing sophistication of music for the silent picture. However, many cinema organs built after 1915 continued to be equipped with a wide range of traps.[2]

Contemporary reactions tell us a great deal about what effects were usually like and what they were expected to achieve but seldom did. In most instances they were unsatisfactory because they were too loud or were ludicrously inaccurate; this was especially true before the emergence of the special effects machines. Quite often the effects succeeded only in obliterating the voices of the actors, singers, or speakers who were endeavoring to accompany the film. Music critic H. F. Hoffman tells an amusing anecdote about this problem:

> I was lecturing once at a large theater that held a thousand people on the ground floor and it required some vocal effort on my part. Behind the screen they had a prop-worker who felt the importance of his position, very much to my discomfort. He never missed a horse's step; every time a door closed he would rap on a box; the waiter's tip always jingled on the table; the chickens outcackled me; the cows "mooed" me into silence, and I was lost in the ocean's roar. I said nothing to him because he was peevish and very jealous of his playthings. One evening we had the interior scene of a peasant's cottage, and a painful parting between two lovers was taking place. All at once a bird began to sing with great violence. I looked at the piano player in wonderment and found him looking the same at me. "What's that for?" he asked. "You've got me," I replied, "I'll go and see." I found my friend with his cheeks and his eyes bulging out, blowing for his very life. "What's the trouble?" says I. "The bird! The bird!" says he, without removing the whistle. "Where?" says I. "There," says he, pointing triumphantly with a stick to a diminutive canary in a tiny wooden cage on a top shelf at the far corner of the room. "Good boy!" I cried, giving him a wallop on the back that made him almost swallow his blooming whistle.[3]

Frequently the sound effects were incorrect. Hence the answer given by the editor of *Moving Picture World* to the question whether it was best to undertake to reproduce the sounds to go with the picture or not: "The imitations," he observed, "should be fairly accurate or they shouldn't be attempted. Inaccuracy is worse than nothing. It creates wrong impressions and often it wrongly interprets the pictures. They must correspond or else they should be let alone."[4] W. Stephen Bush, another critic writing for the same journal, had nothing but contempt for most of the sound effects he heard in movie theaters, but he also had very definite ideas of what they should have been like and how they should have been used. His fellow critics seem generally to have concurred with his views whenever they expressed their opinions on the matter:

> Now effects to help the picture must be few, simple and well rehearsed for each separate and particular picture. The idea that a set of mechanical contrivances for the production of a limited number of sounds can be made to fit most pictures or even a small percentage of them is utterly absurd. The moment an effect is repeated too often it becomes monotonous, then tires one, and at last is ridiculous. Each picture must be studied by itself and only such effects introduced as have a psychological bearing on the situation as depicted on the screen. . . . At all times, effects must be original, novel, simple, quickly understood and appreciated by the audience. The proper moments for introducing them must be judged from picture to picture and no set of stereotyped rules can be laid down.[5]

Lyman Howe was the only person repeatedly mentioned for his creative use of sound effects. In the 1890s Howe was making a living touring Pennsylvania with his Phonograph Concerts. He used a large tin horn to amplify the sounds of cylinder records played on an Edison phonograph. Up to 3,000 people at a time were said to have attended his programs.[6] When Howe got into the business of supplying sound effects for movies, he discerned instinctively that if the job were to be done well the sort of principles outlined by Bush would have to be put into practice. His effects were selected and rehearsed with great care, and the public response, especially during 1908–12, was appreciative—and lucrative for Howe. The editor of *Moving Picture World* noted in 1909, "One exhibitor has made a special study of this phase of motion picture shows, and has achieved a high degree of perfection. Reference is here made to Lyman

H. Howe. His sounds imitate and to the mind of a great many who see his pictures they add to the attraction of the entertainment."[7] And Clyde Martin, a columnist for the same journal, commented two years later,

> Lyman Howe shows several pictures on his programs that the public has seen in five cent theaters. Howe projection is fine, but there are many picture houses over the country that are putting on just as good pictures. Mr. Howe does not use a symphony orchestra and still his admission prices range from twenty-five cents to a dollar. There's a reason. In the Lyman Howe show they never lose a chance to work an appropriate sound effect, and he can come into your city and show pictures that you have shown a year ago and people will pay a dollar to see them and wish he would come back, which he does, and the same people pass your place up and pay him another dollar. I have put up this argument to many exhibitors in my travels and they all say, "It's his reputation." I agree that it is his reputation, but how did he make it? Good pictures with sound effects.[8]

Unfortunately for the audiences of the period, there were no other Lyman Howes.

Film music, in itself the subject of quite a number of books, is too extensive a study to be given adequate treatment here. Even the music of the silent period would require an additional volume, and so the reader who wishes to explore the topic beyond the limited consideration it is given here should consult the primary information sources. Several have been reprinted in the Arno Press The Literature of Cinema series: Edith Lang and George West's *Musical Accompaniment of Moving Pictures* (originally published in 1920); Erno Rapee's *Moving Picture Moods for Pianists and Organists* (originally 1924) and *Encyclopaedia of Music for Pictures* (originally 1925); and Kurt London's *Film Music* (originally 1936). George W. Beynon's *Musical Presentation of Motion Pictures* is invaluable, but difficult to obtain: it has not been republished since it first appeared, in 1921.

Many journals of the silent period ran articles on film music, and the determined student should become familiar especially with Clarence Sinn's series on "Music for the Picture" in *Moving Picture World,* and with the various pieces on the topic appearing during the teens in the *Film Index* and *Motion Picture News*. A thesis by G. D. Pasquella (University of Iowa, 1968) contains two well-informed chapters on film music from 1908 to 1919. That work, regrettably, is unpublished, but other published sources appearing later than the silent period include Hanns Eisler's *Composing for the Films* (1947; reprint edition, Freeport, N. Y.: Books for Libraries); Roger Manvell and John Huntley's *The Technique of Film Music* (New York: Focal Press, 1957), which contains an admirable section on music and the silent film and an invaluable appendix, listing, year by year, the major developments in film music since 1895; Reginald Foort's *The Cinema Organ,* 2d ed. (Vestal, N. Y.: Vestal Press, 1970); Charles Hofmann's *Sounds for Silents* (New York: DBS Publications, 1970), which, most usefully, comes supplied with a record of musical examples; and, most recently, Tony Thomas's *Music for the Movies* (Cranbury, N. J.: A. S. Barnes, 1973), which is richly informative on the sound period but has little to say about what occurred before 1930, and James L. Limbacher's *Film Music from Violins to Video* (Metuchen, N. J.: Scarecrow Press, 1974) which contains authoritative listings of film music credits.

As Kracauer said (see quotation at the head of this chapter) the need for music to accompany the silent images was recognized from the beginnings of cinema. The first *public* movie show appears to have been a presentation by the brothers Max and Emil Skladanowsky, using their Bioskop apparatus, at the Wintergarten, Berlin, November 1, 1895. It is not known whether any musical accompaniment to the films was provided on that historic evening. But a pianist was employed to play during France's first public movie show: the Lumière program, given in Paris at the Grand-Café on the Boulevard des Capucines, December 28, 1895.[9] Pianists were at work in most store-front theaters or nickelodeons in the first eight or ten years of the present century. Affluent exhibitors would also employ a drummer and a violinist. "Of course," wrote George W. Beynon, "it was not to be expected that they should play continuously. . . . They played only during those scenes which appealed to them as holding possibilities for music with which they were conversant. In other words, they made no pretense to fitting the music to the scenes but waited until a scene should appear that fitted the music. They had little or no [sheet music] library, and 'faked' selections by ear. Technically the music was abominable."[10] At times the musicians also played what they knew or could "fake" even when it did not fit the scene, and sometimes they played in competition with one another.

As G. W. Beynon saw it, the accompaniment frequently "resolved itself into a question in the minds of the performers as to who could make the most commotion. . . ."[11] The drummer usually won without much difficulty, and, no doubt, to his great satisfaction, since, according to H. F. Hoffman, the drummer assumed "that the audience came there to hear him and him only. His object," insisted Hoffman, "is to drown the piano player and prove his worth by the amount of noise he can make. . . . His noisy fault is apt to abide with him, and that is why we have so many irritating men behind the drum in moving picture houses."[12] Thus, music, which was originally intended both to render the absence of sound tolerable and to heighten the effect of the visual images, often became an annoying distraction from the motion picture. Even when the musicians were inclined to play in harmony, their selections would vary from the banal to the ludicrous. "Stock pieces" such as "Hearts and Flowers" or a butchered version of the *William Tell* Overture were the pinnacles of musical taste in many nickelodeons. But standards were changing even before 1910.

In the period between *The Great Train Robbery* (1903) and *The Birth of a Nation* (1915) the standard length of the dramatic motion picture increased from the thousand-foot single reel (12 to 15 minutes' showing time) to features of six to ten reels (60 to 90 minutes' showing time.) As film stories became more elaborate and sophisticated, the need for more elaborate and sophisticated musical accompaniments became increasingly evident. The practice of musicians playing only intermittently during film shows gradually gave way to continuous musical accompaniments, and among many musicians a controversy arose as to whether music should be selected with regard to the prevailing mood of the picture or whether the nature of each scene should determine the kind of music played with it. The second alternative, which failed to serve the increasing complexity of film stories after 1910, was usually abandoned in favor of the first.[13]

Meanwhile, the nickelodeons were giving way to movie palaces that could accommodate several thousand patrons at one sitting and also orchestras of a hundred or more musicians. Pasquella cites two examples of orchestras playing in movie theaters as early as 1908, but that was a rare occurrence until the teens.[14] Around this time, organs began to be installed in many larger movie palaces whose proprietors could not (or would not) provide the luxury of a full orchestra. Beynon maintained that Mitchell Mark's Alhamabra Theatre on English Avenue in Cleveland, Ohio, contained the first organ installed in a movie theater[15]—this was in 1910, according to Pasquella.[16] Some exhibitors tried to eliminate the need for any musicians by introducing player pianos, but they soon found that machines lacked the versatility of live musicians, who, of course, could vary the musical mood along with the twists and turns of the film story.

As movie musicians began to take greater pride in their work, their interest in widening the choice of appropriate music also increased. Between 1910 and 1913 a number of publishing houses started issuing collections of relevant sheet music, consisting invariably of pieces that had not been composed with movies in mind. Cue sheets giving suggestions for music linked to specific scenes seem to have appeared first around 1910.[17] In that year, *Edison Kinetogram* started publishing a series of articles giving appropriate musical selections and musical cues for Edison Company releases.[18] Other movie companies were quick to follow the example.

J. S. Zamecnik introduced the idea of publishing collections of "classified mood music," beginning in 1913 with the issue of his *Sam Fox Moving Picture Music Volumes*. Zamecnik's was perhaps the most widely used collection in the teens; it was supplanted in Europe by Giuseppe Becce's *Kinothek* or *Kino-bibliothek* (Berlin, 1919), a more extensive compilation, and in the U. S. by Erno Rapee's one-volume *Moving Picture Moods for Pianists and Organists* (1924). From 1915 to 1928 scoring for silent features could either mean assembling a pot-pourri mainly or entirely from the works of composers unconnected with film or else an original composition commissioned (usually by the studio) to be played along with the movie. An outstanding example of the pot-pourri was the score concocted by D. W. Griffith and Joseph Carl Breil for *The Birth of a Nation* (1915): the selection ranged from songs like "Dixie" through Wagner's "Ride of the Valkyries."[19] With the pot-pourri as with the original score, the method of using leitmotifs and linking themes to specific characters and key incidents was well established by 1915.

The composition of original film music seems to have begun in France in 1907, when Camille Saint-Saens wrote a score for the Film d'Art production *L'Assassinat du Duc de Guise*. It was subsequently published as his Opus 128 for strings, piano, and harmonium. The score cued each musical segment (an Introduction and five Tableaux) to specific scenes of the movie.[20] In the same year or in 1908, Russian composer Ippolitov-Ivanov provided the music for a film about Stenka Razin and the revolt of the Don Cossacks. Perhaps the first American composer to follow the direction pointed by Saint-Saens and Ippolitov-Ivanov was Walter Cleveland Simon, who wrote an original score for the screen adaptation of Dion Boucicault's *Arrah-na-Pogue* (directed by Sidney Olcott for Kalem, 1911).

With the rise of the feature film and the establishment of orchestras in the movie palaces of most cities, studios began to take film music more seriously, and composers were assigned to write original compositions as well as to prepare the usual pastiches. In the teens and twenties, a number of talented composers became distinguished exclusively or mainly for their film scores—most notably Joseph Carl Breil (*The Lily and the Rose, Intolerance*), Victor Schertzinger (*Civilization, Robin Hood*), Hugo Riesenfeld (*Joan the Woman, The Blue Bird, Humoresque, The Covered Wagon, The Ten Commandments, Grass, Beggar on Horseback*), Louis F. Gottschalk (*Broken Blossoms, Orphans of the Storm*), Mortimer Wilson (*The Thief of Bagdad*), William Frederick Peters (*Way Down East, The Enemies of Women*), Erno Rapee (*The Iron Horse, Sunrise*), and Leo Kempinski (*Greed*). Max Steiner, the most prolific composer of film music, began his career in 1916 with a score for *The Bond-*

man; but his best-known work (the music for *King Kong, Gone with the Wind, Casablanca,* and *The Big Sleep*) would belong to the sound era. In Europe during the twenties, Edmund Meisel wrote memorable scores for Eisenstein's *Potemkin* and *October,* while Gottfried Huppertz was critically acclaimed for the music he provided for Fritz Lang's *Siegfried* and *Metropolis.*

A number of European composers whose work was to become part of the regular concert repertoire supplied original music for other important films of the twenties. Among them were George Antheil (*Ballet Mécanique*), Erik Satie (*Entr'acte*), Darius Milhaud (*L'Inhumaine*), Arthur Honegger (*Fait Divers, Napoléon*), Jacques Ibert (*The Italian Straw Hat*), Jean Sibelius (*The Unknown Soldier*), Roger Desormière (*À Quoi Rêvent Les Jeunes Filles*), Paul Hindemith (*Krazy Kat at the Circus, Ghosts Before Breakfast*), and Dmitri Shostakovich (*The New Babylon*). J. S. Zamecnik and Giuseppe Becce, compilers of the leading mood music collections, were also active film composers: the former wrote scores for *Abie's Irish Rose* and *The Wedding March;* the latter the music for *Tartuffe.*

After special effects and music, a third method of adding sound to the silent film was via the voices of live singers, actors, or lecturers.

During the period before 1915, singers were most commonly used for "illustrated songs" or accompanied tableaux, and for operatic scenes. As these two art forms are sometimes confused by film historians, it is worth distinguishing between them.

With the illustrated song or accompanied tableau, a filmed scene representing a well-known melody or musical piece was accompanied by a singer (or singers) behind a screen. Thus Stephen Foster's "Swanee River" would be represented by a short film (often in color) of a plantation in the Old South, while the song was being sung by singers invisible to the audience. Ketelby's "In a Monastery Garden," an intensely popular piece of program music, was sometimes depicted in a filmed tableau of a beautiful arbor where cowled monks paraded to the strains of a chorus hidden behind the screen. Sometimes there were no singers behind the screen, but a pianist accompanied the illustrated song or tableau while the audience sang along, aided by large display cards or printed sheets giving the lyrics of "Daisy," "Lily of Laguna," or other popular songs of the time. This was a not uncommon variation on the song slide, which became a popular interlude attraction in movie programs from about 1909 onwards.

With the operatic scenes, the film subjects were not fanciful creations suggested by the words of a song or the title of a piece of music but were filmed excerpts from operas—or at least scenes whose settings were appropriate (more or less) to the arias sung by the hidden singers. Although the use of live singers to accompany silent operatic scenes reached the peak of popularity between 1908 and 1915, the most ambitious effort along these lines did not occur until 1922. On May 19 of that year, an audience in Berlin, Germany, saw and heard *Across the Stream,* an original film-opera conceived and directed by Ludwig Czerny with music by Ferdinand Hummel. A correspondent for the London *Times* (May 20, 1922) attended the presentation and noted that

> The problem resolved itself into one of synchronization, the orchestra and the singers behind the screen timing their efforts to fit exactly with the action of the film. Though they were, on the whole, successful in keeping pace with the rapid action of the film, the illusion of an opera was not created, as the close association between voice and gesture was entirely wanting. It might have been better if the characters of the film had actually sung their parts at the time of production; but this was not done, and the impression always remained that one person was acting and another singing.

In the same city, only five months after this stillborn venture, American inventor Lee De Forest gave the first public demonstration of his sound-on-film experiments, the ultimate success of which would sweep such efforts as *Across the Stream* into oblivion.

The use of the actor behind the screen or the lecturer alongside it was the most familiar form of nonmusical accompaniment to silent film from about 1905 to 1915. The movie lecturer's art was never as developed in the West as it became in the Far East; in Japan, for example, the speaker was known as the *benshi.* Anderson and Richie in their history of the Japanese film note that

From the very first the *benshi* tended to dominate the film and, since the audience liked to be instructed, he would rarely let an opportunity slip by. . . . As his popularity grew so did his importance. In the larger theaters a fanfare would sound before every show . . . and the *benshi* would enter with great dignity to sit on his platform beside the screen. . . . The more famous had different techniques and sometimes differed widely in interpreting the film. . . . Eventually the *benshi* rather than the film became the box office attraction. . . . His pay became equivalent to that of the highest paid Japanese film actor, and his position was further secured by the producers and distributors, who liked the *benshi*, saying he saved the cost of printing titles.[21]

The Western movie lecturer never attained such glorious heights. More frequently he was the subject of fundamental advice from long-suffering columnists in trade papers. "A thorough and patient study of the picture is essential," wrote W. Stephen Bush in 1911.

If you have seen a picture ten times you can be of great help to the man who sees it for the first time. You can explain and point out things that at the first exhibition of the release even a man of average intelligence and good education might very easily miss. Do not, however, attempt to lecture on a film unless you feel in your heart and soul that there is need for it and that you are competent to fill that need.[22]

In the West, the typical movie lecturer engaged in little more than such elementary exposition; there was seldom any attempt to provide dramatic characterizations similar to those skilfully undertaken by the *benshi*.

Such performances were, however, expected of actors behind the screen, who, at their best, probably anticipated the techniques of acting for radio. One performer, the Baroness Blanc, claimed to have spent three years studying the art of talking to pictures, "noting each detail, and seeking to cultivate that particular vocal method combining flexibility and adaptability, which is essential, in order to make the figures on the screen absolutely true to life."[23] However, not all performers were so painstaking; from time to time the trade press erupted with complaints about amateurs and inadequately trained professionals who were lowering the standards of acting behind the screen; they made no attempt to synchronize their voices with the characters on screen, or their voices were unsuitable or characterless, or they uttered dialogue that was irrelevant or absurd.

Acting behind the screen, sometimes known as the "Talking Picture Play," seems to have originated with Lyman Howe as early as 1897, but it did not become popular or professionally organized until ten years later. Commentators of the period sometimes distinguished between two kinds of Talking Picture Play: standard film subjects to which dialogue, not necessarily intended for the picture, was subsequently added; and movies "specially posed with completely spoken dialogue by all characters and with the same dialogue rendered from manuscript during projection by the speakers behind the screen."[24] The second kind clearly involved close association between the production company and the performing group(s), but it is not known how frequently this arrangement occurred or even which companies were most involved with it. We do know that in the heyday of the Talking Picture Play, about 1908 to 1912, troupes, generally consisting of two men and a woman, would tour theater circuits with several films for which they had rehearsed dialogue for all the roles. After a week's performance at a specific location, a particular troupe would move on to the next theater, together with their films, to be followed by the next troupe, along with *their* films and rehearsed dialogue. Mogul-to-be Adolph Zukor at one time managed no fewer than twenty-two such talking trios, which he called Humanuva Troupes.[25]

Thus far, except for sound effects machines and player pianos, all the methods we have considered for supplying sound for silent films involved the active presence of live performers or live special effects men. But before the coming of talkies, two other methods of making sound films were investigated and applied with varying degrees of success. The first involved the combination of the phonograph and the motion picture; the second, which we shall discuss in the next chapter, involved the use of a sound track on the film itself.

Numerous attempts to combine the phonograph and the motion picture were made during a period of nearly forty years following the commercial beginnings of cinema in 1895.* The remainder of this chapter is concerned with the more significant, ingenious, or spectacular of these attempts before the inception of Vitaphone, the sound system which marked the culmination of all efforts at linking phonograph recordings and the cinematograph.

All the attempts we shall discuss fall into three main categories: (1) Films made first and then supplied with a phonograph record accompaniment which provided varying degrees of synchronization. (2) Films made to "illustrate visually" previously made phonograph records. Usually the singers or actors were filmed while miming to the sound of a record—the same record that was later played when the film was projected. The usual reason for this procedure was that before 1910 adequate recordings could only be made if the performer was as close as possible to the microphone. Thus, to film while the recording was being made would have meant revealing the microphone in the movie. (3) Films made simultaneously with the recording of the relevant sound and subsequently shown with the same sound accompaniment; this type was rarely attempted with any success before 1910. To a greater or lesser extent all these categories of sound films were affected by the same problems— those of synchronization, amplification, and brevity of recorded disks in relation to the standard lengths of movies. It will be convenient here to consider each of these problems separately before turning to actual achievements in combining the phonograph and the cinematograph.

Synchronization generally involved difficulties at two separate stages: first in *recording,* and then in *reproducing* the visuals and the accompanying sound. Success at the first stage did not automatically guarantee success at the second. Accordingly, inventors sought various methods of obtaining a precise relationship between the recording and the reproducing machines. The methods that evolved were, basically, the use of unitary machines, the use of dependent machines, and the use of dial-regulated and operator-adjusted machines.[26]

With the unitary method, the phonograph and cinemato-

* See list of patents in Appendix C.

graph (in recording) or the phonograph and projector (in reproducing) used synchronous electric motors or were driven by the same power source, which worked a single main shaft connecting the two machines. This main shaft might be fairly short in the film studio, where the camera and the phonograph were often placed in close proximity. In the movie theater, by contrast, the main shaft was often very long. It would frequently be located under the floor of the auditorium, extending from the phonograph, which was placed behind or alongside the screen, to the projector, situated in a booth behind the audience. This arrangement was considered necessary because it seemed unnatural for the audience to listen to the sound coming from behind their seats while they were facing the picture. The alternative method of projecting the picture from behind a translucent screen would have allowed for a short connecting shaft between the two machines, but for some obscure reason this procedure was not regarded as acceptable or satisfactory.

In its conception the unitary method may have seemed promising, but in order for it to work satisfactorily it was necessary for picture and sound to start off in exact synchronization —or for some means to be provided whereby the operator could slow down or speed up either machine if synchronization was not maintained. A problem could arise if there was a defect in the record or a splice in the film where a repair had necessitated the removal of a number of frames. A loss of three frames would reduce a film's showing time—at the silent speed of 16 frames per second—by approximately one-fifth of a second; thus a long film with many splices would gradually run seconds or minutes ahead of the sound accompaniment. A typical solution to the problem was the use of a clutch mechanism that allowed the projectionist to disengage the projector from the main shaft. He could then adjust the speed of the projector by hand-cranking it until synchronization was regained—at which time he could use the clutch to reengage the projector and the main shaft.

With the dependent method, one machine depended on, that is, was driven or controlled by, the other. Usually it was the phonograph motor that controlled the speed of the projector. Any change in the speed of the phonograph effected a corresponding change in projector speed. The phonograph could not normally be the dependent machine because any adjustment that involved varying the speed of the phonograph would change the pitch of the sounds being reproduced, and that was usually undesirable or even objectionable, particularly with music. As with the unitary method, clutch-like devices were introduced that allowed the projectionist to disengage the projector from the controlling drive of the phonograph whenever it was necessary to restore synchronization by hand-cranking the projector.

By contrast, there were no connections between the separate machines in the dial-regulated or operator-adjusted methods. The first provided the operator with dials that gave readings of the speed of each machine. By watching the dials and where necessary making hand-crank adjustments to the speed of the projector, the operator was able to maintain approximate synchronization. The operator-adjusted method was the simplest: the operator did not rely on dials but listened to the sound either directly, as it filtered through to him from the auditorium, or as he heard it over an internal telephone system. While listening to the sound he adjusted the speed of the projector to coincide with it.

None of these synchronization techniques was perfect, and usually they were less than adequate. Until the arrival of Vitaphone, sound systems using phonographs or Graphophones achieved synchronization on a hit-or-miss basis at best, though some inventors, including Edison and Gaumont, made exaggerated claims of having attained perfection.

In 1912, the London *Times* noted the observations of an eminent scientist, Professor W. Stirling, on the conditions that had to be fulfilled for the successful making of sound films. Much of what he had to say concerned amplification, which would have to be sufficient for large audiences to "hear the sound and observe the exact correlation between the movements of the speakers, actors, or singers, and the audible sounds as regards pitch, loudness, and quality of tone."[27] That, of course, was the ideal, and it was not to be realized for many years. At the outset, when only one horn speaker was used, amplification was as serious a problem as synchronization. However, it became less of a problem from about 1908 onwards, when theaters presenting sound films would, typically, be equipped with numerous horn speakers arranged behind a perforated screen (where they were sometimes moved about by hand in relation to the on-screen action), or assembled in a battery below a slightly raised screen, or scattered at various locations throughout the auditorium. Around 1910, various methods of increasing the volume of sound by compressed air devices were tried in the U. S. and Europe.[28] Audiences were thus quite often able to hear the sound fairly well, but what they heard seemed just like old phonograph records with plenty of surface noise.

The brevity of sound recordings posed another serious problem for inventors. Even as early as 1905, the average story film ran longer than the four minutes of a cylinder record or the five minutes of a 12″ disk recording. Theoretically there was no limit to the length of recorded sound that could be supplied with a film provided that several records were used; but switching from record to record generally resulted in loss of synchronization. The development of auto-change systems (c.1910) or the use of several phonographs never totally overcame this particular difficulty. Some European inventors tried using oversize disks that played for as long as twenty minutes, but they found that sound quality would deteriorate markedly as the needle approached the center of the recording.

Bearing in mind these general observations on the problems of combining the phonograph and the motion picture, let us now turn to specific work in this area of sound cinema.

A selective listing, compiled by *Film Daily,* giving details of patents for sound-on-disk apparatus, shows that more than one hundred inventors in France, Germany, Britain, and the U. S. were at work in this field before 1929.[29] Since we cannot discuss all of them and their achievements, we shall concentrate on the highlights.

In America the impulse to harness the phonograph to the motion picture declined temporarily between 1897 and 1908, the years following the debut of the Vitascope. The main inventive development of the period was the introduction of the Biograph projector, which reduced the flicker of the projected image to a tolerable minimum, and which, in 1897, began to supplant the Vitascope.* Most film activity before 1900 was concentrated on the commercial development of the silent motion picture. Independent inventors were soon overshadowed by the rise of the entrepreneur, the small businessman who bought or rented a movie projector, obtained a few short, crudely made films, and presented them at fair grounds, as a vaudeville turn, or, most ambitiously, as a separate show in a converted store. Early in the twentieth century, the more successful of these converted store-theaters sometimes became nickelodeons, the first established movie houses. Despite some spectacular success stories, the majority of entrepreneurs did not become millionaires. In fact, by 1900, periods of fluctuating profits had already demonstrated the fickleness of the public with regard to motion pictures. Not unnaturally, the entrepreneurs were more interested in consolidating their business enterprises than in sinking money into new technical developments, such as sound and color, which might turn out to be a nine days' wonder as far as the public was concerned.

It is hardly surprising, therefore, that no one showed much interest in marketing the invention of one George W. Brown, which received U. S. patent no.576,542, on February 9, 1897. Brown constructed an apparatus that synchronized a moving picture film and a phonograph. The pictures he used were not projected; they could only be viewed (as in the Kinetoscope) through an eyepiece as they ran, on an endless loop, over a drum which was rotated by a belt worked from the drive mechanism of a phonograph. The playing of the phonograph was automatically adjusted to the speed at which the picture strip passed under the eyepiece. The invention was, obviously,

---

* In the summer of 1901 the Biograph was used in conjunction with the Graphophone to provide an exhibit of moving pictures with sound accompaniment at the Pan-American Exposition in Buffalo, New York. The films showed work in the institutions of the U.S. Bureau of Education, and the nonsynchronized cylinder records accompanying them contained the voices of teachers and pupils at those institutions. There is no evidence that the experiment was continued after the Exposition. See further, reproduction of the souvenir card advertising the exhibit in Kemp R. Niver, *Biograph Bulletins 1896–1908* (Los Angeles: Locare Research Group, 1971), p. 58.

a variation on the Kinetophone, developed too late to be an exploitable novelty.

Alas for Brown, the immediate future of the motion picture generally and of sound film in particular lay not in the peep show machine but in the use of projected film in movie theaters. The initiative now shifted to France, where for nearly ten years after Edison abandoned his earliest efforts to make sound movies, a number of inventors tackled, with varying degrees of success, the problems of linking the phonograph and the motion picture.[30]

The first of these inventors was Auguste Baron. Fired by the commercial success of the Lumière Cinématographe, Baron sank his personal fortune of 200,000 francs into a series of attempts to make sound pictures. His work evidently passed through three main phases:

On April 16, 1896, Baron and a collaborator named Burnon took out a patent for an apparatus that would record and reproduce scenes and sounds. There is no evidence that at this time they actually constructed such a machine. In fact, the Lumières, claiming priority as pioneers of sound film, were later to maintain that they had actually accomplished synchronization of sound and image (using their Cinématographe and an Edison phonograph) four days later than the "theoretical" patent of Baron and Burnon. But their claim remains conjectural.

In the second phase of his activity, Baron seems to have actually constructed an improved version of his apparatus. On April 4, 1898, he took out French patent no.276,628 for a machine "perfected to record and reproduce simultaneously animated scenes and the sounds which accompany them." The invention was a combination of a phonograph and a "chronophotographic apparatus"—the latter most probably being an adapted Lumière Cinématographe obtained from Félix Mesguisch, who had worked for the Lumières and who became Baron's assistant in 1897. Mesguisch in his *Tour de Manivelle* (Paris, 1933) claims that Baron was the first person ever to synchronize the phonograph with a projected motion picture, and he provides a fairly detailed description of the sound system patented by Baron in 1898. Its major innovation was an electrical device which controlled the motor of the "chronophoto-graphic" apparatus and was linked to the motor of a phono-graph. Mesguisch maintains that during 1897–98, at Baron's modest laboratory in Alma Street, Asnières, he assisted the inventor in making several films that utilized the new sound system. They included a number of song and dance scenes, utilizing stars from the Opéra Comique and the Eldorado, and a "talkie" in which Mme. Baron supplied the spoken com-mentary. Baron appears to have supervised the sound recording while Mesguisch shot the films.

Probably in 1898, Baron demonstrated his sound films to Marey and was delighted to receive the latter's praise and en-couragement. But, as noted in the previous chapter in connec-tion with Demeny, Marey placed his faith in science and not in money, and Baron soon began to realize that the heavy expense of his work made strong financial backing more desirable than idealistic enthusiasm. Potential backers were generous with their encouragement but would not put up a franc to develop or exploit Baron's system. What they must have recognized very quickly was that Baron had failed to find a reliable and inexpensive method of duplicating the wax cylinders on which he recorded the sounds that accompanied his films. It was im-possible to make copies of the same sound films; to make the equivalent of a copy it was necessary to reshoot the picture and re-record the sound.

In 1899, Baron gave a presentation of his sound films to the Institute of Sciences in Paris. His brief program included movies of Miss Duval of the Lyric Gaiety Theatre singing a popular song and Trewey, the famous magician and friend of the Lumières, giving one of his celebrated shadow shows. Whatever impression this program may have had on the members of the Institute, it did nothing to improve Baron's deteriorating financial position.

About this time, Baron's eyesight began to fail. Nevertheless, in the midst of his increasing difficulties, he became involved in a third stage of experimentation—an attempt to make stereo-scopic sound films. While engaged in this work, Baron went blind. His efforts to perfect sound films came to a sudden end. Mesguisch left his employ shortly before 1900, and Baron gradually drifted into poverty. He lived on until 1938, dying at the age of 83 in an old people's home in Neuilly. His end came in the same year as the deaths of Georges Méliès and Emile Cohl, two other French pioneers of the cinema.

Almost contemporaneously with Baron, other French inventors were concentrating their efforts on solving the problems of amplification—in using the phonograph to provide sound accompaniment to films shown before large audiences. One "solution" was that described by G.-Michael Coissac in his *Histoire du Cinématographe.* A certain Jacques Ducom described to Coissac a presentation of talking pictures at the Olympia in Paris, about 1898. Adequate amplification was provided by supplying individual telephone receivers for each member of the audience. These receivers were connected to a phonograph which provided the sound accompaniment to projected movies.[31] Unfortunately, nothing more is known of this curious experiment though it may well have influenced the *Phonorama* of Dussaud, Berthon, and Jaubert, of which we shall be hearing shortly.

According to Georges Sadoul, the eminent film historian, French pioneers of the cinema Charles Pathé and Ferdinand Zecca experimented with talking films as early as 1899.[32] But like the Olympia show of the previous year little is known of the success or failure of their efforts at this time. Pathé was variously an inventor, entrepreneur, and showman. In the 1890s he made a fortune by importing into France British-made phonographs and Kinetoscopes that infringed Edison's patents and which he sold at prices that undercut the Edison machines. He established a recording studio at which he made some of the earliest cylinder recordings in France. And in June 1895 he formed a business partnership with H. Joly, who, in 1906, would patent one of the first dial-regulated sound systems. Years later, Pathé was to observe, "The phonograph for me was only a preparation for the cinema. Just as the phonograph preceded the gramophone, so too the Edison Kinetoscope preceded the cinema. . . . The principle of cinema . . . was achieved by the Kinetoscope . . . which I obtained in London and . . . which I sold in large numbers before the Lumière Cinématographe had made its appearance."[33] Zecca was to become one of France's first notable film makers. Inspired by Georges Méliès, he tried his hand at making trick and fantasy films; independently he discovered the dramatic possibilities of the close-up, which he used as early as 1901; he made some of the earliest story films to embody social commentary; and in 1905 he filmed the very first reconstruction of the Potemkin mutiny.

A more obscure figure than either Pathé or Zecca was the French inventor Gariel. On March 31, 1900 he patented a system for "combining in the same cinematographic apparatus the mechanisms for recording and reproducing the words used in the phonograph."[34] This system was, presumably, a method of synchronization. But there is no evidence that the apparatus was constructed or demonstrated, and Gariel's name does not figure in connection with subsequent attempts to make sound movies.

More spectacular than the efforts of Baron, Pathé, Zecca, or Gariel were the exhibitions of sound-on-film systems at the Paris Exposition of 1900. The first of these systems was the Phonorama of L. A. Berthon, C. F. Dussaud, and G. F. Jaubert. The development of Phonorama appears to have been as follows: Before 1897, Dussaud found a way to combine simultaneous recordings made by at least twelve phonographs. Rather like multi-channel recording on a modern tape recorder, it was a means of capturing clearly all the various sounds that might be audible in one location: music, conversation, natural sound, etc. Dussaud called his apparatus the Macrophonograph. Subsequently he joined forces with Berthon and Jaubert to find a way of combining the Macrophonograph and the cinematograph. The machine they constructed was given the elephantine name of Cinemacrophonograph, and patented on January 1, 1898. News of the invention came to the attention of Eugène Pereire, president of the General Transatlantic Company of Le Havre, and he decided that it could be exploited as a novel advertisement for his company, which had reserved a booth at the Paris Exposition. Pereire's company thereupon acquired an interest in the invention, which was mercifully renamed Phonorama.

Félix Mesguisch, who had worked for the Lumières and for Auguste Baron, was employed to shoot the films that would be shown in the Phonorama exhibit. Mesguisch evidently made three films for the show: views of maritime life in Le Havre and Marseilles, some Paris street scenes, and a singer performing with an orchestral accompaniment. In making the films, the same electrically powered shaft was used to drive the movie apparatus and twelve phonographs, thus insuring some degree of synchronization during the recording and playback. In filming the singer's performance, some of the phonographs were placed on stage, while others were located in the orchestra. Subsequently, the films were colored by hand at the Gaumont studios, so that Phonorama was actually a presentation of sound films in color! The sound system used inside the Phonorama booth at the Exposition was similar to that used at the Olympia two years earlier. Each member of the audience watched Mesguisch's films while simultaneously listening through an earphone to the synchronized sounds being supplied by the twelve phonographs.

More impressive than Phonorama, and in certain respects more spectacular than any presentation in the history of sound film, was the Phono-Cinéma-Théâtre of Clément-Maurice Gratioulet and Henri Lioret, which had its public premiere at the Paris Exposition on June 8, 1900.

Gratioulet (who called himself Clément-Maurice) is said to have introduced the Lumières to the Kinetoscope; he was the concessionaire who had arranged for the showing of the Lumière program at the Grand-Café on the Boulevard des Capucines, Paris, on December 28, 1895. He was a fashionable photographer who specialized in making portraits of the stars of theater, opera, ballet, and vaudeville. His dual interests in the cinematograph and show business led him to the idea of making sound movies of many of the stage personalities he had photographed. His associate, Lioret, was an horologist by training and an inventor by inclination. In the 1890s he patented a cylinder talking-machine which he called the Lioretographe: its recording and amplification qualities were said to have been superior to Edison's phonograph, and Lioret had already marketed it profitably before he went into partnership with Clément-Maurice. The Lioretographe was to become the basis of the sound system used in the Phono-Cinéma-Théâtre. Film historians René Jeanne and Charles Ford claimed that Léon Gaumont had a hand in developing it, but that may be purely conjectural.[35]

Lioret's system was less complex than that used in the Phonorama. Apparently there was no mechanical connection of the cinematograph and the Lioretographe. It was the first (or one of the first) systems using the operator-adjusted method. The scenes to be shown were first filmed, and then the performers recorded their dialogue or songs on the Lioretographe, endeavoring to adjust their cadences to the film performance. In showing the films, synchronization of sorts was achieved by adjusting the film image to conform to the sounds issuing from the Lioretographe. The projectionist was equipped with a telephone through which he listened to the cylinder machine, which was located in the orchestra pit. While following the sound, he regulated the speed of the projector, which was hand-cranked. The sound reached the audience by way of a large morning-glory horn attached to the Lioretographe. It has been claimed—by Georges Sadoul and others—that the ubiquitous Félix Mesguisch was the projectionist at the Phono-Cinéma-Théâtre for its run at the Exposition, but that is questionable since Mesguisch was then involved with Phonorama. However, Mesguisch, assisted by a young man named Berst, who later became the agent for Pathé Frères' New York office, did take the Phono-Cinéma-Théâtre on a successful European tour in the fall and winter of 1900–1901.

Before this tour the first home of the Phono-Cinéma-Théâtre was a beautiful pavilion in the Cours la Reine. The building was a reconstruction of the Salon Frais at the Trianon, and in this lovely setting, for the modest sum of one franc, the visitor to the Paris Exposition could see and hear films of the great stars of theater and opera, ballet and vaudeville. The program included such attractions as Sarah Bernhardt in the duel scene from *Hamlet*, Coquelin the Elder in scenes from Rostand's *Cyrano de Bergerac* and Molière's *Les Précieuses Ridicules*, Réjane in *Madame Sans-Gêne* and *Ma Cousine*, and Victor Maurel in *Falstaff* and *Don Juan*; it offered dance attractions such as Zambelli in *Le Cid* and *Sylvia*, Rosita Mauri, Violat, and Mante of the Paris Opéra in *La Korrigane*, Cléo and

Merode performing a Javanese dance, and Félicia Mallet in a ballet, *The Prodigal Son* (in three tableaux); it presented Cossira, vocal star of the Paris Opéra, and such vaudeville celebrities as Little Tich (the British comedian), Mason and Forbes (American vaudeville artists), and popular singers Polin and Milly Meyer. The only bill that approached this galaxy of stars was the one offered by Warner Bros. twenty-six years later in one of the programs used to introduce Vitaphone.

The Paris press gave the Phono-Cinéma-Théâtre rave notices. One journal, quoted by Georges Sadoul, rhapsodized over the scenes showing Coquelin in the Molière play: "It is really Coquelin whom we see before us; it is his voice that we hear! It is stupendous!"[36] *L'Intransigéant* described the large audiences that enthusiastically applauded the "arresting presentation" of the ballet *The Prodigal Son* and the shouts of triumph that greeted the screening of the duel scene in *Hamlet,* in which the divine "Sarah Bernhardt is so tragically beautiful." *Le Figaro* noted:

> The success of this very original enterprise surpasses all that can be said about it. The artists themselves, after graciously posing before the *Phono-Cinéma-Théâtre* apparatus, go to see themselves again, to hear themselves again, and, what is also satisfying, to hear themselves being applauded just as if they were acting in person before the public. . . . The duel scene from *Hamlet* . . . is a wonder of art at the same time that it is a masterpiece of accurate representation. Réjane plays in *Ma Cousine* and *Madame Sans-Gêne* with such spirit that the spectator believes himself transported to the vaudeville theatre. Coquelin . . . brings the show to an end with [a scene from] *Les Précieuses Ridicules,* and his resonant and splendid voice is drowned by the thunder of applause.[37]

Summing up the experience, a reviewer for *Le Matin* observed:

> Beyond the very real pleasure which one feels at this spectacle, one cannot help entertaining the agreeable and consoling thought that here are beautiful sounds and beautiful gestures which are fixed for eternity; and while the people of our generation know of Talma and Rachel only through hearsay, our descendants will admire [through these films] the performance of the divine Sarah and will be able to relive our emotions and our joys at her artistry.[38]

With such notices the success of the show was almost guaranteed. It played to packed houses until the Exposition closed and then, on November 10, 1900, was transferred to a new location, at 42 bis Boulevard Bonne-Nouvelle. Mesguisch and Berst took charge of the touring version of the show which, during the fall and winter of 1900–1901 visited Sweden, Germany, Austria, Switzerland, and Spain. They were back in Paris by the spring of 1901, when the Phono-Cinéma-Théâtre was transferred to the Olympia. By this time, however, several other programs of sound films (including Phonorama) were being presented in Paris. Competition was vigorous, and there were even attempts to sabotage the program at the Olympia—which was commercially the most successful of the sound film enterprises and had received the most favorable publicity. One attempt to disrupt the show was described thus, by Mesguisch:

> One evening, when I was in the projection booth on the second floor while Berst was working the phonograph in the orchestra, an ill-disposed workman cut the wire of the telephone by which I was supposed to follow the sound coming from the phonograph. Without interrupting the performance, I actually succeeded in finishing my projection in perfect synchronization with the phonograph. No one noticed that the projectionist had for a short time been 'struck deaf.'[39]

The Phono-Cinéma-Théâtre did not survive more than two or three years, but sabotage was not responsible for its demise. Its fate was sealed by two factors. First, contrary to the extravagant claims of its promoters and the press reviewers, the sound it provided was unsatisfactory. It was harsh, strident, and seldom more than approximately synchronized. Some of the original cylinders and films still survive, unearthed in 1930 by Mesguisch and Clément-Maurice's son in the archives of their firm, the Compagnie de Tirage Maurice. At that time, the beginning of the sound era, the cylinders and films were played and projected under conditions that simulated the original presentations. The latest methods of sound reproduction were also applied, but neither approach resulted in a satisfactory experience. Sadoul comments, "The sound was sharp and nasal, and it was difficult to follow the words. As soon as the first flush of success due to public curiosity had ended, this defect, even more than the imperfections of the synchronization, prevented the novel attraction from becoming established in a seasonal or permanent fashion, in the programs of the great music-halls."[40]

The second reason that the success of the Phono-Cinéma-Théâtre was brief was probably that the main attraction it held for the public was not the "Phono" or "Cinéma" but its "Théâtre." The novelty was in seeing great stars at little expense and in unusual circumstances, and when the novelty had worn thin, the public went back to seeing the same stars, in person, in full-length stage productions rather than in poorly recorded excerpts. Phonorama aroused less interest than the Phono-Cinéma-Théâtre because, though its sound quality and synchronization were probably better, it could not rival the theatrical galaxy presented by Clément-Maurice. Phono-Cinéma-Théâtre did little or nothing to create an enduring public interest in sound films; but it is still memorable for having demonstrated, more than a decade before Adolph Zukor rediscovered it, the box-office appeal of famous players in film versions of famous plays.

Following Berthon–Dussaud–Jaubert and Clément-Maurice, the most formidable rivals in the phono-film field were Edison and French film pioneer Léon Gaumont, both of whom marketed systems that for a while seemed to promise commercial success—even though they too were far from perfect.

Gaumont's interest in creating sound movies was evident as early as 1900, when, in his photographic company's display case at the Paris Exposition, he exhibited a movie projector mechanically linked to a phonograph. Years later, he admitted that it was "basically nothing but a variant of the coupling of the Kinetoscope apparatus of Edison [with a standard phonograph]."[41] In the following year he was granted French patent no.312,613 for his method of driving a projector electrically from a phonograph. This method was demonstrated for the first time on September 12, 1902, before the French Photographic Society. Frederick Talbot wrote in 1912 that Gaumont's apparatus

> was not yet perfect, but it served to demonstrate that synchronous production of sound and movement by the aid of the cinematograph and the talking machine was within measurable

distance of attainment. The demonstration was held primarily to show how perfect a synchronizing mechanism had been evolved. The great difficulty encountered was in regard to the sensitive character of the material required for taking the records of sounds from a distance.[42]

A second Gaumont patent, granted on November 18, 1902, provided a clutch device for correcting faulty synchronization. A third, dated 1903, introduced a microphone and telephone connection from the phonograph, which was located beside the projector, to the loudspeakers, which were placed behind the screen. Gaumont's system also required that the loudspeakers be moved about in order to follow the on-screen action. (This movement was done by hand, not automatically.) Gaumont created an alternative system in 1904, by devising a phonograph whose speed was controlled from the projection machine. It had rather dubious advantages, since any change in record speed was bound to distort the sound. In 1907 he improved both systems. He patented a gearing device, connecting the phonograph and the projector, which worked a dial that would clearly indicate to the operator when the machines were running in synchronization, and he devised a method for rapidly switching from one record to the next. An electrical circuit that closed when the needle of the phonograph arrived at the end of the record was used to start a second phonograph. In this way, a sufficiently long sound accompaniment could be provided for the average one-reel film of the period. Gaumont never satisfactorily solved the problems of amplification any more than he was able to refine the sensitivity of the phonograph. His most advanced technique for increasing the volume of sound was to use several loudspeakers or morning-glory horns while also intensifying the sound waves by means of compressed air. This method was basically one adopted from the Auxetophone of C. A. Parsons.

The general name for the Gaumont systems was Chronophone, while the sound films it presented were variously known as Filmsparlants or Phono-Scènes. Before 1910, Gaumont had to make each of his Phono-Scènes in two sessions because it was impossible to get anything like a distinct recording unless the singer or speaker projected his voice directly into the microphone. To avoid having to film the microphone as well as the performer, Gaumont's practice was first to make the recording, then to play it back while the performer was filmed mouthing the same piece. Inevitably, synchronization was often a hit-or-miss matter. But in 1910, improvements in the Chronophone made it possible for Gaumont to place the horn out of range of the camera and to achieve adequate synchronization by filming and recording simultaneously. In that year, the International Congress of Photographers in Brussels and the French Academy of Sciences applauded demonstrations of Gaumont's sound system. Within a short time thereafter, a program of Phono-Scènes was prepared for commercial presentation.

It was found that songs made better Chronophone subjects than did spoken dialogue. With the former, the music was usually audible even if the words were indistinct, and imprecise synchrony was generally more tolerable with singing than with speech. Nevertheless, in 1908 the Gaumont company made Phono-Scènes of Sarah Bernhardt, Réjane, and other notable stars of the French theater (it was like a replay of Clément-Maurice's production), and it was announced that such dramatists as Edmond Rostand and Henri Lavedan had been contracted to write film plays for the Chronophone. At least one twenty-minute talking picture play was made about 1912.[43] The title, dramatist, and stars are not known, but it can be said for certain that it did nothing to hasten the arrival of the talkies. They were still nearly twenty years away.

The Chronophone was commercially exploited as early as 1902, although it was not until 1910 that Phono-Scènes became regular presentations at the Gaumont-Palace in Paris. During the next three years they were to be seen and heard in most European capitals and in the U. S. The other leading French sound-on-disk systems—Gentilhomme's (sponsored by the Pathé company), Joly's, Couade's, and Gibl's—were basically similar to Gaumont's, but none achieved the international vogue of Chronophone.

The showpiece of Gaumont's system was an ambitious program that he sent on tour in 1912–13. It presented not only sound films but also movies in "natural color." (Gaumont had developed an additive color process that he called Chrono-

chrome; it was later improved and renamed Gaumont Color.)
The subjects of the sound films included a rooster crowing, a
lion tamer cracking his whip in a den of roaring lions, a banjo
player, a sailor reciting "The Battle of the Clampherdown," and
Gaumont's magnum opus: the twenty-minute talking picture
play.[44] The program was the accomplishment of more than ten
years' experiment and considerable financial investment by the
inventor and his backers, but for the public in Europe and the
U. S., it was little more than a novelty.

Even when the Chronophone's synchronization was perfect,
its sound quality was crude and its amplification left much to
be desired. Jeanne and Ford maintain that exhibitors were
deterred by the expense of installing Chronophone in their
theaters, though Edison's rival system does not seem to have met
with comparable objections. More significantly, compared with
the increasing sophistication of the story material in silent
cinema, the subject matter of even the most elaborate of Gaumont's sound films seemed ludicrously primitive to European
and American audiences in 1913.

World War I interrupted Gaumont's work with sound-on-
disk. Thereafter he resumed his experiments without the
impetus of his prewar years. The culmination of this final phase
of his work appears to have been a well-received demonstration
in Paris, in June 1922, of two short sound-on-disk movies. One
presented General Buat speaking about the necessity of con-
scription; the other was an address by M. Paisant about "the
solemn duty of France and her Unknown Warrior." The
London *Times* noted that the "synchronization of the pictures
and words was irreproachable, and the audience could well
imagine that they were in the presence of living orators. Some
slight imperfections were noticeable in the timbres of the voices,
but the speeches were delivered in clear and sonorous tones."[45]

Years later Gaumont was to claim that some time after 1913
he had been in touch with Danish sound-on-film pioneers
M. Valdemar Poulsen and P. O. Pedersen. He noted, "We made
an agreement which led to the improvement [or rectification] of
the sound films which we used."[46] This statement sounds as if
Gaumont himself was turning toward experimentation with
sound-on-film, but in fact the "agreement" he refers to was a

contract enabling the Gaumont Company to promote a sound-on-film system invented by Poulsen and Pedersen. Marketed in the 1920s under the name GPP [Gaumont-Poulsen-Pedersen system], it used a 35 mm sound record film separate from the film carrying the photographic images. GPP had faulty synchronization and failed commercially. It was never directly associated with Gaumont's own attempts at making sound movies.

As we have seen, in the first ten years or so after the birth of cinema, French creativity in the field of sound movies overshadowed everyone else's. However, inventors *were* busy in other countries.

In Germany, phono-film activity was dominated by Oskar Messter, who describes his work at this period in a memoir, *Mein Weg mit dem Film* (Berlin, 1936). Max and Emil Skladanowsky had presented the first public film shows in Germany —at the Wintergarten, Berlin, in 1895—but commercial film production on a regular basis did not begin in Germany until 1897, when Messter opened his Berlin studio on Friedrichstrasse.[47] Messter had already produced several hunded short silent films by 1903, when he made his first venture into sound movies—a brief film of comedian Robert Steidl accompanied by a record of his patter. Details of the system used at this time are unclear, but it is known that in 1905 Messter patented an operator-adjusted disk system which he improved with patented devices of 1906 and 1909. Before 1908 he went into partnership with inventor Alfred Duskes,* who was to construct a unitary disk system using synchronous motors and (hopefully) avoiding the need for operator adjustments (French patent of 1908). By this time Messter was customarily supplying recorded musical accompaniments to his films, including those in which Henny Porten, Germany's first real movie star, was making her appearance. Among the synchronized dialogue films he made about 1908–10 were a short movie of Giampetro of the Metropol Theatre and a longer effort, *The Green Forest*, starring Henny Porten and Alfred Stein. Messter had major problems with amplification, which, along with waning public interest in his

---

* In the teens the firm of Messter and Duskes became a subsidiary of the great UFA organization.

sound films, persuaded him to give up his experiments soon after 1911. German inventor Ernest Vorbeck tackled the amplification problem in 1913, but whatever he accomplished never got beyond the laboratory.[48]

The first British "sound movie" was perhaps the achievement of William Friese-Greene. If his biographer is correct, as early as spring 1889, Friese-Greene used a camera he had invented to take "some moving pictures of a man singing in time with a phonograph record, and . . . played the record during the showing of the film."[49] The record was made on an Edison machine that Friese-Greene had acquired two years earlier. As noted in chapter 1, he wrote to Edison later in 1889 telling him of "the experiments he had made in using the phonograph in conjunction with the motion picture camera, and suggested that Edison and he should combine in finding a method of making what, nearly forty years later, was announced as 'talkies.' "[50] He received only a perfunctory reply, and the proposed collaboration never materialized.

Friese-Greene's experiments—however successful or prophetic they might have been—remained in the privacy of his laboratory. It was not until 1901 that the British public had its first experience of sound movies. They were Clément-Maurice's, imported from the Paris Exposition. Gary Alligham prints the text of a 1901 playbill advertising the

> Cine-Phono-Matagraph [sic], illustrating in a most marvellous manner, vocal selections from the Royal Italian Opera in Paris. A new kind of Phonograph reproduces the voice, while the Cinematograph shows the singers, their actions, and surroundings. Thus you get scenes from the Royal Italian Opera in Paris brought to your very doors.[51]

The same playbill also indicates an additional program, of strong local appeal, made with the Phono-Cinéma-Théâtre system at the London Hippodrome:

> Mr. Poole has arranged with Mr. Gibbons, of the London Hippodrome, to introduce his latest Singing Pictures—Vesta Tilley, the London Idol, singing 'The Midnight Sun'; Lil Hawthorne, the famous American comedienne in 'Kitty Malone'; Alec Hurley, the coster comedian in 'The Lambeth Cake Walk'; and the American Comedy Four will introduce 'Sally in Our Alley.'

The film of English comedian Little Tich, shown at the Paris Exposition, but curiously omitted from the 1901–1902 programs in Britain, was presented in London in 1903, along with some of Clément-Maurice's other sound films. It was acclaimed by the press as one of the entertainment "triumphs" of the year.

An early version of Gaumont's Chronophone was, according to British film historian Rachel Low, the first disk system to be marketed in England, after being demonstrated at the London Hippodrome in 1904: "By 1906 it was being exploited in the provinces and film subjects for it were selling at 1s. a foot, with 7s. 6d. for a 10-inch disc and 10s. 6d. for one of 12 inches. This early machine apparently sold well and was followed at the end of the year by an improved model called the 'Chronomegaphone,' which was also shown at the Hippodrome and ran there for months with great success."[52] Alligham quotes a 1908 advertisement of the Gaumont Company indicating a further development of their apparatus for the British market—a Hand Chronomegaphone, a "living-picture, singing and talking machine" for £150; it was "worked almost entirely by hand," and was described as a companion to the "renowned Chronomegaphone."[53]

Around 1906, British agents for the Pathé and Edison companies began importing their sound systems along with films and records to be used with the apparatus. Contemporaneously, home-produced systems began to make their appearance. The most prominent were Cinematophone (1907), marketed by the firm of Walturdaw Ltd.; Vivaphone (1907), marketed by the Hepworth Manufacturing Company; Cinephone (1909), patented and marketed by Harold Jeapes; and Animatophone (1910), developed by F. A. Thomassin and marketed by a syndicate formed by Thomassin and Harry Nathan.[54] This last was reputedly the best British disk system, though it survived only until 1911 when the syndicate was dissolved. Rachel Low comments,

> it is not difficult to explain the sound film's failure to become general at this date . . . for the most part sound films were merely unpretentious turns by music-hall artists, thus remaining stationary at one of the very earliest stages of the development of film technique. The technical obstacles to any change on this pattern

were formidable. Not only was the actual sound reproduction often faulty and indistinct, but the size of the disc tended to restrict the duration of the film to a few minutes. The much-discussed synchronization of sound and picture, moreover, was necessarily poor where there was no automatic regulation of the speeds of the four different machines needed to record and project sound and picture.[55]

The British public's interest in sound movies seems to have dried up shortly before World War I. It revived again briefly in 1920, when veteran inventor-producer-director Cecil Hepworth (who in 1910 had patented a disk system using electrical circuit breakers) presented his new feature film, *Anna the Adventuress,* starring Alma Taylor, James Carew, and Ronald Colman, with synchronized sound effects supplied by some unspecified apparatus. Whether it employed disks or sound-on-film is not known. The London *Times* reviewer noted:

> The new process is Mr. Hepworth's secret. . . . To the onlooker the synchronization seems to be perfect. In one scene, for instance, Miss Alma Taylor, as the innocent girl, is seen in the act of packing her trunk. Miss Taylor [also doubling] as the adventuress, throws her a nightdress across the room to include in the trunk, and Miss Taylor as the innocent one, deftly catches it. Obviously, the synchronization to secure such a result must be correct to within a fraction of a second.[56]

E. E. Norton's Cameraphone was the first American disk system to gain a measure of commercial success in the new century. It was promoted by the National Cameraphone Company of New York City. In 1908, when the apparatus became available for lease to exhibitors, demand for it was so great that the company's Bridgeport, Connecticut plant was worked to capacity. *Moving Picture World* described Cameraphone as

> a combination of the moving picture and the graphophone.* The two are operated by one man, who controls them by electricity. The moving picture machine is operated by a spring motor, as is the graphophone, which is concealed behind the screen on which

---

* Norton had been a mechanical engineer for the American Graphophone Company, one of Edison's major business competitors in the field of talking machines.

the pictures appear. The gestures, steps, or sounds indicated in the pictures are heard, if there is any sound connected with them, from the graphophone behind the screen, thus giving the effect of speaking, as well as moving pictures. They are perfectly synchronized; that is, the movement of the lips in the pictures coincides with the words from the graphophone.* . . . The operator, if he finds the pictures slightly ahead or behind the graphophone record, can control the two so absolutely as to bring them in unison. The Cameraphone Company purchases the projecting machine and the graphophones from the companies which make them. They then combine the two in a way never before successfully accomplished. . . .The [Cameraphone] Company, at its New York gallery, rehearses the players and makes the moving picture exposures and graphophone records, thus obtaining the music, noises or sounds which properly accompany the action.[57]

A typical Cameraphone program of 1909 consisted of "I Guess I'm Bad," "the well-known coon song . . . posed by Miss Stella Mayhew," a scene in a Turkish bathhouse (presumably a comedy), and a short drama, *The Corsican Brothers*. Synchronization and sound quality ranged all the way from nonexistent to impressive. Concerning the film of Miss Mayhew, one reviewer remarked, "Of course the pictures were good, but the deep metallic voice of the concealed phonograph detracted somewhat from the illusion. It was not a woman's voice that spoke." In the Turkish bathhouse scene, "neither action nor words were in accord any of the time," but with *The Corsican Brothers*

> the work was much better than in the lighter pieces. The deliberate action required was conducive to consonance between the words and the movement of the speakers, and there was less facing of the audience when the characters were speaking, which permitted more illusion regarding the speeches. On the whole there was nothing to be desired in the production. The voices of the characters are notably heavy, anyhow, and that helped the phonograph materially in reproducing the text. On the whole, this ambitious third number was a success.

* At least in some instances; *Moving Picture World* was later to have reservations about Cameraphone's "perfect" synchronization.

There were no complaints about inadequate amplification, but the reviewer commented generally about the synchronization, "Perhaps in the near future it will be properly adjusted and the text and the pictures will coincide so closely that the action of the pictures will be in perfect consonance with the words."[58] These expectations were not to be fulfilled with Cameraphone during its short vogue.

Nor were they to be realized with such rival devices as L. P. Valiquet's "combined Mutoscope and Phonograph," which he called the Photophone (1908); Jules Greenbaum's Synchroscope, which Carl Laemmle presented for one summer (also 1908) at the Majestic Theatre in Evansville, Indiana (the program included a sound film of Caruso); the nameless system heralded by the Vitagraph Company (also 1908); the British Cinephone, premiered in New York by the Warwick Trading Company in March 1909; or by the Photokinema apparatus promoted in Los Angeles by Orlando Kellum's Talking Picture Company (c.1910–14.)[59] Not even Edison was able to succeed where all these inventors and entrepreneurs had failed.

Edison got back into the race to perfect sound movies in 1911, with a system he called the Cinephonograph. The inventor promptly announced that as far as he was concerned all the problems of making talking pictures were either solved or near solution. Others were less optimistic. Film columnist Robert Grau, who attended a Cinephonograph showing of the sextette from Donizetti's *Lucia di Lammermoor* (sung by Caruso, Plançon, and others), was impressed but admitted that "perfection has not yet been achieved."[60] Movie exhibitors, who were *not* impressed, lost no time in letting the inventor know the shortcomings of his system. Aside from the general limitations in tone quality and amplification that it shared with most other commercial systems, the Cinephonograph was restricted to playing no more than one five-minute record. As the exhibitors pointed out, the average story film in 1911 ran for twenty to thirty minutes. (Edison's problem here was the exact reverse of that experienced with his Kinetophone of 1895—in which the record continued playing some time after the moving pictures had come to an end.) Edison, like Gaumont, was also confronted with insensitive microphones, which forced his performers to stand as close as possible to them while singing or speaking. He, too, could have synchronization at the expense of allowing the apparatus to be visible in the picture.

Heeding the objections to his Cinephonograph, Edison took it back to the drawing board, and within a year he had come up with a somewhat modified system which he named the Kinetophone after his 1895 invention. It was to be launched commercially in 1913.

Isaac F. Marcosson, who saw the system in operation, described it thus:

A receiving-horn attached to the delicate recorder is placed alongside, and is connected with the camera. The operator turns the crank, and the picture and record begin. Frequently a good many feet of film are reeled off before there is any definite sound-wave to be registerd. All this is automatically adjusted.

In making a talking picture, the actor or singer moves about just as if he or she were on the real stage. Every word, every action —even the slightest footfalls—are recorded simultaneously. The action is taken at the usual rate of sixteen pictures a second, and is on ordinary celluloid film, from which the finished positives are printed.

The sound is recorded on soft wax cylinders, resembling in shape the early phonographic records. They are nearly a foot in length and four or five inches in diameter. From this soft 'master' record the indestructible records of commerce are made. Mr. Edison told me that these duplicates, in time, could be made for a dollar apiece.

At this point the question naturally arises, what sets the pace —the action or the sound? In the case of the Kinetophone, the film goes at a pace dictated or set by the phonograph. The speech has the right of way, and the picture must follow. In this way perfect accord is secured, and there can be no runaway dialogue.

. . . The reproduction of the talking motion picture seems to be a comparatively simple matter. A horn attached to the phonographic record is placed behind the screen. It is connected by wires with the projecting-machine back in the gallery of the theater or the hall. The machine operator can regulate the phonograph from his station. Once released, it sets the pace for the film; and, the synchronization now established, the machine controls the operator. He can turn his back to the picture while operating the machine and the record.[61]

These details are augmented by Eddie O'Connor, another contemporary commentator who noted that

> For the picture itself the regular sheet, or film screen of the day was used. In the center, at the bottom, a hole was cut and covered with gauze or muslin, behind which the phonograph which played the record was placed, with its horn against the muslin. Under the phonograph a trap was cut in the stage floor and as it finished the trap opened, the phonograph descended, the screen was rolled up, and behold the stage was bare![62]

O'Connor was employed, in 1913, as an actor at Edison's studio in the Bronx, New York City, where films for the commercial Kinetophone programs were made. The production manager was W. E. Wardell. Allen Ramsey was director and Joe Physiog cameraman on all Kinetophone pictures. O'Connor recalled, sixteen years later, that the first talking film made in the studio was a demonstration picture in which Ramsey was seen and heard delivering the following speech:

> Ladies and Gentlemen, a few years ago Mr. Thomas A. Edison presented to the world 'The Kinetoscope' and today countless millions of people in every section of the civilized world are enjoying his 'Phonograph.' It remained for Mr. Edison to combine two great inventions in one that is now entertaining you and is called 'The Kinetophone.' The Edison Kinetophone is absolutely the only genuine talking picture ever produced.[63]

Then came scenes showing a waiter dropping a pile of dishes, a piano solo by Justus Ring, a violin solo, and some dogs barking.

As O'Connor remembered it, "Every performance, vocal, instrumental or dramatic had to take just five minutes and fifty-five seconds, no more and no less." (The sound was synchronized to accompany 400 feet of film—the greatest length that Edison was at that time receiving from the Eastman Kodak Company.)

After the demonstration film came *A Minstrel Show*. "The orchestra was arrayed in costumes of the Court of Louis XIV and the actors were in Court Dress. But the end men were blacked up, and while the Interlocutor was in Court Costume, William H. Meadowcraft, Mr. Edison's assistant and right-hand man, wore full evening dress and conducted the performance."[64]

Subsequent films were *Julius Caesar,* act 4 scene 3 (the quarrel of Brutus and Cassius), *The Transformation of Faust, Her Redemption,* and the "Miser Scene" from *The Chimes of Normandy.* O'Connor himself appeared in *The Irish Politician,* which, he maintained, was "the first real comedy talking picture which told a story."

There were no soundproof stages and no means of eliminating or excluding unwanted sounds. Shooting and recording were often done at night when there was less noise in the neighborhood. But whether it was by night or day, the microphones unavoidably picked up the splutter of the arc lights, whose heat also softened the wax coatings on the cylinders and sometimes blurred the recordings. A dozen years later the same problem of arc lamp noise would bedevil the making of the first Vitaphone pictures, but unlike the Vitaphone engineers, Edison never managed to solve the matter. The director also had his difficulties. O'Connor noted that Ramsey could not direct in any way that had previously been attempted. "He had to sit on the floor or on a low chair just out of range and direct in pantomime, or by signals given with a handkerchief, or in any way that his inventive faculties suggested. But it must not record and it should not divert too much attention of his actors." There were problems also for the cameraman, who had to do what little he could to keep his cranking quiet, to make as little noise as possible while moving his equipment—if he was foolhardy enough to attempt any camera movement. No one came up with the idea of using a soundproof booth of the kind that would become commonplace in the sound studios of the late twenties. But it is evident that all concerned had a good foretaste of what it would be like to make talkies in Hollywood.

Edison discounted such difficulties in an interview he gave to Isaac Marcosson in 1913, shortly before the commercial premiere of Kinetophone. He was satisfied with the system and as optimistic about its future as he had been with the Cinephonograph.

> The Kinetophone is an old idea of mine that has finally been realized. . . . The problem of actual synchronization was the least difficult of my tasks. The hardest job was to make a phonographic recorder which would be sensitive to sound a considerable distance away and which would not show within the range

of the lens. . . . The difficulty has now been overcome, although I expect to make my recorder much more effective than it is at present. . . . I believe that its greatest use, for the present and for a considerable time to come, will be for music. By this I mean opera, musical plays, and kindred entertainment. . . . I am interested in the man I call the five-cent fellow. I want him to be able to go to his regular motion-picture house, and for five cents hear the great artists and the immortal music that for years have been denied him. Thus we can reduce the high cost of amusement, if we cannot put down the high cost of living. Of course, as you have seen, the Kinetophone is and will continue to be more and more effective in the interpretation of the shorter and more intimate plays. I do not think that it will be used, for some time at least, for long, sustained dramas.[65]

Edison was to awaken from his dreams with a sharp jolt. The Keith and Orpheum vaudeville circuits booked Kinetophone programs as star attractions. But the system that had worked well in the controlled conditions of the Edison laboratories or in the Bronx studio, developed unexpected imperfections when transferred to the theater. The Palace, in New York City, was one of several theaters where the Kinetophone lost synchronization or broke down completely. Audiences hissed Edison's talking pictures off the screen, and Keith-Orpheum paid the Edison Company to terminate the contract and withdraw its talking pictures.

In the wake of this experience, Edison's attitude toward sound movies underwent a marked change. He no longer considered them worthy of further improvement or experimentation, and persistently ridiculed or underrated the efforts of other inventors to accomplish what he had failed to do with the Kinetophone.

Except for a brief resurgence of activity at the beginning of the twenties, American sound-on-disk ventures remained more or less dormant until the meteoric appearance of Vitaphone. Iris Barry notes that D. W. Griffith used Orlando Kellum's Photokinema disk system to make records for several scenes in his feature, *Dream Street* (1921),

> but, displeased with the results, limited public performances to a love song [sung] by Ralph Graves. Before the feature Griffith himself appeared on the screen and talked optimistically about

"The Evolution of Motion Pictures," but his sound experiment was unsatisfactory—both the recording techniques and the synchronization were imperfect—and he did not repeat its use after the Town Hall [theater, New York] run.[66]

Griffith's next essay in using recorded sound would be the synchronized sound-on-film score for *The Battle of the Sexes* (1928).

Contemporaneously with the *Dream Street* experiment, George Regester Webb of Baltimore demonstrated what looked like a more promising disk system at London's Westminster Cathedral Hall. A correspondent for the London *Times* attended the demonstration, which consisted of the voice of Enrico Caruso (singing "On with the Motley") synchronized with the projected image of another "singer." "The illusion was complete and unusually effective," noted the *Times* correspondent. He observed that it was created with apparatus that could be used with all standard projectors. Webb's system comprised

> a transmitter, electrically connected by means of an ordinary telephone wire to the reproducing instruments, which are placed in the frame of the screen, and a double turntable . . . [carrying] the musical records, which are automatically controlled by the film in such a way that the change from one record to another is made without pause and in absolute conjunction with the movement of the pictures.[67]

Despite the success of the demonstration, Webb's system had limited practical and no commercial possibilities. It could be used for supplying sound for short films, but "enormous difficulties" would have had to be overcome if it were ever to be used to provide sound accompaniments to films longer than the playing time of two standard-sized phonograph disks. Among the other problems Webb had not solved was the question of how to regain synchronization when the film ripped and sections of it had to be removed. Like all the other disk systems before Vitaphone, it was an invention without a future.

However, during most of the years in which one disk system after another had come and gone, other inventors were exploring very different ideas for making sound movies. As we shall see, none involved using the phonograph.

CHAPTER THREE

SOUND-ON-FILM:

FRITTS TO

DE FOREST

When Chladni showed his vibrating plates to the Emperor
Napoleon, the latter cried out in surprise, "Marvellous! This
Chladni lets us see sounds!"
ERNEST RÜHMER, 1908

All in all, it is pretty well admitted today that any successful
system of talking motion pictures must combine the sound record
and pictures on a single film; any other plan only leads to trouble.
SCIENTIFIC AMERICAN, January 1923

The evolution of sound-on-film involved three different techniques: the groove-on-film, magnetic sound, and optical sound
systems. The first never reached a satisfactory stage of technological development nor did it ever arouse any strong commercial interest, although in its most advanced form—as Madalatone
—it was briefly but unsuccessfully marketed in 1927–28 in
competition with various other systems. By contrast, optical
sound was to challenge and eclipse sound-on-disk; then, in the
late 1950s, after more than twenty years of universal use, it in
turn was to be virtually eclipsed by the widespread use of
magnetic sound systems.

vv

GROOVE-ON-FILM

In effect, groove-on-film was nothing more than a variation of sound-on-disk with a track on the film performing the same function as the grooves on a record. The earliest such system was probably the invention of an American, John Ballance. It was covered by U. S. patent no.823,022, dated June 12, 1906. Ballance's apparatus required the use of a stylus supported on a sound box at one edge of a phonograph horn. The stylus ran along a groove or track formed near the edge of the film and extending along its entire length. All later groove-on-film systems were merely variations and elaborations of this one.

Propjectophone, patented in 1916 by Katherina von Madaler, recorded sound by means of an electrically heated stylus connected to the diaphragm of a microphone. Sounds caused the diaphragm to vibrate and make the heated needle burn a wavy sound track in the film on which it was resting. The system was far from perfect; its major shortcoming was the same as that of most sound systems before De Forest's Phonofilm: inadequate means of amplification. Madalatone was a development of Propjectophone patented by Ferdinand von Madaler (presumably a relative of Katherina). It reached its final form in the late twenties, when it was described as follows by one of Ferdinand's contemporaries:

> Madaler . . . photographs the picture on the emulsion side of the film in the usual manner, but upon the unsensitized, or plain, side of the celluloid film strip, by the use of a diamond stylus, he engraves the voice in the form of a wave-line record similar to the recording of the voice upon a disk record. The film appears not unlike an ordinary motion picture positive film, but close examination with a powerful magnifying glass discloses a fine line, containing hills and valleys, so to speak, close to the perforation, and just outside the picture frame. . . . The film, including the emulsion, is but .005's of an inch in thickness. The engraved record line is only .002's deep. A speaker unit is employed, with an electrical circuit, to pick up the voice, or music record on the film, and this is again reproduced with suitable apparatus, employing cone speakers.[1]

In some versions of groove-on-film, two separate synchronized projectors were used, one for the projection of the film carrying the photographic images, the other for the film carrying the groove or track. Groove-on-film was never more than a curious byway in the history of sound cinema. No films of significance were made using any of the varieties of this system.

wwwwwwwwwwwwwwwwwwwwwwwwwwwwwwwwwwwwwwwwwwwwwwwwwwwwwwwwwwwwwwwwwwwww

MAGNETIC SOUND

The basic principles of magnetic recording were first established by Danish inventor M. Valdemar Poulsen, a pioneer of wireless telegraphy. Poulsen found that

> if an iron disk similar to a phonograph disk be rotated and an electro-magnet arranged to travel over the disk in the same manner as the stylus travels over the ordinary phonograph disk, and if the traveling electro-magnet be energized with intensity varying with, and controlled by sound waves through a microphone of the usual type, a spiral magnetic path of varying intensity will be formed in the steel or iron disk. If the disk is then rotated and a solenoid [electromagnetic coil] be passed over the spiral path while connected with a suitable reproducing and amplifying mechanism, the sounds recorded magnetically on the iron disk will be reproduced in a manner similar to that of the ordinary disk phonograph. This method of recording and reproducing sounds had, of course, the advantage of eliminating the scratching effects of the needle or stylus on the record such as occurs in the ordinary type of phonograph.[2]

Poulsen named his system Telegraphone, and patented it in Germany and in the U. S. in 1900. It was first applied in a device for the magnetic recording of messages received by wireless telegraph, and then used for making a dictating machine (given the same name as Poulsen's system), which the American Telegraphone Company marketed in 1917 in unsuccessful competition with the already established cylinder dictating machines. It worked satisfactorily by the standards of the period, but was more complicated to use than the cylinder machines.

About the same time, Poulsen, working in collaboration with a fellow-Dane, P. O. Pedersen (director of the Polytechnic High

School in Copenhagen), was applying his discovery of the principles of electromagnetic sound recording to the development of a method of making sound motion pictures. Instead of using an iron disk with a spiral track, Poulsen and Pedersen employed a magnetic ribbon or wire either running along the edge of the film that carried the visual images or on a strip of film separate from the images but synchronized with them.* Electric currents, controlled by a microphone arrangement, were used to magnetize the wire or ribbon while the movie was being shot. When the developed film or films were run through projectors with the requisite soundhead and loudspeaker system, the recorded sound was reproduced from the magnetized ribbon in synchronization with the projected images.

The two inventors gave their first public demonstration of the system in Copenhagen on October 12, 1923.[3] Demonstrations in other European cities and in the U. S. soon followed. However, the system was not a success. At that period, in terms of clarity, tone, and amplification, magnetic sound-on-film compared unfavorably with the leading optical sound systems, particularly with Phonofilm. Poulsen and Pedersen were unable to get sufficient financial backing to perfect and promote magnetic sound-on-film. Magnetic sound would eventually triumph, but the story of that development is beyond the scope of this book.

~~~~~~

OPTICAL SOUND

The origins of the recording of sound photographically may be traced to 1862, when the Viennese Czmark (or Czermak) took still photographs of the workings of the vocal cords. In 1876, the German scientist Sigmund Theodor Stein photographed the vibrations of violin strings and tuning forks, and two years later, Francis Alexander Blake of Brown University made a series of photographs showing the vibrations of a mirror connected to the diaphragm of a microphone. Blake used a clock mechanism to keep his photographic plates in motion. Like Czmark and

---

* As we saw in the previous chapter, a two-film system of Poulsen and Pedersen was exploited by the Gaumont Company. GPP, as the system was called, used optical sound-on-film—not the magnetic principle.

Stein before him, Blake found no means of reproducing the sounds he had photographed.

An American, Charles E. Fritts, seems to have been the first to devise a method of recreating photographically recorded sounds, more than a decade before the inception of the motion picture! Fritts applied for a U. S. patent on October 22, 1880, though it was not actually granted until 1916, some time after his death. Earl Theisen, historian of photography and onetime curator of the Los Angeles Museum, described Fritts's patent as

> one of the broadest ever issued on any invention. It covers, basically, all the elements of sound recording as practised today. [The patent application describes] various systems of recording sounds by photographic means. . . . [It] specifies various slits, or shutters . . . which were coupled to a microphone diaphragm, as well as various optical systems in conjunction with mirrors for creating the sound record. These records were to be recorded on long photographic bands. Selenium bars were used in recreating the photographed sound record from a radiant energy into a pulsating electric current that vibrated a diaphragm to recreate the sounds. Selenium [was also utilized here perhaps for the first time in sound reproduction] as . . . an electrical resistor whose conductivity . . . [could be] increased with light intensity.[4]

During 1901–1902, the British physicist William Du Bois Duddell (designer of the Duddell oscillograph), taking advantage of developments in motion picture technology, conducted a series of experiments in sound recording by means of light, but was unable to improve significantly on Fritts's work.

Rather more success was achieved by the German inventor Ernst Walter Rühmer, whose Photographophone was used to record and reproduce sound-on-film—but without accompanying visual images. It was first demonstrated on December 12, 1901 at the Berlin Polytechnic. The invention is described in detail in chapter 4 of Rühmer's *Wireless Telephony in Theory and Practice* (1908). Rühmer used microphone sound currents (activated by the human voice) to produce variations in the intensity of a light ray issuing from an arc lamp. This ray was concentrated onto an undeveloped film that moved at a constant speed. The sounds originally transmitted through the microphone currents were photographically recorded when the film was developed and fixed. To reproduce these sounds, the inventor passed a beam of light through the photographically recorded film strip onto a light-sensitive selenium cell, whose currents operated a telephone. The recorded sounds could be heard through the telephone earpiece. Hence the system was sometimes referred to as "light telephony."[5] Unfortunately, serious limitations of the Photographophone prevented its being used to make talking pictures. Its carbon microphone was extremely insensitive; the casual fluctuations of its arc lamp produced unwanted noises; and its selenium cell generated sound currents that could be heard only faintly through the head telephone.

From 1901 to 1904 an entertainment known as the Singing Arc Light appeared in vaudeville shows in Europe and the U. S.[6] It may have been an offshoot of Rühmer's device, although the possibilities of the speaking arc had been known to scientists since 1897. The *Radiophone,* a booklet distributed at the Louisiana Purchase Exposition in St. Louis, 1904, described a photophonic transmitter based on the speaking-arc principle; it had been patented on June 1, 1897 by one Hammond V. Hayes. H. Simon, a German scientist, also appears to have anticipated Rühmer's use of the arc lamp in a demonstration of light telephony that he gave to the Physical Society of Frankfort a/M on September 8, 1900.[7] But neither Hayes nor Simon used the arc lamp in connection with film. The precise nature of the Singing Arc Light entertainment has not been ascertained. One description simply indicates that it used a beam of light to carry human voices. Here, too, there is no evidence that film was involved.

The French inventor Eugene Augustin Lauste was evidently the first to make a motion picture with visual images and a photographically recorded sound track on the same strip of film. Lauste was a pioneer inventor of motion picture apparatus long before he became involved with sound recording. It is said that in 1867, at the tender age of ten, he conceived the idea of taking a paper strip from a Zoetrope (a moving picture toy based on persistence of vision) and oiling it to make it transparent—like a film before the invention of celluloid. Then he passed the strip through a magic lantern, covering up the lens between each projection of the pictures on the strip. Although the method was crude and not very effective, it was, undoubtedly, a primitive anticipation of cinematography.

Between 1887 and 1892 Lauste was mechanical assistant to W. K. L. Dickson at Edison's laboratory in Orange, New Jersey. He assisted Dickson in the research that eventually led to the invention of the Kinetoscope. In 1894–95 he joined forces with Major Woodville Latham in constructing and marketing the Eidoloscope, the first projector to use wide gauge film. It was first publicly demonstrated in New York in May 1895, a year before the commercial beginnings of American cinema. Lauste returned to France in 1896 and for several years thereafter was director of the American Biograph Company's laboratory near Paris.

According to Merritt Crawford, an authority on the inventor's life and work,[8] Lauste first conceived the possibility of recording sound photographically in 1888, while he was employed by the Edison organization. But it was 1904 before he was able to find the time and money to work on his idea. He was not slow in achieving results once he got started. On August 10, 1907 Lauste and two others (they were not coinventors but financial backers) were granted British patent no.18,057 for a system called Photocinematophone. Crawford describes it as the "master patent in the field of synchronized sound and movement photography." The system was improved in 1910 by Lauste's invention of the string galvanometer, which enabled him to achieve sound recording by variable area exposure—a method that was to become basic to RCA Photophone, one of the two major sound-on-film systems to be adopted by many Hollywood studios in the late twenties and early thirties.

Crawford asserts that Lauste "first photographed sound and scene on the same film at his Brixton, London, studio" in 1910. However, another inventor, Elias E. Ries, applied, in 1913, for a U. S. patent on a single-film system. This patent was actually granted to Ries some ten years later and was to lead to considerable litigation over infringement of patent rights.[9] In 1911, Lauste visited the U. S. and demonstrated his Photocinematophone. He sought, unsuccessfully, to interest the film industry in his system, but the timing of his demonstration coincided with the presentations of the then more advanced disk systems of

Gaumont (Chronophone) and Edison (Kinetophone). And he also made a short sound film (subject unknown), which Crawford claims was "the first true sound picture to be taken in America."

So far Lauste had been preoccupied with improving the quality of his sound recording and reproduction. But from 1912 on he increasingly turned his attention to the problem of amplification. Regrettably, he was never able to provide Photocinematophone with sufficient amplification for the system to be used satisfactorily in theaters. Nevertheless, between 1910 and 1914 he shot thousands of feet of sound films, none of which were commercially exhibited. Their subjects were of limited scope, as may be gauged from this brief account in the *Kinematograph Year Book* for 1915:

> M. Eugene Lauste, an elderly French experimenter and former assistant of Edison himself, has succeeded in constructing a wonderful apparatus whereby sound waves may be *photographed* upon a kinematograph film in such a way that the kinematograph record is capable of being made to reproduce the original sound again, not through contact of any needle or sapphire, but by the simple action of light acting through it upon an electrically energised resistance cell. When you have sat and heard the *Temptation Rag* played to you in rousing style through the means of an arc light, a kinematograph film, and a couple of telephone receivers you begin to realize something of what Shakespeare had in mind when he wrote: 'There are more things in Heaven and earth than are dreamed of in your philosophy' [*sic*].[10]

Crawford maintains that if Lauste's work had not been interrupted by lack of capital and the outbreak of World War I, and if he had been able to make use of electronic amplifiers, the sound era would have begun a decade earlier than it actually did.

Webb's Electrical Pictures, premiered at New York's Fulton Theatre on May 3, 1914, seem to have used a system essentially the same as Lauste's Phonocinematophone. The *New York Times* noted that "The sound of the voices in Mr. Webb's 'Electrical Pictures' is reproduced by a device whereby electrical vibrations are converted into natural tones. Both picture and voice are produced by the same apparatus and therefore the voice and action are synchronous." Webb's show presented a minstrel act and scenes from vaudeville and opera. Not much more is known about his short-lived enterprise, and it is not known whether Lauste ever came to hear about it.

In 1923, Photocinematophone in its most perfected form was demonstrated by Lauste to the editor of *Scientific American*, who published the following description of it:

> The motion pictures are made in the usual manner, either on standard film or on film of a larger width. The sound record is made alongside the motion picture 'frames.' The film moves intermittently—frame by frame—through the motion picture camera mechanism, and continuously before and after. While it is moving steadily the sound record is made. For this purpose the sounds to be registered are gathered by sensitive microphones, which modulate or vary an electric current accordingly. This modulated current is brought to the fine wires of a string galvanometer—a device consisting of fine wires placed in a powerful magnetic field, so that the slightest current flowing through the wires causes the latter to warp. A powerful beam of light is projected through the galvanometer strings and on to the sensitized motion picture film. Then, according to how much or how little the wires are warped by the current flowing through them, more or less shadow falls on the film which registers the results. Thus the finished sound record resembles the teeth of a saw, or the characteristic 'peaks' of a statistician's graph. For exhibition purposes the same film is passed through the projector and sound-reproducing device. The film goes through the projector mechanism intermittently, frame by frame, and steadily through the sound-reproducing device. A beam of light is passed through the sound record, and the varying degree of shadow, falling on a light-sensitive cell, causes a current of fluctuating strength to pass through a circuit which includes loud-speaking devices. Lauste has made use of selenium for his light-sensitive cell, which, as is well-known, varies its electrical conductivity according to the amount of light falling on its surface. However, this mineral is somewhat sluggish in its response to light variations, and that sluggishness is often sufficient to interfere with successful results.[11]

Lauste was never to profit financially from his achievement, but he has earned a permanent niche in film history as "the first to record sound and scene on the same film and to reproduce it. . . . The importance of his researches and early experiments," as Merritt Crawford has maintained, "will become increasingly apparent with the passing of the years."

Lauste is not exactly a household name even among film specialists. But for every hundred who know something about him and his work, it is doubtful if there is one who has even heard the name of Joseph Tykocinski-Tykociner, who gave a public exhibition of his optical sound system at the University of Illinois on June 9, 1922. In certain minor respects, however, Tykociner's accomplishment was more remarkable than Lauste's. His system cost less than $1,000 to construct (the university footed most of the bill), and he actually netted a profit of $100—his fee for writing an article on his invention and on the future of talking pictures.

Tykociner was born in Vloclawek, Poland, in 1867 or 1877[12] and first visited the U. S. as a student in 1896. Soon after his arrival he attempted, without success, to design an "improved phonograph" that would avoid sound loss from inertia or friction by using photographic film instead of wax cylinders. His idea for recording sound was to connect the diaphragm of a telephone receiver to a device that controlled a light source, and then to photograph the variations of light intensity. He proposed to reproduce the recorded sound by passing a ray of light through the film's sound track and converting it into a variable electric current. The sound would, he hoped, be received when the current was amplified through a telephone receiver system. Tykociner did not get very far with this invention, but in 1896, while it was still occupying his thoughts, he happened to see his first movie. A quarter of a century later he described the conjunction of the phonograph idea and the movie experience in an article he wrote for the *New York World*.

> I saw projected upon the screen athletic, military and simple dramatic scenes. . . . In a dark room marching soldiers were seen on the wall, performing movements under command of officers. No sound was heard other than the clicking noise of the projecting machine.
>
> I was impressed by the technical achievement, but the absence of sound made the show unnatural, and especially the mute dramatic scenes seemed to me unendurable. The necessity of

sounds and especially speech in addition to the visual illusion was so manifest that I could not help associating the working of my new phonograph combined with the projection of moving pictures.[13]

Tykociner immediately set to work to realize what he had imagined. And by the end of the summer of 1896, he had already constructed two different kinds of sound recording camera.

In the first he used sound to control the pressure of a gas jet in a lantern, and moved a photographic plate past the flickering flame. It is remarkable that this model worked at all. Most photographic negatives of the day were made on glass plates, and Tykociner had to develop intricate methods of dropping the plates past the slit. He was unaware that flexible film had recently become available. Nor was he able to get fluctuations in the flame that corresponded exactly to the very small fluctuations of sound waves. In his second model, the light passed through the opening of a vibrating shutter controlled by the diaphragm of a telephone receiver. This model was severely hampered because the shutters could not be moved rapidly enough. But Tykociner had discovered and purchased some flexible film which made it easier to photograph the light fluctuations.[14]

That was as far as he was to get for more than twenty years. What held him up was not a shortage of ideas but lack of money. He could not afford the selenium cell he needed for the apparatus to reproduce photographically recorded sounds.

Between 1901 and 1918 Tykociner worked in Europe. He undertook radio research for the Marconi Wireless Telegraph Company in England and the Telefunken Company in Germany. At the start of World War I he was employed by the czarist government to install radio links between the Russian fleets operating in the Baltic and Black seas. Then came the Revolution. Forced to flee from Russia, Tykociner decided to return to America. Back in the U. S., his thoughts returned to the old dream of recording and reproducing sound photographically. He obtained a position in the laboratories of Westinghouse Electric in Pittsburgh, but resigned when he found that the company was not interested in supporting his researches into sound-on-film. At this juncture, Tykociner resolved to seek a university appointment, preferably in a school that would encourage his project. The opportunity arose in 1921 when he was invited to join the faculty of the University of Illinois as research professor of electrical engineering.

When Tykociner met Ellery Paine, his department chairman, he was asked which area of research he wished to investigate. Tykociner promptly replied:

"I want to record sound on film."

Paine was surprised. "You can't photograph sound."

"Certainly not," Tykociner said. "But it is possible to photograph a light modulated by sound."

Most of the Department's research was in power engineering, so Tykociner's idea was in an area unfamiliar to Paine. "Can you prove it will work?" he asked.

The question annoyed Tykociner. "Prove it? That's why you do research."

Paine was still cautious. "If you can show a committee of engineering faculty that your idea of photographing sound has merit, we will support your research."

The demonstration, which was of urgent importance to Tykociner, took three weeks to prepare. After explaining his ideas about converting sound into variations of light on film . . . Tykociner pushed a button and a small bar of light appeared on a screen. As he spoke into a telephone transmitter the intensity of the light changed noticeably and bands formed across the slit, approximately corresponding to the sound of his voice.

Tykociner explained that he needed to refine his equipment to produce a more accurate image of sound, photograph it, and find a way to convert the photographic record back to sound. Excited by the idea, the committee members offered the support which Tykociner had sought over two continents for 25 years.[15]

By a remarkable coincidence, the answer to Tykociner's major technical problem—the same one that had confounded him twenty years earlier—lay just across the hall from his laboratory in the Physics Building. Tykociner soon became acquainted with Jacob Kuntz, inventor of the photoelectric cell (1913), and almost immediately realized that he could reproduce sound by using a photoelectric cell instead of a selenium cell. It would, in fact, prove better for his purposes than selenium, which, as he probably knew, had never solved the amplification problem for Lauste.

What happened next was a triumph of improvisation.

Tykociner borrowed vacuum tubes from the student-operated radio station and a motion picture projector from the College of Agriculture. The tubes had to be returned to the radio station each evening so that it could go on the air, and Agriculture would not allow Tykociner to remodel its projector. Film and electronic equipment were expensive, and the Department's research budget was small. He was forced to make a great deal of his own equipment and supervise the development of his film.

Tykociner's "microphone" was a carbon-grain telephone transmitter; his sound-reproducing apparatus included a Magnavox speaker with a morning-glory horn; his camera was a Bell & Howell "Professional" model to which he had connected a penthouse sound recorder; and his projector was a Simplex. A modulated mercury vapor lamp was used in exposing the film, and the sound reproduction was, of course, dependent on the use of one of Professor Kuntz's photoelectric cells. But this heterogenous array of apparatus produced results that were at least as good as Lauste's and at times were considerably better.[16]

Tykociner completed his first talking picture in October 1921, within the same month that he initiated his experiments. It was a voice-only movie with the sound track running down the center of the film. The voice was Tykociner's, stating that this was "an experiment in the reproduction of sound," then counting from one to ten, and completing the test with a shout of "Hello!"[17] When Tykociner proceeded to make films with images, too, he shifted the sound track to the side of the film—but it was the opposite side from where it was to be located in most subsequent sound-on-film movies.

The public demonstration of the system, on June 9, 1922, took place in the auditorium of the Physics Building on the University of Illinois campus. Tykociner presented a "double feature." His first film showed a woman in a white dress (Mrs. Tykociner) holding a bell. Her lips could be seen to move as she spoke words that were clearly audible throughout the hall. "I will ring," she said. The sound of the bell could be heard next, as she shook it. Then, after a brief pause, she could be heard to ask, "Did you hear the bell ring?" The second film showed Ellery Paine delivering Lincoln's Gettysburg Address. Resounding applause followed the two brief films. Apparently everyone present was impressed. But many of Tykociner's colleagues subsequently voiced the opinion that what they had been shown was a toy, not a scientific achievement.[18]

At this stage, however, Tykociner was not to be depressed by such an attitude. His demonstration made headlines across the country, and he was asked to write an article for the *New York World*. Ironically, this was to earn him his only recompense for anything connected with sound pictures. Another article, by a reporter for the *World*, quoted Tykociner as saying,

> The voices in an opera, the music, the orchestra, the dialogue can be recorded and reproduced. Many noted plays, comedies and farces that are not adapted to the screen because of the wit and humor of the dialogue, the personality of the actors, may now be revived and find new favor. I have great hopes that it will cause a revival of the masterpieces of dramatic art.[19]

His hopes were to be short-lived. The Board of Trustees of the University of Illinois refused to promote any further research by Tykociner unless he agreed to assign to the university any and all patent rights to inventions he had accomplished with the institution's resources. Tykociner rejected the idea and headed for New York, where he expected to find a promoter in the film industry. But he was flatly turned down by every producer he approached as well as by executives of the General Electric Company. George Eastman delivered the *coup de grace* by telling the frustrated inventor, "I wouldn't give a dime for all the possibilities of that invention. The public will never accept it."[20] Tykociner headed back to Urbana, gave up any further thought of sound movies, and turned his attention to less sensational research in photoelectricity.

Perhaps Tykociner would have been less easily discouraged if he had known the real reason for General Electric's apparent lack of interest in his work. At the very moment when the company was rejecting his invention, a research team headed by Charles A. Hoxie and C. W. Hewlett was engaged in perfecting GE's own sound-on-film system at the company's laboratories in Schenectady. The Hoxie-Hewlett system was named Pallophotophone (Greek for "shaking light sound"). It used a single film for the images and the sound track. A special feature of the recording process was the use of a mirror smaller than a pinhead. This minute mirror was made to vibrate by a fluctuating current from a radio microphone. It then threw a vibrating beam of light onto the edge of the unexposed film. The developed motion picture carried a photographic tracing of the sound vibrations in a zigzag pattern 1/10 inch wide along the entire length of the film. In reproducing the sound, the system employed a photoelectric cell, radio amplifiers, and a radio loudspeaker.

Curiously, Pallophotophone sound was first used publicly not for a movie presentation but for a radio broadcast. In the fall of 1922, the process was used to record the voice of announcer K. Hagar, which was then broadcast over GE's radio station WGY (Schenectady). The press gave widespread publicity to the experimental broadcast, viewing it as an important potential for radio. Typical reactions were these:[21]

A few weeks ago a mysterious announcement buzzed off the aerial wires of our friend WGY at Schenectady. The announcement ran as follows:

'The next selection is for the benefit of the Edison convention at White Sulphur Springs, W. Va., to which WGY sends greetings. These greetings are being transmitted by a new device, not a phonograph, constructed by the General Electric Company, and by means of which the voice has been recorded and is now being reproduced. We would like to have comments from our listeners telling whether this last announcement came through as clearly as the other announcements on our evening program.'

Mr. Hagar, studio manager of WGY, spoke those words a week before the radio audience heard them. No, his voice was not recorded on a phonographic disk; a new instrument, the Pallophotophone, was used. . . . Before describing the Pallophotophone it is interesting to know that WGY received many answers to their announcement, and every one of the fans who took the trouble to write was firm in the belief that Mr. Hagar's voice was more distinct than it had ever been before. Thus a new invention was introduced to the world over the radio. It was not only introduced, but it was given the acid test.

[*Literary Digest*]

Recently the Pallophotophone was employed to operate the radio broadcasting station WGY of the General Electric Company. The well-known voice of the WGY announcer, KH, was recorded on a photographic film and sent out over the radio phone with such accuracy that it was almost impossible to distinguish it from the living voice as ordinarily transmitted from that station. Indeed, it appears very likely that such applications of the photographic recording of sounds will become quite common in the future, and that lectures and important speeches may be simultaneously broadcast from several radio stations. This system has a definite application in recorded speeches, songs and other sounds for future generations. Its application to the theatre is, of course, obvious.   [*Scientific American*]

Subsequent radio broadcasts using Pallophotophone included the recorded voices of President Calvin Coolidge and various other public figures.

Initially, General Electric's interest in sound-on-film was limited to its use in radio broadcasting, mainly because Hoxie and Hewlett at first spread their variable-area sound tracks across almost the entire width of the film, leaving no room for any photographic images. It was not until Hoxie demonstrated the effectiveness of Pallophotophone with a narrow variable-density sound track (it was only 1/16 inch wide) that the company decided to promote the system for use with motion pictures (c.1925). L. T. Robinson, chief of GE's General Engineering Laboratory, was appointed head of the research program for developing sound-on-film apparatus for commercial use. Improved loudspeakers were developed by Chester W. Rice and Edward W. Kellogg. And Professor A. C. Hardy provided a method for satisfactorily reducing the width of variable-area sound tracks so that they were an improvement over Hoxie's variable-density tracks.

Pallophotophone in its improved form was renamed Kinegraphone. As such it attracted the interest of Paramount, and in 1927 the studio took the option of using it to provide synchronized sound for William Wellmann's *Wings*, which premiered at the Criterion Theatre, New York, on April 12, 1927, less than two months before the momentous first night of *The Jazz Singer*.[22] The sound effects and music were actually added after the film had been shot. There were no recorded dialogue scenes. *Wings* was a spectacular, wide-screen (Magnascope) film about World War I aviators, starring Richard Arlen, Clara Bow, Charles "Buddy" Rogers, Gary Cooper, and Jobyna Ralston. Following its New York opening, the movie went on a series of road show tours. Simultaneously, the film was released in a silent version, but the road show presentations were all supplied with synchronized sound by Kinegraphone, for GE had leased to Paramount about a dozen separate sets of Kinegraphone apparatus for use with the road shows. Despite the commercial success of the experiment, Paramount did not use the system after the initial venture with *Wings*. Either the studio was unable to come to any long-term arrangements with General Electric, or else Paramount's executives considered the system less satisfactory than Movietone—which they contracted to use less than a year later. We shall hear more, subsequently, about these rival systems and their use by the Hollywood studios.

In 1921, a British inventor, H. Grindell-Matthews, was working, quite independently of Hoxie and Hewlett, on a sound-on-film process that was similar in several respects to Pallophotophone. A commentator for the London *Times* attended one of Grindell-Matthews's demonstrations and was impressed by the simplicity of his system which, he claimed, "involved only the addition of an adapter to ordinary projection apparatus."[23] Like Pallophotophone, the British system used only a single film for the images and the sound. In the process of recording, sound vibrations caused a "tiny mirror of stainless steel to vibrate two pencils of light, which in turn . . . [were] focused on the edge of the film. The film . . . [was] shown in the ordinary way, while from beneath the screen a 'sound shoot' . . . [amplified] the record[ing]." Although Grindell-Matthews's system may have been as effective as Pallophotophone—at least in the earlier stages of that system's development—it was never to be commercially exploited. The few sound films made by this inventor—entirely for demonstration purposes—included a farewell address by the explorer Sir Ernest Shackleton, who was filmed before leaving on one of his Antarctic expeditions.

Contemporaneously with Grindell-Matthews, a Swedish team headed by Sven Aison Berglund was working on a sound-on-film system using two cameras and two projectors and employing a selenium cell in its recording unit. W. Bayard Hale was among those who attended a demonstration of the Berglund system (named Photophone but not connected with a later system developed by RCA) at the experimental laboratory of Brevik, ten miles from Stockholm. Hale's description of the experience was published in the London *Times* on September 24 1921. "What we saw," he wrote, "was Mr. Montelius [a Swedish professor] in his capacity as Royal Antiquarian and Director of the National Museum, at his lecture desk or moving freely about the platform without thought of a camera or a receiver, and what we heard were his words in a reproduction so perfect that it was almost impossible to believe that Montelius was sitting, with silent lips, at my side."[24] Notwithstanding its impressiveness at this presentation, Berglund's Photophone was to have no commercial future. In the early twenties it was already clear to those who had kept abreast of developments in the U. S. and Europe that if sound-on-film was to have any commercial prospects it would be through a single-film system that would use either a photocell or a magnetic recording method.

The most successful European development along these lines was the work of three Swiss-German inventors, Josef Engl, Joseph Massolle, and Hans Vogt. Beginning in 1918 and continuing into the early twenties, this trio collaborated on a sound-on-film system they called Tri-Ergon ("the work of three"), a single-film process. In a Berlin movie theater on September 17, 1922, Tri-Ergon's first audience saw and heard comedian Friedl Hintze recite Goethe's poem "Heideroslein."

Rights to the system were acquired about this time by the Swiss firm Ton-F. Zwecke, Glimmlampe für Licht-Tonaufnahme. Thereafter, through lack of promotional initiative and wavering interest in the possibilities of sound films, the rights were bounced from one organization to another. Ton-F. Zwecke sold them to the German UFA organization. In 1926, another Swiss company, Hauszer-Staub, Heberlein und Iklé, bought the European rights from UFA, and soon afterwards sold them yet again, to Tonbild Syndicat AG—usually abbreviated to Tobis. It was Tobis that commercially promoted the system in Europe, beginning in 1928–29.[25] The organization immediately became embroiled in litigation with RCA and Western Electric over alleged infringements of the Tri-Ergon patents. But the disputes were settled amicably in 1930.

Tri-Ergon used a photocell for sound reproduction. Its inventors discovered, as did Tykociner, that it was more effective than using selenium, which Lauste and others had found to be unreliable in response to fluctuations in illumination. The photocell was to be used contemporaneously in several other sound-on-film systems. But Tri-Ergon had another feature that was unique, a device for avoiding variations in speed as the film passed the photocell. It was a flywheel mechanism on a sprocket, a relatively simple device, but one that was to have devastating consequences for the American film industry. It was heavily protected by patents (most notably by U. S. patent no. 1,713,726). Between 1928 and 1934 every manufacturer of sound film equipment who did not work out a deal with Tri-Ergon's patent holders had the choice of infringing the flywheel patents (and facing the consequences) or marketing apparatus that was mechanically inferior to or more complicated than the Tri-Ergon equipment.

In 1925, William Fox, president of the Fox Film Corporation, acquired 90 percent of the Western Hemisphere rights to Tri-Ergon,[26] including, of course, the flywheel patents. In Hollywood, Fox's expenditure of $60,000 for a sound system must have seemed an absurd waste of money. But that was a year before the commercial beginnings of sound cinema by any Hollywood studio. By 1930, Fox was claiming innumerable infringements of his flywheel patent rights. On March 19, 1931 he brought matters to a head by filing suit against Electrical Research Products, Inc. (generally known as ERPI), Altoona Publix Theatres, and many other exhibitors. After due deliberation, a Delaware court declared that the Tri-Ergon patents were invalid on the grounds of "want of invention." On appeal, the case was heard by Judge Albert W. Johnson of the U. S. District Court in Scranton, Pennsylvania, who overturned the decision and upheld the validity of the patents. Fox now had the legal right to claim damages from countless producers and exhibitors across the U. S., Canada, and South America. Inevitably, the defendants appealed Judge Johnson's decision. But the U. S. Circuit Court sustained his verdict.

Now in addition to the defendants specified in the original suit, the two mammoth organizations, RCA and AT&T (through ERPI and Western Electric), were liable for vast sums for infringing the Tri-Ergon patents. Accordingly, they took the matter to the Supreme Court, where on October 8, 1934, by unanimous decision, the associate justices reaffirmed the verdict of the Circuit Court. They directed the U. S. District Court to appoint arbitrators to determine the specific fines to be levied against all the companies, organizations, producers, and exhibitors who had infringed Fox's patent rights.

The matter appeared to have been settled entirely to Fox's advantage, but his triumph was short-lived. An impressive array of senators and lawyers representing Wall Street business interests, theater owners, and Hollywood studios appealed to the Supreme Court to reconsider its verdict. Incredibly, the Court agreed to reopen the case. Even more incredibly, on March 14, 1935, the same associate justices decided that "in the public interest" their previous decision should be overturned. The Tri-Ergon patents were, thereupon, declared invalid. No further appeal was possible. Now Fox, who had gambled heavily on collecting immense sums in damages, who had overextended himself financially, and who owed millions of dollars in legal fees, suddenly found that he was holding all the wrong cards. In 1930 his personal fortune had exceeded $100 million. In June 1936, he filed for bankruptcy, listing his total assets as $100. (Tykociner may have derived some wry amusement from that.) Meanwhile, Sidney Kent, the new president of the Fox Film Corporation, arranged for his company to merge with Twentieth Century Productions in order to secure the latter studio's Darryl F. Zanuck as his production chief. Thus, a fortune was lost and a studio born—on account of a flywheel patent.

Despite the overthrow of Tri-Ergon's American rights, the patents were still recognized in Germany. There, the major production companies, UFA and Klangfilm, obtained licenses to use Tri-Ergon in making their first sound movies.

Tonfilm, a rival optical sound system available in Germany during the twenties and thirties, was another development of the Danish inventors Poulsen and Pedersen. It used an oscillograph in the recording process and a selenium cell in the reproducing/amplifying process. Though less satisfactory than Tri-Ergon, Tonfilm was the system licensed by the Gaumont Company (in France) and was one of the systems licensed by British Acoustic, Ltd. (in England).

None of the pioneers whose work we have considered thus far contributed more to the perfection of sound-on-film than the American inventor Lee De Forest. Unfortunately, in his own lifetime, De Forest's achievements were almost forgotten in the wake of the tremendous commercial success of Vitaphone sound-on-disk and in consequence of the legal battles that consumed his time and money and deprived him of rights to some of his own patented inventions.

For most of our knowledge of De Forest we are indebted to the researches of film historian and archivist Maurice H. Zouary, whose invaluable collection of more than 100 of the inventor's pre-1928 synchronous optical sound films was recently acquired by the Library of Congress. Here we can only provide a brief outline of the work that Zouary surveys in various detailed articles, that Georgette Carneal discusses in her book *A Conqueror of Space* (the authorized biography of Lee De Forest), and that De Forest himself considered at length in his autobiography, *Father of Radio*.

As we have noted, other inventors before and contemporaneously with De Forest succeeded in making sound-on-film movies. But it was De Forest who found the solution to the problem of amplification. His key invention was the Audion Three-Electrode Amplifier Tube (U. S. patent no.841,386, dated January 15, 1907), which he originally conceived as a means of improving the reception of radio broadcasting. Through the Audion Tube, weak sounds received via radio (and also over telephone cable) could be greatly amplified. In 1912, when De Forest discovered that his amplifier could also be used as an oscillator, he realized that the invention could be applied to the making of sound movies. Hitherto he had been preoccupied with the development of radio, now he turned his attention wholly to the problems of talking pictures. In 1923, looking back on this period he observed:

Perhaps the one consideration which, more than any other, prompted me to enter this field was my desire personally to develop a new and useful application of the audion amplifier—one which I could expect to develop largely by my own efforts as distinguished from its application to long-distance telephony, where obviously the intensive efforts of large corps of engineers, backed by a gigantic business organization, were indispensable. Another motive was my desire to see a phonographic device which would be free of many of the inherent shortcomings of the disk machine, notably the short length of record, the necessity for frequent changings of needles, and the belief that by means of a pencil of light, instead of a steel needle, it might be possible completely to escape from the surface scratch which has always been inseparable from the existing types of phonographs.

Early in the spring of 1919 I filed patent applications on the methods which I believed would accomplish the above laid-down conditions, and began actual research on the various means which might be successfully employed. At that time I figured that the work involved should require at most two years—a period one-half as long as that which has actually been demanded. The work has been almost uninterrupted, and of the most exacting and discouraging nature. Literally hundreds of experiments have been made and thousands of feet of film have been photographed only to be thrown away.[27]

De Forest experimented with magnetic wire recordings separate from the film carrying the visual images and also with two other methods involving a speaking flame (a method anticipated by Rühmer and others) and miniature incandescent filaments. At the outset the synchronization was imperfect, but he overcame that problem in due course; while almost from the beginning his Audion Tube provided more amplification than was possible with any other system at that period. The system he evolved used standard film with a variable density sound track (approximately 3/32 inch wide) running alongside the visual images.

In 1922 he outlined his process in general terms to one of his representatives:

Taking the picture:
1   Sound waves (voice of the actor) translated into electrical waves.
2   Electrical waves translated into light waves.
3   Light waves recorded on the edge of the film.

Reproducing the picture:
1   Light waves translated back into electrical waves.
2   Electrical waves translated back into sound waves.
3   Sound waves amplified with loud-speakers placed near the screen for the audience.[28]

In more detail, his recording system required three transformation processes: first, sound waves had to be changed into electric telephonic currents; second, these currents had to be amplified into light waves; and finally, the light waves had to be recorded photographically on film. To accomplish these processes, De Forest used a microphone transmitter that could pick up sounds up to fifteen feet from their source. The transmitter transformed them into weak telephonic currents, which were then amplified some 100,000 times so that they could activate a Photion tube in the motion picture camera. The Photion was an oxide-coated cathode located close to the objective lens. It generated light whose intensity fluctuated in exact rhythm with the strength of the telephonic currents reaching the tube. The light waves emitted by the Photion were directed through a narrow slit* onto the margin of the moving negative film, where they were registered photographically. Simultaneously, visual images were recorded on the same strip of film.

In order to reproduce synchronous sound and image, a positive print was made from the negative that carried both image and sound recordings. The print was then run through a standard projector to which had been added an attachment

---

*   The slit idea originated with Elias E. Ries and was patented by him in 1924. However, De Forest seems to have come across it independently, as early as 1920. In 1924, when he discovered the existence of the patent, he bought the rights to it from Ries. The slit idea was, of course, basic to the De Forest system. See further Georgette Carneal, pp. 288–289.

containing an incandescent lamp and a photoelectric cell. As the film moved through the projector, it passed between the lamp and the cell. Light from the lamp was focused through a narrow slit (like the one used in the camera), through the film's sound track, and onto the photoelectric cell, whose resistance was controlled by the intensity of the light falling on it. A small battery was connected to the photoelectric cell; its current, controlled by the intensity of the light activating the cell, was made to reproduce the currents originally transmitted during the recording process. But these currents were weak, and had to be strengthened greatly by the use of audion amplifiers. The now-powerful currents were sent through loudspeakers behind or beside the screen on which the motion picture was being projected. And in this complex manner audiences could see and hear a sound movie.[29]

Maurice Zouary quotes a speech by Dr. Elman Meyers, who assisted De Forest in 1913 with the first test of his single-film optical sound process. The test subject was a barking dog that turned a somersault. "Projecting the film with its sound on a De Forest invented projector sound device, marked this experiment as the first sound ever to be heard loud and clear, coming directly from a motion picture film."[30]

The inventor's first *talking* movie was made in 1921. De Forest noted in his diary for July 9 of that year:

> Today I made my first "talking movie" picture—of myself, very hot and somewhat flurried; talked too loud, and the photography was poor, due to white "back drop" and bad placing of the light. But it was *at last made,* despite all jinxes and hoodoos—two months behind schedule, and after two years of hard work in preparation—a definite promise of great things to come.[31]

De Forest was invited to Germany by the firm of Erich Huth G.m.b.H., and continued his experiments in Berlin. There he made his first sound movies for public presentation. His principal subject seems to have been his German assistant, Dr. Fritz Holborn, playing his violin—a rather curious parallel to the Edison Kinetophone film of 1894, in which that inventor's assistant, W. K. L. Dickson, had also played the violin. In September 1922 De Forest demonstrated, before an invited audience in a Berlin theater, what he had accomplished to date. German press reaction, he noted, was "polite, if not enthusiastically laudatory." He himself admitted that the "audio output was disappointing but adequate for the immediate purpose."[32] He had been forced to work with makeshift equipment and less-than-competent assistance, so he decided to pack up and return to the U. S.

Conditions at his Highbridge, New York, laboratory were as ideal as he could afford to make them. And back in the U. S. in the fall of 1923, he was also fortunate to receive encouragement and support from Dr. Hugo Riesenfeld, silent film composer and musical director of New York's Rialto and Rivoli theaters. When De Forest informed Riesenfeld that his experiments were advanced enough for him to proceed with the making of sound films for commercial exhibition, the composer offered to find him a studio, technicians, musicians, and the necessary equipment for film production, and to provide the Rivoli Theatre as a showcase for the De Forest movies as soon as they were ready.

The inventor decided to call his system Phonofilm, and in November 1922 he established the De Forest Phonofilm Corporation. A sister organization, founded at the same time, was the De Forest Patent Holding Company, which controlled all his patents in the field of sound recording and reproducing (more than 70 patents were involved). Production of Phonofilms began in the old Talmadge studio ("that ancient remodelled brewery of Tec-Art," De Forest called it) on East Forty-eighth Street in New York. The cameraman was Harry Owens, whom Riesenfeld sent over to assist De Forest. In the studio's heyday (1923–25) several short Phonofilms a week were being produced —a routine that anticipated Warner Bros.' regular production of Vitaphone shorts, beginning in 1926.

Interviewed by the *New York World* in May 1922 and the *New York American* in March 1923, De Forest offered some acute predictions about what his invention would mean to the development of the feature film:

> They'll have to direct pictures by the sign language. What will happen is that they will have to use real artists—actors who have a voice as well as a camera face. I think it will add brains to the movies.

[Silent film] dramas are especially written for the screen and are designed to be without the human voice. But forward-looking screen writers will evolve something for the application of the Phonofilm to drama.[33]

At the East Forty-eighth Street studio at the beginning of March 1923, a reporter from the *New York American* was privileged to witness a demonstration of one of the films that De Forest would present publicly the following month.

As I watched the movie of an orchestra performing, I heard the music it made. Piano, flute, clarinet, cello—I could distinguish the notes from the several instruments. The music played came from out of nowhere, from the direction of the screen. Measure by measure, it harmonized exactly with the movements of the shadow players.[34]

A preview of the public premiere of Phonofilm was held on April 12, 1923 before the New York Electrical Society in the auditorium of the Engineering Societies' Building. A packed audience saw short Phonofilms of Henry Cass describing the workings of the De Forest system, Eddie Cantor singing "The dumber they come the better I like 'em" and "Oh Gee Georgie," and Lillian Powell doing a bubble dance to the strains of a Brahms melody. De Forest noted in his autobiography, "Other numbers, exquisitely beautiful or rollicking comedy, followed in unbroken succession."[35] Phonofilm was launched publicly at the Rialto and Rivoli theaters three days after the preview. Its initial success led to the showing of Phonofilm programs in no fewer than thirty-four movie theaters on the East Coast between 1923 and 1925, as well as in Canada, South America, Britain, South Africa, Australia, and Japan.

Zouary estimated that De Forest made more than a thousand short optical sound movies by 1927. His Phonofilm system (at least *by name*) does not appear to have been used for a full-length talking feature film until the Weiss-Artclass production *Unmasked* (1929). The full range of Phonofilm short subjects is too vast to recount here. It included a variety of entertainment for all tastes: grand opera (scenes from *Lakmé, Rigoletto, Lucia di Lammermoor*); Pavlova and Fokina, each in a separate

"swan dance"; various numbers played by the bands of Roger
Wolfe Kahn, Ben Bernie, Paul Specht, xylophonist Teddy
Brown, and Helen Lewis (with her All-Girl orchestra); Clyde
Doerr and his Sax-o-phone Sextet; a short speech by Bernard
Shaw (anticipating his sensational Movietone appearance of
1928); Chauncey Depew giving his personal recollections of
Abraham Lincoln, and Edwin Markham reading "Lincoln, the
Man of the People"; DeWolf Hopper reciting "Casey at the
Bat," Monroe Silver in "Cohen on the Telephone," Elsa Lan-
chester in "Mr. Smith Wakes Up," Fannie Ward wisecracking
about her age and singing "Father Time"; as well as perform-
ances by Eddie Cantor, George Jessel, Sir Harry Lauder, and
Chic Sale; dialogues by Gloria Swanson and Thomas Meighan;
Weber and Fields in their famous poolroom scene; sketches
starring Raymond Hitchcock, Frank McHugh, and singer Harry
Richman with a very young Joan Bennett; Una Merkel singing
"Love's Old Sweet Song"; Max Fleischer's bouncing-ball song
cartoons; the Jubilee Four (quartet of black male singers); many
blackface minstrel acts and various "Mammy" singers, both
Negro and blackface. Perhaps as early as 1923, De Forest also
took Phonofilm outside the studio to make a short sound movie
of New York City streets and people—a feat that would be considered a technological breakthrough when Sam Wood did it
for the talkie feature *So this is College?* (1929). De forest was
probably the first to shoot a sound picture outdoors—though
that achievement has sometimes been attributed to the Fox
Movietone engineers who filmed a parade of West Point cadets
in 1927.

In 1973 the author was permitted to examine a number of the
De Forest Phonofilms in the Zouary collection at the Library
of Congress. A typical good example was a short sound movie
of Norah Blaney at the piano, singing several of her songs, including "He's Funny That Way" and "How About Me?" The
picture consisted of one 35mm reel (about 650 feet) with excellent synchronization but much surface noise. It was directed
by Philip Braham, probably in 1922 or 1923. There were,
interestingly enough for so short an experimental film, several
camera setups and the use of fades as transitional devices. A
poorer example was the outdoor Phonofilm of President Calvin

Coolidge, taken on the White House lawn in the spring of 1924. Coolidge was seen against a background of trees, holding the notes of the speech that he delivered for the De Forest cameras: "The costs of government are all assessed on the people. . . . One of the greatest favors that can be bestowed on the American people is economy in government." This movie consisted of only 320 feet of 35mm film. The synchronization was found to be imperfect—the President's lip movements and gestures lagged behind his words—and the picture was static.

After the Phonofilm premiere in 1923, De Forest and Riesenfeld sat back and waited for the big offers to pour in from Hollywood. Could the studios be deaf to the miracle of sound? Could they possibly resist the opportunity offered by the dream De Forest had now realized? De Forest and Riesenfeld were in for a dismal awakening. Years later, the inventor reflected bitterly, "what stone walls of indifference, stupidity, and solid negativity did we unearth among the dead bones and concrete skulls of motion picture 'magnates'!"[36] Until the Vitaphone disk system (1926) suggested that there might be something in sound movies after all, not a single Hollywood executive showed serious interest in De Forest's enterprise. They generally wrote it off as a passing novelty that would bring financial ruin to anyone foolish enough to sink money into it. The reasons for Hollywood's indifference and even hostility to sound movies will be considered in more detail in the next chapter. Here it will suffice to mention that in 1923 movie mogul Carl Laemmle, one of the studio heads invited to a presentation of De Forest's sound movies, was too busy to attend. He sent an assistant, whose enthusiasm for what he saw and heard was promptly slapped down by other executives at Universal. Adolph Zukor *did* find time to sample a De Forest program, but he could still recall the failure of Edison's venture with the 1913 Kinetophone, and so he decided not to throw any of *his* money away on yet another crackpot invention without a future.[37]

Where Hollywood's reaction to Phonofilm was bland indifference, critical response vacillated between the apathy of Karl Kitchen, who headlined his review of the Rivoli premiere "New Talking Picture Is Shown—But What of It?",[38] and the excitement of Iris Barry, who described the film of Fokina performing

her swan dance as "a most uncanny and delightful experience
. . . it was just like seeing the ballerina herself."[39]

A technical objection was raised by De Forest's friend C. F.
Elwell when he demonstrated a program of Phonofilms before
the Royal Society of Arts in London, on November 26, 1924.
After acclaiming the inventor's achievement of excellent amplification and perfect synchronization, Elwell went on to observe
that there remained unsolved the further problem of "obtaining
perfect mechanical reproduction of sound. The reproduction
by the loud speaker, though extraordinarily good, does not yet
render perfectly all the qualities of the human voice."[40]

Meanwhile, De Forest was temporarily less concerned about
tone quality than about the promotion of the system to which
he had already devoted so much time and money. He started a
regular talking newsreel series in the spring of 1924—three years
earlier than the famed Movietone. It was a presidential campaign year, and De Forest lost no opportunity of filming the
candidates. Using "a pickup truck with battery-operated sound
camera and amplifier," he journeyed to Washington to make
the aforementioned Phonofilm of President Coolidge. The same
day he filmed a speech by Progressive candidate Senator Robert
La Follette, and then drove north to Long Island, where he
recorded the opinions of Democratic candidate John W. Davis.
Audiences in more than thirty East Coast theaters saw and
heard these three preelection statements.[41] The following year,
both Franklin D. Roosevelt and Al Smith made Phonofilm ad-
dresses prior to their campaigns for governor of New York.[42]

More ambitious than any of these short Phonofilms was De
Forest's synchronized recording, in 1924, of a musical score by
Riesenfeld, for James Cruze's epic Western, *The Covered
Wagon*. In a 1941 article in *American Cinematographer,* De
Forest claimed that it was with this film that he first introduced
the method of "dubbed sound recorded in synchronism with a
projected picture."[43] He notes in his autobiography that he first
tried post-dubbing for a 1924 film of Sarova's dancers performing to the music of Grieg's "Song of Spring." He recalls that
"They danced to the music of a single violin and cello, but the
developed film was then projected on the studio screen while
the full Rivoli orchestra replayed the music in perfect synchroni-

zation with the dancers."[44] The recorded score for *The Covered Wagon* presents the film historian with a possible controversy. Georgette Carneal, De Forest's biographer, states that the music was supplied for only two reels of the film during a special showing of *The Covered Wagon*.[45] But somewhat ambiguous comments by De Forest himself[46] lead one to believe that the Riesenfeld score was recorded for the entire movie, possibly anticipating by three years what Warner Bros. later claimed had been first undertaken with William Axt's score for *Don Juan* (1926). De Forest said that it was Riesenfeld's score that largely accounted for the Broadway triumph of Cruze's film.[47] But he may not have been referring to the synchronized recording of that score. There was a "live" orchestra at the Rivoli, and De Forest may have been speaking about their playing of the Riesenfeld music during regular showings of *The Covered Wagon*. Anyhow, in 1925, a year before *Don Juan*, Riesenfeld's score for Fritz Lang's *Siegfried* (1922) was recorded "in the Century Theatre while the orchestra was playing to the projected picture." Carneal says nothing about it, and De Forest nowhere intimates that the recording was for anything less than the whole film.

The years 1924–25 were remarkably prophetic as well as active ones for Phonofilm. *Domen* (1924), a short Phonofilm "talking picture play," was produced in Swedish by Arthur Donaldson; an English-language version, titled *Retribution,* was made early in 1925. De Forest proudly noted in his autobiography, "This was two years before Al Jolson's much-exploited *Jazz Singer*."[48] In spring of the same year, De Forest essayed a Technicolor sound film: "Balieff's entire Chauve Souris was . . . recorded, using a sound camera synchronized to the color camera. . . . The sound-track was then printed on the green positive, which dyed surface, although serving better than the red, was found quite unsuitable. Nevertheless, certain numbers of this production were exhibited . . . to enthusiastic audiences in the London Tivoli, and in Japan and Australia."[49] Zouary states that in 1925 De Forest made the first industrial sound film, which was shown at the Atlantic City Exposition.[50] But this claim is challenged by E. S. Gregg's reference[51] to the showing in 1924, at the Hotel Astor, of Western Electric's *Hawthorne,* a talking (disk-system) film about the Western Electric factory in the Chicago suburbs. It was in 1925 that De Forest unfortunately turned down the opportunity of buying U. S. rights to Tri-Ergon. Soon afterwards, William Fox acquired what De Forest had allowed to slip through his fingers, and within a year or so the movie tycoon was engaged in litigation with De Forest over the patent priorities of Tri-Ergon versus Phonofilm.

From 1926 to 1935 lawsuits were to consume much of the time and money that De Forest could have spent creatively and profitably in developing and promoting Phonofilm. The most unfortunate of these legal actions—regrettable because they brought into opposition two considerable inventive talents— arose out of De Forest's association with fellow inventor Theodore W. Case.

Case began his experiments in sound recording before World War I, while he was a graduate student at Yale. One of the earliest of his many patents was for the Thalifide cell, used by the army in 1917–18 in their infrared communications system, and by De Forest, in 1919, as a light-recording source in place of less-sensitive Kuntz photocells. In the early twenties Case visited De Forest's laboratory and got to know a great deal about the sound-on-film system he was working on. De Forest in turn visited Case's laboratory at Auburn, New York, and observed the gas-discharge amplifier tube devised by Case and his assistant, E. I. Sponable. "Forthwith," says De Forest, "I sketched out the first oxide-coated cathode glow-tube," which Case and Sponable then went ahead and constructed. It was the Aeolight, which Case patented in 1927 (U. S. patent no.1,816,825), and which was to become fundamental to the Movietone system.[52] At one period De Forest employed the Aeo-light in his Phonofilm, but after 1925 he designed and used a new metal cathode recording tube and substituted improved photoelectric cells for the Case Thalifide cells he had been using since 1919.

Since his visits to De Forest's laboratory, Case had been working with Sponable on the development of a sound system that in most respects was identical with De Forest's. Georgette Carneal tells what happened next, according to De Forest:

De Forest heard nothing further from Case other than that the latter was making talking pictures in Auburn and exhibiting them in Auburn theatres with equipment based on that which De Forest had loaned to these theatres long previously. Nevertheless De Forest made no move to stop Case, whose ideas had after all proved useful, until one year later, in 1926, De Forest learned that Case had set up his reproducing equipment in the Fox studios in New York. As a result of this demonstration Case had succeeded in interesting William Fox, who, not knowing De Forest's end of the patent situation, had immediately entered into contract with him and formed the Fox-Case Company to make pictures and exhibit them in the Fox Theatres under the title of 'Movietone.' De Forest observed with amazement that this name, Movietone, was, in his estimation, the chief distinction between the Case pictures and the De Forest Phonofilm pictures. He immediately brought suit against the Fox-Case Corporation for infringement of several of his patents.[53]

He also sued Tri-Ergon inventors Vogt, Massolle, and Engl (see further, Appendix E), the Stanley Company of America, and Western Electric (the two latter organizations on a charge of infringing his rights to the slit patent).[54] By 1935 all his patent claims had been upheld by the U. S. courts. He demanded and received less than $100,000 in compensation (he had spent more than $200,000 on Phonofilm and the compensation was eaten up by legal fees) and the legitimate right to call himself the inventor of sound-on-film. Unlike Fox, he had no desire to monopolize the American film industry.

The major Hollywood studios—not De Forest—were to profit by his invention. His Phonofilm Company—later renamed General Talking Pictures—never really gained a foothold in the movie capital. The organizations and companies De Forest had sued for patent infringements, and even those that brought suit against him, had what De Forest lacked: the resources to develop large-scale production of sound films while they were simultaneously engaged in litigation.

After 1926 hardly anyone outside a law court could be bothered with De Forest and Phonofilm. As we have seen, he could have brought Hollywood into the sound era in the early twenties. But the ears and eyes of the American film industry were to be caught at last not by sound-on-film but by the retrograde return of sound-on-disk, manifesting itself in a most spectacular swan song.

CHAPTER FOUR

THE VOICE OF

VITAPHONE

The decisive events leading to the coming of talkies occurred during the mid-twenties and involved the association of Warner Bros. Pictures, Inc., with Western Electric and Bell Telephone Laboratories.

Warner Bros. followed no long-term policy with regard to the development of sound cinema. Indeed, they were to be directed by the unpredictable nature of public response (particularly as far as reception of *The Jazz Singer* was concerned) rather than by any astute insight into the future of the medium. However, in retrospect, we can now discern three major phases in Warner Bros.' involvement with sound films. The first culminated with the making of *Don Juan* (1926), in which, following the tradition of silent cinema, the sound used was primarily musical accompaniment. The second phase was to produce *The Jazz Singer* (1927), out of which the transitional concept of the part-talkie emerged. The third and final phase was realized with *Lights of New York* (1928), which inaugurated the conventional dialogue film of the sound era.

Some three years before the Warners were to come into the picture, a little-publicized experiment took place. It was eventually to have shattering consequences on film industries all over the world, but at the time not one studio head seems to have bothered about it. In October 1922 at Woolsey Hall in Yale University, Edward B. Craft demonstrated the synchronization of a phonograph record and a projected motion picture.

Sound engineers, the only people seriously interested in the experiment, were more concerned with the record itself than with the synchronization, for Craft was giving the first public demonstration of a system for the electrical recording of phonograph disks. It was the outcome of combining electromagnetic reproducers (the work of Crandall, Kranz, and H. D. Arnold, c.1913–15) with improvements (by J. P. Maxfield and his associates and H. C. Harrison) in wax disk recording and the phonograph.[1]

The recording system was imperfect, but its possibilities aroused the interest and activity of researchers at Bell Telephone Laboratories. Bell Labs and Western Electric Company were both subsidiaries of American Telephone and Telegraph Company; the former was the research branch, the latter the manufacturing and marketing arm. These organizations had obvious, vested interests in technological developments relating to sound.

Mainly through their invention of a mechanical filter that greatly refined the quality of sound recording, Bell engineers managed to improve considerably upon Craft's system. Their apparatus was ready by 1924, and RCA, Victor, and Columbia, the major phonograph recording companies, promptly obtained licenses from Western Electric to use the new system (whose advancement of the art and science of sound recording was to be paralleled only by the much later development of the long-playing high-fidelity microgroove record). This successful and lucrative outcome of their work encouraged Bell engineers to consider further applications of the new sound system. Recalling Craft's attempt to synchronize film and phonograph record, they proceeded to experiment along the same lines. Only after the expenditure of millions of dollars did they become aware of Hollywood's indifference—even downright hostility—to sound pictures. Then it became clear to them that most, if not all, film companies regarded sound pictures as the kiss of death.

It was well known in Hollywood that previous dabblings with such innovations had proved to be technical failures and financial disasters. And even if a new system turned out to be technically perfect, it was generally agreed among studio heads that the transition to sound would be a very costly gamble that could be disastrous to the whole industry. Sound studios would have to be built, and theaters would have to be equipped with the new apparatus. And what would happen to all those millions already invested in silent films? What would be the effect on the industry's lucrative overseas market if talking pictures with American dialogue replaced silent films whose titles could be easily translated? What would become of silent movie stars who were not trained to deliver spoken dialogue, but whose reputation as silent stars had been "created" by expensive promotional campaigns and whose popularity sustained the studios and represented their greatest assets? "What," as *Variety* asked, "would happen to the class theatres with expensive orchestras and stage shows, if any jerk-water movie joint was to be able to give its patrons gorgeous feasts of music via the screen?" Oblivious to these and other questions, Western Electric and Bell sank more and more time and money into experiments they felt sure would interest the film industry as eagerly as the development of electric recording had interested the phonograph record industry.

The energies of the Bell people were concentrated on perfecting a sound-on-disk system. Their ignorance of the needs of the film industry may be gauged from the fact that the apparatus they originally built was designed to synchronize records with films running at 75 feet per minute. As film was normally projected at 90 feet per minute, their system would have required modifications to every projector wired to their apparatus. Fortunately, this little oversight was corrected when, in due course, Warner Bros. came onto the scene. But, as we shall see, other shortcomings were not discovered until their system was already in use for the production of sound movies for commercial exhibition.

As Edward Kellogg noted, "To provide sound for pictures, using the disk-record system, it was necessary to have records which would play continuously for at least the projection time of a 1000-ft. reel (about 11 min.), to plan a synchronous drive, and to use electrical reproduction in order that, with the help of amplifiers, adequate sound output could be had."[2]

After much trial and error, what the Bell people eventually produced was a combination of several important technical developments: First, "an electrical system of recording, employing a high quality microphone and a record-cutting mechanism . . . second . . . an electrical needle reproducer in the grooves of a sound record [where it was sensitized] by electrical vibrations. The electrical currents from this device pass[ed] into an amplifier and then operate[d] a high quality speaker capable of filling the largest motion picture auditorium."[3] Third, a method for making the change from one record to the next without any interruption in the recorded sound.

Sixteen-inch one-sided disks were used; when played at 33⅓ rpm, the speed at which the sound had been recorded, this size supplied the sound equivalent of a standard thousand-foot reel of film. Interconnected projectors providing imperceptible transitions from reel to reel were already in general use in most cinemas. The corresponding switch from one record to another was managed by the use of a double-amplifying rheostat, "the points on one side of which led to the electrical 'pick-up' of one reproducing instrument, those on the other side leading to the other. These points were numbered, and the switch served both as amplifier control and as switch-over. If record number one was being played on point 5, record number two could be switched to by a single quick turn of the dial to point 5 on the other side. This would open the circuit between number one's pickup and the loudspeaker, and close that between number two's pickup and the same loudspeaker. The amplification would be the same in both cases."[4] The final development in the Bell system was the use of a "link between the reproducer and the audience in a theater. An adaptation of the public address system . . . [made] it possible to pick up electric vibrations from the reproducer, amplify them, and by means of properly located loudspeaking telephones, transform them into sound."[5]

One of the first uses of the new system was the completion, in 1924, of *Hawthorne*, a talking picture about the Western Electric factory in suburban Chicago. E. S. Gregg has described it as "the first industrial sound picture ever to be seen and heard."[6] During the same year, Bell technicians prepared a number of short test films of songs and dance bands to demonstrate their newly developed system to the heads of the most important

Hollywood film companies. The Warner brothers were not invited. Their company was too small and insignificant at that time. But Edison, Jesse Lasky, and several executives from MGM were among those who attended the demonstration programs. Their responses, when enthusiastic, stopped short at investing in the system or at expressing any interest in the production of sound movies in Hollywood.

Meanwhile, separate and more aggressive approaches to the film industry were being made by Walter J. Rich, an independent entrepreneur with little direct knowledge of Hollywood. He nevertheless convinced Western Electric that he was the man to promote the new synchronization system and to persuade the Hollywood companies that the sound era had arrived and that they should make haste to join it. Rich's agreement with Western Electric provided that licenses to use the system were to be negotiated with him as well as with Western Electric. (In due course this provision was to involve him in dealings with Warner Bros., whom he had not bothered to contact during his promotional efforts.) By spring 1925, before Warner Bros. came into the picture, Rich had spent $36,000 of his own money in promoting the system without managing to sign up a single company. He thought and talked on the grand scale but achieved little and was never more than incidental to events that led to the coming of sound.

Despite Rich's activities, during 1923–25, events were transpiring that would involve Warner Bros. in the experiments of Bell Laboratories. Since 1903, when they traveled through Pennsylvania and Ohio, exhibiting an overworked print of *The Great Train Robbery*, Sam, Harry, Jack, and Albert Warner had been active in the film industry—first as small-time exhibitors, and later, with increasing success, as distributors and producers. In 1923 they established Warner Bros. Pictures, Inc., a production company whose greatest assets were the popular dog-star Rin-Tin-Tin and the talents of John Barrymore (in that order of importance). When the new corporation began to rack up healthy profits and a rapid increase in production became desirable, more studio space and equipment and an effective, widespread distribution system were needed. These requirements were fulfilled by buying the ailing Vitagraph company, with its acres of well-equipped studios and an established network of foreign film exchanges.

Stepped-up production meant that more publicity would be needed. At that period radio offered the most exciting medium for advertising films, and a film company that was affluent enough owned a radio station or even a radio network. Warner Bros. could not afford to establish a new radio network, but late in 1924 it did buy the equipment of a radio station that had gone bankrupt. It was the best investment the company ever made. As Jack Warner notes: it was "one of those freak rolls of dice—a radio station was almost directly responsible for the fantastic upheaval which took us from a net income of $30,000 for the first eight months of 1927, to a staggering profit of $17,000,000 for a similar period only two years later."[7] However, such a development was inconceivable in 1924. The immediate concern of the Warners was to transport the heap of apparatus to their studio and get it working.

The installation job was given to Western Electric. As a result, Benjamin Levinson, a radio expert and Western Electric's engineer in charge of the work of setting up KFWB (as Warner Bros.' station came to be known), got to meet Sam Warner. The two men became close friends, and Levinson enjoyed explaining to Sam Warner the intricacies and marvels of the apparatus that the studio had just acquired.

Early in 1925, Levinson visited Bell Labs in New York and chanced upon a showing of one of the short test films that had been prepared the year before to demonstrate the new system to the Hollywood executives. According to E. S. Gregg, "He heard the natural sounds of the steps of a pianist going to his instrument; he heard the clicks as the pianist unbuttoned his gloves, the life-like sounds as cane, gloves, hat and coat were tossed aside. He heard for the first time the music of the piano as it came from the screen with startling fidelity. He was greatly impressed."[8] Back in Los Angeles and in the company of Sam Warner, Levinson could not contain his enthusiasm.

> "Listen," he said, "I'm bringing you hot news. I just saw in our New York Laboratories the most wonderful thing I ever looked at in my life. A moving picture that talks!"

... "Benny," said Sam with a shake of the head, "haven't you been around the show world long enough now to know that a picture that talks is something to run away from?"

"I know, I know," said Levinson impatiently. "You're thinking about the old ones. 'Cameraphone,' 'Kinetophone,' all those things. But this is different. This is a talking picture that works like radio! Vacuum tubes. Amplifiers. Listen while I explain it to you. . . ."9

According to Fitzhugh Green, Levinson made Sam Warner promise to attend a demonstration at Bell Labs, telling him, persuasively, "there's more money in it than there ever was in movies." Green, writing close to the events, nowhere mentions that Jack Warner influenced Sam's decision to attend the demonstration. However, as recently as 1965, Jack Warner claimed in his autobiography that it was on his "enthusiastic urging" that his brother "went to New York and there, with eyes popping like a kid at a French peep show . . . saw a series of shorts in which voices and music came from the screen."10 It is not clear why Jack Warner should have been so enthusiastic about an invention he had never seen or heard. What is clear is that he wants his readers to believe that he was the most prescient of the Warner brothers. (Later in the same book he states, "I started production on our first sound film, *Don Juan*." [Notice the "I."] Elsewhere brother Jack speaks of "we" [all the Warner brothers], but here he claims credit for being the sole, personal producer of the first sound feature film, a claim that this writer has been unable to substantiate in Warner Bros. promotional material, in trade advertising for the film, or in any of the published and unpublished sources he has consulted. It should be noted, incidentally, that while Jack Warner clearly identifies himself as the producer of *Don Juan*, he somehow omits to mention the name of the man who directed the picture. He does remember Alan Crosland when he gives his account of the making of *The Jazz Singer*, but this little piece of information is overshadowed by the revelation that it was none other than Jack Warner who had the brilliant idea of offering the lead to Al Jolson.)

With or without the inspiration of his brother, Sam Warner attended a demonstration of sound films at Bell Labs in April

1925, when he was visiting New York to finalize the takeover of Vitagraph. If anything, he was even more impressed than Levinson. The synchronization and the sound quality seemed remarkably natural and clear to him. The idea of producing sound movies began to appeal to his imagination. Back in California he tried to convey his excitement to his brother Harry. But Harry was ice-cold on the subject of talking pictures; he knew all the horror stories about earlier ventures into sound movies. Also, as he was in charge of the company's financial affairs, he knew better than Sam did how heavily it had gone into debt to buy Vitagraph. It would be lunacy to gamble even more borrowed money on an untried novelty. Accordingly, he refused to see the invention or even talk about it.

Undaunted, Sam arranged what was ostensibly a social meeting between his brothers and officials from Bell Labs and Western Electric. Actually, it was a ruse to get Harry Warner to attend a demonstration of sound movies, and it worked. Harry "was very much impressed, but didn't want the Western people to know it. It was when they showed an orchestra that he got his great inspiration of providing film with musical accompaniment."[11] He was to explain subsequently:

> "The thought occurred to me that if we quit the idea of a talking picture and brought about something the motion picture theatre of the present day really needs—music adapted to the picture—we could ultimately develop it to a point at which people would ask us for talking pictures. If I myself would not have gone across the street to see or hear a talking picture, I surely could not expect the public to do it. But Music! That is another story. . . ."[12]

Later, when he was alone with his brother, Harry admitted that he thought the system had possibilities.

> "But Sam," he added, "I wouldn't be so foolish as to try to make talking pictures. That's what everybody has done, and lost. No, we'll do better than that: we can use this thing for other purposes. We can use it *for musical accompaniment to our pictures!* We can film and record vaudeville and musical acts, and make up programs for houses that can't afford the real thing or can't get big-time acts. Think of what it would mean to a small independent theatre owner to buy his orchestra with his picture!

Not to have an organ! Not a musician in the house! Not an actor—and yet his whole show. . . ."[13]

Thus was envisaged what was to be the first of the three major phases of Warner Bros.' development of sound cinema.

Now that Sam and Harry were both seriously interested in the new sound system, Warner Bros. was ready to open negotiations with Western Electric. At this point it was discovered that the company would first have to settle with Walter J. Rich. Rich was promptly approached, and having given up hope of interesting any of the big film companies, he was more than willing to deal with Warner Bros. For a fee of $72,000 he agreed to "go in with [Warners] on a share and share alike basis"[14] and permit them to negotiate freely with Western Electric for permission to use the new sound system.

In June 1925, "Stanley Watkins, who had been head of [J.P.] Maxfield's experimental sound crew at Western Electric, took his men to the Vitagraph studio, in Brooklyn, and set up shop. Inside the big glass stages, they built a box 50 feet square and 30 feet high. This would be their new set, but it had to be sound-proofed. So the crew and Sam Warner, who . . . left the studio only to sleep, hung rugs over the walls of the box stage to insulate the place for sound."[15] Vitagraph studios had not, of course, been designed for the making of sound movies. Despite the efforts of Watkins and his crew, acoustic problems arose from the outset. "Draperies were hung up in the rafters to muffle sound. . . . Ed DuPar . . . was the cameraman on this early project. He achieved as much camera mobility as possible by running four cameras on a take. One master camera ran continuously on a long-shot set-up while the others were used to get cut-in shots. Sometimes he would make ten or twelve changes on the close-up camera in the course of one ten-minute recording."[16] At this period, the sound system was being used at Vitagraph on the basis of Rich's agreement with Western Electric and his recently-formed partnership with Warner Bros. So far Warner Bros. had not signed a contract with Western Electric.

By spring 1926 short test films using the new sound system were being made quite regularly at Vitagraph. Two of the short experimental pictures made at this time were later released for public exhibition. The first was a speech by elderly Dr. Watson, who had collaborated with Alexander Graham Bell in inventing the telephone. The second, rather more ambitious effort was titled *The Volga Boatmen*. It required the construction of a studio set depicting a river bank along which eight sturdy men —two quartets of Russian singers—proceeded laboriously while singing the "Volga Boat Song" and tugging at a rope supposedly attached to an unseen boat. "For this opus they imported loads of salt to simulate snow and braced one hefty member of the [sound] crew off stage so the 'boatmen' could have something to pull on."[17] The inspiration for this masterpiece, reputedly directed by Sam Warner himself, was doubtless the release, early in April 1926, of Cecil B. DeMille's feature film *The Volga Boatman*, starring William Boyd, Robert Edeson, and Victor Varconi. If DeMille heard about the competition he was unlikely to have been disturbed by it. The Warners would have a much longer haul than their boatmen before they could make sound pictures that offered any serious opposition to the ambitious silent features of the major studios.

Before legalizing their arrangements with Western Electric, the Warners decided to keep their venture into sound films separate from the regular, silent film-making activities of their Hollywood studios. Early in April 1926 they established a new company, Vitaphone Corporation (no doubt a deliberate echo of Vitagraph), and named the sound system Vitaphone. On April 20, 1926, the new corporation formally leased the Vitaphone system from Western Electric and also secured rights to sublicense the system to other film companies. In due course, Warner Bros.' control of these sublicensing rights was to antagonize other studios when they in turn sought to make the transition to sound; and more than any other single factor it was to lead to the promotion of rival systems and the eventual triumph of sound-on-film over sound-on-disk.

But at this stage Warner Bros. had the field to itself. It was a questionable advantage when none of the other studios had shown any interest in sound movies, but nevertheless one that had to be exploited in view of the company's heavy and increasing investments in the system. Rich suggested arranging demonstration programs for film exhibitors, who might thereby be induced to sink some of *their* money into Vitaphone. But the Warners knew show business better than Rich did. Realizing that they had something unique, they decided that the best way to exploit it was to use it in a unique way—to present it in a package that no other film company could offer. Instead of demonstrating experimental films to exhibitors, they would use the system to create a spectacular show that everyone would want to see. (The same idea was behind Clément-Maurice's Phono-Cinéma-Théâtre of 1900 and in the exploitation, years later, of such technical developments as Cinerama and 3-D). Thus, from the outset the public would associate Vitaphone with entertainment of the highest order. The inspiration was Harry Warner's. As he subsequently explained, "I said to my partners, 'Let's get the greatest artists and the best orchestra in the country. Let's have confidence in this and put all our muscle behind it. We'll know the result after we have opened the first show. . . .' "[18] He conceived a long, elaborate program, consisting of a number of short films exhibiting the talents of musical virtuosi of the concert stage and opera house, followed by a lavish feature film. In every part of the show the "miracle" of Vitaphone would be evident.

Once the die had been cast and the Warners were firmly committed to promoting Vitaphone on the grand scale, it became imperative for them to raise large amounts of capital. The creation of the whole program for the premiere of Vitaphone would finally involve Warner Bros. in an expenditure of almost $3 million. Within a year after the agreement with Western Electric, the company had so overextended itself that the future of Warner Bros. Pictures, Inc., depended entirely on the success or failure of the gamble with Vitaphone.

For the short films that would make up the first part of the program the Warners planned to present leading artists of the Metropolitan Opera Company of New York. Eventually, upwards of a million dollars was spent in hiring the chosen artists, obtaining their temporary release from contracts with Metropolitan Opera and various record companies, hiring the New York Philharmonic Orchestra, and securing rights to use certain copyrighted music.

It was decided that the program's feature film would be *Don Juan,* the latest vehicle for John Barrymore. Originally intended as a silent movie, the film was already in production in Warner Bros.' Hollywood studios. Its budget had been fixed at half a million dollars, but when the decision was made to include the movie in the Vitaphone program, an additional $200,000 was ploughed into the picture, thus insuring that it would be one of the most expensive films of 1926, and certainly the costliest Warner production up to that time. This additional investment did not include the considerable expense of supplying the sound accompaniment, which utilized a specially commissioned score.

The short films for the premiere program were made in Manhattan. Vitagraph studios proved to be totally unsatisfactory. The production crew was "isolated in Flatbush from everything, except the subway. The Coney Island line of the BMT ran above the surface—right past the studio windows. Every time a train passed, the record needle jumped in anguish. Working conditions in Flatbush went from bad to worse."[19]

Obviously, at this period no sound studio where feature films could be made existed anywhere in the world, and Warner Bros. had no immediate plans to build one. A compromise location had to be found, and the old Manhattan Opera House, which was known to have good acoustics, was chosen. The Vitaphone Corporation took a year's lease on the building, and soon electricians, carpenters, and sound engineers were swarming over the place, installing miles of wiring, and setting up arc lamps, cameras, and recording equipment.

"S. S. A. Watkins was in charge for Western Electric. He had a group of men including H. C. Humphrey, R. C. Sawyer, and George Grove. Sam Warner carried on the Warner Brothers' end. With him he had Ed DuPar, a cameraman, and Bert Frank, a cutter. On occasion Herman Heller, musical director of the Warner Theatre in New York, came over. Heller was the first 'Talkie' director because all the first numbers were musical."[20]

Now that production had begun, in earnest, on a program intended for the largest possible public audience, a series of difficulties became apparent that had been latent or nonexistent while the test films were being made. As Fitzhugh Green observed: "It was easy to make pictures, easy to make records; but another matter to make them together. Conditions that were ideal for the one were so often not at all ideal for the other."[21] The Manhattan Opera House turned out to be scarcely any improvement over the Vitagraph studios. The most serious problems arose from noise of all kinds, which impaired the quality of the sound recording. Close to the Opera House, part of the New York City subway system was being excavated, and workmen were blasting into the rocky surface of Manhattan while recording sessions were in progress. Aside from the disruptive sounds of explosions, shock waves would knock the stylus out of the groove and ruin a well-nigh perfect disk.

A host of other unexpected noises plagued the recording engineers: interference from static electricity; echoes, resonances, and various extraneous sounds (such as coughs, footsteps, passing traffic), most of which were inaudible to listeners in the Opera House but were nevertheless picked up and amplified by the Vitaphone system. The system also proved to be ultrasensitive to the sounds emitted by the studio arc lights: not only the barely audible "sizzle" but also the normally inaudible emission of radio waves and harmonics. In addition, the records themselves produced uncontrollable surface noise, and it was discovered that the Vitaphone apparatus was sensitive to radio broadcasts and was sometimes unexpectedly recording radio programs along with the intended sounds.

But the most serious obstacles were created by the cameras themselves. First, they were hand-cranked, which meant that even the most assiduous and unwearying cameraman could not maintain a speed regular enough to insure perfect synchronization with phonograph recordings. Motor-driven cameras had to be devised to replace the standard hand-cranked apparatus, but the sound of their whirring mechanism was clearly discernible on every recording made at the outset of production in the Manhattan Opera House. Most, if not all these difficulties had to be mastered quickly. Unfortunately, not all the immediate solutions were ideal ones for the art of motion picture making. Thus by housing the camera in a soundproof booth, camera noise was eliminated—but at the cost of the camera's former mobility and flexibility. The booth constructed for this purpose was about seven feet high, four feet deep and three feet wide, mounted on rubber tired swivel wheels, with a door cut in the back for the ingress and egress of the camerman and his machine. There was a square hole in the front of it for the camera to "shoot" through. And in order that no camera noise should come through this hole, felt sound insulating material was fastened, in the shape of an inverted pyramid between its edges and the outer part of the lens; the lens stuck its glassy eye out from the depths of a felt-sided tunnel.[22]

After one occasion when the door of the booth had been left open accidentally and the camera noise ruined the take, it became the practice to lock cameramen into the booth during the recording sessions. But no way was found to avoid frequent disruptions from noises outside the Opera House; this problem was not solved until the construction of sound studios insulated against exterior noise.

The other difficulties were easier to cope with. Radio sounds and some surface noise were prevented by covering every part of the Vitaphone apparatus with a metallic "shield" that was impervious to static and radio waves. Unfortunately, this shield proved ineffective as a barrier to sounds emanating from the arc lamps; the only solution here was for Frank N. Murphy, Warner Bros.' chief electrician, to devise an entirely new lighting system employing incandescent lamps. The system he developed was a major advance in studio lighting, and within a short time in most studios it had entirely replaced the old arc lighting that had been used during the silent era. Echoes and resonances inside the building were reduced or eliminated by hanging heavy drapes or placing scenery flats at suitable locations to break up extensive wall surfaces. With these and other quickly improvised methods, the shooting and recording sessions were able to proceed more or less on schedule.

As mentioned earlier, the Warners expected that the effectiveness of Vitaphone in providing musical accompaniment of silent pictures would decide the future of the system. Accordingly, special consideration was given to the score of *Don Juan*. Since the film would have to demonstrate unequivocally Vitaphone's superiority over the live cinema orchestra, organist, or pianist, it was essential to provide a memorable, original score played in perfect or nearly perfect synchronization with the picture. William Axt, David Mendoza, and Major Edward Bowes were selected to write the music. Axt, a film composer of some eminence, had previously written the music played by theater orchestras as accompaniment to *The Big Parade* and *Ben Hur* (both 1925). His success with the music for *Don Juan* was to earn him the first studio contract ever given to a film composer —though curiously it was to come from MGM not Warner Bros. Axt went on to provide the scores for numerous films during the first years of the sound era. By contrast, the careers of Mendoza and Bowes were short-lived. Mendoza *did* collaborate with Axt on at least three other films before 1929, including the score for Fred Niblo's *Camille* (1927), starring Norma Talmadge and Gilbert Roland. Bowes also supplied music for *Camille*. Axt, Mendoza, and Bowes watched *Don Juan* many times, familiarizing themselves with the moods, actions, and personalities they would have to express or intensify musically. They timed every shot with stop watches and then set to work to write a score which compounded original themes and melodies from classical compositions and which, when played at the correct speed, would synchronize with the film.

When the score was ready, Henry Hadley, conductor of the New York Philharmonic, rehearsed it while watching the picture on a screen behind the orchestra. The speed of the music was carefully adjusted to the picture, and various additions, excisions, and changes were made to the score until the timing was perfect. The recording sessions could now begin. One visitor to these sessions was a reporter for *Moving Picture World,* who rapturously noted his impressions in that journal's issue for July 10, 1926, less than a month before the film's premiere:

> The other afternoon at the Manhattan Opera House we heard the New York Philharmonic Orchestra recording for *Don Juan* via the Vitaphone. . . . It was playing what will be admitted as one of the finest scores that ever accompanied a picture . . . Warner Bros., with the Vitaphone, are in a fair way to rewrite a big chapter of picture presentation. . . . The influence of a beautiful and appealing musical score, going hand in hand with the picture, will be profound in every center, large or small. The effect on the social structure of the country, aside from its effect

on the picture business will be as marked as the influences of any one of the great inventions in electrical and physical science.

In August 1926, the Warners believed that the future of their organization depended on the accuracy of this prediction. No one was discussing talking pictures: synchronized music would decide the success or failure of Vitaphone and Warner Bros.

Meanwhile, Warners' Theatre, in New York, where the first Vitaphone show was to be premiered, was being wired for sound and decorated for the gala event. What the latter involved may be imagined from this description by Peter Milne in *Moving Picture World* for August 14, 1926:

> The theatre had been closed for a week prior to the opening, during which time an army of workmen transformed the interior of the house to more closely resemble a legitimate theatre. There is novelty in the new decorations from the lighting of the interior itself to the dressing of the lobby of the house.

The technical installations were another matter. They required less labor but were far more complex. First, the projection booth had to be equipped with amplifiers, a monitor or control horn (to enable the operator to gauge the sound in the auditorium), a disk attachment for the projector, and a "Control gear by means of which one or other projector" might be "put in use at will and the volume of sound adjusted to any particular requirement."[23] (Contrasting photos of Warner projection booths in 1926 and 1928 appear in F. Green's *The Film Finds Its Tongue,* 1929.) Next, in order to insure the existence of a self-sufficient power supply, a power room, containing a generator, a transformer, a battery charger, and a generous supply of batteries, was installed. Finally, the stage was equipped with concealed speakers in duplex form. A contemporary account describes them as four horns "twelve and fourteen feet long, and coiled . . . they are placed in back of a special screen . . . two mounted at the line of the stage and pointed upward towards the balconies, and two mounted at the upper edge or above the screen, and pointed downward."[24] This arrangement was found to provide satisfactory sound distribution throughout the auditorium.

The first Vitaphone show had been prepared hurriedly. Work

began late in April 1926 and was completed only three months later, on August 1, 1926. Three days later the show was given its first preview, for all those who had been involved in its production. The next evening, August 5, there was a preview for executives and engineers of Western Electric and Bell Telephone. Everyone was impressed. But then, of course, it was "their baby." The big question remained unanswered. What would the reviewers and the public think of Vitaphone?

Advertisements were already doing everything possible to influence their reactions. The striking four-page, red and black announcement that appeared in the leading trade journals was typical:

EXHIBITORS!
If you think the world has been thrilled before, wait until August 6th when WARNER BROS. will present the

V I T A P H O N E
At the Warner Theatre, New York, in conjunction with the World Premiere showing of

"DON JUAN"
Story by Bess Meredyth   Directed by Alan Crosland
With the world's greatest actor

JOHN BARRYMORE
Opening night $10 Admission Plus Tax. . . .

The rest of the announcement detailed the supporting program of short films, which offered the talents of Giovanni Martinelli ("the world famous Metropolitan Opera tenor"), Efrem Zimbalist ("acclaimed the master violinist in both Europe and America"), Mischa Elman ("known to every man, woman and child that loves music"), Harold Bauer ("the pianist numbered among the immortals of music"), Marion Talley ("the Metropolitan Opera Sensation of the Year"), Anna Case ("the favorite of Europe's royalty and the American public"), the Metropolitan Opera Chorus ("singers heretofore appearing only with the Metropolitan Opera Company"), and Henry Hadley and the New York Philharmonic Orchestra ("Mr. Hadley himself, conducting this unparalleled aggregation of 107 symphony artists")

—all "presented on the Vitaphone by Warner Bros. by arrangement with the Western Electric Company and the Bell Telephone Laboratories."

Another, prophetic and even more boastful advertisement appeared a week later, in the August 7 issue of *Moving Picture World:*

> EXHIBITORS! Do you realize that on August 6th motion pictures will have been completely revolutionized by "VITAPHONE"? On that day "VITAPHONE" will bring the realization of a new future to the theatres of the world; a future brighter in its aspects, broader in its scope, and greater in its possibilities than any other period in the development of motion pictures.
>
> What the telephone means to modern life; what the railroad means to modern travel; what the world's greatest inventions mean to civilization today—that is what Warner Bros. bring to motion pictures in "VITAPHONE."
>
> Nothing in the history of motion pictures compares with the importance of this one event! Through "VITAPHONE" it will now be possible for the world at large to see and hear that which was heretofore impossible. . . .
>
> Like the rumblings of a coming storm, word-of-mouth comment comes low and slowly, but gathering power as it sweeps onward, it carries like lightning to the far corners of the world. Such will be the praise for "VITAPHONE"! Already you have heard of it. And on August 6th the whole world will thrill to the greatest news the entire motion picture industry has ever heard. The World Premiere of "VITAPHONE"—remember the date, August 6th, 1926.

In August 1926 Warners' Theatre, at Fifty-second Street and Broadway, New York, was the only theater in the world equipped to present Vitaphone. The public premiere attracted a distinguished and formally attired audience, which included Hollywood moguls William Fox and Adolph Zukor; theater producers and impresarios Lee Shubert, Marc Klaw, and E. F. Albee; singer Amelita Galli-Curci; financier Otto Kahn; entrepreneur Walter J. Rich; and most of the performers whose talents were displayed in the short films. As the audience filed into the theater on that historic Friday evening, they were handed programs in which they read the following statement expressing Warner Bros.' high aims and hopes for Vitaphone and the ease with which the system could be operated, but patently excluding any mention of plans to make talking feature films:

> The Vitaphone will revolutionize the presentation of motion pictures in the largest metropolitan theatres as well as in the smallest theatres in the smallest towns. It will bring to audiences in every corner of the world the music of the greatest symphony orchestras and the vocal entertainment of the most popular stars of the operatic and theatrical fields. Its use is not confined by any means, to the presentation of pictures. It will be available for use in legitimate theatre, and, in the educational, commercial and religious fields as well as in the field of amusement.

> The invention will make it possible for every performance in a motion picture theatre to have a full orchestral accompaniment to the picture regardless of the size of the house. The apparatus, by means of which the combination of motion pictures and sound will be reproduced in theatres, is no more complicated, from the standpoint of operation, than an ordinary motion picture projector. No special skill or technique is required by the operator. If the film breaks there is no interference with the accuracy of synchronization. The sound system is not controlled by the film itself.[25]

Such claims were soon found to be more than a little exaggerated, but at this stage they served to impress potential investors and exhibitors who might easily be discouraged at learning not only that it would cost a minimum of $16,000 to install Vitaphone equipment in the average movie theater but also that the system was not simple to operate (or fix, if anything went wrong) and that all the bugs were not yet out of it.

With so much at stake, the Warners were leaving as little as possible to chance. Only a week before the premiere, Harry Warner was to announce that "no time would be lost in taking steps to put the Vitaphone accompaniment within the reach of all exhibitors."[26] Publicly the premiere and the advertised claims about Vitaphone *seemed* to be having the desired effect. A boxed news item on the front page of *Moving Picture World* noted that "Other producers and distributors present at the Vitaphone premiere . . . were keenly interested in the possibilities the invention offers. There is the probability that an arrangement will be effected whereby other producers will employ the Vitaphone."[27]

At first, however, the truth was rather different. Shortly after the *Don Juan* premiere, Harry Warner was confronting his brothers with a serious question. "The show is open and everything is fine, but who is going to buy our machines? . . . I have gone around to the heads of several companies and tried to persuade them to participate, but as yet I must admit we have not succeeded."[28] And in March 1927, at an interview with Joseph P. Kennedy, held at the Harvard Graduate School of Business, Harry revealed the hard facts involved in trying to persuade exhibitors to install Vitaphone in their theaters.

> **Mr. Kennedy:** Do you lease or sell the Vitaphone?
> **Mr. Warner:** We take the cost of the machine and we lease it on that basis to the man who runs the theatre. . . . Then we charge him a tax of ten cents a seat a week. . . . That does not mean that that is the way it is ultimately going to be done, because I personally believe that the man who has a small theatre in a small town will not be able to pay that much money. . . . We shall have to modify our policy to meet the requirements of the situation.
> **Mr. Kennedy:** What, approximately, does it cost to install?
> **Mr. Warner:** We have got it down to the cheapest figure. In a theatre of nine hundred or one thousand seats, it costs $16,000; in the next size, the theatre of about fifteen hundred seats, $18,000; in the larger theatres, $22,000; in a theatre like the Roxy, $25,000. That is the actual cost to us.[29]

The dubious gamble with Vitaphone must be seen in the context of Warner Bros.' economic standing in 1926. The company was almost incalculably in debt, and had shown a net loss of more than a million dollars for the year ending March 1926 (according to *Kinematograph Weekly*, London, July 15, 1926).[30] Though part of this deficit was the price of becoming national distributors—and included the purchase of Vitagraph—most of the loss could be attributed to the declining appeal of Warner Bros.' silent movies. It was no exaggeration in the fall of 1926 to say that Vitaphone would make or break the company.

But meanwhile, economics aside, what exactly did the audience see and hear as they settled into their seats in Warners' Theatre on the evening of August 6, 1926?

At 8:30 the house lights dimmed. As the curtains opened, on the screen, in long shot, could be seen the willowy figure of Will H. Hays, president of the Motion Picture Producers Association and nominal head of the American film industry. Hays began to approach the audience. As he came nearer, the first sounds could be heard coming from the screen: the image was clearing its throat. It took up a stiff, formal pose standing between an ornate chair and a book-laden table. Then it began to speak. The words were clearly audible throughout the theater and were perfectly synchronized with the movements of the speaker's lips:

> No story ever written for the screen is as dramatic as the story of the screen itself.
>
> Tonight marks another step in that story.
>
> Far indeed have we advanced from that few seconds of the shadow of a serpentine dancer thirty years ago when the motion picture was born—to this, the first public demonstration of the Vitaphone which synchronizes the reproduction of sound with the reproduction of action.
>
> And farther and farther ahead is the future of pictures, as far-flung as all the tomorrows, rendering greater and still greater service as the chief amusement of the majority of all our people and the sole amusement of millions and millions, exercising an immeasurable influence as a living, breathing thing on the ideas and ideals, the customs and costumes, the hopes and ambitions of countless men, women and children.
>
> In the presentation of these pictures, music plays an invaluable part. Too, the motion picture is a most potent factor in the development of a national appreciation of good music. Now that service will be extended as the Vitaphone shall carry symphony orchestrations to the town halls of the hamlets.
>
> It has been said that the art of the musician is ephemeral, that he creates but for the moment. Now neither the artist nor his art will ever die.
>
> Long experimentation and research by the Western Electric and the Bell Laboratories, supplemented by the efforts of Warner Brothers, have made this great new instrument possible, and to

them and to all who have contributed to this achievement I offer my congratulations and best wishes.

To the Warner Brothers, to whom is due credit for this great premiere, marking the beginning of a new era in music and motion pictures, I offer my felicitations and sincerest appreciation.

It is an occasion with which the public and the motion picture industry are equally gratified.

It is another great service—and 'Service is the supreme commitment of life.'[31]

At the end of his speech, the figure on the screen stood silent for a moment. Whereupon the audience spontaneously applauded, as if responding to a live figure. The illusion was complete as the image bowed, apparently acknowledging the applause. "No closer approach to resurrection has ever been made by science," observed Professor Michael Pupin of Columbia University, after witnessing this, his first "talkie."[32]

When the picture faded out it was followed by titles announcing the "Overture 'Tannhäuser' by Richard Wagner, played by the New York Philharmonic Orchestra, Henry Hadley conducting. Presented by the Vitaphone Corporation (a subsidiary of Warner Bros.)."

Mordaunt Hall, who attended the Vitaphone premiere for the *New York Times,* was greatly impressed with the lifelike quality of the Hays speech. "There was no muffled utterance nor lisping in the course of the talk," he noticed. "It was the voice of Hays, and had any of his friends closed their eyes to the picture on the screen they would have immediately recognized the voice. Every syllable was audible and clear."[33] Charles Edward Hastings, writing for *Moving Picture World,* observed that the speech "was delivered with singular clarity, the tones coming clear, distinct and natural."[34] Neither Hall nor Hastings lend any support to the much later recollection (or assumption?) by Richard Griffith that Hays's "flat, middle-Western voice was slightly 'out of sync.' with his image on the screen. . . ."[35] Possibly Griffith's impression was that of the speech as it is preserved in the sound-on-film conversion of the original—a form in which the speech is, indeed, somewhat "out of sync." with the image. At any rate, his comment should warn us to beware of assumptions or conclusions based either on recollections long after the event or on questionable familiarity with the original experience.

Hall was as impressed with the overture as he had been with the speech. The orchestral rendering seemed to him remarkable not only for the "clarity of the tonal colors and softer interludes" but also for the "thrilling volumes of the full orchestra." Hastings offered a more guarded assessment. After describing how the overture was presented—"with 'close-ups' of sections of the orchestra, according as strings or horns were carrying the theme" —he added: "the work of Mr. Hadley, when directing, was accurately timed. The full tone, in the closing movement, illustrated fully what may be expected from the Vitaphone." Epes W. Sargent, also reviewing the show for *Moving Picture World*, went on to clarify what *could* be expected.

> In the work of the Philharmonic orchestra, the string section came out as brilliantly as though the players were in the pit. The wood choir was a bit muffled and tubby, and when the heavy brasses came in there developed a curious covered effect, as though the instrument had too much tone to deliver. On the other hand, the tympani, of even deeper tone, came through clearly. . . . In brief, the Vitaphone seems to work best at opposite ends of the scale; the high notes and the low. The middle registers, whether instrumental or vocal, still lack clarity. The volume of tone seems to govern clearness to a considerable degree, for the solos were much better than the concerted numbers. However, the device gives far greater audibility, a far more correct rendition of tonal values and at most points is free from the suggestion of the phonograph horn.[36]

Promotion for the program placed much emphasis on the fact that Vitaphone had recorded the full complement of the New York Philharmonic's 107 players. But shortly afterwards, Harry Warner was to admit that the recording people had discovered that an 80-piece orchestra sounded better than a 107-piece orchestra when recorded on Vitaphone—"because, if you crowd too many musicians into a small room, naturally you get a very large volume of tone."[37]

When we see this filmed overture today—in a sound-on-film

version, the only one that is occasionally accessible—its static cinematography seems to outweigh the importance it once possessed as a masterly achievement in sound recording. It is dullness incarnate and seems interminable. In fact, the only persistent complaint about the first Vitaphone show in 1926 was that some of the items in the concert section went on too long. The overture was the longest, and the experience of having to sit through it probably influenced the decision to restrict future short Vitaphone films to seven or eight minutes instead of the eleven to fifteen that was typical of the first show.

In filming the overture, the orchestra was placed in the orchestra pit; the stage was concealed by a closed curtain that was flanked by two twisted columns. As with sequences in many musicals of the thirties, the audience was being invited to believe that what they were watching was a live show in the theater. Indeed, in all the concert items that preceded the feature film a conscious effort was made to persuade the audience that they were in an opera house or concert hall rather than a movie theater. In the overture this impression may have been supplied by the limitations imposed on the camera; but in most of the other items the sense that one was watching theater was mainly created by the obviously theatrical scenery. The overture opens with a long shot of the entire orchestra and soon cuts to a slow pan across the string section. Thereafter, the same long shot and slow pan are monotonously repeated. The string section receives most of the camera's attention, simply because it is in the foreground and thus the most accessible to the camera. One expects—but does not get—close-ups of the percussion and woodwind players. They are more remote from the camera. It would have taken a zoom lens or mobile camera to focus on them, but neither was available. The camera was imprisoned in a soundproof booth whose rubber wheels allowed for a minimum of movement. (By comparison with this filmed overture, the celebrated film *Instruments of the Orchestra* [directed by Muir Mathieson, 1946], in which Sir Malcolm Sargent used Britten's *Variations and Fugue on a Theme of Purcell* as a means of demonstrating the orchestral role of various instruments, seems like a brilliant essay in montage.)

The overture film concludes with an irritating visual incongruity. Hadley lowers his baton and takes his bow in the usual long shot that shows the entire orchestra. Then there is a sudden cut to Hadley alone, in medium shot, bowing in front of the closed curtain on the stage above the orchestra pit. With another abrupt cut we are back to the familiar long shot and Hadley is requesting the orchestra to rise and acknowledge the applause. Presumably the problems of editing the film in relation to the recorded sound required the insertion of the disconcerting cutaway to Hadley alone on stage: the shot was probably filmed after the rest of the shooting, when the full orchestra was no longer available.

The solo performance films that followed the overture were no less static, but this fault was less evident because of their comparative brevity. Published accounts of the Vitaphone premiere appear unanimous in praise of violinist Mischa Elman playing Dvořák's "Humoresque," accompanied by Joseph Bonime at the piano. Charles Edward Hastings found this part of the program "one of the most entrancing things, as interpreted by the Vitaphone, that we have listened to."[38] Mordaunt Hall observed that "every note that came to one's ears synchronized with the gliding bow and the movements of the musician's fingers."[39] Elman followed "Humoresque" with another piece, not listed on the program, which Hastings described as apparently "selected . . . for the purpose of illustrating the synchronization purpose of the new invention. As Elman swayed to right or left and touched the bow against the strings, sound and movement touched it off in perfect accord."

A light interlude in this mainly classical presentation was provided by a short film of guitarist Roy Smeck in his "Pastimes" —performances on the banjo, ukelele, harmonica, and Hawaiian guitar. "The numbers were jazzy, and the production wholly satisfying, the audience relishing this offering."[40] The particularly favorable audience response to this part of the show was to play an important part in determining the character of the next Vitaphone program.

After Roy Smeck came Marion Talley, star of the Metropolitan Opera Company, singing "Caro Nome" from Verdi's *Rigoletto*. This part of the show was the most severely criticized for its real or apparent shortcomings in synchronization. Hastings,

rising to the defense, charitably ascribed these shortcomings not
to any defects in the Vitaphone system but to the fact that the
"movements of Miss Talley's lips limped . . . Miss Talley's tones
are formed in her throat before the lips have apparently been
framed for these tones, as we, the audience, watch the young
lady. The Vitaphone caught the tones as formed."

Marion Talley was followed by "An Evening on the Don," a
medley of Russian songs and dances which did not, however,
include that earlier Vitaphone masterpiece, *The Volga Boatmen.*

The last three short films were among the most memorable.
First, Efrem Zimbalist (violin) accompanied by Harold Bauer
(piano) performed variations on a theme from the *Kreutzer*
Sonata. Even today, with their original Vitaphone performance
rechanneled and filtered through an entirely different sound
system, Zimbalist and Bauer offer a sensitive interpretation of
Beethoven's work. What followed their duet was widely considered to be the highlight of the show—Giovanni Martinelli's
impassioned rendering of the aria "Vesti la guibba" from
Leoncavallo's *I Pagliacci*. Martinelli appeared in Pierrot costume and sang the famous aria against a simple theatrical set.
Mordaunt Hall went into raptures over the performance, proclaiming that "Nothing like it had ever been heard in a motion
picture theatre. . . ." Hastings was more restrained but nevertheless considered Martinelli to be "the individual hit of the
Vitaphone prelude. His voice seemed to blend more naturally
with whatever Vitaphone has to offer, than the other soloists."[41]

To conclude this concert of stars that preceded the feature
film, there was an impressive finale in which Anna Case sang
the Spanish number, "La Fiesta," accompanied by a dance
divertissement by the Cansinos, the Metropolitan Opera Company's Chorus, and the 107-piece New York Philharmonic
now under the baton of Herman Heller. The finale was staged
in an elaborate hacienda courtyard set, and the singer and her
accompanying dance troupe were appropriately and ornately
costumed. Music, costumes, and setting prepared the audience
for the feature that was to follow.

The Vitaphone prelude lasted approximately an hour. It was

followed by a ten-minute intermission and then by the feature, which ran for one hour and forty-nine minutes.

The feature opens with an epigraph-title: *The tale they tell of Don Juan, immortal lover and doubter of women, is bold with life and color—a merry, insolent tale slashed with intrigue—yet its beginning is as gray as the old Spanish castle of Juan's earliest memory.*

There follows a prologue in which Don Juan de Marana is shown at the age of five. In an episode somewhat reminiscent of Poe's tale "A Cask of Amontillado," the boy's father, Don José (John Barrymore), is informed by his servant, a vindictive, hunchbacked dwarf, that his wife, Donna Isabel, is having an *affaire.* The outraged husband pretends to leave his castle, but suddenly reappears when the dwarf apprises him that Donna Isabel and her lover are together in her bedchamber. Aware that his presence is about to be discovered, the hapless lover hides in a recess in the wall that was left open when a hidden treasure chest was removed. But Don José realizes what has happened and orders the recess to be sealed up permanently. As the servants begin to brick up the wall, Don José mockingly asks his wife, "Think you of any reason why they should not seal the wall?" She remains silent, endeavoring to conceal her guilt. Her lover is entombed alive. But Donna Isabel's silence is of no avail, for in the presence of their tearful child, Don José turns on her, denounces her infidelity, and drives her from the castle forever.

Five years elapse. Don José's disillusionment with women is complete. Convinced that the entire female sex is as wanton and unfaithful as his wife, he expresses his contempt for women by surrounding himself with sycophantic courtesans, with whom he indulges his unbridled lust. At length, Elvira, one of his mistresses, goaded by jealousy at his display of interest in another woman, stabs him in full view of his impressionable, ten-year-old son. Before dying, Don José tells Elvira, "My three-fold debt to woman is now complete: life—disillusionment—death." And he enjoins young Don Juan: "Beware giving your love to women. Go out into the world and take their love when it pleases you—smile—and forget!" With that the prologue comes to an end. The story begins.

Ten more years have passed. The scene has now shifted to Rome: *The mighty Vatican soaring heavenward amid a seethe of corruption—scented velvets brushing against the plague sores of the wretched. Incense—purple—wine—gold.* The city is divided by the rival factions of the Borgias and the Orsinis. Don Juan (John Barrymore), already notorious throughout Europe as the irresistible lover, the man of countless *affaires,* has taken up residence in the Eternal City. His home is a place "where innocence might enter but never depart."

Cesare Borgia (Warner Oland) and his sister Lucrezia (Estelle Taylor) are proceeding through the streets of Rome in the company of their lecherous kinsman Donati (Montague Love). (Lucrezia's lady-in-waiting, Mai, is played by a very young and beautiful Myrna Loy.) Lucrezia, hearing about the celebrated Don Juan, commands him to attend an audience at the Borgia palace, the Palazzo Santa Maria. To the same audience she invites the Orsini Duke Della Varnese (Josef Swickard) and his lovely daughter Adriana (Mary Astor), whom she plans, in due course, to marry to Donati as a way of bringing Varnese's wealth and power under the control of the Borgias.

Meanwhile, Don Juan's humor and adroitness in handling numerous assignations are depicted in a sequence in which he juggles his latest inamorati—the wife, niece, and mistress of Duke Margoni (Lionel Braham)—in and out of his palazzo under the very nose of the suspicious nobleman. Margoni is actually persuaded that the rumors that had sent him angrily to Don Juan's home were spread by his jealous wife as part of a trap to compromise the Duke himself. Don Juan tells Margoni: "Your lovely wife suspects your affair with Imperia and sent messages to bring you both here. She came herself to catch you together." Margoni hurriedly departs, expressing his gratitude to Don Juan.

En route to Lucrezia's reception, Juan takes time out to philander with one of Lucrezia's maids. On the verge of being discovered by Lucrezia, he extricates himself, dextrously leaves his manservant, the effeminate Pedrillo (Willard Louis), in the arms of the maid, and proceeds to the audience with Lucrezia, with whom he promptly makes an assignation. But when he beholds Adriana, he is instantly more attracted by her than by Lucrezia.

At the reception he frustrates a Borgia attempt to poison Varnese, and as an expression of her gratitude, the innocent Adriana promises Juan anything he wishes. Juan interprets her promise as an invitation to yet another assignation. And so, while Lucrezia impatiently awaits his arrival in her bedchamber, he climbs instead up to Adriana's balcony and enters her room. The unsuspecting girl is taken completely by surprise. Her horror and revulsion at his passionate advances are new experiences for the Great Lover.* Accepting his first defeat, he retreats from Adriana's presence, suddenly aware that the pangs of true love— a sensation hitherto unknown to him—are stirring in his breast. Later, the couple meet in the chapel garden, and a more sympathetic Adriana listens to Juan's plea: "You have given me a new faith—faith in the goodness of women. Teach me—help me—so that I may never lose that faith again."

Juan's new faith is soon put to the test and found wanting. Discovering Adriana in the company of Donati, he misinterprets their being together as a demonstration of her fickleness. He does not realize that Adriana and Varnese are in the power of the Borgias and that the girl is being forced to marry Donati in order to save her father's life. Without more ado, Juan throws himself into the arms of Lucrezia. And soon he has resumed his old libertine existence.

Meanwhile, plans for Adriana's forced marriage go forward. On the day of the wedding, Juan becomes involved in a tragic love triangle. One of his mistresses commits suicide when her husband discovers her intrigue with Juan. The jealous, griefstricken husband goes insane. He calls the wrath of God down upon Don Juan. Conscience-stricken, the Great Lover watches as the man he has wronged is taken off to jail, charged with murdering his wife. Simultaneously, wedding bells ring out. Unable to suppress his love for Adriana, Don Juan sets out for the Borgia palace.

As Donati comes to claim his bride, Juan suddenly appears and challenges him to a duel. A savage fight ensues. Juan kills Donati, but upon the orders of Cesare Borgia, he is immediately

---

* According to *Variety*, Barrymore bestowed 127 kisses during the film; many were unwillingly received by Mary Astor in this scene.

seized and thrown into a dungeon. Adriana is dispatched to a torture chamber, her punishment for being implicated in Donati's death. In his cell, Juan is visited by Lucrezia, who offers him a seductive alternative to death. But this time he proves immune to her charms. Whereupon she tells him that Adriana had been faithful to him and that the girl had been forced into a marriage contract with Donati. Lucrezia then departs, leaving Juan to ponder these facts and his imminent fate.

After she has left, the prisoner in the adjoining cell dislodges a stone in the wall, and Juan crawls through the hole to meet him. Juan's fellow prisoner turns out to be the deranged husband of his dead mistress. The insane prisoner instantly assumes that God has thrown Juan into his clutches. But before he can wreak revenge, the unexpected occurs again. The dungeon wall had been weakened by the breakthrough, and another stone is dislodged, allowing the Tiber's waters to pour into the cell; it also allows Juan to make a hasty escape.

Overpowering Neri, Adriana's would-be torturer, Juan assumes the man's garb, tricks and defies Borgia, and then escapes from the palace with Adriana, who is now obviously in love with her rescuer. A wild pursuit follows, but as a swordsman and horseman Don Juan is more than a match for the Borgia cavalry. After giving the *coup de grace* to his most persistent pursuers, Juan, with the adoring Adriana beside him, rides off towards Spain, into the sunset and into the pages of legend.

Love and infidelity are the central themes of *Don Juan*. The prologue and story contrast these themes by effective plot inversions. The experiences of Don José and Don Juan are closely paralleled and closely contrasted. In the prologue the father repudiates love and turns to libertinism; in the story the son does the opposite. Don José discovers his wife's infidelity and rejects her forever, after entombing her lover in a wall. Don Juan mistakenly assumes that Adriana is unfaithful and promiscuous when he finds Donati in her bedroom. He decides to reject her forever, but his love compels him to return to the Borgia palace and kill the man she is being forced to marry. For that *he* is entombed in a dungeon; he escapes through a breach in the wall made by none other than a man whose wife *he* had seduced.

Such interrelationships of plot and theme are interesting but superficial. The film's passions and motivations, situations and resolutions are movie clichés, and *Don Juan* would scarcely merit further attention if they were all it had to offer. But it is not all. *Don Juan* was and still is a charming "swashbuckler," whose individual performances are never less than highly competent and in several instances are outstanding.

Barrymore, of course, is the most memorable. In general, he is at no disadvantage in comparison with the Errol Flynn of *Captain Blood* and *The Sea Hawk*. His Don Juan is, by turns, impudent, sardonic, witty, graceful, and athletic (in the "balletic" style of Douglas Fairbanks, Sr.). Perhaps the strongest objection to Barrymore's performance is that he follows Don José's injunction to "Smile!" with such irritating persistence that he might, at times, be rehearsing for a toothpaste commercial. But this complaint is trivial and cannot minimize the quality of his interpretation. Estelle Taylor's Lucrezia Borgia plausibly combines poise and elegance with a feline malice, cunning, and seductiveness. As Donati, Montague Love gives us a lusty, full-blooded villain, whose open rascality and eagerness for the fray mark a refreshing change from the more conventional, secretive, foxy, and cowardly villains of silent screen melodrama. As the innocent heroine, Mary Astor provides a delicate, delicious, and altogether desirable alternative to the evil Lucrezia; while supporting actors Willard Louis (Pedrillo), Warner Oland (Cesare Borgia), and John Roche (Leandro, the deranged husband) give impressive performances.

Aside from being an actors' vehicle, *Don Juan* is a film of considerable visual beauty—especially in its sets and costumes. Among the most striking sets are Don José's opulent banqueting hall, the circular, sunken lounge in Don Juan's Roman residence, and the interior of the Palazzo Santa Maria—a detailed reconstruction of a Renaissance palace.

The multi-colored souvenir program of the first Vitaphone show contained a brief but informative article titled "Behind the Scenes with the Makers of *Don Juan*." This anonymous piece noted that the carefully designed Spanish-Moorish and Italian buildings in the film had been built with great fidelity to original palaces in Spain and had been erected as if they were permanent structures. Even the dungeon in which Don Juan is incarcerated was a replica of a real dungeon in the prison of the castle of St. Angelo.

The flower-decked chapel garden scene in which Juan declares his "new faith" in women combines beauty of setting with impeccable costuming. Barrymore moves gracefully through this scene clad in a flowing, elegantly draped white robe that tastefully contrasts with his dark costume, the somber trees, and the gray, ivy-covered, ancient chapel walls. Other costumes are no less impressive in themselves and in relation to their settings—Lucrezia's sumptuous gowns, the gorgeous dresses of the courtesans, and the striped, tight breeches that Barrymore wears during the great duel scene—these and other examples of the costumer's art are in abundant evidence in this film.

However, our primary interest here is not visual but aural—namely the film's musical accompaniment, response to which is bound to be primarily subjective. And so, whether or not it is effective as incidental music, the listener may be inclined to dismiss it as trite and uninteresting. The present writer finds it generally effective, seldom trite, and sometimes enchanting. In particular, he considers the main title theme to be a perfect musical expression of the film's romantic mood—as memorable as Angelo Lavagnino's lovely score for *The Naked Maja* (1959) and André Previn's rich, brooding music for Minnelli's *The Four Horsemen of the Apocalypse* (1962)—the compositions with which it should most obviously be compared.[42]

But aside from these personal judgments, there are more objective aspects to the music for *Don Juan*. It is a remarkably sophisticated score, which supplies, develops, and counterpoints separate themes for the main characters and for important incidents and moods. Don Juan himself is provided with two themes: a "love" theme (first heard across the main title and credits) and a "lust" theme (first heard in the prologue when the boy Juan and his father, Don José, enter the hall of the courtesans in the Marana castle).[43] Adriana and Lucrezia each have distinct themes—the first appropriately plaintive and wistful, the second appropriately seductive and sinister. A somber "Borgia" theme is used indiscriminately for Donati, Cesare, or all the Borgias. A striking fanfare and march tune are heard repeatedly in scenes showing the Borgia troops or as the prelude to scenes of combat or the great duel. Ironically, the same music is used when the faithless Donna Isabel is given her "marching orders" by Don Juan's father. The aid of Tchaikovsky is summoned on two occasions—in the banqueting scene at the Marana castle and at the wedding feast in the Borgia palace—when a well-known passage from his *Capriccio Italien* is quoted. Parts of the prologue music sound like *ersatz* Wagner, and the phrases that introduce Rome under the Borgias suggest Berlioz in one of his off moments. But these are brief lapses in an otherwise original score.

The sophistication and effectiveness with which the music is employed can be exemplified by two sequences. Early in the film, Juan climbs up to Adriana's balcony, enters her bed-chamber, and tries to seduce her. When she resists and spurns him, he suddenly realizes that he is in love with her. The sudden change in Juan is conveyed mainly by the music. As he seizes her, the "lust" theme is fully developed; its jauntiness emphasizes his mockery of Adriana's ineffectual resistance. When the girl faints and Juan takes her in his arms, the "lust" theme gives way to the tender, romantic "love" theme. The music and the cuts from the unconscious Adriana to Barrymore's changing expression tell us all we need to know: love has supplanted lust—the Great Lover is in the grip of the Grand Passion.

In a subsequent scene, Don Juan and Lucrezia are standing on a balcony in the Borgia palace. Suddenly, below them, they observe Adriana being accosted by Donati. The scene is brief and there are no helpful intertitles, but the music alone makes us aware of various attitudes and cross-purposes at work. Thus, Lucrezia's theme is obliterated by Adriana's as Juan notices her in the garden below. It is immediately clear who dominates his interest. His feelings for Adriana, and perhaps her developing love for him, are then succinctly expressed by a snatch of the "love" theme. But it is suddenly drowned by the somber Borgia motif, as Donati appears from out of the shadows. The music here conveys to us not only the impending rivalry of Don Juan and Donati for the possession of Adriana but also the impression that the evil Borgia power is in the ascendant. In the scoring for this scene, as in many others, one notices the effectiveness with which Vitaphone was used to permit precise synchronization of shots lasting as little as three or four seconds with comparably brief musical passages.

With the film as a whole, one also notices that although music is provided throughout the picture, there are only two places in which sound effects are used, and they have been skillfully worked into the score: the ringing of cathedral bells for the wedding of Adriana and Donati and the sound of the deranged husband rhythmically beating on Juan's door. A possible third use of sound effects occurs in the duel scene, where there are faint suggestions of the clash of swords, but the volume of the music and the surface noise on this part of the sound recording make it difficult to determine whether the effect is real or imagined. The two sound effects that are indubitably in the film function psychologically as well as realistically: as symbols of Juan's aroused conscience (the beating on the door and the tragedy that follows it) and irresistible love (Juan's reaction to the wedding bells). There is even a rudimentary but intelligent attempt to create a montage of these sound effects: they are intercut, suggesting Juan's inner conflicts that compel him, despite his conviction that Adriana is as "Faithless as all women," to return to the Palazzo Santa Maria and rescue her. In short, *Don Juan* demonstrates a creative and sometimes original use of music and sound effects. Lack of historical and critical interest in the film indicates that most of the historians and critics who have made an effort to see it have neither looked at nor listened to it very carefully.

Surprisingly little is known or has been written about Alan Crosland, the man who had the distinction of directing the first two sound feature films. Few directors of importance have suffered from comparable indifference. Lewis Jacobs in his *Rise of the American Film* (1939) mentions him in passing as one of a number of former Army Signal Corps cameramen who became movie directors—as if this trivial fact was more significant than having directed both *Don Juan* and *The Jazz Singer*. Paul Rotha in *The Film Till Now* (1930; revised edition 1949) dismisses Crosland as the "maker of *Bobbed Hair, Three Weeks,* and that abominable costume picture with John Barrymore, *Don Juan,* followed by another as bad, *The Beloved Rogue.*" The place of *Don Juan* in film history seems to have eluded him, though several hundred pages later in the same door-stopping volume, his cowriter, Richard Griffith, shows a better awareness of the film's importance. In their recent histories of cinema, both Gerald Mast and David Robinson refer to *Don Juan* without bothering to mention who directed the picture. Kevin Brownlow in *The Parade's Gone By* is one of the few film historians to show any interest in Crosland—though his book adds little to the generally available knowledge of this central figure in the transition from silent to sound cinema. However brief, an attempt to repair the deficiency is worth making.

The bare facts of Crosland's life and career are these. He was born in New York on August 10, 1894. After receiving an education at Dartmouth, he embarked on a career as an actor and stage manager, most notably for the Annie Russell company. For some three years he played minor roles in productions of Shakespeare and such classic comedies as *She Stoops to Conquer* and *The Rivals*. It was here, presumably, that the lasting influences of period drama and comedy of manners originated: both are abundantly evident in his surviving films. Crosland's acting career suddenly ended when he switched to journalism. He became the drama critic for the *New York Globe* and simultaneously began writing short stories for movie magazines. The stories caught the attention of the Edison (Film) Company, and in 1912 he accepted an appointment as that company's publicity director. Subsequently he became Edison's casting director. Various conflicting sources indicate (1) that in 1914 he left Edison and joined the Pomona Company, for which he worked until 1917, mainly as Alice Brady's director; (2) that he left Edison only briefly between 1912 and 1917, in order to direct a picture sponsored by the Curtis Publishing Company. He was so successful in this undertaking that on his return to Edison he was made a full-fledged director. During 1917 and 1919 Crosland served in the Army Signal Corps as a cameraman.

Upon his discharge from the military, he became a director for the Selig Company, and before joining Warner Bros., in 1925, he directed numerous pictures for Selznick Films, Cosmopolitan Pictures, and various other companies. His earliest films for Warner Bros. seem to have been *Compromise* (1925), starring Clive Brook, Irene Rich, and Louise Fazenda; and *Bobbed Hair*

(1925), starring Marie Prevost, Kenneth Harlan, and Dolores Costello; the latter film, anticipating a certain notorious best seller of recent years, was based on a novel by twenty different authors. Prior to *Compromise* and *Bobbed Hair* Crosland directed at least twenty-six films. *Kidnapped* (1917), evidently an adaptation of Stevenson's novel, appears to be his first identifiable film. He also directed commercially successful adaptations of Stanley Weyman's *Under the Red Robe* (1923) and Elinor Glyn's "scandalous" novel, *Three Weeks* (1924). One of his specialities was movies about flappers and the flaming youth of the jazz age: *The Flapper* (1920), *Youthful Folly* (1920), and *Sinners in Heaven* (1924) typified this side of his work. *Under the Red Robe* exemplified another aspect that was to culminate in *Don Juan:* namely, Crosland's special interest in lavish costume pictures.

The anonymous *New York Times* reviewer of *Under the Red Robe* passed over the film's cliché-ridden plot and had little to say about the acting. Instead, he commented mostly on the movie's pictorial qualities.

> The scenes in many sequences of this film are so attractive that without much else they would be worth viewing. . . . There is an especially beautiful sequence where cavaliers are shown tackling each other in the middle of a shallow, fast-running brook, and other scenes in a forest, which might just as well be that of Fontainebleau. . . . The costumes in this film are especially good. . . . This picture, like many others, may have outstanding failings, but the costumes, the exteriors and some of the sets make it a production that is satisfying on many points.[44]

When Crosland joined Warner Bros. in 1925 he was already established as a major director with the reputation of making pictures that responded, with commercial success, to the popular tastes of the twenties. He was the perfect choice to direct the pictures that would gauge the popular appeal of Vitaphone. The Warners' faith in him was not misplaced. *The Jazz Singer,* which he directed the year after *Don Juan,* broke all existing box-office records. Doubtless Crosland's name would be better known today if his most celebrated films had been artistic triumphs. Even now his films give us a clearer sense of the taste of the period than such critically admired but far less popular movies

as *The Crowd* (1928) and *A Woman of Paris* (1923)—though
for every hundred or more revivals of silent films by Vidor,
Chaplin, Stroheim, and Griffith there is barely a single opportunity to see *Don Juan*. *The Jazz Singer* is shown more frequently, but what merits that film possesses are usually ascribed
to Jolson at the expense of Crosland.

But before Jolson arrived on the scene, Crosland was already
the world's most experienced (indeed *only*) director of sound
feature films. And in the late twenties, Warner Bros. kept him
busier than any other director on the lot. Thus, between his
completion of *Don Juan* and the start of shooting of *The Jazz
Singer,* he directed three major features. Typical of Crosland,
two were romantic costume dramas: *When a Man Loves* (1927),
with a script by Bess Meredyth and starring John Barrymore and
Dolores Costello; and *The Beloved Rogue* (1927), based on a
story by Paul Bern (later to become the ill-fated husband of
Jean Harlow), with art direction by William Cameron Menzies
(subsequently director of *Things to Come,* 1935) and starring
Barrymore and Conrad Veidt. The third film, *Old San Francisco*
(1927), was a melodrama based on a story by a young man named
Darryl F. Zanuck; it starred Dolores Costello and Warner Oland
and employed a Vitaphone accompaniment consisting of a
musical score by Hugo Riesenfeld and ear-splitting sound effects
of the earthquake of 1906. Although Bryan Foy was to have the
honor of directing the first all-talking feature, nearly three
months before the release of Foy's *Lights of New York* (1928),
Warner Bros. premiered Crosland's *Glorious Betsy* (1928), a
costume drama with talking sequences, starring Dolores Costello
and Conrad Nagel.

All of Crosland's twenty-two subsequent films were sound
movies. They included *On with the Show* (1929) and *General
Crack* (1929), which used Technicolor as well as sound—the first
combination of these technical advances in feature film-making.
Among his films of the thirties were the Technicolor *Song of the
Flame* (1930), an operetta by Otto Harbach, Oscar Hammerstein
II, George Gershwin, and Herbert Stothart; *Big Boy* (1930), in
which Al Jolson played a jockey (in blackface) and sang "Liza
Lee"; *Viennese Nights* (1930), an original operetta (also in
Technicolor) written for the screen by Sigmund Romberg and

Oscar Hammerstein II, and starring Walter Pidgeon and Jean Hersholt; *Captain Thunder* (1931), a Mexican bandit picture starring Victor Varconi and Fay Wray—some two years before King Kong was to lift her to immortality atop the Empire State Building; *Hello Sister!* (1933), Crosland's completion of the last, abortive directorial effort of Erich von Stroheim; *Massacre* (1934), a pro-Indian Western starring Richard Barthelmess and Ann Dvorak; and *The Case of the Howling Dog* (1934), the first Perry Mason film, starring Warren William and Mary Astor.

Crosland was married twice. His first wife, Juanita Crawford, whom he divorced in 1930, was the mother of his son, Alan Crosland, Jr., who was eventually to follow him into the film industry. His second wife was the actress Natalie Moorhead. They were divorced in 1935, the year before his untimely death at the age of 42. On July 10, 1936, Crosland sustained serious injuries when his car crashed into an obstacle beside a street excavation on Sunset Boulevard. He died shortly after his arrival at Beverly Hills Emergency Hospital. A professional to the end, in his last moments he asked the nurse to convey to his assistant, Carol Sax, directions for shooting certain scenes in the film he had been working on when the accident occurred.

An even more neglected figure than Crosland is his screen-writer, Bess Meredyth. She started as a film actress (appearing, for example, in Kalem's *The Desert's Sting*, 1914) and in 1917 she gravitated to writing photoplays. According to Lewis Jacobs, between 1917 and 1919 she wrote the scripts of no fewer than ninety feature films. Her credits during the twenties included the screenplays of *Ben Hur* (1925) and *The Sea Beast* (1926) (an adaptation of *Moby Dick,* starring John Barrymore as Captain Ahab) as well as *Don Juan.* In the late thirties Jacobs referred to her as "one of the top-ranking writers" in Hollywood. She was still active in the late forties, writing original screenplays and adapting the work of other writers. Today, general in-difference to her numerous and significant contributions to American film is exemplified by her omission from Richard Corliss's *The Hollywood Screenwriters,* with its detailed ap-pendix of fifty filmographies of important Hollywood screen-writers. Like Crosland, her career is a subject eminently worthy of further research.

To return to the premiere of Vitaphone: there can be no question that initial public response was encouraging. The show drew crowded audiences, and their prolonged applause expressed positive enjoyment of the concert items and the feature film. The New York run lasted nearly eight months (until April 1927), during which the program was seen by over half a million persons and grossed $789,963. It was a record run for a Barrymore picture, and when it left New York, it was equally successful in Chicago, Los Angeles, Boston, Detroit, and St. Louis, as well as in many European capitals.

Many reviewers were ecstatic about Vitaphone. A reporter for London's *Kinematograph Weekly* described the show as a "sensation," and went on to say that "It was universally admitted that no earlier experiments had achieved anything like the same degree of success in regard either to exact synchronization, volume or tone. The 'Vitaphone' is amazing in all three particulars. . . . There is general agreement here that if the test was typical and if the apparatus is portable and 'commercial' it opens up amazing possibilities of the reproduction of the finest music in the meanest theatres." Charles Divine *(New York Evening Telegram)* described it as a "miracle of sound." "Marvellous invention," wrote Rose Pelswick in the *New York Evening Journal,* "It is almost uncanny in its excellence. Vitaphone is revolutionizing. Go see it for yourself and be convinced." "It is impossible to imagine," said Regina Cannon *(New York Graphic),* "Vitaphone is the eighth wonder of the world." John S. Cohen *(New York Evening Sun)* offered a similar assessment: "Vitaphone is unquestionably one of the wonders of the world. It marks a new development in the history of motion pictures." Dorothy Herzog *(New York Daily Mirror)* also announced without reservation that Vitaphone "marks a new era in the amusement world: a glorious credit to those who have worked to perfect it." With comparable conviction, Eileen Creelman *(New York American)* declared that Vitaphone has "marched triumphantly into the motion picture industry. So remarkable is this synchronizing machine it seemed incredible that the figures on the screen were only shadows." No less enthusiastic, if rather more restrained, were comments by F. D. Perkins *(New York Herald-Tribune),* who recognized the show as a "complete success," and Palmer Smith *(Evening World)*, who described it as "highly effective," adding his belief that "Vitaphone is making possible high quality presentations and adequate thematic musical accompaniments for films generally."

Despite such a glowing critical reception and the considerable public interest in Vitaphone, the results of the first presentation were fairly inconclusive. It was not clear whether the public interest could be developed and exploited or whether it was merely transitory. However, Warners had too much at stake to accept the idea that Vitaphone might be an ephemeral novelty —while the rest of the film industry had too much at stake to entertain the notion that it might not. The latter assumed that the success of the first Vitaphone show was a mere fluke or the passing appeal of a mere curiosity. The public would soon get over it and Warner Bros. would collapse if they were foolish enough to go on sinking their money into such a gimmick.

However, Warner Bros. *had* learned a few things from preparing and presenting the first show. First, they had become aware of the technical problems and limitations involved in using Vitaphone for making several different kinds of sound movie. A speech, virtuoso musical performances, an orchestra, a dance ensemble, and a full-length feature film—each had raised different problems and had taught different lessons in the use of sound in film-making. Solutions had been found for many of the worst problems, and technicians were already at work finding ways to cope with the others. Epes W. Sargent summed up the technical situation thus: "Vitaphone . . . is a gigantic step forward, but not yet a perfect step."

Second, the recorded musical accompaniment to *Don Juan* had certainly heightened the moods and dramatic intensity of the picture, and the job of writing the score had introduced composers William Axt, David Mendoza, and Edward Bowes to the problems and opportunities of composing for sound movies. But the advantages of Vitaphone were primarily evident to exhibitors who could not afford live orchestras in their theaters. Yet the question still remained: how many could or would want to afford the alternative expense of the system. During the late teens and twenties, the public had increasingly taken for granted the provision of specially composed music for silent films, but there was no reason to suppose that they were conscious of or interested in Vitaphone's value in supplying synchronized scores.

Finally, critical and popular acclaim for concert items in the first Vitaphone program convinced the Warners—temporarily—that they were on the right track in using Vitaphone as a medium for vocal, instrumental, and orchestral music, while the enthusiasm shown by the audience for the short film of Roy Smeck playing the guitar supported the view that its use could also be extended, quite lucratively, to presenting vaudeville acts.

The Warners proceeded to affirm their faith in Vitaphone by having two more of their New York theaters, the Colony and the Selwyn, wired for sound. They also announced that all their silent films for 1927 would be provided with Vitaphone accompaniments. Several Vitaphone short films of a lighter and more popular nature were already in production. Clearly, Warner Bros. was now in the grip of the sound revolution. The year 1927 would reveal whether that revolution was to be triumph or a disaster.

CHAPTER FIVE

"YOU AIN'T HEARD NOTHIN' YET!"

. . . Blessed ones
of this—and every other—succeeding generation
who can, do, and shall discover
for their first time
the Voice of Jolson
and who'll thrill to It
and who, hence, will love him.

EDNA ST. VINCENT MILLAY

The Blue Boy is a beautiful picture, but comparatively few
people have seen it. . . . My answer to that is people want
entertainment. If The Blue Boy sang like Jolson, they'd go to
see him.

MERVIN LeROY

There is little question that here was an example, like the
performance of Dr. Johnson's dog, of something being
remarkable not because it was well done but because it had been
done at all.

IRIS BARRY on *The Jazz Singer*

The film concludes with a scene in the theatre, with Mammy of
Mine in the stalls . . . and the son . . . warbling down at her the
most penetratingly vulgar mammy song that it has ever been my
lot to hear. My flesh crept as the loud speaker poured out those
sodden words, that greasy, sagging melody. I felt ashamed of
myself for listening to such things, for even being a member of
the species to which such things are addressed.

ALDOUS HUXLEY on *The Jazz Singer*

I won't say that I'm the best singer in the world—
I'll just say I sound better than anybody else!
AL JOLSON

Let me sing of Dixie's charms,
Cotton fields and Mammy's arms,
And if my song can make you homesick—I'm happy.
Popular Jolson song

While the *Don Juan* program was playing to full capacity houses, several other, relevant developments were taking place. On August 23, 1926 Rudolph Valentino died suddenly, only thirty-one years old and at the height of his career. The Great Arab had been born in the year that the Lumières presented France's first public movie program. Ominously, he folded his tent for the last time on the eve of the coming of sound.

Early in September 1926, Warner Bros. announced its intention of providing means for enabling the deaf to hear and the blind to see their miraculous Vitaphone programs. Fifty selected seats in Warner theaters were equipped with headphones that would amplify the sound for patrons who were hard of hearing or would supply descriptive commentaries for patrons who had little or no eyesight. The reactions of the deaf and blind were given little or no publicity in 1926, but three years later, as we shall see in a later chapter, they were to respond to the talkie revolution in ways that were not anticipated by Warner Bros. It is unlikely that the innovations of 1926 actually made much difference to the afflicted, but doubtless the expense of the installations was worth the publicity Warners received from it. More significant was the announcement later in September that Warner Bros. was arranging to secure at least one important cinema in every big city in the U.S., and that the company would have control of at least fifty major movie theaters by the start of the fall season. This policy of rapid expansion showed no evidence of the imminent collapse that the rest of Hollywood had been expecting ever since Warner Bros. had begun pouring money into Vitaphone. To the contrary, the Warners radiated optimism, and their growing chain of movie theaters obviously had something to do with public interest in sound pictures and the Warners' ability to communicate their faith in Vitaphone to the financiers who were providing the capital for their expansion.

Meanwhile, executives of the big movie studios were closely observing developments but saying as little as possible about it. Immediately after the opening night of *Don Juan,* movie tycoon William Fox took time out to remark, "I don't think that there will ever be the much-dreamed of talking pictures on a large scale. To have conversation would strain the eyesight and the sense of hearing at once, taking away the restfulness one gets from viewing pictures alone." (He was to have second thoughts on the subject sooner than anyone else in Hollywood.) But the rest of the movie industry, assuming that Warner Bros. would be overtaken by the inevitable, refrained from making even the obvious predictions.[1] In mid-September the silence was broken briefly when Fred Niblo, one of MGM's leading directors, ventured the belated prediction that synchronized music would replace cinema orchestras. Probably as a counterblast to Vitaphone, he also suggested that radio would be used in conjunction with silent movies to supply synchronized sound effects, music, and even dialogue. However, for the time being it was Vitaphone that held the public interest. That now seems remarkable when measured against the tremendous competition offered by the rest of the movie industry during the brief period between the premiere of *Don Juan* (August 6, 1926) and the premiere of *The Jazz Singer* (October 6, 1927).

The last year of the silents, 1926, was a golden age for moviegoers. Across innumerable screens in America flashed the silent forms of Ronald Colman and Alice Joyce in *Beau Geste,* Greta Garbo and John Gilbert in *Flesh and the Devil,* Lillian Gish and Lars Hanson in *The Scarlet Letter,* Victor McLaglen and Dolores Del Rio in *What Price Glory?* (subsequently reissued in a synchronized sound version), Eddie Cantor and Clara Bow in *Kid Boots,* Rod la Rocque and Dolores Del Rio in *Resurrection,* Warner Baxter in *The Great Gatsby,* Lon Chaney in *Mr. Wu,* Mary Pickford in *Sparrows,* Pola Negri in *Hotel Imperial,* H. B. Warner in DeMille's *The King of Kings,* Adolphe Menjou in D. W. Griffith's *The Sorrows of Satan,* George Bancroft in von Sternberg's *Underworld,* Laura La Plante in *The Cat and the Canary,* Richard Barthelmess in *The Patent-Leather Kid,* Buster Keaton in *The General,* and Harry Langdon in *Long Pants.* There were also the American premieres of Eisenstein's *Potemkin,* Fritz Lang's *Metropolis* and *Dr. Mabuse,* Murnau's *Faust* and *Tartuffe,* and Pabst's *Secrets of a Soul.* In addition there were the attractions of color films (including color sequences in important feature films), wide-screen movies using the Magnascope or Widescope processes, and various less-publicized, less-developed, or inferior sound systems, including Vocafilm, Phonofilm, and Remaphone. But it was still Vitaphone that held the public interest.

Its promise became clearer with the second Vitaphone show, which premiered on October 5, 1926 at B. S. Moss's Colony Theatre in New York. Like the *Don Juan* program, the new show consisted of a number of short films followed by a feature picture. But this time the offerings were in a much lighter vein: a comedy, *The Better 'Ole,* preceded by a concert of vaudeville sketches and songs. In two respects the program anticipated the shape of things to come for Vitaphone. First, Al Jolson appeared in one of the short films entitled *Al Jolson in a Plantation Act.* And with more prescience than he could have realized at the time, Mordaunt Hall, who reviewed the show for the *New York Times* commented on Jolson: "This Vitaphone [short] assuredly destroys the old silent tradition of the screen."[2] A month after its New York premiere, the second Vitaphone show opened on the West Coast, and by this time the trade papers were singling out the Jolson short as the hit of the program.[3] The second development, which received comparatively little comment, was that in several of the other short films there were snatches of dialogue and sound effects, and in the short movie of George Jessel there was a fairly lengthy monologue. Talk was, almost imperceptibly, creeping into what had been conceived by the Warners as a medium for recorded music.

The second Vitaphone program, like the first, opened with an orchestral overture. It was followed by Reinald Werrenrath singing "The Long, Long Trail" and a medley of other melodies, and then by Elsie Janis, atop an army truck, dancing and singing the songs she had popularized on her wartime tours:

"Madelon," "In the Army," "The Good Old War," and "Good Bye-ee." She was accompanied by a chorus of soldiers from the 107th Regiment of the U. S. Army. Next, Willie and Eugene Howard appeared in a vaudeville sketch entitled *Between the Acts at the Opera,* which was one of the items provided with such sound effects as a starter's whistle and a taxi horn—effects used in developing the comic situation. There was also a jazz quartet. And then came Jolson, in blackface, singing to the accompaniment of Al Goodman's orchestra (off-camera) three of the songs always associated with him: "The Red, Red Robin," "April Showers," and "Rock-a-Bye Your Baby with a Dixie Melody." Jolson's movie audience was "silent, so keen was everybody to catch every word and note of the popular entertainer, and when each number was ended it was obvious that there was not a still pair of hands in the house."[4] The Jolson short, produced by Robert Green and directed by Philip Roscoe, had been observed in production early in September 1926 by a reporter for *Moving Picture World:*

> Al Jolson made his debut on the Vitaphone last week at the Manhattan Opera House. Workmen for over a week there were busy night and day building the setting for the comedian's number, which is to be one of the big features of the [new] Vitaphone prelude. . . . A representation of an old Southern plantation was built especially for Mr. Jolson's "act," which took up the whole of the stage and the auditorium of the opera house. All the props were in evidence, including cotton in bloom, corn tasselling and water-melons ripening. A little old log cabin was constructed, from which Jolson emerged when he sang. . . .

By ironic coincidence the Jolson film was followed by the short movie of George Jessel, who was currently starring in the Broadway stage production of Samson Raphaelson's play *The Jazz Singer.* (In June 1926 Warners had bought the screen rights to the play. They subsequently announced that they would spend half a million dollars making the film and that Jessel would be the star. But things were to turn out very differently from the way they looked in the fall of 1926.) Jessel's short Vitaphone movie had nothing to do with *The Jazz Singer.* It opened with a comic monologue and concluded with a scene in which Jessel, seen only in shadow, gave a spirited rendering of Irving Berlin's song "At Peace with the World and You." The monologue was particularly well received; the audience laughed longer than expected. But the response to Jessel was patently less than the applause that had followed Jolson's performance. The first star of sound movies was already rising, and his name was not George Jessel.

The *New York Times* reviewer noted that during the intermission "the conversation in the lobby was wholly devoted to a eulogy of the Vitaphone."[5] The program resumed with a live performance—a medley of war tunes played by the Vitaphone Symphony Orchestra under the baton of Herman Heller. It set the mood for the synchronized feature, *The Better 'Ole,* a comedy of World War I based on a play by Bruce Bairnsfather and Arthur Eliot. The film's title was taken not only from the play but also from a celebrated newspaper cartoon depicting Old Bill, an imperturbable British Tommy, resignedly puffing at his pipe in a waterlogged trench and commenting, "If yer know a better 'ole, go to it." The Bairnsfather-Eliot play, previously filmed in England in 1919 (when its stars were Charles Rock and Arthur Cleave), was heavily influenced by Chaplin's *Shoulder Arms* (1918). The Vitaphone version was adapted to the screen by Darryl F. Zanuck and Charles F. Reisner; the latter also directed the picture. Chaplin's brother, Sydney (who had appeared in *Shoulder Arms*), played the lead role of Old Bill, and Jack Ackroyd and Harold Goodwin appeared as Alf and Bert, his two sidekicks. Essentially a mixture of broad farce and slapstick, the movie focused on Old Bill's exploits following his discovery that his major is a German spy. The level of humor can be gauged from the fact that the film's most hilarious scene shows Bill and Alf escaping from the enemy by disguising themselves as the front and rear ends of a pantomime horse. Another scene, located rather improbably in an opera house where Bill and Alf were supposed to be performing (it was obviously the Manhattan Opera House, where the movie was made), reveals Warner Bros.' cost-cutting efforts at improvising within the limits of immediately available facilities.

As an experiment in the use of Vitaphone, *The Better 'Ole* was of little or no significance. Most of its comedy was visual or based on intertitles. When it was released as a silent movie for theaters that were not equipped for Vitaphone, audiences were unaware that anything was lacking. Sound had been used in *The Better 'Ole* for rather obvious effects: explosions, pistol shots, the neighing of a horse. The film's score, consisting mainly of a medley of war songs, was unmemorable and unobtrusive except for a few brief scenes in which music added to the comic effect. A typical example was the use of the song "Horses, Horses, Horses" as an accompaniment to the pantomime horse sequence.

Although little or no progress seemed to have been made in using Vitaphone, the second show demonstrated that the potential of Vitaphone went beyond filmed concerts, operas, and synchronized music scores. It offered a new dimension in popular entertainment. The whole range of vaudeville could now be presented on the screen. And as we shall see, the business interests behind vaudeville were not slow in recognizing this new departure of Vitaphone as a threat to their exclusive control of popular theatrical entertainment.

An encouraging view of Vitaphone's future was expressed by Epes W. Sargent, who reviewed the show for *Moving Picture World*. Sargent maintained that the second show was probably "more in line with the immediate development of Vitaphone . . . notwithstanding a general tendency to regard Vitaphone as a musical matter." This tendency, he asserted, was a

popular but decided error. Music is but one phase of Vitaphone activities. The device is all-embracing. It brings to a single medium every phase of amusements from opera and concert to the circus. It is, in its own peculiar way, the most elastic amusement medium ever developed. Its possibilities are limited only by the restrictions of human ingenuity, and for the time being it is probable that straight orchestral and instrumental music, unless presented by internationally known stars, is the least of these possibilities. . . . Any house with sufficient appropriation may achieve an orchestra of symphonic instrumentation. This is merely a matter of having at command sufficient money to pay salaries. But no house can, for example, command the money and the influence necessary to draw Al Jolson from his current musical comedy.[6]

Despite future development implicit in the second show, no one at Warner Bros. was ready to talk seriously about talking pictures or even feature-length musicals. The third Vitaphone program, premiered at the Selwyn Theatre, New York, on February 3, 1927, merely marked time with an awkward attempt to combine the appeals of the first two shows. Selections from grand opera were interspersed with musical-comedy pieces. The total effect was at best incoherent, at worst downright ludicrous. The operatic arias were, however, superior to those presented in the first show—both in choice of artists and quality of sound recording. The highlight was the quartet from *Rigoletto* sung by Beniamino Gigli, Marion Talley, Giuseppe de Luca, and Jeanne Gordon. The popularity of this performance was so great that it was frequently added to later Warner programs. Almost as well received were the solo arias by Marion Talley and Charles Hackett. One reviewer, commenting on the operatic pieces, observed that "there were moments when the vocal renditions came with marvellous precision from the images on the screen, and then there were moments when the tonal quality was burdened with the resonance of the reproducing horns. The stronger and more vibrant voices came forth with better effect than the weaker ones. But the synchronization was in all cases a triumph for the producers."[7]

The feature that provided the second half of the program was *When a Man Loves,* directed by Alan Crosland and starring John Barrymore, Dolores Costello, Warner Oland, and Eugenie Besserer. Adapted by Bess Meredyth from Prevost's *Manon Lescaut,* the film, despite its source, bore more than a superficial resemblance, in plot and character, to *Don Juan,* which, of course, had starred some of the same leading players. The composer of the synchronized music score for *When a Man Loves* has not been ascertained, and the music itself does not appear to have survived in either sheet music or recorded form. However, Mordaunt Hall noted that the "orchestra effect was so good that there were many in the audience who forgot until the last moment that there were no musicians in the pit. They were reminded of the absence of the orchestra when the body of musicians was depicted on the screen, and then the spectators were moved to applaud."[8]

Before turning to Al Jolson and *The Jazz Singer,* it will be enlightening to review the off-screen developments preceding the momentous premiere of that movie. Some of them bear little or no direct relationship to one another, but collectively they suggest the vacillations and speculations, the optimism and uncertainty that prevailed in Hollywood (and vaudeville) during the months that followed the first Vitaphone show.

In November 1926 the Vitaphone Corporation set up its executive offices in the General Motors Building at Fifty-seventh Street and Broadway, New York. At the first meeting of the board of directors it was publicly announced that Vitaphone had plans for worldwide distribution. The system would be made available to "all producers of high class pictures and to producers and exhibitors of standing."

By the end of the year the success of the first two Vitaphone programs was beginning to arouse the interest—and concern— of other Hollywood studios. According to Fitzhugh Green,

In December 1926, the leading silent film people held a Council of War. They had watched the Vitaphone opening, confidently expectant that like all other talking [*sic*] movies, this would fail. Now that it had not, they saw it as a threat to the conventional movie and movie show. Talkies, they felt, was something that if it came to be demanded by the public would cost them a dozen fortunes in modifying their present equipment and technique. It would rock the movie world. It would, as they foresaw perfectly, do exactly what it has done. And they were afraid. The so-called Big Five [at this time MGM, Universal, Paramount, First National, and Producers' Distributing Corp. (P.D.C.)] decided to try to buck it. In the first place, they planned to undo the Warners. Secondly, if they were forced to adopt talking pictures, they decided that they were entirely unwilling to take sub-licences from Warners. They could not bear to pay Warner, a competing film company, royalties for the use of the Talkies; they felt that to acknowledge use of Warner or Vitaphone devices would cause them to suffer loss of prestige. They also engaged an engineer who spent about $500,000 in the next year and a half investigating and trying to perfect other devices. There was no doubt about their concern. As a final step in this defensive move, they mutually agreed, so that they would have a bartering point, that none of them would adopt talking pictures until they all did; and that "in the interests of standardization in the industry," they would, when they did adopt the thing, all use the same device. . . . The Big Five believed that this threat of uniform equipment in the industry would be a strong bulwark against the inroads of Vitaphone on their precious properties. If they decided to use another set of inventions than those used by Warners they would be safe enough. With their huge combined outfit they could undoubtedly cause their type to be the standard equipment used by the bulk of the theatres in the country. They hoped further it would be one that Warner would not be able to use, so that the majority of theatres would be closed to the Warner product. . . . All these elaborate plans failed for just one reason. The Western Electric apparatus was [at that time] really the best of all the apparatus on the market. If the others had been able to find one even two-thirds as good they would have signed up and played freeze-out against the Warners in a minute.[9]

The Big Five must have been particularly apprehensive at the news that the Fox Company, which had not joined the council of war, was about to swallow its pride and open negotiations to secure the use of Vitaphone. In late December 1926, undenied rumors were circulating in Wall Street that William Fox, president of the Fox Film Corporation, was trying to contract with Warner Bros. "for the right to present the Vitaphone in all Fox theatres of reasonable size no matter where located." Shortly afterwards there were other undenied rumors that MGM, oblivious of its agreement with the other major studios, had endeavored, without success, to tie up with Vitaphone on an exclusive basis. The Vitaphone Corporation went some way towards confirming some of these rumors by issuing a declaration that no exclusive rights to Vitaphone would be granted to any company or companies.

The stories about Fox's interest in Vitaphone were confirmed on January 8, when *Moving Picture World* revealed that the Vitaphone and Fox-Case corporations had signed reciprocal contracts—each licensing the other to use the sound systems over which it had legal control. (Fox had recently established the Fox-Case Corporation to develop and promote the sound-on-film system he had bought from Theodore W. Case and E. I. Sponable.) Less than two months later the trade papers announced that Fox had already ordered Vitaphone equipment to be installed in his theaters "as soon as possible."[10] The Vitaphone-Fox agreements also extended to mutual use of studio and theater facilities and the exchange of artists and technicians. The announcement of cooperation was accompanied by brief statements by Harry Warner and William Fox. Warner offered his congratulations to the Fox interests "for the foresighted step they have taken in obtaining a licence from the Vitaphone Corporation. I consider this," he added, "one of the greatest forward moves that has taken place in the industry since the inception of motion pictures. . . ."[11] Some months later he was to announce: "We have developed our machine with an extra attachment that costs less than a thousand dollars, which enables us to use also the Fox . . . method. So that a theatre putting in a Vitaphone can use either the method now used by us or the one on the film [i.e., the Fox-Case sound-on-film system]."[12]

Fox's statement, following his corporation's agreement with the Vitaphone people, revealed his personal vision of the future of sound cinema: "The amazing accomplishment, now perfected, is destined to have far-reaching influence in the world. Its influence will be felt not only in picture theatres everywhere, but in 150,000 churches for religious purposes and in 170,000 schools for educational purposes, and in 20,000,000 American homes."[13] He went on to acknowledge those who were responsible for Vitaphone and the Fox-Case sound system: the engineers of Western Electric Company and Bell Telephone Laboratories, and Case Research Laboratories of Auburn, New York.

Fox's eagerness to tie up with Vitaphone can be explained in part as a means of covering his bets just in case the disk system won out. Another reason, suggested Fitzhugh Green, is that Fox discovered that he could not introduce his newly acquired sound-on-film system into theaters without using patents belonging to Western Electric. "The outcome of this situation was that . . . [Fox] approached Western and learned that Vitaphone had an exclusive sub-licence, which, however, required that Vitaphone sub-licence others in the industry as they applied, sharing the royalty fees with Western."[14] Fox was thus obligated to negotiate with Vitaphone if his system was to be put before the public.

In the previous chapter we heard about the origins of that system. It is time now to take the story further. On May 2, 1926, four months before the *Don Juan* premiere, Case and Sponable demonstrated "their" system (it was essentially De Forest's) privately at the Nemo Theatre on 110 Street and Broadway in New York. One of those present was Courtland Smith, who brought the system to the attention of William Fox. Fox attended another Case-Sponable demonstration and decided that what they had to offer was worth an investment. (It is not known whether he had heard that the system had previously been turned down by RCA, General Electric, and Western Electric.) Fox's interest in the Case-Sponable apparatus is rather puzzling since, the previous year, he had ordered the removal of De Forest equipment from several of his theaters where it had been installed without his personal consent. Also, in that same year, as we have seen, he had acquired 90 percent of the Western Hemisphere rights to Tri-Ergon.

Curiously, as Maurice Zouary has noted, while Fox was obtaining, through Case and Sponable, what was basically the invention of Lee De Forest, he was simultaneously involved in litigation against De Forest in an effort to prove that "his" Tri-Ergon patents antedated De Forest's Phonofilm system. A U. S. federal court was to uphold the priority of De Forest's claim in 1935.

But that was a long way off. In 1926, Fox may have been genuinely unaware that he was really buying rights to De Forest's work. Anyhow, the Fox Film Corporation acquired patent rights to Case-Sponable on July 23, 1926. Fox promptly established the Fox-Case Corporation to promote the system, which he renamed Movietone. Courtland Smith was assigned the task of developing it, which meant combining the best elements of Tri-Ergon with an improved Fox-Case system. Work on Fox-Case shifted to the Fox studios in Hollywood, where, in the second half of 1926, the system was used to make several synchronized film sequences. One of the private demonstrations of these films was attended by Adolph Zukor, who, as in his sampling of Phonofilm, was quite unimpressed; another was attended by Jesse L. Lasky, who was enthusiastic—as long as he was not going to put any of his own money into it. Fox himself waxed hot and cold. On at least three occasions before the end of 1926 he ordered Smith to stop work on sound movies. However, efforts to improve Fox-Case were continued despite Fox's sporadic apathy. The first Movietone program was ready for presentation at the Sam H. Harris Theatre in New York on January 21, 1927. Considerably less ambitious than the Vitaphone premiere, Movietone's initial offering consisted of a cycle of songs sung by the Spanish artiste Requel Meller. It provided a supporting program to the silent feature *What Price Glory?**

In the first half of 1927, Fox was in no particular hurry to promote his system through regular and frequent programs. The public had to wait several months before seeing the next Movietone. When it did appear, at last, on the same program as the silent feature, *Yankee Clipper* (Roxy Theatre, New York, May 2, 1927), it turned out to be an important, if little-noticed, advance for the Fox-Case system. For the Movietone engineers had taken their apparatus out of the studio and made an outdoor sound movie—a short film of cadets parading at West Point. The sound quality was evidently adequate; at least, there appear to have been no adverse critical comments about it. The next Movietone films were premiered on May 25, 1927, also at the Sam H. Harris Theatre. This time the program was an ambitious one: First, Movietone had been used to supply the feature film, *Seventh Heaven* (directed by Frank Borzage) with a synchronized score by Erno Rapee—including a dubbed-in performance of his song hit "Diane"—and sound effects. Second, there were three Movietone short films appealing to a variety of tastes. Requel Meller made a second Movietone appearance in a "Corpus Christi" recitation; Gertrude Lawrence sang a song from one of her revues; and Chic Sale supplied some comedy with a brief sketch entitled *They're Coming to Get Me,* which had the distinction of being the first Movietone with

---

*   "Charmaine," Erno Rapee's theme song for this film, became one of the first *hit* theme songs in the history of the cinema.

dialogue. But this innovation was overshadowed by the critical acclaim for *Seventh Heaven*.

However, Movietone's next offering, which opened at the Roxy Theatre, New York, on June 14, 1927, received worldwide attention. On the same bill as the silent feature *Secret Studio* were Movietone shorts of Lindbergh's reception in Washington by President Coolidge and Mussolini making brief speeches in English and Italian. This time the feature was scarcely noticed, but the shorts received press comment throughout the world. The great public interest they had generated led to their revival on September 23, 1927, when they were shown at the Times Square Theatre, New York, along with Murnau's *Sunrise,* which was provided with synchronized music and sound effects (Movietone), and additional Movietone shorts—of the Italian Army on parade and the Vatican Choir. Again the Mussolini and Lindbergh films were widely discussed. And their success was a major reason for the establishment of the regular series of Fox Movietone Newsreels (beginning October 28, 1927, at the Roxy Theatre).

So far we have emphasized the value of the Vitaphone-Fox agreements to the Fox interests. For different reasons the agreements were no less valuable to Warner Bros. The contracts minimized the danger of Warner Bros. being wiped out by the policy of the Big Five or by the emergence of a superior or more commercially viable sound system. The latter danger was already clearly discernible during the second half of 1926. For in the U. S. De Forest's Phonofilm was available to any studio offering terms that were favorable enough to De Forest, and Vocafilm was already receiving advance publicity for its first program (some sound shorts and a Babe Ruth baseball film supplied with music and special effects)—which would actually be delayed until July 25, 1927. In Britain there were other ominous developments. In her *History of the British Film: 1918–1929,* Rachel Low notes that less than two months after the *Don Juan* premiere, an advertisement appeared in England for the Gaumont system, British Acoustic.

This was a sound-on-film system, using a separate film for the sound which, according to [Sir Michael] Balcon, ran 50 per cent faster than the picture and through a separate projector. The company had been busy with the system for some time and claimed in its favor that it gave fidelity, volume, distinction, a wide range of production, and that it was practicable outdoors [which Vitaphone, of course, was not] and unaffected by mixes, fades and chemical manipulation during development. [The subjects of the British Acoustic test films included the Changing of the Guard at Buckingham Palace and Sybil Thorndike delivering speeches from Shaw's *Saint Joan.*] No public demonstration took place at this date, however. At the same time, the Phonofilm system, with sound on the side of the picture film, was demonstrated in a program of shorts of British vaudeville artists, the best known of whom was Billy Merson, at the Capitol, Haymarket, on September 27th 1926.[15]

Meanwhile, inventors in France, Germany, Austria, Scandinavia, and elsewhere were no less active. However, systems were only one side of the development of sound cinema. Financial resources, promotion, exhibition outlets were another, and equally important. These assets Fox could provide in abundance— whether or not Movietone (Fox-Case) turned out to be more viable than Vitaphone. Between them, Fox and Warner Bros. controlled sufficient theaters and adequate capital to insure the survival, if not the dominance, of the sound systems they were jointly promoting.

At the end of January 1927, MGM executives began dickering with Vitaphone again.[16] Their objective was to buy a controlling amount of stock in the Vitaphone Corporation. They lost interest, however, when Warner Bros. revealed that it held 70 percent of the stock and had the option of buying the rest. The Warners announced defiantly that they had "shouldered the responsibility for Vitaphone and took all the risks in the beginning, and that now . . . [they were] entitled to control the stock." Again they affirmed that exclusive rights to Vitaphone would not be granted and any studio wishing to use the system would have to accept Warner Bros.' terms. In February 1927, the perplexity of the major Hollywood studios in the face of the mounting sound revolution led the Big Five—MGM, First National, Universal, Paramount, and PDC (Producers' Distributing Corporation)—to approach the Motion Picture

Producers and Distributors Association (generally known as the Hays Office) with a request for an expert study of existing sound systems as a basis for determining which should be adopted, if necessary. It is not known whether this study was actually conducted.

Meanwhile, to add to the growing vexation of executives at MGM and other studios, Will C. Durant, the so-called Wall Street Wizard, declared in an interview for *Forbes* magazine that Vitaphone was "The thing that has the biggest possibilities of anything and everything I have come across in the last forty years."[17] Such enthusiasm was tempered, however, by the elderly Edison, who remarked, blandly, that he had made a talking picture system (the Kinetophone, of course) some fifteen years earlier, but "discarded it as having no permanent value."[18] As we know, it was the public, not Edison, who had "discarded" the Kinetophone; but memories of what had happened in 1913 were probably vague in 1927. No one contradicted the aged inventor, but he was to change his tune only nine months later, after attending a private screening of some Fox Movietone Newsreels at his laboratory in Orange, New Jersey. "There is," he said, "no question but that Movietone is a distinct advance towards the perfection of talking pictures . . . and I believe that it will go a long way toward creating a better understanding among the peoples of all the world."[19]

A potentially serious blast at Warners came late in March, when J. J. Murdock, general manager of the nationwide Keith-Albee Theatre Exchange, which handled vaudeville interests, announced that henceforth players contracted to Keith-Albee would not be permitted to perform for sound movies. To this declaration of open hostilities between vaudeville and Vitaphone, Sam Warner defiantly responded with the assertion that vaudeville had more to worry about than Vitaphone, which "has and is doing more to publicize artists than any other form of entertainment." He warned that "unless a sensible attitude is taken by vaudeville, *it* will be the sufferer not *Vitaphone,* as we can give well-known artists a yearly contract for as much salary as any vaudeville circuit can afford to pay, and they can work all season without leaving New York or Los Angeles."[20]

Murdock began taking a "sensible attitude" rather sooner

than was generally expected. Early in April, barely two weeks after disclosing Keith-Albee's hostile policy towards sound movies, he realized that he had shot his mouth off too hastily. The way things were going, vaudeville might, after all, have to compromise with sound movies. But as he had already antagonized the Warners, he would have to seek a compromise with another viable system. There was no point in approaching Fox, since he was now contractually associated with Warner Bros. But Phonofilm was still up for grabs. De Forest had installed his system in the Palace Theatre in New York, and was giving private demonstrations of short Phonofilms to potential investors. Murdock and other executives of Keith-Albee attended one of these demonstrations. Their initial response was guarded. They were satisfied, more or less, with the system, but realized that De Forest was not yet in a position to supply sufficient apparatus and an adequate number of sound films to equip and supply the Keith-Albee circuit with strong counter-attractions to Vitaphone.

Murdock left the demonstration without making any commitments, but promptly announced a Keith-Albee policy change. Henceforward, movie stars might be booked into special vaudeville acts while they were marking time between film productions. Warner Bros. presumably interpreted this offer as a reply to Sam's tempting bait of yearly contracts to vaudeville stars: if the Warners knew how to lure vaudeville people into movies, Murdock had ways to entice movie stars into vaudeville. However, the Keith-Albee policy shift was actually an expression of compromise rather than another salvo against sound movies. In announcing that vaudeville was prepared to accommodate movie stars, Murdock was really persuading himself (and vaudeville) that show business could even accommodate movies.

On April 9 it was revealed that the Vitaphone Corporation was coping with an average of twelve installations per week and that the system would soon be active in 150 movie theaters in the U. S. The announcement spurred Murdock to a flurry of activity. Within two weeks he had arranged with the Pathe Corporation to exhibit Pathe (silent) movies in Keith-Albee theaters. A month later, he had begun formal negotiations with

De Forest for the purpose of securing rights to Phonofilm. Warner Bros. responded to these developments by advertising "considerable reductions" in the installation costs of Vitaphone, leaving exhibitors in no doubt that Vitaphone— the tried, tested, and well-publicized system—would be cheaper to install than Phonofilm or any other process whose reliability was still open to question.

Within a short time, Murdock, having realized that sound movies would deal a devastating blow to vaudeville,

> merged with the film interests of Joseph P. Kennedy, a Boston promoter, and with the Radio Corporation of America [soon to develop the Photophone sound-on-film system]. Kennedy, backed by John J. Raskob and Mike Meehan of Wall Street, had bought the American interests of Pathé and an English firm, Film Booking Offices, popularly called F.B.O. David Sarnoff, president of R.C.A., became chairman of the board of the combined corporation, known as Radio-Keith-Orpheum (R.K.O.).[21]

Meanwhile, in mid-1927, it was announced in the trade papers that Warner Bros. had bought out Walter J. Rich and were now the main controllers of Vitaphone Corporation. Harry Warner replaced Rich as the corporation's president, and Jack L. Warner was appointed vice president. The directors of the corporation were the brothers Warner and Waddill Catchings of the brokerage firm of Goldman, Sachs & Co.[22] It was further revealed that henceforth installation of Vitaphone apparatus and the licensing of producers to use Vitaphone and/ or Movietone would be conducted exclusively by Electrical Research Products, Inc. (ERPI), a subsidiary of Western Electric. Warner Bros. and Vitaphone would be responsible for insuring that there would be sufficient programs of sound movies to keep pace with the rapid spread of installations.

Preparations for increasing the production of Vitaphone films were soon under way. The first and most important step was the construction of a sound studio on Warner Bros.' thirteen-acre lot on Sunset Boulevard in Hollywood. Begun in April 1927 and more or less completed by October of the same year, the new studio became officially known as Stage Three. "At that time there was no other talking picture studio in the world— nor was there to be for nearly a year following!"[23] *The Jazz*

Singer was to be filmed at Stage Three shortly after it was ready—in May 1927, and even before that picture was completed, Stage Four was under construction and Stage Five was being planned.

The world's first sound studio was provided with everything the Manhattan Opera House had lacked. It had double, insulated, soundproofed walls and floors lined with felt and Celotex.

> Thought had been given to its acoustics, to its qualities of resonance; its echoes had been scientifically considered. It had all the specific fittings of the movie studio. For the first time lighting and scenic work could be carried out with ease, instead of in the makeshift manner of the Manhattan. And in addition, it had talking-picture-making innovations.[24]

First there was the monitor room, or "mixing booth." Situated some 15 feet above one side of the large stage (it was approximately 75 feet wide by 100 feet long), the monitor room was a doubly soundproofed, glass-enclosed box in which an operator could observe the action on stage and regulate the sound so that it was recorded at the required levels of tone and volume.[25] Then there was the "playback room," which was equipped with a loudspeaker

> wired through the mixer to the recording room and the recording apparatus. Through this system any "wax" [recording] could be played back as soon as it was made. . . . The actors and director, then, could go to the playback room as soon as they had finished their work, and hear the "sounds" they had just recorded. This was invaluable as an aid to better recording, as an actor could tell just how his voice sounded, where he should speak louder, etc.[26]

The camera booths used in the Manhattan Opera House, "with their felt masks around the front opening, designed to keep the sound in, had been very limited."[27] They had restricted the camera to shooting in only one direction, usually straight ahead. The new, improved booths gave the camera somewhat more freedom. They were soundproofed and moveable—they could be "swung" to follow action—and were provided with nonrefracting windows, three feet square, through which the camera could shoot. (However, compared to silent film-making, shooting a sound picture at Stage Three still involved considerable restrictions of camera movement and setup.)

There was also a new lighting system. Applying his experiences at the Manhattan Opera House, Warner Bros.' chief electrician, Frank Murphy, discontinued the use of carbon arcs (then in general use throughout movie studios) and installed noiseless, incandescent globes. They were suspended from beams at the top of the studio and were supplied with special reflectors to strengthen their candlepower. Since "incandescent light brings out colors of the spectrum, inconspicuous under carbon lighting," it was necessary to use a new kind of film stock, panchromatic film, "a type of negative vastly more sensitive than that previously used."[28]

A regular production unit was assembled to handle all the technicalities of the new studio. The production chief was Bryan Foy (son of Eddie Foy, the vaudevillian), who had directed a number of the sound shorts made at the Manhattan Opera House. Aside from his general responsibilities for Vitaphone production, Foy handled all matters pertaining to booking and casting of actors and performers, and he continued to undertake directorial assignments. Ed DuPar, another veteran of the Manhattan experiments, became chief cameraman. Colonel Nugent Slaughter, a technician who had worked for Western Electric, was appointed chief recording engineer. A. M. "Doc" Salomon became superintendent of the studio's 700 employees, and George Grove was placed in charge of sound "mixing." Vitaphone had now been put on a regular production basis.[29] By early October 1927, Warner Bros. announced that all its films would henceforth be made with "a complete synchronized Vitaphone accompaniment."[30]

Almost every week since April 5, 1927, Warner Bros. had been able to provide its programs with a selection of short Vitaphone pictures, mainly opera arias and vaudeville sketches. On June 28 an anonymous *New York Times* reviewer noted: "As is usual with the Warner Brothers' presentations nowadays, [the] . . . feature is prefaced by a Vitaphone concert." These "concerts" included Cantor Joseph Rosenblatt singing two songs at a New York recital (he was later to appear in *The Jazz*

Singer); Bernardo Pace (mandolin) and Beniamino Gigli in a scene from *Cavalleria Rusticana* (released April 5, 1927); "Whispering" Jack Smith, "The Rollickers," Vincent Lopez and his orchestra, and Giovanni Martinelli and Jeanne Gordon in a scene from act 2 of *Carmen* (released April 12); "The Revellers," the Vitaphone orchestra playing the Overture to *Orpheus in the Underworld,* and John Charles Thomas in the Prologue to *I Pagliacci* (April 20); Mary Lewis (soprano), Albert Spalding (violin), and Margaret McKee—the whistling "bird in a cage" (released April 26); Leo Carillo in *At the Ball Game* and George Jessel in *A Theatrical Booking Office* (released May 6); and John Charles Thomas and Vivienne Segal singing "Will You Remember?" from *Maytime* (released late May 1927).

A particularly interesting concert selection accompanied the June 21 premiere of Alan Crosland's feature *Old San Francisco*. In fact, the *New York Times* reviewer described the short films as "infinitely more sane and far more interesting than the principal film subject."[31] The concert items included Gigli singing arias from *La Giaconda,* William and Eugene Howard, and Blossom Seeley with Tom Brown and the Six Brown Brothers.

Despite critical objections, the feature film *did* give a spectacular demonstration of Vitaphone's ability to provide powerful sound effects combined with a synchronized score. *Old San Francisco,* which starred Warner Oland, Dolores Costello, Anna May Wong, and William Demarest, was based on a story by Darryl F. Zanuck. Although its visuals were completed before the erection of Stage Three, it was one of the first features scored in the new sound studio. Because of the improved technical and acoustic conditions, the recording was the best achieved up to that time. But, unpredictably, New York censors ordered that cuts be made in one reel of the movie, which meant the synchronization would be destroyed. It was easy to cut footage from the film, but there was no way known to remove the equivalent sound passage from the wax recording. The idea of doing a new recording of the music was rejected. It had cost $900 an hour to hire the Los Angeles Philharmonic Orchestra to play the score for the film. An easier and less expensive solution had to be found, one that could be used again whenever similar difficulties arose. After some trial and error, the Vitaphone sound engineers solved the problem by re-recording the sound of the original Vitaphone disk, deleting the unwanted sound passages. This method, which became standard procedure in sound recording, was promptly nicknamed "duping," a contraction of the word *duplicating*.

Aware that similar problems would arise when film broke during a theater showing, Vitaphone engineers came up with another solution, which was promptly passed on to the movie theater operators. Vitaphone films were sent out to the theaters together with a reel of blank footage so that if a break occurred in the film the operator could simply replace the damaged or useless footage with exactly the same number of frames of blank film. In this way, the synchronization could be preserved even with a Vitaphone film that had many cuts and splices. The problems arising out of censorship of *Old San Francisco* thus turned out to be a blessing in disguise.[32]

But Crosland's film was something of an endurance test for audiences who were becoming accustomed to more sensitive and melodious uses of Vitaphone. Culminating in scenes of the great earthquake of 1906, *Old San Francisco* was enlivened by screams, thunderous crashes, and an intense musical score by Hugo Riesenfeld. The sensational sound effects were created by Herman Heller, Warner Bros.' musical director, who had been experimenting with sound dubbing since the earliest Vitaphone shorts. Heller provided earthquake noises by having "tons of bricks . . . rolled down a chute and recorded, then the assembled voices of several extras were dubbed in over the sound."[33] The ear-splitting, horrendous climax was sufficient to drive the most prejudiced admirers of Vitaphone back to the tranquil sanctuary of silent cinema. Alan Crosland's next feature film would be far less noisy, but its repercussions would be unimaginably vaster.

The Jazz Singer was to be the start of Warner Bros.' regular production of features conceived for Vitaphone and made generally available for distribution to all Vitaphone-equipped theaters. It was to be a prestigious picture and was promoted in advance publicity as the studio's "supreme achievement." In mid-1927, however, not even the wildest optimist at Warner

Bros., nor anyone else in Hollywood, vaudeville, or Wall Street, would have predicted that this movie—and more specifically the charisma of its star, Al Jolson—would decide the fate of silent cinema and determine the future of sound pictures.

In his book *Stardom,* Alexander Walker corrects the oft-repeated assertion that *The Jazz Singer* made Jolson into a star. As he states, *"The Jazz Singer* owed far more of *its* success to the celebrity he already possessed."[34] During the twenty years preceding *The Jazz Singer,* Jolson was America's most popular vaudeville artist. He played the lead in nine consecutive Broadway hits between 1911 and 1925. Walker notes that in the early 1920s Jolson's "phonograph royalties for one month alone amounted to 120,000 dollars; his musical, *Big Boy,* grossed 1,419,000 dollars plus half the net profit which could well have totalled another 150,000 dollars."[35] In 1921, when the Shuberts built a new theater at Seventh Avenue and Fifty-ninth Street, they acknowledged his enduring appeal by naming it the Jolson. During the 1926–27 season he was earning $17,000 per week at the Los Angeles Metropolitan, and for a single appearance at San Francisco's Warfield Theatre he received $16,500. The $350,000 he received for the entire season broke all box office records for the twenties.

As a singer, Jolson's style was fixed and familiar long before it became internationally famous with *The Jazz Singer.* In 1913, while appearing in blackface as Gus in *Honeymoon Express,* he had the inspiration of getting down on one knee and delivering his songs with arms outstretched. According to one of his biographers, the source of this inspiration was an ingrown toenail, which made it painful for the singer to stand up. Whatever the reason, the response of his adoring audiences encouraged him to adopt this manner of delivery as part of his regular routine.

It is widely assumed that Jolson made his screen debut in *The Jazz Singer.* But, as noted earlier, in the previous year he had appeared in the second Vitaphone program, and, in fact, he was involved in other movie projects even before Vitaphone. As early as 1915 Jolson had appeared in a short silent film (title unknown), in which he burlesqued screen acting. A production of the California Motion Picture Corporation, the movie was made for presentation at the 1915 Panama Exposition. About this time Jolson turned down an offer of $50,000 to star in a silent feature film. In 1916 he was persuaded to make a short silent movie for the Vitagraph Company on the understanding that the picture was to have a limited showing and that all profits were to go to a benefit fund for traffic policemen. A viewing of this film left Jolson unimpressed. ("I'm no good if I can't sing.") Later, he ordered the picture to be suppressed when he discovered that Vitagraph had released it for general exhibition and that some of the profits were not going to the prescribed fund.[36]

Jolson's already unfavorable attitude towards movies and the film industry was aggravated by his dealings with D. W. Griffith, the director of *The Birth of a Nation*. Griffith repeatedly tried to induce Jolson to star in one of his movies, and he was so persistent and persuasive that at last, in 1923, Jolson accepted the lead in a film tentatively entitled either *Black and White* or *Mammy's Boy*. Jolson's role was that of an attorney who disguised himself as a Negro in order to solve a crime. The masquerade was, of course, a device for presenting him in his familiar blackface appearance. It is unlikely that *Black and White* was conceived even in part as a sound film. As we noted in chapter 2, two years earlier Griffith had tried to use synchronized sound (Orlando Kellum's sound-on-disk system) in connection with his film *Dream Street*, in which Ralph Graves sang a love song. The results were so unsatisfactory that he discontinued the experiment after a short trial run. And in an article published in *Collier's* in 1924, Griffith assured his readers that "It will never be possible to synchronize the voice with the pictures. This is true because the very nature of the films forgoes not only the necessity for but the propriety of the spoken voice."[37]

At the outset of work on *Black and White*, Jolson threw himself into the production with his characteristic drive and enthusiasm. All went well until he saw the rushes. The comic scenes (in blackface) looked fine, but he was appalled at the love scenes, which he had played seriously, in whiteface. Immediately, he resolved to pull out of the picture, and to make sure that Griffith would not be in a position to change his mind, Jolson boarded the first available ship for Europe. Only six reels of the movie had been shot when the cameras stopped rolling. The picture was never completed. Griffith was furious. He promptly sued Jolson for half a million dollars. But an unsympathetic judge (perhaps one of Jolson's innumerable fans) allowed him to collect a meagre $2,627.

After this misadventure there was every reason to expect that Jolson would never again set foot inside a movie studio, but only two years later he accepted $10,000 for singing a song in one of De Forest's short experimental Phonofilms. It was Jolson's first experience in making sound movies. His reaction was lukewarm. He considered sound movies just a passing curiosity; they could never replace or challenge vaudeville. But the money he received for making the Phonofilm was excellent, and the time and effort involved were negligible and did not interfere with his stage career. So he agreed to perform for the second Vitaphone show, in 1926. That, presumably, was to be the limit of his association with Warner Bros. and Vitaphone. Certainly no one considered the possibility of getting Jolson to play the lead in *The Jazz Singer*. George Jessel had been the star of the Broadway production and had signed a $2,000-a-week contract with Warner Bros. to do the movie version. Advance advertising for the film announced that Jessel would be the star. Then the unexpected happened. Warner Bros. announced that Al Jolson would replace Jessel.

There are at least four versions of what occurred. According to a confused account in *Moving Picture World,* Jessel understood that he was going to make a silent film and agreed to play the title role for $100,000.

After his trunks had arrived at the Santa Fe station and the actor was introduced to the Vitaphone annex to the regular Warner Studio, we hear that for 'Vitaphoning' he must receive something like a second one hundred 'thou.' About this time, we gather, Warners decided that they could get that internationally known crooner of black babbles to do the two jobs [i.e., acting and singing] for just a couple of hundred thousand. [Presumably Warner Bros. considered that Jolson was worth $200,000 but that Jessel wasn't.] On checking up all of this at the Warner Studio, we learned that 'something like that' did happen. . . .[38]

The account given by Pearl Sieben, one of Jolson's biographers, is that

Jessel signed a contract to make the picture, but when he saw the finished script, he had misgivings. The ending had been changed considerably and he did not like it. Another thing that made him reluctant to make the film was his belief that the movie would kill his chances of keeping on with the stage play, and in those days an actor could run for years in the same show. He told Warners that he did not want to fulfill the contract. The Warners argued with him, but they finally gave in and allowed him to work out the contract with two silent pictures.[39]

Alexander Walker more or less combines both of these explanations:

Jessel . . . pointed out that since he would be expected to make two or three records for Vitaphone . . . he ought to get an additional fee. Negotiations with him were abruptly broken off—and opened with Jolson. Jessel is also believed to have claimed that he could get two more years out of the stage version of *The Jazz Singer* and he did not want to see the Vitaphone disks sold in competition with himself![40]

The version provided by Michael Freedland, Jolson's latest biographer is that

with the uncertainties of a talkie and the effect it might have on his career, Jessel wanted insurance to the tune of one hundred thousand dollars. Warners said no and approached Eddie Cantor. He, too, said he was too worried about the effects of talking pictures on his career to contemplate the idea. Darryl Zanuck suggested they try to get Jolson. They knew Jolson loved a gamble. "What about asking Al Jolson to put money into the picture and draw stock from its takings?" Zanuck asked. Jolson insisted on complete secrecy about the whole matter while he thought it over. . . . The next day [Jessel] read in the papers that Jolson had signed with Warner Brothers to make *The Jazz Singer*. "Is it any wonder I always felt bitter?" Jessel asks. "I felt sick. It

was my part and partly my story. Jolson got the role because he
put money into it. But he *was* better at it than I would have
been."[41]

Leo Guild, in his recent biography of movie tycoon Darryl
F. Zanuck, rather dubiously explains what occurred as the outcome of a personality conflict between Jessel and Jack Warner.
This "explanation" is sandwiched between even more dubious
accounts of how Guild's "hero" originated the idea of filming
The Jazz Singer and later came up with the inspiration for the
spoken dialogue sequences:

> Zanuck was called into Warner's office and Warner's orders were
> to find a property that they could use to introduce sound. [What
> had they been doing since *Don Juan?*] When Zanuck did find
> the property, *The Jazz Singer,* Harry Warner threw up his hands.
> He refused to buy it.
>
> "No," he said, "it's too strongly Jewish. Therefore it limits its
> appeal."
>
> Zanuck argued, "Look, Harry, you've seen *Nanook of the
> North*. Well, when that Eskimo woman loses her child on the
> ice cap do the audiences stop to ask what religion she is? No,
> they just burst out crying."
>
> Harry shook his head. Jack Warner chewed on his cigar and
> said, "Let him do it. He usually knows what he's doing."
>
> . . . So Harry went along with it. They had long conferences
> and decided they'd put Georgie Jessel into the lead of *The Jazz
> Singer*. He had done it on Broadway and everyone thought he
> was just right for it.
>
> But Jessel and Jack Warner couldn't get together. They ended
> cursing each other. Jessel said they didn't have enough money
> to make it worth his while. Zanuck wanted Jack to give him
> what he wanted but Warner, always stubborn, refused. So Jack
> went to Al Jolson.
>
> Zanuck always said, "I paid for twelve dinners before Al
> agreed to do the picture."
>
> While the picture was being done Zanuck put some words in
> it too. He couldn't stand just using music with this great inven-
> tion of sound. So several sentences were added. . . . It was a big hit
> from the beginning and the beginning of sound in film [really?]
> and it was Zanuck who had the courage and the necessary stickto-
> itiveness to get it on the screen.[42]

Aside from their inconsistencies, each of these explanations is open to question on specific details. *Moving Picture World* was later to contradict its own, earlier, confused report (quoted above) that Jolson had received $200,000 for playing in *The Jazz Singer* by announcing, on September 10, 1927, that he had actually received only $150,000. Sieben's story indicates, unconvincingly, a complete lack of foresight on the part of Jessel (or his agents). Warner Bros.' heavy investment in the screen rights to *The Jazz Singer* would obviously have made it necessary to find an attractive replacement for the lead role (Al Jolson, Eddie Cantor) if Jessel backed out. We are expected to believe that Jessel would not have realized that or would have been unconcerned by it. Finally, we are asked to assume that it was only *after* he had signed the contract that Jessel realized that a film version with or without Jessel might pose a threat to the stage show. The problem of Freedland's version is that it is ambiguous and there is no factual support for it. What was the "insurance" of a hundred thousand dollars that Jessel allegedly asked for? Was it his fee or a sum over and above the fee? Freedland maintains that it was Zanuck's idea to replace Jessel by Jolson, but, as we saw in the previous chapter, Jack Warner has also claimed credit for that. Freedland also intimates that Jolson received no fee for making the picture but actually invested in it. And he quotes Jessel's assertion—which is hardly credible—that Jolson only got the part *because* of his investment. Jessel's remark has the distinct flavor of sour grapes. It is the comment of a man who does not want to admit to the worst mistake of his career. Leo Guild's account indicates that the personal animosity between Jessel and Jack Warner was the root cause of the former's replacement by Jolson. And that may indeed have been an important factor in what occurred—although it is rather curious that Guild seems to be the only writer who has ever mentioned it.

Whatever actually happened, as the years passed, Jessel evidently became increasingly aware that he had been deprived (or had deprived himself) of a fortune and a permanent niche in film history. For on one item all the sources agree—it was Jessel's withdrawal that led to Jolson's becoming the star of *The Jazz Singer*. Jolson's own, brief account of the events that led to his appearance in *The Jazz Singer* is curiously vague. Diplomatically, perhaps, he avoids any mention of Jessel.

> I couldn't be convinced that the silent screen was a proper medium for me to use to reach an audience. Several producers and directors tried to persuade me but I was always dubious. I went so far as to make tests and to plan a story, but I was still dubious and finally decided that the silver screen was not for me. I'm still skeptical—about silent pictures—but the public has been kind in its approval of *The Jazz Singer*. . . . I had resisted some tempting offers to try the silent picture and was on the road with my show *Big Boy* when the suggestion that I make a "singing picture" was first discussed. We were in Denver with the show and before we left there I had thought the proposition over and decided to make the experiment. Warner Brothers who had just then perfected the Vitaphone and who had approached me with the proposal that I make their first full length talking [*sic*] and singing picture, were notified that I would accept their offer to make one Vitaphone picture. During the rest of the tour of *Big Boy* we planned the story of *The Jazz Singer* and when the road show closed I went to Hollywood for the first tests. I was not easily won away from my intention to make the legitimate stage the only medium between the public and me but the Vitaphone offered me an opportunity I could not resist. The success of *The Jazz Singer* is now motion picture history. It did 'break' into the movies with a loud bang which is echoing yet, and I found a new and satisfactory way of reaching a vastly increased audience. Having made the break, it followed naturally that Warner Brothers wanted more pictures and that I was willing to make them. . . . I looked a long time before I leaped but once the leap was made into movies I had no regrets.[43]

It should be noted that Jolson does not mention his experiences with D. W. Griffith. His recollections were written in 1929, six years after the fiasco of *Black and White*, but the memory was still a painful one. Jolson says that he was approached with a suggestion to appear in a "singing picture"; later he amplifies it into a proposal to make Warner Bros.' "first full length talking and singing picture." The word "talking" is, of course, slipped in to convey the idea that *The Jazz Singer* was actually planned as a talkie. In fact, there is not a shred of evidence to support this notion, but good reason for believing that the dialogue passages on the sound track were the results of Jolson's unexpected ad-libbing.

Particularly dubious is Jolson's motive in remarking that he was involved in "planning" the story of *The Jazz Singer* during the road tour of *Big Boy*. There was obviously no need to plan what already existed in theatrical form (as a successful Broadway show) and in screenplay form (as a potential vehicle for a Jessel movie). However, Jolson ungenerously ignores Samson Raphaelson, who wrote the play (it was based on his original short story "The Day of Atonement"), and Alfred A. Cohn, who adapted it to the screen. In his version, *The Jazz Singer* was planned by Al Jolson and some other individuals whose names are not worth mentioning. Except for the Warners, who are allowed the credit of having "perfected" Vitaphone and the inspiration of having approached Jolson, we are expected to believe that the achievement was by, with, and from Jolson and all for the benefit of his adoring and ever-widening public.

The switch from Jessel to Jolson occurred in the course of a week at the end of May and the beginning of June 1927. *Moving Picture World* for May 28 reported that Jessel had arrived in Hollywood and *The Jazz Singer* would go into production in a week. Alan Crosland was to direct the picture, May McAvoy would costar with Jessel, and vaudevillian William Demarest, a recent "discovery" of Warner Bros., would make his feature film debut in one of the minor roles. A week later, the same journal announced that Jolson was to get the title role in *The Jazz Singer*. With the news that Jolson had replaced Jessel came the first reports that there was something unusual about the picture. Like *Don Juan,* it would have intertitles and a synchronized music score provided by Vitaphone, but this time songs and sounds would somehow be incorporated into the movie's dramatic structure.

Alan Crosland began shooting the picture in mid-June. It was not, of course, the only movie then in production at Warner Bros., but because of its importance in the development of Vitaphone and because its star was Al Jolson, *The Jazz Singer* generated more interest than all the other films in progress at the studio.

Cantor Joseph Rosenblatt had been contracted to sing in the

picture, and his arrival in Hollywood on June 7 made headlines in the trade papers.

> Joseph Rosenblatt, the greatest cantor in America, if not in the
> world, is to appear in *The Jazz Singer*. . . . Cantor Rosenblatt
> was signed this week by H. M. Warner and is to appear as a
> singer not as an actor. . . . He has already made two songs [in
> New York] on the Vitaphone which will be used, and the
> finishing touches will be made at Warners' Hollywood studio.
> . . . The Cantor has had all sorts of offers to appear in motion
> pictures, both here and abroad, but has refused to appear on
> the screen other than as a singer, which is made possible only
> by Vitaphone.[44]

During the second week in August a writer for *Moving Picture World* visited Warner Bros. and reported that

> Work throughout the entire Warner Studio—except on the set
> where Alan Crosland is filming *The Jazz Singer*—was suspended
> for one day this week while the whole production staff listened
> to Al Jolson, star of the picture, sing for the sequences which are
> to bring the Vitaphone into the dramatic action of a feature for
> the first time. *The Jazz Singer* has been under way for about ten
> weeks and the shooting schedule has now progressed to the
> point calling for the making of the several song numbers that
> are to be included as an integral part of the plot's development.
> These numbers will take several more weeks to complete.[45]

According to Fitzhugh Green, it was Jolson who made the
most innovative contributions to the picture. They also turned
out to be its most sensational aspects. During the shooting of one
scene

> Jolson became imbued with the spirit of the thing. He began to
> 'ad lib.' He is a natural 'ad libber.' When he is confined to tight
> lines his style is cramped. He works best when he can simply
> let himself go, put his own words into the thought that he is
> trying to get across—play it naturally, entirely in character. . . .
> They were working on a song which he was singing to his mother.
> The script called for him to summon her to the piano, and then
> to start singing it for her. All the action up to the start of the
> song was supposed to take place in the silent part of the film.
> They rehearsed, lined up, started the take. And before he sang,
> Jolson spoke to his "mother," spontaneously. "Come on, Ma,"

he said. "Listen to this!" She went over to the piano, and he began to sing. The action went ahead. Sam Warner and Alan Crosland had not expected Jolson to speak. But when they heard it in the play-back, that spontaneous bit sounded good. They decided to leave it in. That decision made history.[46]

The filming of Jolson's songs occupied much of the last month of production. "The remainder of the time was consumed in shooting interiors at the Warner Studio and in allowing Director Alan Crosland to make a location trip to New York with several of the principals."[47] The purpose of the trip was to film scenes of the Lower East Side that were to appear at the beginning of the movie.

At the end of September, immediately after the completion of the picture, Warner Bros. announced to the press that the premiere of *The Jazz Singer* would take place in New York, at the Warner Theatre, on Thursday evening, October 6, 1927. There followed a week-long, rapid-fire promotional campaign involving a flurry of billboard and press-release activity, collaboration with Grosset and Dunlap, who published a novelized version of the film story (it was the work of Arline De Haas, who also prepared a serialized version that was made available free of charge to newspapers from coast to coast), and a tie-in with Brunswick Records, Inc., who were to issue recordings of songs from the film.[48] A trailer for *The Jazz Singer* was actually made after the premiere and was used in connection with the general release of the picture following the first three months of its run in New York. A landmark of sorts, the trailer was the first in which sound was used. It showed not only scenes from the film but also the crowds outside the Warner Theatre on opening night and some of the show-business personalities who had turned up for the big event.

Richard Watts, Jr., who reviewed *The Jazz Singer* for the *New York Herald Tribune,* voiced the opinion of many critics in describing it as "a pleasant enough sentimental orgy" that was "inherently far from sensational." This impression was not, however, shared by the "milling, battling mob" that swarmed outside the theater before and after the premiere. Even the thousands who did not manage to get in to see the picture evidently considered the combination of Al Jolson, Vitaphone, and the show in which Jessel had triumphed on Broadway as unique an event as Lindbergh's solo flight across the Atlantic some six months earlier. It wasn't just any premiere: it was the movie sensation of 1927—and they had to be there. As they waited, a steady procession of celebrities—from composer Irving Berlin and comedian Johnny Hines to Mayor Jimmy Walker—stepped out of their limousines and paused on the sidewalk to entertain the crowd with a song, a dance, or some small talk before passing out of sight into the foyer. Among the last to arrive was the star of the show, Al Jolson, escorting a very young Ruby Keeler (to whom he was not yet married).

Al's brother Harry Jolson recollected that when the show started its star was ensconced

> in an orchestra seat, nervous and worried. Never before had he sat in an audience to see and hear himself on the stage. There was tremendous applause when his voice came from the screen. Tears were in every eye when the picture ended, with the jazz singer chanting the prayers in the synagogue. Al broke down completely, for tears always came easily to his eyes. The critics joined in a paean of praise. Talking pictures were here to stay.[49]

There are some inaccuracies in this description. The picture does not end with the jazz singer chanting in the synagogue but with the jazz singer singing "My Mammy" in a theater. Also, the critics did not "join in a paean of praise." Critical opinion of the picture ranged from ecstatic to antipathetic; mostly it was lukewarm. But Harry was probably correct about his brother's nervousness on that momentous opening night. Jolson was, above all, a performer. Passive observation—even of himself—was unnatural, even intolerable to him. Then, as we have already seen, he had long been dubious about appearing in movies; he was probably even more doubtful about the future of Vitaphone. If *The Jazz Singer* flopped what would it do to his reputation? Above all, he was probably reacting to the fact that the story unfolding on the screen was in certain respects his own. He too was a jazz singer, and like the hero of the film, his career was a reaction against an orthodox Jewish background.

The plot of *The Jazz Singer* is concerned with a conflict between old-world and new-world values, represented in the refusal of a Jewish cantor to tolerate his son's commitment to popular music. The father wants him to become a cantor, but the boy wants to be a jazz singer.

Thirteen-year-old Jakie Rabinowitz has run away from New York and his orthodox Jewish parents after his father (Warner Oland) has punished him for singing popular songs in a tavern. "Years later—and three thousands miles from home," Jakie, who now calls himself Jack Robin (Al Jolson) begins his show-business career as a singer in Coffee Dan's nightclub. Here he meets and falls in love with Mary Dale (May McAvoy), who is already a rising star in vaudeville. His talents and her assistance and encouragement eventually land him a part in a big Broadway show. Back in New York for rehearsals, he visits his parents' home. His mother (Eugenie Besserer) is overjoyed to see him, but his father refuses to acknowledge a jazz singer as his son and orders Jack out of the house. On the opening night of the show, Jack hears that his father is dying and that the old man's last wish is to hear his son sing in his place as cantor of the synagogue. Forced to make a painful choice between losing his big chance on Broadway or breaking his father's heart, Jack deserts the show and goes to the synagogue to sing "Kol Nidre." The old cantor, having expressed his love for his son, passes joyfully away to the strains of Jack's voice drifting in from the neighboring synagogue. Time passes. Although Jack had let the show down, all is forgiven. Once again he gets his big break. But this time there are no conflicts. He goes on stage and proves to be a tremendous success—much to the delight of his ecstatic mother and an adoring Mary, who are in the theater to join the rapturous applause as he sings "My Mammy."

As the picture faded out on Jolson (in blackface), the on-screen applause was taken up and amplified by countless audiences throughout the world. But what the public applauded, many critics deplored. Leading the chorus of critical denunciation was the novelist Aldous Huxley, who, predictably, was revolted by his first experiences of sound movies. He summed them up in an essay titled "Silence is Golden" (first published in 1929), an eight-page tirade against sound movies in general and *The Jazz Singer* in particular.[50] The subject provided him with an opportunity for making odious comparisons between his own elevated aesthetic standards and the decadent taste of his less-cultivated fellowmen. Curiously, despite his sophistication and refinement, he was not above indulging in cheap anti-Semitic jibes. The program in which he saw *The Jazz Singer* included a short movie of a jazz band. He describes it as a performance by "dark and polished young Hebrews, whose souls were in those mournfully sagging, seasickishly undulating melodies of mother love and nostalgia and yammering amorousness and clotted sensuality which have been the characteristically Jewish contributions to modern popular music." (Aside from its anti-Semitism, the comment displays total insensitivity to the work of such composers as George Gershwin, Jerome Kern, Irving Berlin, and Harold Arlen.)

When Huxley turns to *The Jazz Singer* he has already made it clear from his prejudice against "dark . . . young Hebrews" and his deeply rooted antipathy to what he called "standardized entertainment" that he is not going to attempt an objective assessment of the picture. He starts out by satirizing the plot, which he considered sheer absurdity. (Actually it is the summit of intelligence and credibility compared to the heroic drama of Dryden, in whose work Huxley professed admiration.) His treatment of the plot is too long to quote in full; a few choice passages will suffice:

When, after what seemed hours, the jazz band concluded its dreadful performance, I sighed in thankfulness. But the thankfulness was premature. For the film which followed was hardly less distressing. It was the story of the child of a cantor in a synagogue, afflicted, to his father's justifiable fury, with an itch for jazz. This itch, assisted by the cantor's boot, sends him out into the world, where in due course and thanks to My Baby, his dreams come tree-ue, and he is employed as a jazz singer on the music-hall stage. . . . The crisis of the drama arrives when, the cantor being mortally sick and unable to fulfill his functions at the synagogue, Mammy of Mine and the Friends of his Childhood implore the young man to come and sing the atonement service in his father's place. Unhappily, this religious function is booked to take place at the same hour as that other act of worship vulgarly known as the First Night. There ensues a terrific struggle, worthy of the pen of a Racine or a Dryden, between love and honor. Love for

Mammy of Mine draws the jazz singer toward the synagogue; but love for My Baby draws the cantor's son toward the theatre. . . . Honor also calls from either side; for honor demands that he should serve the God of his fathers at the synagogue, but it also demands that he should serve the jazz-voiced god of his adoption at the theatre. . . . With the air of a Seventeenth Century hero, the jazz singer protests that he must put his career before even his love. The nature of the dilemma has changed, it will be seen, since Dryden's day. In the old dramas it was love that had to be sacrificed to painful duty. In the modern instance the sacrifice is at the shrine of what William James called "the Bitch Goddess, Success." Love is to be abandoned for the stern pursuit of newspaper notoriety and dollars.

Huxley's mockery of *The Jazz Singer's* plot could, of course, be extended to the story lines of innumerable operas and musicals (in both theater and film), but in the final analysis his ridicule is insensitive because it ignores the intensification and enrichment that comes with the interaction of dramatic and musical elements that in themselves may seem trite. His snobbish critique anticipates the kind of imperceptive objection to the musical and other popular screen genres that has persisted among a certain type of intellectual since the beginnings of film criticism.

Anyone who has seen *The Jazz Singer* will realize that Huxley's satirical account of it is inaccurate. The hero as a child is not booted out by his father—he leaves home of his own accord. It is not "Friends of his Childhood" who implore Jack to sing in his father's place but Yudelson the Kibbitzer, who had betrayed young Jakie to his father when the boy was singing in a tavern. And it is not love for Mary (or My Baby, as Huxley calls her, in mocking echo of the lyrics of popular songs of the period) that pulls Jack toward the theater; it is clear in the film that being a jazz singer had meant everything to Jack even before he met her. Aside from such specific details, the struggle to which Huxley refers is not between Love and Honor (or Success and Duty) but between Personal Ambition and Duty—or, more precisely, between Narcissism and Responsibility. It is a struggle in which, quite exceptionally, no value judgments are involved. The hero's commitment is to the modern world and his own self-expression, to getting theater audiences to listen to him singing the kind of music he loves best—that obviously counts for him much more than "newspaper notoriety and dollars." (Significantly, the first piece of recorded dialogue to be heard in the film is Jack's speech to the audience in the nightclub: "Wait a minute. Wait a minute. You ain't heard nothin' yet. . . .") By contrast, the cantor's commitment is to tradition and to expressing what man owes to God rather than what he considers due to himself. There is a genuine, meaningful conflict here. It cannot be trivialized by deliberate distortion and mockery.

While other critical reactions to *The Jazz Singer* never approached the cynical prejudice of Huxley's, many were equally irrelevant. The film was most persistently criticized for being nostalgic and sentimental: a rather pointless objection since that is precisely what it was intended to be. Little consideration was given to the more valid questions of whether it was a good film *of its kind* (there are standards in sentimental and nostalgic movies) and why it was so much more conspicuously successful than the numerous other nostalgic and sentimental films of the period.

In fact, there has been no serious thought about this historically important film until very recently. Alexander Walker, in his book *Stardom* (1970), notes that *The Jazz Singer* is concerned with

> three of the most emotionally charged themes round which any film has been built—Jewish traditions, showbiz sentiment and mother love. All three are interwoven in a mawkish, yet crudely effective story. . . . It is undoubtedly this calculated pitch to the basic sentiments of an audience which makes the film's poorly recorded sound so emotionally effective even today and which, in its day, gave it what one might call a heart-start over the other part-talkies on the screen. . . . One may be pardoned for the irreverent thought that the only trick the film-makers missed was having Jolson sing *Kol Nidre* in blackface, thus achieving an unbeatable concentrate of racial sentiment.[51]

Perceptive as his commentary is, Walker actually gives a rather limited impression of the film's themes. For the movie was also concerned with modern reaction against traditional

values, with duty to parents, and with the desire for self-fulfill-
ment. Moreover, the central conflict was patently Oedipal, and
this familiar situation together with the universality of most of
the aforementioned themes extended the film's appeal far beyond its focus on Jewish characters. Thus *The Jazz Singer*
reached out to the widest possible public: to young and old,
parents and children, modernists and traditionalists, the ambitious and the dutiful. Added to all that, *The Jazz Singer*
attracted its audiences with memorable popular songs sung
inimitably by one of the great stars of vaudeville. It moved
them with the intensity and sincerity of its performances (particularly Jolson's and Warner Oland's). And last but by no
means least, it offered the novelty of Vitaphone used in a new
and unexpected way. For *The Jazz Singer* was a film that talked!

Robert E. Sherwood was one of the film's few contemporary
critics to rise above superciliousness or mindless glorification
and recognize the potential importance of the picture. In October 1927 he wrote:

> There is no question of doubt that the Vitaphone justifies itself
> in *The Jazz Singer*. Furthermore, it proves that talking movies are
> considerably more than a lively possibility: they are close to an
> accomplished fact. *The Jazz Singer* isn't much of a moving pic-
> ture, as moving pictures go . . . and Al Jolson as an actor is only
> fair. But when Al Jolson starts to sing . . . well, bring on your
> super-spectacles, your million-dollar thrills, your long-shots of
> Calvary against the setting sun, your close-ups of a glycerine tear
> on Norma Talmadge's cheek—I'll trade them all for one instant
> of any ham song that Al cares to put over, and the hammier it is,
> the better I'll like it. In view of the imminence of talking movies,
> I wonder what Clara Bow's voice will sound like. [He was very
> soon to find out.]

Sherwood added, with more foresight than he could have
realized: "I wonder whether the speeches that the Hollywood
sub-title writers compose will be as painful to hear as they are
to read."[52]

Curiously, although millions heard what Jolson said, there is
widespread inaccuracy and confusion among film historians
about the recorded dialogue in *The Jazz Singer*. Here are some
typical examples: According to Lewis Jacobs "The audience

responded riotously to Al Jolson's 'Come on, Ma! Listen to this. . . .' "[53] But Jolson never uttered that line in the film. Richard Griffith writes that Jolson spoke only at the end of the picture, when he said, "Hey, Mom, listen to this." Then, continues Griffith, "he sang two songs. To hear these two songs and the five words that introduced them, New York and the world queued up for months."[54] This account is totally incorrect: Jolson speaks *twice* in the film and when he talks to his Mom (Eugenie Besserer) it is midway through the picture, not at the end. At that point in the movie he sings only one song, "Blue Skies." Also, as we shall see, he says considerably more than five words to Eugenie Besserer, and what he says does not include "Hey, Mom, listen to this." In David Robinson's version, the film has only "a line or two of dialogue, including a catch phrase: 'You ain't heard nothin' yet.' "[55] Robinson is correct about the catch phrase, but quite wrong about there being only a line or two of dialogue. Finally, according to Gerald Mast, the film contains only two sequences using synchronized speech (and he is correct in this statement); he accurately identifies one of them, but then incorrectly states that the other sequence is the one in which Jolson sings "My Mammy."[56]

Admittedly, *The Jazz Singer* is not one of the masterpieces of world cinema, but it will always have a permanent place in film history. Therefore, once and for all it is worthwhile getting the details straight.

The two sequences in which synchronized speech occurs are: (1) Coffee Dan's nightclub near the start of the picture, and (2) the episode, halfway through the film, when Jack Robin visits his parents' home for the first time since he was a boy.

In the nightclub sequence, Jolson has just finished singing "Dirty Hands, Dirty Face." (That is *his* first song in the movie —it is also the first time we are shown the adult Jack Robin.) As his audience applauds, Jolson raises his hands for silence and says: "Wait a minute. Wait a minute. You ain't heard nothin' yet! Wait a minute, I tell you. You ain't heard nothin'. You wanna hear 'Toot-toot-tootsie'? All right. Hold on." He turns to the band and says: "Now listen: play 'Toot-toot-tootsie.' Three choruses. In the first chorus I whistle. . . ." He then goes into his song. Jolson is the only person whose speech is recorded in this part of the movie. The scene concludes with Jack's first meeting with Mary Dale. Their conversation is presented in typical silent cinema fashion—with visual intertitles.

Most of the recorded speech in the film occurs in the famous scene between Jolson and Eugenie Besserer, the scene that Robert E. Sherwood considered "fraught with tremendous significance" when he viewed it in the fall of 1927. "I for one," he observed, "suddenly realized that the end of the silent drama is in sight. . . ."[57] The scene begins when Jack, seated at the piano with his adoring mother beside him, stops between verses of "Blue Skies" to involve her in the following exchange:

Jack: Did you like that, Mama?

Mama: Yes.

Jack: I'm glad of it. I'd rather please you than anybody I know of. Oh, darlin'—will you give me something?

Mama: What?

Jack: You'll never guess. Shut your eyes, Mama. Shut 'em for little Jackie. Ha! I'm gonna steal something. Ha, ha, ha, ha, ha, ha!

(He kisses her and Mama mock-protests.)

I'll give it back to you someday too—you see if I don't.

(She laughs.)

Mama darlin'—if I'm a success in this show, well, we're gonna move from here.

(She protests.)

Oh yes, we're—we're gonna move up in the Bronx. A lot of nice green grass up there. A whole lot of people you know. There's the Ginsburgs, the Guttenbergs and the Goldbergs. Oh, a whole lot of bergs. I dunno 'em all. And I'm gonna buy you a nice black, silk dress, Mama. You see, Mrs. Freedman, the butcher's wife, she'll be jealous of you.

Mama: Oh no—

Jack: Yes she will. You see if she isn't. And I'm gonna get you a nice pink dress that'll go with your brown eyes.

Mama: No—I—I—No, No—

Jack: Just what do you mean, "No"? Who—who's tellin' ya? Whadda ya mean, "No"? Yes, you'll wear pink or else—Or else you'll wear pink.

(He laughs.)

And darlin'—Oh, I'm gonna take you to Coney Island.

Mama: Yes?

Jack: Yes—for a ride on the Shoot-the-Shoot. And, you know, in the Dark Mill.

Mama: Yes?

Jack: Ever been in the Dark Mill?

Mama: Oh no!—I wouldn't . . .

Jack: Well with me it's all right. I'll kiss ya and hug ya. You see if I don't. Oh Mama, Mama! Stop now! Will you? Kiss me! Mama —Listen, I'm gonna sing this like I will if I go on the stage. You know—with this show. I'm gonna sing it Jazzy. Now get this— (He sings a verse of "Blue Skies" and then interrupts with:) You like that slap in the tune? (Papa enters and yells: Stop!)

There is no other synchronized speech in the rest of the film. Examination of screenplays of the film confirms the oft-repeated assertion of film historians that the recorded dialogue was unplanned.[58] Alfred A. Cohn's screenplay was delightfully vague on the question of how Vitaphone was to be used. Such directions as the following indicate the relative freedom with which Crosland was able to use the recording system:

Scene 43 MEDIUM SHOT OF PIANO PLAYER
The player plays the introduction to "Mighty Lak a Rose" [the song was not used for the film] and the boy starts to sing. (The various shots for this will have to be in accordance with Vitaphone and its necessities.) *Vitaphone singing stops* when cut is made.

Scene 74 CLOSE UP PIANO PLAYER
Getting the humor of the situation, he [Jakie] starts playing something appropriate, like "Stay in your own Backyard" [the song was not used for the film] or perhaps something more modern and more to the point.

Scene 123 CLOSE UP JACK
He starts to sing his song. (The song which is to be Vitaphoned should be one especially written for the occasion as any current number would be out of date long before the picture has played every theatre equipped for Vitaphone by release time.) [Actually, several of the songs in the movie were not current numbers. "Toot-toot-tootsie," for example, was a hit five years before *The Jazz Singer* was made.]

Obviously, the screenplay encouraged—or at least permitted —the director to improvise in using Vitaphone. And in the course of his own improvisations, Crosland was, presumably, receptive to Jolson's. But there is no reason to believe that Crosland and Jolson considered the ad-libbed lines as having any dramatic significance or that they anticipated the public reaction to them. Nevertheless, it has frequently been said that the film's original audiences were excited by the integration of recorded speech into the action of the story. The movie itself demonstrates the inaccuracy of this notion. Jolson's ad-libbing has no dramatic function. It develops neither situation nor character. True, it provides in one scene a transition from song to song and in another a transition from one verse of "Blue Skies" to another. But these transitions were unnecessary. Their omission would have passed unnoticed and would not, in any way, have impaired the film. The original audiences were excited not by a *dramatic* use of recorded dialogue but by synchronized speech being used *naturally* in contrast to "performed" songs and the conventions of the silent drama.[59]

There was no novelty in recorded speech and songs coming from the screen. As mentioned in the previous chapter, a year earlier than *The Jazz Singer* the image and voice of Will Hays had addressed the audience at the first Vitaphone program, and in the intervening months Jolson himself had been among the many artists who had sung for short Vitaphone films. But the Hays film had presented a formal, prepared speech, whereas Jolson's ad-libbing was exactly that: unexpected, informal, spontaneous. In those two scenes of *The Jazz Singer,* the occurrence of recorded speech created the illusion of a real experience. For a few moments, Jolson wasn't merely an image on the screen— he was, or seemed to be, actually there, in person, speaking just the way people did when they tried to break in on conversation or applause, when they were kidding or making small talk. The earlier uses of Vitaphone had, at best, succeeded in recreating other synthetic experiences—opera, vaudeville, sound effects— but here, suddenly, inadvertently, it was creating realism.

While its synchronized speech received most attention, *The Jazz Singer* was also innovative, though less obviously, in its use of synchronized music.* Here Crosland was able to apply and develop ideas and techniques he had first employed in making *Don Juan*. As with the earlier film, music provided most of the synchronized sound in *The Jazz Singer*. However, where *Don Juan* was supplied with an original orchestral score, the music to *The Jazz Singer* was more varied and in some respects rather more complex. It consisted of popular songs (new and traditional), Jewish cantorial music, and an orchestral score composed partly of variations on the themes of popular songs and partly of excerpts from works by Debussy, Tchaikovsky, and Rimsky-Korsakov.

Seven popular songs were scattered through the picture. The first two—"My Gal Sal" by Paul Dresser and "Waiting for the Robert E. Lee" by L. Wolfe Gilbert and Lewis F. Muir—were lip-synced by Bobbie Gordon, who played Jakie Rabinowitz as a boy. They were reputedly sung by Jolson, though that seems impossible as the voice is quite unlike his. The remaining five were all definitely sung by Jolson. "Dirty Hands, Dirty Face" (by Jolson, Grant Clarke, Edgar Leslie, and James V. Monaco) and "Toot, Toot, Tootsie" (by Gus Kahn, Ernie Erdman, and Dan Russo) both occurred during the scene in Coffee Dan's nightclub. (This setting, incidentally, had been used in 1926 for a Vitaphone short starring William Demarest, who also appeared in the nightclub sequence of *The Jazz Singer*.) "Blue Skies" (by Irving Berlin) was sung by Jolson in his famous scene with Eugenie Besserer. It had originally been written for Belle Baker, who sang it in the show *Betsy* (1926). But the song did not become popular until Jolson sang it in *The Jazz Singer*. The fourth number, "Mother O' Mine" (by Jolson, Grant Clarke, and Lou Silvers) was the first of two that Jolson sang in blackface. The other blackface number was, of course, "My Mammy" (by Sam M. Lewis, Joe Young, and Walter Donaldson), which provided the film's finale. Aside from these numbers, several more traditional songs were used as background music. These pieces—which were not sung—included "The Sidewalks of New

---

* A recording of the complete soundtrack of *The Jazz Singer* has appeared on Sountrak ST-102 (Van Nuys, Cal.: Sunbeam Records, 1974) .

York," "In the Good Old Summertime," "If a Girl Like You Loved a Boy Like Me," and "Give My Regards to Broadway."

The cantorial music consisted of excerpts from "Kol Nidre" and the "Yahrzeit," both sung in Hebrew. The first was lip-synced by Warner Oland and actually sung by Cantor Rosenblatt, and Jolson himself sang part of "Kol Nidre" in the synagogue scene that occurs near the end of the film. In another scene, Jolson as Jack Robin goes to a concert of Jewish music and hears Rosenblatt, in person, singing the "Yahrzeit."

The orchestral score consists mainly of excerpts from Tchaikovsky's *Romeo and Juliet* Overture, brief snatches of Rimsky-Korsakov's *Scheherazade,* Debussy's "Beau soir," and orchestrations of "Mother O' Mine," "My Mammy," "Kol Nidre," and the more traditional popular songs.

The great achievement of Alan Crosland and Lou Silvers* (who was the film's musical director) was the integration of these very different musical styles into the same picture without any incongruity. They successfully realized stylistic combinations that had been attempted less effectively in the third Vitaphone program. Much of *The Jazz Singer*'s music may have sounded hackneyed even in 1927, and all of it was distasteful to sophisticated tastes such as Aldous Huxley's. But it appears that no one complained about the *combination* of popular songs and orchestral music, and of both of them with traditional cantorial melodies.

The skill with which the musical material was interwoven with the visual fabric of the picture can be exemplified by the opening of the movie—between the appearance of the film's title and our first view of the boy Jakie singing in a Lower East Side tavern. The music heard across the credits is a quotation from the opening of Tchaikovsky's *Romeo and Juliet* overture, which leads directly into the first of three brief, Hebraic-sounding themes (the other two are to be associated with Jakie's mother and father, respectively). The first theme, a tragic melody scored rather heavily for strings, accompanies the following

---

* Silvers had previously written scores for three D. W. Griffith films: *Way Down East* (1920), *Dream Street* (1921), and *Isn't Life Wonderful* (1924).

intertitles: "In every living soul a spirit cries for expression—perhaps this plaintive wailing song of Jazz is, after all, the misunderstood utterance of a prayer," and "The New York Ghetto throbbing to that rhythm of music which is older than civilization." Significantly, the mention of jazz is accompanied not by jazz or popular music of any kind but by the Jewish theme: that is, jazz and the Jewish spirit are immediately set in conflict—suggesting from the very outset the antagonism that will dominate the picture.

Although it is Jolson's songs that one remembers, from a dramatic standpoint it is the classical and cantorial music that pervades the film. This music is, of course, strongly associated with Jackie's father. Repeatedly, Tchaikovsky's themes interrupt and cut short the popular melodies that we identify with Jakie and his career in show business. But the fact that the Tchaikovsky passages are "love" music suggests the force that will eventually prevail over Jakie's rebellious spirit.

This force is particularly evident in two of the film's major sequences: Jakie's return home, and his ultimate decision to sacrifice his big opportunity and sing for his father. Jakie's arrival at his parents' home is accompanied not by a jazz theme but by a brief quotation from "Kol Nidre." We see Mama before she has noticed that her boy has come back. The music is now the gentle, Hebraic-sounding melody associated with Sara, the cantor's wife. Then, as she turns and sees Jakie, we hear, for the first time, the tune "Mother O' Mine" (it will not actually be sung until much later in the picture) followed by its preamble. So far there is no thematic or stylistic dominant in these musical snatches. Then Jakie takes his seat at the piano. In a moment, "Blue Skies" has established a new, buoyant tone: the jazz singer's spirit is in the ascendant. Suddenly, the cantor appears. His peremptory "Stop!" (*heard* over the sound track) receives the response of a *silent* intertitle ("Papa!") from Jakie.* Thereupon the interrupted piano piece gives way to the love theme from *Romeo and Juliet*. It is developed in full (the

---

* One commentator has made the following interesting observation about Papa's "Stop!" "It was the first word spoken on the screen that ever advanced a plot." Ben M. Hall, *The Best Remaining Seats* (New York: Bramhall House, 1961), p.249.

orchestral sound replacing the solo piano) as Jakie, in a smiling, conciliatory manner offers his father the prayer shawl he has bought for the cantor's sixtieth birthday. The development of the "love" theme continues as both gift and Jakie are rejected. But then, as Jakie leaves—with a resentful "Some day you'll understand as Mama does"—the strains of "Mother O'Mine" are picked up briefly. The juxtaposition of musical themes clearly emphasizes both the father's dominance and the son's allegiance to his mother.

Later in the film, Jakie is in his dressing room, blacking his face before going on stage. His girlfriend, Mary Dale, is watching him. Over the sound track we hear not a theme associated with Mary but "Mother O'Mine." Mary is encouraging him before his first big appearance on Broadway, but the music tells us that he is thinking of Mama. (This is one of many places in the film where music is used to reveal characters' thoughts or states of mind: it demonstrates the effective application of techniques that had been tried out to a much more limited degree in the making of *Don Juan*.) As Jakie completes his makeup, the music cuts to "My Mammy." Momentarily, the jazz singer is his buoyant self and the lively tune indicates that his concern for Mama has been absorbed into concern for the show. But at this point Mary mentions Jakie's father, and "My Mammy" suddenly cuts out. In its place we start to hear a wistful cantorial theme. A haggard-looking Jakie confesses that the songs of his people are tugging at his heart. He looks at himself in a mirror, but what he sees is a vision of a synagogue service. By now, the strains of "Kol Nidre" have developed out of the wistful cantorial melody. Meanwhile, Mama has arrived at the theater. As she enters Jakie's dressing room, "Kol Nidre" gives way to the Tchaikovsky "love" theme. The music alone tells us that the cantor will really be speaking through Mama. At first, Jakie resists her appeal to come to his father. He goes on stage, in blackface, and sings "Mother O'Mine," in rejection of the cantor. But afterwards he *does* go to see his father. Debussy's lovely melody "Beau soir" is heard during the death-bed scene, but when the picture cuts to the theater, where the producer of the show is announcing that the performance has been cancelled, we hear, once again, the strains of *Romeo and*

Juliet. The father's leitmotif has obliterated the music of the jazz singer. However, the movie ends with an expression of the mother's dominance when Jakie returns to the theater to sing "My Mammy."

In contrast to this overtly dramatic scoring, there are several scenes in the film where music is used for satiric effect. At the station where Jakie is about to hear the news that he is wanted for a Broadway show, one of his show-business colleagues is making envious comments about him. Our attitude towards her is influenced by the mocking, classical theme that accompanies her remarks. In another part of the movie, Yudelson the Kibbitzer is holding a meeting of the synagogue elders to determine who is to sing in place of the sick cantor (Jakie's father). An absurd quarrel develops, which is satirized in some comic variations on Hassidic themes.

These few examples are sufficient to demonstrate that *The Jazz Singer* is scored like a modern picture. Music is used to create moods and psychological effects, to build an inner drama parallel to the outer action, to suggest and emphasize dramatic conflicts, and to create and develop character. It is hardly an exaggeration to say that after having seen the film only once, one can look away from the screen during a second showing and follow the narrative entirely through the music.

No observations on *The Jazz Singer* would be complete without a few words about the songs. They were obviously selected to display Jolson's range as a performer. Accordingly, we have dramatic/pathetic numbers like "Dirty Hands, Dirty Face," lively, rhythmic songs like "Blue Skies," and sentimental/ nostalgic melodies like "Mother O'Mine." "My Mammy," the number that concludes the film, is a kind of summation of all the previous song styles. Characteristically, Jolson gives it everything he has. No one who has seen the film is ever likely to forget his impassioned rendering of that song as he goes down on one knee, arms thrown out to embrace the world, and with the light gradually fading out on his blackface, leaving only his white lips, white gloves, and tie momentarily visible.

The most vivid impression of Jolson at the summit of his career is Alexander Walker's recollection of him in the film's concluding scene:

Heavy-lidded, dark-eyebrowed, a skull-cap of hair, a lean, streaky, ever-eager look and a style that punches his personality over a row of imaginary footlights—Jolson plays the part like one who knows he is the star of the show. But what must have been striking at the time was the new dimension that sound could add even to this star personality. May McAvoy, as the singer's girl-friend, sums it up in one line when she tells him [in an earlier scene], "There are lots of jazz singers, but you have a tear in your voice."[60]

Many of the reviewers who were unenthusiastic about the film as a whole, considered *The Jazz Singer* a personal triumph for Jolson. Thus, Richard Watts, Jr., observed,

What they [the audience at the premiere] saw was an impressive triumph of both Mr. Jolson and the Vitaphone over the formerly silent drama. . . . But it should be recalled that this is not essentially a motion picture, but rather a chance to capture, for comparative immortality, the sight and sound of a great performer. . . . The Vitaphone makes the entertainment . . . a great show, but hardly a transcendent motion picture. . . . But, of course, the evening was Jolson's.[61]

An anonymous reviewer for *Picture Play* (January 1928) had praise for Jolson the singer, but was less than favorable about his acting or his interpretation of the lead role:

The Jazz Singer is important because of Al Jolson and the Vitaphone. As a picture it is second-rate, but with the comedian actually heard singing some of his famous numbers in conjunction with the story, *The Jazz Singer* offers genuine entertainment. As almost everyone knows, the comedy depicts the conflict between Jewish tradition and the glamor of theatrical life. . . . All this is perfectly fitted to Al Jolson's songs . . . and he sings them as only Jolson can. It is too bad that he does nothing to make his rôle real. Instead of being a wise-cracking youth, as the character was played on stage, Jack Robin in Jolson's hands becomes a veteran performer, who knows that he is the star of the picture and takes that fact with gravity. Thus it becomes no characterization at all, but simply an opportunity to see Jolson on the screen and hear his inimitable art. . . . Bobbie Gordon plays Jakie at thirteen. The boy makes you wish that Jakie hadn't stopped being such a good actor when he became Mr. Jolson.

Among the relatively few reviews that were unqualified in their admiration for every aspect of the picture was another anonymous one, in the trade paper *Moving Picture World,* which welcomed the picture as "The Best Show on Broadway," and described it as

> Entertainment all the way through, the sort of box-office combination of tears and smiles that will always be sure-fire. *The Jazz Singer* is nothing short of a magnificent triumph for Warner Brothers, for the Vitaphone, for Al Jolson, and for Director Alan Crosland. It should do tremendous business. . . . [62]

It did—wherever it was shown in its full Vitaphone version with synchronized sound. But in some theaters that were not wired for Vitaphone, the picture was presented with an accompaniment of ordinary phonograph records of Jolson played during appropriate scenes of the film. At such theaters, the box office returns were moderate at best. And in other theaters, where not even a record accompaniment was provided, the returns were far worse. The lesson was not lost on Warner Bros. Recorded music helped to "sell" the picture, but it was the unique, synchronized dialogue passages that were making it the big movie hit of the year.

At the end of 1927, as *The Jazz Singer* began its triumphal tour of the world's capitals, vast sums of money began to pour into Warner Bros.' empty coffers. The great gamble with sound was paying off. The burgeoning spirit of success was not dimmed by the untimely death of Sam Warner, who had led his brothers into the involvement with Vitaphone, or by the resignation of Alan Crosland and his screenwriter Bess Meredyth, who were seeking potentially greener pastures at Columbia Pictures.

Warner Bros.' optimism was symbolized by the newly approved trademark for the Vitaphone Corporation. Designed by Jack R. Keegan, the head of Vitaphone's publicity department, the trademark first appeared on the credits for *The Jazz Singer* and was subsequently to become a familiar sight on Warner and First National pictures. In its August 27, 1927 issue, *Moving Picture World* described it as

> simple and effective. The single word Vitaphone is strongly in the foreground across two tangential globes, each showing half of the

world. Around the background, tieing the whole together, is the motto that Vitaphone has adopted. This gives the complete message. "The Voice of the Screen—Vitaphone—is Thrilling the World."

It was. Ironically, only six years later it was rumored that the picture whose success Jolson had helped insure might be remade with Jolson in the lead role in order to help the star "recapture some of his *former* appeal."[63] The rumor was unfounded. Instead of a remake, Warner Bros. had actually decided to find out whether the original film still had any box-office attraction. As there were no longer any theaters equipped for showing Vitaphone, the film was re-released, in 1935, with its original sound-on-disk transferred to sound-on-film. The revival passed almost unnoticed. But A. F., in *Today's Cinema,* one of the few reviewers who considered the film worthy of comment, noted with surprise that despite its "flowery verbiage" and "frank sentimentality," its story was told with an admirable compactness. "Its sum total of entertainment is far from negligible for it has a vitality all its own and its well recorded score and camera qualities are on the credit side rather than the debit side."[64]

Jolson himself was never to do a remake of *The Jazz Singer. The Jolson Story* (1946), a Columbia production directed by Alfred E. Green, was a fanciful musical biography of the star, but it contained no scenes or recreations of scenes from *The Jazz Singer.* Jolson himself appeared, unrecognizably, in a long shot during one scene of *The Jolson Story,*[65] and his singing for the film was lip-synced by Larry Parks, who played the title role.

In their book, *Show Biz from Vaude to Video,* Abel Green and Joe Laurie quote the remark of *Variety's* editor Sime Silverman, "Al Jolson without a talking picture wouldn't mean a thing on the screen." They then comment:

> But a talking picture without Al Jolson could mean plenty—as long as it was about him, and had his voice—as *The Jolson Story* and its sequel, *Jolson Sings Again* [1949, a Columbia production directed by Henry Levin], proved almost twenty years later. Where *The Jazz Singer* earned $3,000,000 for Warners, and put them into the big league, the two "Jolson" pictures, via Columbia —Jack L. Warner had nixed the first one—grossed $15,000,000,

and over \$5,000,000 of that . . . accrued to Jolson as his net. Thus, already a legend within his own time, did Jolie complete the cycle from vaudeville to minstrelsy, to star at the Winter Garden, to the historic impetus that gave soundpix their start, and finally to glorification in celluloid as the subject, twice-over, of two bio-pix.[66]

In 1952, three years after Jolson's death, Warner Bros. decided, at last, to produce a remake of *The Jazz Singer*. Why? Presumably because Jack Warner wished to rectify his costly mistake in turning down the opportunity of making *The Jolson Story*. One *New York Times* film reviewer also suggested that there had been some "theorizing [at Warner Bros.] to the effect that the present generation would cotton to the remake of *The Jazz Singer* as much as its forebears did to the original."

The new version was directed by Michael Curtiz and starred Danny Thomas. It was made in Technicolor, had an updated plot, and except for "Kol Nidre," contained entirely different music from the original. The film's hero (played, of course, by Danny Thomas) was renamed Jerry Golding. Jerry is a Korean war veteran, "who returns to his Philadelphia home to find that he cannot carry on the family tradition, since his heart really does not belong to daddy, but to Miss [Peggy] Lee and life behind the footlights." The *New York Times* reviewer found this new version "well dressed" and "well mounted," but concluded, "They are not likely to change the course of film history with this *Jazz Singer*."[67]

CHAPTER SIX

LIGHTS OF

NEW YORK

AND SOUNDS

OF HOLLYWOOD

Something of the fragrance and mystery of the screen departed
on the echoes of *Sonny Boy*.
R. F. DELDERFIELD

1928: Hollywood's year of decision—Hollywood's year of transition. As it began, across the length and breadth of America there were still only 157, out of some 20,000 theaters, wired to show sound movies. And a mere 55 of them were equipped for sound-on-film. But within a year, no fewer than 1,046 theaters would be showing sound movies, and 1,032 of them would be equipped for both disk and film systems.[1]

1928: the brakes were off at Warner Bros. At Stages Three, Four, and Five production was in full swing. The Warner studio would, in fact, provide more than 30 percent of the eighty or so feature-length sound films that were to be made in Hollywood during this crucial year.

Four types of Vitaphone movie were produced for release to the rapidly increasing number of theaters that were wired for sound: silent features with added sound effects and/or musical accompaniments, short subjects, part-talkies, and, eventually, "100% all-talkies"—or "talkers," as they were sometimes called in 1928–29.

The first of the ten silent features supplied only with Vitaphone sound effects and/or a musical score was *Beware of Married Men* (premiered January 4, 1928), a farce about infidelity and divorce, directed by Archie L. Mayo and starring Irene Rich, Clyde Cook, Myrna Loy, and Richard Tucker. It was followed by: *A Race for Life* (January 28), a Rin-Tin-Tin melodrama, directed by D. Ross Lederman and starring (in addition to the celebrated dog star) Bobby Gordon, Carroll Nye, and Virginia Brown Faire; *The Little Snob* (February 11), a social comedy directed by John G. Adolfi and starring May McAvoy, John Miljan, and Robert Frazier; *Across the Atlantic* (February 25), a romantic drama about an air pilot—rather obviously exploiting the interest in Lindbergh's 1927 flight—directed by Howard Bretherton and starring Monte Blue, Edna Murphy, and Burr McIntosh; *Powder My Back* (March 10), a comedy-drama about flappers, directed by Roy Del Ruth and starring Irene Rich, Audrey Ferris, Carroll Nye, and André Beranger; *Domestic Troubles* (March 24), a farcical comedy about twins, directed by Ray Enright and starring Clyde Cook, Louise Fazenda, and Betty Blythe; *The Crimson City* (April 7), a melodrama with a Chinese setting, directed by Archie L. Mayo and starring Myrna Loy, John Miljan, Leila Hyams, Anna May Wong, and Richard Tucker; *Rinty of the Desert* (April 21), another Rin-Tin-Tin picture, directed by D. Ross Lederman and starring Rinty, Carroll Nye, Paul Panzer (onetime celebrated villain of the Pearl White serials), and Audrey Ferris; *Pay as You Enter* (May 12), a comedy about a waitress and her boyfriends, directed by Lloyd Bacon and starring Louise Fazenda, Clyde Cook, Myrna Loy, and William Demarest; and, finally, *Five-and-Ten-Cent Annie* (May 26), a slapstick farce about a salesgirl in love with a garbage collector who has inherited a fortune, directed by Roy Del Ruth and starring Louise Fazenda, Clyde Cook, and William Demarest. From this list it can be clearly seen that by 1928 Warner Bros. had established a repertoire of directors and actors specializing in films made for Vitaphone accompaniment.

Meanwhile, the usual variety of Vitaphone shorts—operatic, orchestral, vaudeville—was being produced on a regular schedule. Under Bryan Foy's supervision, the

> making of a one reel "short" was put through just as though it were a ten reel feature. . . . Theatre men had reported from the first that it was the "short," the thing in which the picture talked, that really gripped the audience. . . . Foy, used to the stage where talk was the first tool of the actor, wanted to use his one-reel shorts for talk. He wanted to make brief sketches, or acts. It was an experiment. They were willing to let him try it. They would try them on the public, mix them in with the regular vaudeville shorts, and see what the public's reaction to them was. They would be a feeler as to the acceptability of full-length talking pictures. In July 1927 . . . [Foy had] made a one-reel comedy called *The Bookworm.* In August 1927 he made a one-reel drama called *The Lash,* written by and featuring Hal Crane. It was an act Crane used in legitimate vaudeville. In October 1927, he made a two-reel drama called *Solomon's Children.* The real "Talkie" was expanding. . . . This last two-reeler had just been made when word came for "More Talk." *The Jazz Singer*'s premiere had been a sensation. Simultaneously the first of the one-reel talkies was being released to theatres and proving to be a great success. Talk, then, was going to be the order of the day.[2]

Tenderloin, Glorious Betsy, and *The Lion and the Mouse,* three of the Vitaphone features in production at Warner Bros. early in 1928, had originally been conceived along the lines of the ten features mentioned above; that is, as vehicles for nothing more ambitious than synchronized music and sound effects. But now, in the wake of public reaction to *The Jazz Singer* and to Foy's short talkies, it was hastily decided to supply these three features with recorded dialogue sequences. At this stage there would be no attempt to make a film with all dialogue recorded. After all, the tremendous interest in films that talked might be nothing more than a passing craze. Now that it looked as if Warner Bros. was going to survive the great gamble with Vitaphone, the company was playing a more cautious game.

Tenderloin, the first of the three features to be released, established the interim period of the part-talkie, which had unintentionally been anticipated with *The Jazz Singer.* A crook melodrama directed by Michael Curtiz, *Tenderloin* (premiered March 14, 1928 at Warners' Theatre in New York) starred Dolores Costello, Conrad Nagel, and John Miljan. The film was first shown with four talking sequences, but two of them proved damagingly ludicrous and were removed within the first week of the film's run. The two that were retained were scarcely any better. Movie critics were undecided whether they were more objectionable for being irrelevant or for being absurd.

> After reading the melodramatic phrases in the sub-titles, one is startled by the thundering voice of a sleuth [Fred Kelsey] trying to make our dainty heroine [Rose, played by Dolores Costello] confess that she stole the bag containing $50,000. . . . [Later] one comes to a sequence wherein Rose and the "Professor," a lame but immensely powerful man, are left alone in a country house. For this episode it was thought that the Vitaphone was necessary and therefore one again hears the blasts from shadows on the screen. . . . Mitchell Lewis is capable as the "Professor," but words such as he has to utter would destroy the value of any acting. It looks very much as if the title writer had supplied the words to the actors. At any rate the spectators were moved to loud mirth during the spoken episodes of this lurid film.[3]

Nevertheless, *Tenderloin* and the next two part-talkies "broke box office records . . . the public loved them and nobody but Warners was making them."[4]

Glorious Betsy came next, premiering at Warners' Theatre in New York on April 26, 1928. An historical drama about the love affair of Jerome Bonaparte (brother of Napoleon I) and Elizabeth (Betsy) Patterson, the Belle of Baltimore, this film was Alan Crosland's first deliberate venture into the part-talkie. Its stars were the same as *Tenderloin's*, but this time the reviewers were more receptive. Mordaunt Hall of the *New York Times* actually preferred *Glorious Betsy* to Sidney Olcott's *Monsieur Beaucaire* (1924), one of Valentino's most admired films. Although the spoken dialogue scenes did not impress him as significant contributions to the film ("In this instance it is the picture that matters rather than the spoken word"), he praised Dolores Costello's restrained utterances as "decidedly effective" and singled out another, nondialogue Vitaphone se-

quence for especially favorable comment. This last was an episode in which André de Segurola, a Metropolitan Opera singer,
gave a stirring rendition of "La Marseillaise." On the debit
side, Hall deplored Conrad Nagel's failing even to attempt a
suggestion of French pronunciation in his role as Jerome
Bonaparte. It was already clear from the first two part-talkies
that the coming of sound would demand radical changes on
the part of screenwriters and actors. Nevertheless, the reviewer's
concluding assessment of *Glorious Betsy* was unusually generous
—towards its director. The film was, he maintained, Crosland's
"outstanding pictorial achievement. The narrative flows gently
and there is always a measure of suspense. . . . Crosland is to be
congratulated on his direction of the film."[5]

Glorious Betsy was the first sound movie seen by director
William C. DeMille (Cecil's elder brother). A memorable ac-
count of the experience was recorded in his book, *Hollywood
Saga* (1939):

> In April, 1928 . . . The Warner Brothers were opening their
> new Hollywood Theater with a picture called *Glorious Betsy*. . .
> and, as we had heard that there was some sort of new-fangled
> sound effect connected with the production, I took [my wife]
> Clara [Beranger] along to see what it was all about. We knew,
> of course, that experiments were being made in talking pictures,
> but that sort of thing had been going on for years. In fact, I
> myself had lost a few hundred dollars to oblige a friend who had
> devised a film-phonograph combination which was very scientific
> and most interesting but which, unfortunately, never worked. . . .
>
> We sat in the darkened theater and watched *Glorious Betsy*
> unwind herself. For several reels it was just a regular picture, the
> plot of which I have forgotten, but I shall never forget the mo-
> ment when André de Segurola, playing the part of a military
> officer, stood in the middle of the picture to address the group
> around him.
>
> "Ladies and gentlemen," he said.
> *He said!*
> A thrill ran through the house. The screen had spoken at last;
> an operation had been performed and the man, dumb from
> infancy, could talk. No one minded, at first, the gentle, crackling
> noise [amplified surface noise of the recording] which pervaded

the scene. It sounded like a grass fire, but it was to turn into a conflagration which swept away the Hollywood we had known and forced us to build a new city on the ruins of the old.

Many in that audience missed the full significance of what was happening. The voice was tinny, tubby and bellowy in turn, but what did that matter? It had *spoken* to us from the screen; it had *said:* "Ladies and gentlemen". . . .

As I realized the future possibilities of what I was seeing and hearing, I felt a nervous quiver run through me. . . . The nervous tension and sense of excitement which I felt on that night of April 26, 1928, was to last all through the first two hectic years of "sound."[6]

The Lion and the Mouse, directed by Lloyd Bacon and starring Lionel Barrymore and May McAvoy, received its premiere almost two months after *Glorious Betsy,* on June 15, 1928, at Warners' Theatre, New York. Based on a melodrama by Charles Klein, about a ruthless financier who tries to ruin an innocent judge by accusing him of taking bribes, it had previously been filmed in 1919 with Alice Joyce as the star. The *New York Times* review offered a particularly acute critique of this latest, part-talkie version, and also demonstrated a clear understanding of the drastic improvements that would be necessary if Warner Bros. was to venture further into the making of spoken dialogue movies. The review starts out with high praise of Lionel Barrymore.

Mr. Barrymore's knowledge of diction, linked with his splendid acting, overwhelmed the other players who were evidently handi-capped . . . by the fact that they were aware that they had also to be heard. . . . Mr. Barrymore's work alone . . . demonstrated that with adequate histrionic talent a really laudable picture with speech is not only possible, but virtually on the wing. In each of the three attempts at a speaking picture the Warner Brothers have made strides, but the words spoken in last night's presenta-tion show that they still need far more careful thought given to the lines. William Collier Jr., May McAvoy and even Alec Francis appear merely to speak their lines so that they can be heard . . . and the consequence is that this trio of performers, in what they say via the Vitaphone, are sadly reminiscent of the old melodrama days. . . . Mr. Barrymore is marvellously natural and in speaking he really enhances his characterization. But it is quite disappointing to hear the trite and ineffectual words of his colleagues. . . . It is also a mistake to have silent sequences and then to hear a character who has been silent suddenly boom forth into speech. . . . It is quite obvious from this Vitaphoned picture that the ordinary screen players, who have been noted for their agreeable presence, will find it necessary to go through a course of stage training before they can deliver competent performances in a Vitaphoned feature.[7]

But there was no time for lessons. For *Lights of New York,* Warner Bros.' first all-dialogue picture, opened at the Mark Strand Theatre, New York, on July 8, 1928. The age of the talkies had dawned.

Despite its obvious historical importance, *Lights of New York* is a little-known film today. For every thousand persons who have seen *The Jazz Singer* it is doubtful if there are more than a handful who have even heard of *Lights of New York*. Few film societies have shown any interest in reviving it, and few film historians have made any effort to see it or comment upon it from direct experience. Mel Gussow, a recent biographer of movie tycoon Darryl F. Zanuck, observes that *Lights of New York* was

> probably one of the worst pictures ever made. There are still titles, but more hysterical than ever, as if the titlewriter, with the advent of sound, had decided to speak louder himself. [In fact, the film has only three intertitles and none of them is hysterical.] "In the symphony of jazz," goes a typical title, "there are many blue-notes." [Actually, this title does not appear in the film at all!] Worst of all is the self-conscious use of sound. The picture is a veritable cacophony of cars screeching, whistles, doors slamming —as if a sound man had run amuck.[8] [This totally incorrect statement can only have been made by someone who has imagined what the film was like without having seen it.] *

We have relied too long on inaccurate descriptions of this kind. A more careful look at the picture is long overdue.

---

* Richard Schickel, *The Stars* (New York: Bonanza Books, 1972), p. 113, describes *Lights of New York* as "another banal musical . . . in its first crude form . . . the backstage story of the kid waiting for the first break. . . ." This description is also totally incorrect.

Lights of New York was directed by Bryan Foy, photographed by Ed DuPar, and edited by Jack Killifer. The story, scenario, and dialogue of this Prohibition-era melodrama were by Murray Roth and Hugh Herbert. The film's opening intertitles emphasize both its topicality and the thematic importance of its contrasting small-town and big-city locations:

> This is a story of Main Street and Broadway—a story that might have been torn out of last night's newspaper.
>
> Main Street—forty-five minutes from Broadway—but a thousand miles away.

Two naive barbers, Eddie Morgan (Cullen Landis) and his pal Gene (Eugene Pallette), run their sleepy business in a small-town hotel owned by Eddie's mother. Eddie dreams of having a successful career in New York and also of joining his girlfriend, Kitty Lewis (Helene Costello), who has become a nightclub queen in the big city. A golden opportunity seems to present itself when two amiable hotel guests—actually a couple of con-men—offer Eddie and Gene the chance of buying a lucrative barbershop in New York provided they can put up the necessary capital. The two barbers have no money, and Eddie's mother (Mary Carr) is reluctant to provide it until she is introduced to the con-men and taken in by their apparent honesty.

The scene shifts to New York. Eddie and Gene, now set up in their new barbershop, discover that it is actually a front for a gang of bootleggers. The bootleggers rob a liquor warehouse and kill a cop as they are making their getaway.

In Central Park, Eddie and Kitty talk over their problems. Eddie wants to pull out of the barbershop without losing his mother's money. Kitty is sick of nightclub life. Eddie gives her a gun to protect herself from unwelcome admirers.

Kitty's boss, Hawk Miller (Wheeler Oakman), runs a joint called the Night Hawk. He is also head of the bootlegging racket. Hawk gives the brush-off to Molly Thompson (Gladys Brockwell), his former mistress. He is interested in Kitty. But Molly warns him to keep away from her. Hawk assumes that he can get Kitty for himself if her boyfriend is removed, so he plans a frame-up. Eddie is duped into taking possession of the stolen liquor; then Hawk informs the cops when and where they can find it. By chance, Kitty overhears the dastardly scheme and manages to warn Eddie. Hawk arrives at the barbershop expecting to witness the end of his rival, but he is mysteriously shot just before the police arrive. The killer's identity seems clear when Detective Crosby (Robert Elliott) finds the murder weapon: it is the gun that Eddie had given to Kitty.

The scene shifts to Kitty's apartment. The young couple are about to be arrested by Detective Crosby when Molly appears and confesses that she had shot the Hawk for deserting her and showing interest in another woman. She also reveals that it was Hawk Miller who had shot the cop during the warehouse robbery. Crosby responds to this confession with comforting words. Molly has saved the young couple, and the law will be kind to her. She will actually get a reward for getting rid of a cop-killer. Turning to the young couple, Crosby advises them to leave the big city as soon as possible and go back where they came from. Eddie and Kitty—needing no further encouragement—take the next train out of New York.

With all its absurdities of motivation, plot, and character, *Lights of New York* is no worse than the average crook melodrama of the late twenties. The picture has a familiar major theme and several well-worked minor ones. Its strongest emphasis is on the corruptions and dangers of the big city and the implied virtues and safety of small-town life. (This theme had a venerable melodramatic tradition in the theater long before the movies were born.) In *Lights of New York* it is hammered out with the subtlety of a steamroller. Except for Detective Crosby, the stern, authoritarian opponent of criminal chaos, all the "good guys" are naive, small-town folks. All the "bad guys" are sophisticated city slickers. Eddie's hometown is slow and unglamorous but peaceful, whereas New York is presented as a place of ever-present danger, whose attractive "lights" glamorize a corrupt world of criminals, con-men, seducers, and fallen women, and tempt the innocent and the unsuspecting into a downward spiral of destruction. At the end of the picture, Crosby turns to Eddie and Kitty and reinforces the movie's moral: "If you both will take my tip, you'll get out of this city.

Don't you see how close you've been to tragedy? Take a train to the country where there's trees and flowers and mountains. Leave the roaring Forties to roar without you."

A lesser melodramatic theme related to the main one concerns the evil consequences of wanting more than one has. The moral is evident in countless movies both before and after *Lights of New York:* be satisfied or you'll get your comeuppance. Eddie Morgan's discontent and his desire to make a big success of himself by turning his back on the place where he belongs lead him into the entrapments of the city. He becomes rather like an unfunny Harold Lloyd—melodrama is, in many respects, a serious variation of farce—living out the disillusions of the American dream, discovering and enduring the unforeseen consequences of ambition, but surviving because he has learned his lesson and is now eager to return to his Garden of Eden in upstate New York. Hawk Miller's fate typifies the "poetic justice" of much movie melodrama. The consequences of the villain's attempt to destroy another is to destroy himself. Hawk sets a trap for Eddie, but meets his own death when he tries to spring it. Finally, in a typical melodramatic denouement, justice reasserts itself. Molly, we are assured, will not have to pay the penalty for killing her faithless lover, while Eddie and Kitty will live happily ever after, secure in the haven they should never have left.

It was, of course, the sound and not the story that distinguished Bryan Foy's picture. And in this respect alone it was truly a remarkable film. *Lights of New York* ran for a mere fifty-seven minutes, but twenty-two of its twenty-four sequences contained recorded dialogue. These passages were consistently audible, generally very well synchronized, and often lasted for several minutes at a time. Except for the opening intertitle and a later title introducing the Night Hawk club, the movie relied throughout on the spoken—not the written—word. It would have been meaningless if shown as a silent picture.

Film historians have repeatedly maintained that the coming of sound shackled the movie camera. But strictly speaking, that was no longer true by the time Vitaphone pictures were being made in Hollywood. The newly designed camera booths in operation at Stages Three, Four, and Five allowed for much more camera movement than had been possible at the Manhattan Opera House. However, the

> complete shifting of camera, microphone, and electrical apparatus [involved a] time-taking procedure . . . for almost every "set-up".
> . . . Movies thus shrank to a minimum number of shots, as a stage play is restricted to a limited number of scenes. Synchronization of sound and image was a highly exacting task, curtailing the director's freedom; and editing itself returned to the rudimentary level of pre-war [World War I] days.[9]

It was the actor who was really shackled. He had become the slave of the microphone. In order to achieve a satisfactorily audible recording of the human voice, it was necessary (just as it had been with the pre-1910 disk systems of Gaumont and Edison) for the performer to be as close as possible to the microphones.[10] His restricted range of movement was scarcely apparent in relatively static scenes from grand opera, but it was a very different matter in an incident-packed melodrama.

There were at most two hidden microphone placements on any given set for *Lights of New York,* and the actors were directed to keep as near to them as possible whenever they spoke. The results were frequently ludicrous. Characters who were standing up while making long speeches seemed inexplicably rooted to the same spot; characters who were engaged in conversation often seemed to be huddled ridiculously close together. In one scene, a microphone concealed in a headrest explains Eddie's curious fondness for speaking only when he is standing beside an empty barber chair. In another, the M.C. at the Night Hawk "dances" and sings "Morning Glory" without moving from a fixed spot beneath a bunch of festoons that concealed a microphone. In yet another barbershop scene, Gene crosses the room and stands close to Eddie in order to read the newspaper headlines *aloud!* When Hawk calls a meeting of his "boys" they go into a huddle around a telephone prominently placed in the foreground. It is, of course, another concealed microphone.[11] Unintentionally disconcerting effects are created in several scenes in which there were microphone placements on each side of a room. Actors appearing in these scenes sometimes start out by speaking within earshot of one microphone, then lapse into a silence that lasts until they have crossed the room and are within range of the second microphone. The musical *Singin' in the Rain* (1952) amusingly parodies such absurdities of the early dialogue film—though several scenes of *Lights of New York* are even more hilarious than the parody.

Unnatural movements were not, unfortunately, the only shortcomings of *Lights of New York*. Some of the actors had little or no idea of how to deliver spoken lines, and they received inadequate direction from Bryan Foy. Also, much of the dialogue was repetitive, and some of it was ridiculous and could not have been made to sound any better by even the most experienced actors. Mary Carr's delivery was by far the worst. Although she was a talented veteran of the silent screen (she had received critical acclaim for her performances in *Mrs. Wiggs of the Cabbage Patch,* 1919, and *Over the Hill,* 1920), her misguided notion of rendering lines of spoken dialogue was to say them at a speed equivalent to that of the most painfully slow reader of silent film intertitles. Cullen Landis was scarcely any better. His words trickled out as if he had taken a heavy dose of sleeping pills. Mary Carr soon got the idea of what sound movies required and went on to obtain parts in at least a dozen films during the thirties, as well as to make a late appearance in *Friendly Persuasion* (1956). But for Cullen Landis, *Lights of New York* was almost the end of the road. He had appeared in approximately fifty silent movies, but after *Lights* he went on to make only five more films, including one talkie, *The Convict's Code* (1930). Aside from his inability to adapt to the new demands of sound pictures, Landis suffered from the fact that he looked very much like Richard Arlen without possessing any of Arlen's talent.

The actor with the most sensitivity to the new medium was Wheeler Oakman, who generally knew how to make Hawk Miller's lines sound natural. Oakman had played various roles in Hollywood movies since the teens, and before acquiring his moustache, had costarred with Bill Farnum in the first version of *The Spoilers* (1914), but his performance in *Lights of New York* established him as the ideal heavy for early sound gangster pictures. He was soon to be in great demand and appeared in no fewer than a dozen talkies or part-talkies during 1929. His career continued well into the thirties, and serial addicts still fondly remember the delicious villainy with which he opposed Buster Crabbe in *Flash Gordon's Trip to Mars* (Universal, 1938).

Lights of New York is a rich mine for collectors of movie clichés; here are a few of its choicest gems:

> **Sequence 11:** Kitty's dressing room at the Night Hawk: Kitty and Eddie.
> **Kitty:** . . . Don't you ever get bored looking at me, Eddie?
> **Eddie:** Well I get bored looking at anyone but you. . . . You know, someday I'm going to have a night club all of my own with no one in it but you and me . . .

> **Sequence 24:** Kitty's apartment: Kitty and Eddie, Molly and Crosby—
> **Molly** [having just revealed that *she* had killed the Hawk]: . . . He was no good—but *I* loved him. Well, he's gone now. . . . That's all. [She turns to Detective Crosby] Come on, let's get it over with. I'm not afraid. I've lived—and I've loved—and I've lost!

These phrases were, of course, the well-worn language of stage melodrama. Less familiar and more effective was the slangy gangster dialogue already pointing the way to its racier and more skillful treatment in the screenplays of Francis Faragoh (*Little Caesar,* 1930) and Kubec Glasmon (*The Public Enemy,* 1931):

> **Sequence 21:** Hawk's office: the Hawk with two of his "boys."
> **Hawk:** Now we'd better cover ourselves up. I've planted the stuff in Eddie's shop—
> **1st crook:** Yeah?
> **Hawk:** —and the dicks'll be there at ten o'clock—
> **1st crook:** Uh-huh.
> **Hawk:** BUT–THEY–MUST–NOT–FIND–EDDIE!
> **1st crook** (Puzzled): What do you want *us* to do?
> **Hawk:** I want you guys to make him disappear.
> **1st crook** (even more puzzled): Disappear?
> **Hawk:** Certainly. If they don't find him it will cinch everything for us. Don't you understand?
> **1st crook:** You mean—?
> **Hawk:** TAKE HIM FOR——A RIDE!
> **1st crook** (suddenly seeing the light): O——oh!

Although so much of *Lights of New York* was undeniably ridiculous, there were a few flashes of intelligence in Foy's direction of the picture. Realizing that the limited movements of his actors would prevent him from staging a fast-paced warehouse robbery in full view of the cameras, Foy cleverly shot the sequence as an interplay of shadows and relied on music and sound effects to build suspense. Then, as an anonymous review for the *New York Times* notes, there was also "careful direction . . . in a cabaret scene when a door opens and the music sounds louder . . . when it closes again, the music grows dim."[12]

Throughout much of the film, the music, while not particularly tasteful or original, was used sensibly and with admirable restraint. It occurs naturally enough when the M.C. sings, when Kitty and her all-girl chorus of Dancing Pirates go through their routines, or when one of the con-men turns on the radio; elsewhere, it provides an ironically optimistic mood at the start of the film (light vaudeville music plays behind the dialogue), serves to introduce the New York sequences ("Give My Regards to Broadway" is played during a montage of street scenes), and intensifies both the robbery sequence and Molly's confession. But music is absent from certain sequences (such as the episodes in Hawk's office) in which Foy evidently assumed that it would distract attention from the dialogue.

Shortly after the premiere of *Lights of New York* an editorial in the *Exhibitors' Herald and Moving Picture World* found it

> particularly interesting to note in this picture the development of a new technic—one that differs radically from the practices that have characterized the best motion pictures of recent years. With the introduction of dialogue, the closeup is dispensed with and its absence is hardly noticeable because the spoken word easily and more naturally yields the desired emphasis. Also various kinds of scenes—such as cabaret sequences which never previously meant much except for atmospheric purposes—with dialogue and music become high spots in the production.

The same editorial observed that

> *Lights of New York* is a graphic illustration of where the synchronized picture is leading. . . . Without the synchronization . . . [it] would be a picture that would not materially stir the motion picture market. As a film it is not a subject that even nearly ranks

with the best efforts of Warner Brothers, but under the magic
of the dialogue accompaniment it becomes a thoroughly interesting picture and one that doubtlessly will be a major attraction
for the theatres during the coming season.[13]

It was. As another commentator noted,

> The first all-talking picture, without even a subtitle, caught the
> interest of New York. . . . An audience that ranged from Ina
> Claire to Tammany Young gathered to take a look and a hear.
> . . . [It] drew unusual crowds to the Strand on Monday afternoon,
> a blistering hot day. There was a line at the box office and seats
> were at a premium. At the end of every show the audience broke
> into spontaneous applause.[14]

In a separate article, the same commentator stated:

> The synchronized picture, admittedly the most brilliant develop-
> ment of the film industry in recent years, has captured the
> imagination and the interest of a world intent on motion pictures.
> Synchronized pictures hold the center of the screen. . . .[15]

In the final analysis, there are two important things to be
said about *Lights of New York*. First, it had demonstrated that
a feature-length talking picture could be made. But much more
significantly, it had revealed to the astonished Warner Bros.
and to the disturbed and even more dumbfounded movie industry as a whole that such a film could attract audiences. They
looked, they listened, and sometimes they laughed in the wrong
places—but they kept on coming. And it was the talk, not the
music, that brought them in droves to the Mark Strand Theatre.
The movie industry's reluctant recognition of the film's importance was anticipated by the *New York Times* reviewer:
"*Lights of New York*," he wrote, "is the alpha of what may
develop as the new language of the screen. . . . While the picture
could not be described as the best of entertainment, it is novel
and may, in its halting manner, be pointing the way to the
future."[16]

With the success of *Lights of New York*, Bryan Foy was firmly
established at Warner Bros. But his talents were quickly and
correctly recognized as those of a producer rather than a director. He was, in fact, to direct only a handful of movies, but went

on to become a major producer. During the mid-thirties he headed Warner Bros.'

> "B" or program picture unit . . . [and] was assigned to make twenty-six features with a total budget of $5,000,000.00. (The "A" picture, *The Life of Emile Zola,* cost approximately $1,000,000.00 in 1936.) Foy's pictures featured inserts (newspaper clips) which advanced the story without using actors. He employed many closeups to keep attention diverted from the sets. About half of Foy's pictures were remakes of past Warner Brothers films. . . .[17]

Later, he would occasionally free-lance. For example, he produced *Guadalcanal Diary* (1943) for 20th Century-Fox. But most of his big successes were produced for Warner Bros. Among them were *I Was a Communist for the F.B.I.* (1951); *House of Wax* (1953), the most successful film of the short-lived 3-D craze; and *PT 109* (1963), the movie about John F. Kennedy's wartime exploits. Like Alan Crosland, Foy's career is a subject worthy of future research.

Following *Lights of New York,* Warner Bros. released three all-talkie and seven part-talkie Vitaphone features during 1928.

First came an all-talkie, *The Terror,* a horror-mystery based on a novel by Edgar Wallace. Directed by Roy Del Ruth and starring Edward Everett Horton, May McAvoy, Louise Fazenda, and John Miljan, it was premiered at Warners' Theatre in New York on August 15, 1928. The *New York Times* referred to it as a "titleless talking film," and observed that in this second all-talking Vitaphone production, "it appears to be infra dig. to have the slightest suggestion of the familiar subtitle. Even the main title, the cast of players and the names of those who have contributed to the making of this audible film are announced from the screen by the shadow of a masked man."[18]

The masked man was the Terror, a criminal in a black hood who pursued the heroine through the secret tunnels and passages of an old dark house. There are numerous similarities to Paul Leni's highly successful *The Cat and the Canary* (1927), one of the most interesting being the parallel between the comic character Ferdinand Fane (played by Horton) in Del Ruth's picture and the comic hero Paul Jones (Creighton Hale) in Leni's film. Neither character turned out to be as foolish as he seemed. Mordaunt Hall considered *The Terror* to be the best Vitaphone feature he had seen, and praised Del Ruth for shrewdly combining good motion picture ideas with the sound material. Horton and Otto Hoffman (who played Soapy Marks, a criminal) were singled out for their impressive performances. The picture had its shortcomings, but they were chiefly due

> to the manner in which the performers speak their lines and not to the Vitaphone device. . . . with most of the [actors] . . . the speech comes forth as if by command and with a tardiness that is hardly natural. It also seems as if Miss McAvoy had somebody else do the screaming for her, as the screams at various junctures are far louder than one would expect from Miss McAvoy after hearing her modest attempts at speech.[19]

The Terror quickly eclipsed the appeal of *Lights of New York* to become Warner Bros.' most lucrative picture since *The Jazz Singer*. Its commercial success was immediate on both sides of the Atlantic. Rachel Low notes that *The Jazz Singer,* which received its British premiere on September 27, 1928, was closely followed by *The Terror* (October 1928). "These pictures created a sensation, especially when it was heard later that Warner Brothers' profit for 1928 would be over £1,600,000."[20]

The next Vitaphone feature was the part-talkie *State Street Sadie* (Mark Strand Theatre, September 2, 1928). It was yet another crook melodrama, directed by Archie L. Mayo and starring Conrad Nagel and Myrna Loy. The lead performances were well received; one of them, Myrna Loy, was rising to stardom through her appearances in Vitaphone features. The film itself demonstrated no progress in the handling of recorded dialogue and was only a moderate success at the box office.

It was followed, however, by a box-office triumph, *The Singing Fool*. It was Al Jolson's second feature, and a part-talkie. Warner Bros. released in advance a fifteen-minute preview titled "Al Jolson in Announcement Trailer for *The Singing Fool*." The preview is described as follows in the copyright statement on file in the Library of Congress: "Al Jolson walks on in blackface, to applause offscene. He whistles to stop it and tells his audience of his picture, *The Singing Fool*. He tells of his airplane trip East, and concludes by urging his hearers to see his new picture and thanking them for having seen his old one."

The film had originally been named *Sonny Boy*, after what was to become its best-loved song, but was premiered as *The Singing Fool* at the Winter Garden in New York, on September 19, 1928. It was transferred to the Sam H. Harris Theatre on March 11, 1929 in order to make way for Michael Curtiz's Vitaphone (part-talkie) epic, *Noah's Ark*. *The Singing Fool* was directed by Lloyd Bacon and photographed by Byron Haskin. The screenplay was the work of Leslie S. Barrows and C. Graham Baker, and Jolson's supporting actors were Betty Bronson, Josephine Dunn, Arthur Housman, Robert Emmett O'Connor, and, of course, little Davey Lee, who played Sonny Boy. The brothers Warner, correctly attributing their meteoric surge of prosperity to their association with Jolson and the Vitaphone, had decided to treat this latest golden combination as the opportunity for a gala occasion.

> The price for orchestra seats for this first performance was $11. The tickets were of gilded cardboard with a drawing of Mr. Jolson as he is and then in blackface. The men on the doors did not take up these tickets, but permitted the holders to retain them as souvenirs of the occasion. . . . After the film had faded from the screen Mr. Jolson was called to the stage. The first words he said were:
>
> "What can I say?"
>
> To this a thousand voices shouted, "Sing!"
>
> Mr. Jolson talked, however, and said that he thought that *The Singing Fool* was a better production than his first film, *The Jazz Singer*. He referred to the fact that he had been eighteen years with the Shuberts and that he was going back on the stage under their management, but would make several more pictures, possibly, before doing so.[21]

In its songs and sentiment and in its Pagliacci-like climax of a heartbroken singer performing in spite of himself, the appeal of *The Singing Fool* was much the same as that of *The Jazz Singer,* but it was also touched by the vogue of the gangster melodrama. Jolson plays Al Stone, a singing waiter at Blackie Joe's café. He writes a song hit, becomes a vaudeville star, and marries Molly Winton (Josephine Dunn). In due course, Molly deserts him for a big-time racketeer (Reed Howes); when she leaves she takes their child, Sonny Boy, along with her. Now that he is desolate, Al's fortunes take a nose dive. He becomes a bum with nothing to live for, but is eventually saved by Grace (Betty Bronson), a cigarette girl at Blackie Joe's who encourages him to make a comeback. As Al's fortunes are taking an upward turn, tragedy strikes. Sonny Boy dies. But the show must go on. Brokenhearted, Al goes on stage and sings his child's favorite song ("When there are grey skies,/I don't mind the grey skies,/You make them blue, Sonny Boy. . . ./And the angels grew lonely,/Took you 'cause they were lonely;/I'm lonely too, Sonny Boy.") Time passes. Grace's love helps to relieve Al's anguish. Finally, when he is able to look life in the face once more, Al goes off to California, taking Grace with him.

Mordaunt Hall spoke for the majority of critics and reviewers who were won over by the magnetism of Jolson.

> Mr. Jolson has put a great deal of feeling into both his singing and acting in this new offering, in which there are peculiarly appealing bits of sentiment, especially when Mr. Jolson, as Al Stone, tells bedtime stories and sings to his little boy. . . . It is charming when Al Stone reveals his love for the child and it is wonderfully affective when Sonny Boy's terse utterances are heard from the screen. A child named David Lee figures as Sonny Boy and he is perhaps more natural in his speech than any of the adults in the film. . . . The chief interest in this production, however, is not in its transparent narrative, but in Mr. Jolson's inimitable singing.[22]

Jolson's seven songs for this picture were to sweep the world, reaping fabulous royalties in sheet music and record sales.* Aside from "Sonny Boy" by Lew Brown, B. G. DeSylva, and Ray Henderson, they were "It All Depends on You" and "I'm Sittin' on Top of the World" (also by Brown, DeSylva, and Henderson); and "There's a Rainbow Round My Shoulder," "The Spaniard Who Blighted My Life," "Golden Gate," and "Keep Smilin' at Life" (all by Billy Rose, Al Jolson, and Dave Dreyer). Also, as background and mood music, Lou Silvers, the film's music director, supplied an arrangement of Leoncavallo's "Vesti la guibba" from *I Pagliacci*.

---

* The film itself racked up a box-office record that was not to be broken until ten years later—with the success of *Gone with the Wind*.

The most popular song, beyond question, was "Sonny Boy." Al's brother, Harry, provides an interesting anecdote about its composition.

> Warner Brothers rushed Al into another full-length talking picture, *The Singing Fool.* There was a feature song in it which Al did not like when he heard it at a preview.
>
> He dashed out of the theater, went to a telephone and called Buddy DeSylva who was in Atlantic City. Briefly he stated his woes and demanded a song.
>
> "What is it supposed to be about?" asked DeSylva.
>
> "Well, first I am talking with a boy. Then I sing."
>
> "How old is the boy supposed to be?" DeSylva countered.
>
> "He is about three, and is standing at my knee."
>
> "That's fine," DeSylva said. "I have two lines ready. 'Climb upon my knee, sonny boy; although you're only three, sonny boy.' Why don't you take it from there?"
>
> Al took it from there, and "Sonny Boy" was the hit of *The Singing Fool.* It brought Al a fortune from the sales of sheet music and records.[23]

Jolson's career as a movie star peaked with *The Singing Fool.* He would go on to star in ten or more sound movies, but none of them aroused the universal excitement generated by his first two Vitaphone features. Through *The Jazz Singer* and *The Singing Fool,* Jolson and the talkies became identified in the public mind during the first years of the sound era—although, as we have seen, neither of these films was a true, all-talkie. After attending *The Singing Fool* in October 1928, P. S. Harrison, editor of *Harrison's Reports,* expressed what was rapidly becoming an accepted viewpoint both inside and outside the film industry: "I could not help coming to the conclusion that talking pictures are here to stay, that they are a permanent institution, the kind that fires the imagination of the picturegoer."[24]

After *The Singing Fool,* Warner Bros. released another part-talkie, *Women They Talk About* (premiered at the Strand Theatre, New York, October 14, 1928), a comedy-drama about a career woman whose daughter was a flapper. Directed by Lloyd Bacon, it starred Irene Rich, Audrey Ferris, Claude Gillingwater, and John Miljan. Warner Bros.' third all-talkie, *The Home Towners,* came next. Premiered at Warners' Theatre on

October 23, 1928, this picture was directed by Bryan Foy and starred Doris Kenyon, Richard Bennett, Robert Edeson, and John Miljan. *The Home Towners* was based on a popular play by George M. Cohan and had the added distinction of being the first all-talkie without any song sequences. It was followed by another part-talkie, Roy Del Ruth's *Beware of Bachelors* (October 27, 1928). This picture continued a late-twenties vogue of farces of marital infidelity that had begun with Wesley Ruggles's silent *Beware of Widows* (Universal Pictures, 1927) and progressed through Archie Mayo's aforementioned Vitaphone *Beware of Married Men* and George B. Seitz's silent *Beware of Blondes* (Columbia Pictures, July 1928). Del Ruth's picture starred Audrey Ferris, William Collier, and André Beranger, and it concerned a vamp's involvements with a quarrelsome couple. Thereafter came another part-talkie gangster melodrama: *The Midnight Taxi* (premiered at the Mark Strand, October 28, 1928). Directed by John Adolfi, it starred Helene Costello, Antonio Moreno, and Myrna Loy. The program featuring *The Midnight Taxi* also included a Movietone newsreel that, for the first time, was preceded by a recorded voice announcing what was to become a familiar slogan, "Ladies and Gentlemen, we offer you the news of the world, in sound and pictures. . . ."

Warner Bros.' fourth all-talkie, *On Trial* (premiered November 14 at Warners' Theatre), was based on a courtroom drama by Elmer Rice. Directed by Archie L. Mayo, it starred Pauline Frederick, Lois Wilson, Bert Lytell, Richard Tucker, and Jason Robards. The sound system appears to have been less than satisfactory for this film. At its worst, Vitaphone tended to distort *S* sounds into a pronounced lisp; with *On Trial* the distortion was evidently excessive. At any rate, many reviewers complained about it and also about the poor diction of some of the performers. *On Trial* was followed by the part-talkie *Caught in the Fog* (premiered December 2 at the Mark Strand), a comedy drama about a gang of burglars and a rich young man trying to pass himself off as a butler. It was directed by Howard Bretherton and starred May McAvoy, Conrad Nagel, and Mack Swain. The *New York Times* reviewer found the movie "adroitly directed, cleverly acted and nicely photographed," but noted that the "vocal angle . . . begins with a series of intentional whispers, following which there are mute passages relieved by periodical outbursts of brave dialogue."[25]

Warner Bros. wound up its Vitaphone offerings for 1928 with another box-office blockbuster. This time the star was Fanny Brice, queen of the *Ziegfeld Follies*. The part-talkie *My Man* (premiered at Warners' Theatre, December 21, 1928) was her screen debut. It was directed by Archie L. Mayo and had Guinn Williams, Edna Murphy, and Richard Tucker as supporting players. Some of Fanny Brice's songs for the film were among her best known: "If You Want a Rainbow, You Must Have the Rain" (Billy Rose, Mort Dixon, and Oscar Levant), "I'm an Indian" (Blanche Merrill and Leo Edwards), "I'd Rather Be Blue with You Than Happy with Somebody Else" (Billy Rose and Fred Fisher), and "I Was a Floradora Baby" (Ballard MacDonald and Harry Carroll). There was also, of course, the film's title song (by Channing Pollock and Maurice Yvain).

"My Man," a song of ill-fated love, had been the show-stopping number of the sumptuous 1921 *Ziegfeld Follies*. Florenz Ziegfeld had originally intended it to be sung by French artiste Mistinguett, but at rehearsals he was dissatisfied with her interpretation. According to Charles Higham

> he saw immediately that the song would be ideal for Fanny Brice. It was perfect because Fanny, whom he adored, needed to develop a new image, and her tragic affair with Nicky Arnstein was currently making national headlines. He told her to memorize "My Man" for rehearsal. He was horrified when she walked on stage dressed up like a female impersonator in a grotesque red wig and shawl. Ziegfeld ran up to the stage, ripped off the wig and flung it in the wings. He pulled her shawl off and tore her dress from neck to hem. Then he knelt on the stage, smeared his hands with dust, and covered her arms, legs, and costume with the dirt. Fanny started to cry. "Now sing it!" he cried triumphantly, and with a genuine sob in the voice she delivered the heartbreaking lyrics to perfection. When she sang "My Man" on opening night, the audience was in tears.

As *The Jazz Singer* had immortalized another audience-heartbreaker, so Warner Bros.' last big Vitaphone picture for 1928 would preserve for posterity what Ziegfeld considered to be the supreme moment of his career—that "ragged dust-smeared figure on the stage and the audience too overcome with emotion to applaud."[26]

Most of Hollywood had different reasons for *not* applauding the latest Vitaphone film. "In less than a year, the Warners had reversed their circumstances from a deficit of $1,234,412 to a spectacular first place in the industry through sound."[27]

If 1928 was, financially, an *annus mirabilis* for Warner Bros., it was also a year of invaluable experience for everyone associated with the studio. Vitaphone technicians learned how to cope with many of the problems that had plagued them since they had begun making sound pictures. Warner actors, mostly trained in the mimetic traditions of silent cinema, were coming to realize that the sound film imposed new and unfamiliar demands on their art. To survive they would have to learn how to speak for the microphone and how to adjust their acting to the restraints it imposed on their movements. Warner screenwriters had discovered that language appropriate to silent film intertitles was generally unsuitable for spoken dialogue. And Warner directors and producers were now able to assess the relative popularity of part-talkies and talkies and to determine the kind of feature that would prove most attractive with the addition of sound.

Early in 1928, anticipating the great demand for music that would arise from the advent of talkies (and especially from the popularity of movie musicals), Warner Bros. stole another march on its competitors by buying up three music publishing houses—Harms, Remick, and Witmark—whose combined sheet-music copyrights were estimated to be worth some $10 million. In addition, the studio signed a contract with ASCAP whereby for an annual fee of $125,000 it could use any or all works by members of the Society.[28]

In every important respect Warner Bros. appeared to have far outstripped its competitors. Only one dark cloud crossed the horizon in 1928—but it was to have a gold and silver lining for the rest of the film industry. In 1927, the Fox Film Corporation had been the only studio to follow Warner Bros. into the great gamble with sound. But in the spring of 1928, a crisis developed in the relationship between Warner Bros. and Western Electric which led directly to the involvement of all other, major studios in what had become the sound revolution. There are conflicting explanations of what occurred. One account of the crisis is given by E. S. Gregg:

> Western Electric on January 1, 1927, organized a new corporation, entitled Electrical Research Products, Inc.—almost immediately known as ERPI [whose export department was headed by E. S. Gregg]. . . .
>
> When [Walter J.] Rich had shared his agreement with Warner Brothers, it seemed ERPI might be able to sit back and collect royalties. It did not work out that way. Warner Brothers were picture producers and theatre owners; they did not know how to sell complicated electric and mechanical equipment. They also lacked access to capital. While studios might find it possible to lay hands on the $100,000 or more to install one recording channel and some associated equipment . . . and every studio . . . needed several recording channels . . . the thousands of individual theatre owners could not easily find the $10,000 to $20,000 to install sound reproducing equipment. They wanted three years to pay for such equipment and were unhappy when they could get only one or two years.
>
> In 1928 ERPI had to renegotiate its contract with Vitaphone and to take back the rights to sell, install and service Western Electric talking picture equipment.[29]

Gertrude Jobes's explanation differs sharply from Gregg's:

> Of all the devices, the Western Electric was the most expensive and was constructed to carry only Western Electric recordings. In addition Western Electric was slow in filling orders. The Warners, anxious to have their houses wired, signed up with Pacent, whose apparatus sold for about one tenth the price of Western Electric equipment, and who was in a position to make immediate installations. Western Electric would not tolerate what it considered an infringement, and brought suit against the Warners. The Warners, on their part, claimed Western Electric had promised them a commission on all talkie apparatus sold and were suing for such commissions. [The suit was to drag through the courts until 1935, when at long last the action was settled in favor of Western Electric.[30]]

Yet another explanation is possible: that Western Electric executives had come to the reasonable conclusion that the time was ripe to make lucrative deals with other studios—provided that

ERPI could sever its exclusive relationship with Warner Bros. If that were the case, any basis for disagreement would have served its purpose. Whatever the reason, the immediate outcome was clear. On May 15, 1928, ERPI considered itself free to issue licenses to Paramount, MGM, and United Artists, enabling them to use Western Electric amplifiers and other equipment with Movietone sound-on-film. It was a red-letter day in the history of sound movies: in effect, the true beginning of the sound era, since it signified that the major studios were at last climbing aboard the bandwagon. Gregg's version of what happened is that J. E. Otterson, president of ERPI, approached the heads of the major studios and convinced them that it was time to sign up with Western Electric and thereby get into the lucrative market for sound movies. Gregg attributes the studios' prompt acceptance of Otterson's proposal to his astute psychology: "The President of ERPI . . . told these big Hollywood producers he thought Western Electric equipment and royalties were too expensive for them. To men who wanted 'nothing but the finest,' this was too much to take. They signed up for talking pictures, and the stampede was on to get the huge Hollywood studios equipped."[31] By May 1928, however, the big studios needed little persuasion to get into the business of making sound movies. Economically speaking, except for Warner Bros., 1927 had been a bad year for Hollywood, and 1928 was beginning to look worse. It was only sound movies that were consistently attracting large audiences.

Along with the momentous announcement of May 15, Otterson also issued a public statement: "It is my understanding," he said, "that Paramount, Metro-Goldwyn and United Artists have already begun the installation in their studios of the necessary equipment for introducing sound into their productions. They have placed substantial orders both for the studio equipment thus needed and for reproducing equipment in the theatres owned or controlled by them." He noted that First National had recently adopted the Western Electric system (this, of course, was after that company's brief experiment with Firnatone), and that contracts were being drawn up between ERPI and Universal Pictures and Keith-Albee-Orpheum. Otterson anticipated that a thousand theaters in America, including those already using Vitaphone and Movietone equipment, would be wired for sound before the end of 1928.[32]

The news of May 15 immediately convulsed Hollywood. Less than two months after that momentous day, Chapin Hall, a columnist for the *New York Times,* was noting how

> In a recent trip through the manufacturing areas in Hollywood and elsewhere I found many corrugated brows. The manufacturers don't know just how far to go. They realize that the next year or two will see rapid development in the "talkies" and naturally they hesitate to install expensive equipment which may have to be scrapped before the newness has worn off. On the other hand, the public is clamoring for the latest toy, and theatres featuring sound devices are "packing 'em in" at the expense of less progressive houses. . . . The corrugations in the brows of scenario writers come from the fact that a new type of story must be devised—something that will bridge the gap between action and talk. The present sound films are interesting because of their novelty, but as pictures they are flops, and the abrupt changes of tempo when the words stop and the action resumes is a terrific strain on the credulity of the customers. Most of the performers' brows are lined with worry make-up because they see their fat contracts slipping away into the hands of actors who can make language behave. The zero hour of the "beautiful but dumb" is about to strike.
>
> The beginning of a new era is recognized by all hands, but no one yet knows what it portends. In the meantime, the whole industry is nervous and inclined to jump whenever anyone says "boo."[33]

Six months later, an editorial in the same paper stated

> Something like panic has struck the actor colony of Hollywood since the talking films became popular. If the beautiful blondes could only speak intelligibly and in agreeable voices, they would not be so worried, and some of the more ambitious are frantically at work studying under elocution teachers. . . . Both in New York and in small towns all over the country, figures show that "talkies" are more welcome than silent movies. . . .[34]

The effects of the sound revolution on the American film industry will be considered in more detail in the next chapter. Here, before taking a closer look at the Babel of sound systems that were contributing mightily to Hollywood's confusion, we can pause briefly to survey the spectrum of personal reactions to the coming of sound.

Among the relatively few, immediately favorable observations was that of Hal Roach, veteran producer of slapstick comedy:

> There may be some speculation as to the ultimate place of sound effects and dialogue for full-length pictures, but I don't see any questions about the value of sound in the one or two reel film. . . . It's easy to imagine the variety of humorous and farcical effects possible for a sound comedy. And a good dialogue comedy might be compared to a vaudeville skit, with the extra action that the screen can give. The public has already shown unqualified approval of the short sound pictures, the Movietone news reel and the like.[35]

Movie star Adolphe Menjou, interviewed in Paris while on his honeymoon (with Kathryn Carver), responded excitedly when asked about the sound revolution:

> It is the next forward movement in the entertainment of the universe. . . . Talking movies is [*sic*] the first invention making possible a successful combination of the best of the stage and screen. Mussolini, with his brain, was the first to see the big possibilities of an invention which permits him to remain at home and also to appear and to be heard by thousands at the same time.[36]

Mordaunt Hall, touring the studios in July 1928, found MGM's wonder-boy producer, Irving Thalberg, waxing "enthusiastic about audible pictures" and boasting about the acoustic features and structural immensity of the new sound studios that were under construction on the MGM lot. By contrast, Hall was told by veteran actor Lionel Barrymore that as far as he was concerned, sound movies were still only ten minutes old. When Hall questioned him about the quality of screen voices, Barrymore growled that he believed it was Jefferson who had said that fine voices had killed more good actors than had whiskey.[37]

A leading spokesman for the "play-it-both-ways" position was Jesse L. Lasky, production chief of Paramount–Famous Players. Admitting, somewhat bewilderedly, that he found the "talking and sound picture" to be a "big subject," he nevertheless offered his "firm conviction that it is here to stay." Guardedly, he added, "There will naturally be numerous imperfect productions made in the haste to meet the popular demand. . . . But [there] is not the slightest doubt in my mind but that it will improve. At the same time, I don't think that the silent picture will disappear from the screen. . . ."[38]

A rather more intelligent assessment of the situation was offered by independent producer Sam Goldwyn:

> The present state of excitement over the sound picture is virtually due to the financial success of *The Jazz Singer*. . . . What would this picture have been without Mr. Jolson? Certainly it might have made money, but it would never have been the outstanding hit it was all over the country without that stellar performer.
>
> I am by no means opposed to the sound film, but I do think that the hysteria that reigns here at present may mean that so many inadequate talking subjects will be issued that people will eventually long for the peace and quiet to which they have been accustomed with the silent features. They can make all the sound films they want, but I wonder how many pictures will be made with the new medium that will be as beautiful as Chaplin's *Gold Rush*. . . . It is also a question as to where producers will get their stories or whether they will be able to find sufficiently good ones to stand up under the test of sound. . . .[39]

Among the many voices of opposition to the new development were Joseph M. Schenck, president of United Artists, and directors King Vidor and Herbert Brenon. Schenck openly admitted that he disliked talking pictures and that the only reason his company was going ahead with them was "to give the public what it wants." But, he maintained, "I don't think people will want talking pictures long. . . . Talking doesn't belong in pictures. Pictures are on a silent ground."[40]

King Vidor, on returning from a trip to Europe, remarked to an interviewer,

> I came back, and the first thing that was said was, "What do you think of them?" . . . When I went away I was just beginning to put my finger on that something which makes up the screen; and in Europe many persons also said they felt it. . . . Now everyone is thinking of a new development, and rushing to get in on it. I have asked why they want to start something else when they have just learned straight pictures, but it does no good. Talking

pictures are of a different school—one dealing with voice delivery
—and we will have to begin all over again to learn it.[41]

Brenon's was the most pessimistic and hostile voice:

> In my humble opinion the motion picture joined with the
> cheap novelty of the "talking film," is about to commit suicide
> as a popular form of entertainment. . . . The ideal motion picture
> should tell its story in a completely visual manner. . . . But the
> exploiters of this new craze have thrown this ideal overboard,
> have discarded all technique and tradition and begun to pound
> the drum and shake the cymbals before an exotic sideshow. . . .
> What will be the result? The movie camera will, in time, come to
> be subordinate to the talking machine. . . . That will be a sorry
> day for the movies! . . . Right now "talking films" are a novelty
> and people want to hear them. But I am hoping the novelty will
> wear off, and I think it will. . . .It has no place in the dramatic
> art of the screen. Leave that art alone! . . . These voices and
> noises . . . will merely kill it.[42]

They almost killed Brenon's career instead. However, both he
and King Vidor rose above their initial antipathy to sound pictures and were soon directing their first talkies. Brenon's best
work already lay behind him, in the silent era, while some of
Vidor's finest films (aside from *The Crowd*, 1928) were yet to
be made.

But in July 1928, while King Vidor was still asking why
Hollywood was starting something else when they had just
learned straight pictures, no one in the film industry had time
to answer him. In that month alone Western Electric installed
400 of their sound projector systems leased through ERPI, and
the major studios were working, at white heat, on the production of sound pictures.

On July 14, 1928, the *Exhibitors' Herald* provided the following line-up of film companies involved in the transition to
sound:

Western Electric, licensing both film and disk methods:
1 Warners, with Vitaphone, disk
2 Fox-Case, with Movietone, film
3 Paramount, Movietone, by arrangement with Fox, which may
  be made either on film or disk.

4 Metro-Goldwyn-Mayer, Movietone, by arrangement with Fox, film or disk.

5 United Artists, Movietone, by arrangement with Fox, film or disk.

6 Hal Roach Comedies, expected to use [Movietone] film.

7 Christie Comedies, mostly Movietone, film.

Columbia Pictures and the Tiffany-Stahl film corporation were also on the verge of making a decision to sign up with Western Electric, while Universal, with two of its films (*Uncle Tom's Cabin* and *The Man Who Laughs*) already under contract to be synchronized by Movietone, announced that it would have sound added to sixteen more of its pictures before the end of the year. No one doubted that Universal, too, would shortly be joining the procession to Western Electric.

At the same time, several other systems were attracting Hollywood companies. The most important was Photophone, a sound-on-film recording and reproducing system almost identical to Movietone. It was developed by a research team from General Electric Company working under the supervision of Dr. C. A. Hoxie,[43] and was promoted by RCA Photophone, Inc., a subsidiary of the RCA Company established in 1928

> to carry on the commercial exploitation of the sound-on-film system. Carl Dreher (later with RKO) was its first chief engineer, followed in 1929 by Max C. Batsel from the Westinghouse Co. A laboratory was established in New York to which a number of engineers were transferred from the Technical and Test Dept. of RCA. . . . The first commercial soundhead [the device for adapting existing silent projectors into sound machines] to be offered by the RCA group . . . was of Westinghouse design, but the manufacturing was carried out by both companies. . . . Although the RCA group was convinced of the inherent advantages of sound-on-film for motion picture sound, disk equipment was wanted in all of the earlier theatre installations, and accordingly, combined sound-on-film and synchronous disk equipment was designed and built by the G. E. and Westinghouse companies and supplied by RCA Photophone, Inc.[44]

The promoters of Photophone claimed that its sound reproduction was superior to that of any other system since it was not affected by underdeveloping or overdeveloping of the film or by jumping needles or warped disks. Several years later, further research by RCA, Western Electric, and General Electric would result in Photophone's becoming the first widely used system employing a variable area sound track. Maurice Zouary described that development as "the first true breakaway from the De Forest method of optical photography in the density method and pattern."[45]

In July 1928, four Hollywood studios—Mack Sennett, Pathe Exchange, Tiffany Stahl, and Educational Pictures—contracted to use Photophone after their studio heads attended demonstrations organized by RCA at the Gaiety and Biltmore theaters in New York. Arrangements were made to supply them promptly with the necessary equipment to begin production of sound pictures. Pathe quickly re-released Cecil B. DeMille's *The King of Kings* (1927) with a synchronized score by Hugo Riesenfeld, and started production of Pathe Newsreels in competition with Fox's Movietone Newsreels. As we shall see later, in more detail, Photophone was also to be used by FBO (Film Booking Offices) when that company was taken over by RCA early in the summer of 1928.

Photophone, Movietone, De Forest's Phonofilm, Cinephone (which we shall be considering shortly), and the European Tri-Ergon system promoted by the Tonbild Syndicate (Tobis) were all basically interchangeable with little or no modification—as Tobis was to point out, rather belatedly, in March 1929. Compatibility would have been forced on Hollywood sooner or later, but in fact, with the major exception of Warner Bros., it was there almost from the outset. There were, of course, incompatible systems apart from Vitaphone.

We can review only briefly the more prominent systems other than Vitaphone that were being actively promoted in that decisive, transitional year. Edward W. Kellogg notes that by 1930 there were "234 *different types* of theater sound equipment including the large number which were designed for disk only."[46] All of them, including Vitaphone, were to be swept aside by the dominance of Western Electric Movietone and RCA Photophone and by the rising demand for compatibility of sound systems that became irresistible by the early thirties. It should be noted that in mid-1928, the crucial moment of the transition to sound, the De Forest organization had suspended promotion of its Phonofilm system. The *Exhibitors' Herald* announced: "This company is at present formulating a policy pending legal actions already under way. De Forest, one of the first to present sound-on-film, claims basic patents and contemplates an entry into this competition from the door that leads to the law courts."[47]

The other systems that were being seriously considered by Hollywood companies in 1928 included:

Firnatone.   A disk device similar to Vitaphone that could also be used with Western Electric apparatus. It was used briefly by First National (hence the name FIRst NAtional TONE) before that company adopted the Vitaphone system.

Vocafilm.   A disk system with an amplifying horn placed in front of the screen. As noted in the previous chapter, it was first publicly demonstrated in July 1927, when it provided synchronized sound for a baseball picture, *Babe [Ruth] Comes Home*. A columnist for the *Exhibitors' Herald* noted that Vocafilm had been "demonstrated with success in New York . . . if one will overlook a bad first day. The advantage of this system, it is claimed, is that it promises to be quite inexpensive as compared with some disk machines."[48]

Bristolphone.   Another disk system. This one was produced and promoted by the William H. Bristol Manufacturing Company of Waterbury, Connecticut. The apparatus incorporated a device enabling the sound to be stopped or started without losing synchronization with the picture—an obvious advantage whenever the film broke. The Dictaphone Sales Corporation of Bridgeport, Connecticut, sponsored the first public demonstration of Bristolphone on May 14, 1928, at the Belmont Hotel in New York. The system was presented on that occasion as the most portable of sound systems and a "new method of advertising through eye and ear."[49]

Remaphone.   A disk system invented by Robert E. Machat (R.E.M.), who first demonstrated it publicly in October 1927 at the Wardman Park Theatre in Washington, D. C. Remaphone enabled ordinary stock records to be used in approximate synchronization with the film. According to *Film Daily Yearbook*, the apparatus consisted of a "Victor 'Cadenza' Electrola working on five tubes, with two tuning tables connected by a shaft to the projection machine."[50] The stock records were used together with a mat, devised by Machat, for covering the unwanted segments of the disks.

Han-A-Phone and Kaleidophone.   Disk systems about which little is known except that they were cheap to install.

Madalatone.   A groove-on-film system developed by Ferdinand von Madaler, onetime technical expert for the Columbia Phonograph Co. (It is discussed in chap. 3.) Madalatone apparatus sold for about $1,000 per unit.[51]

Cortellaphone.   A combination system using both disk and film. The sound scoring was provided by a hairline on the film between the photographic image and the sprocket holes. Among the advantages claimed for Cortellaphone were its relative inexpensiveness (less than $500 per unit) and its prompt and easy installation.

The Canton System.   Invented by Allen Canton. This system was based on "the photography of air waves." It employed a microphone that picked up sound and changed it into electrical impulses; it also utilized a new kind of loudspeaker operating from an air blast. For a short time in 1927 Universal Studios considered investing in the system.

Titanifrone.   Invented by Marcus C. Hopkins. Originally demonstrated on October 3, 1928 at the Eltinge Theatre in New York. Titanifrone was not an entire sound system but a device for improving the sound quality of other systems. Basically, it discarded the usual horn speaker in favor of a cone loudspeaker on a large vibrating board. Hopkins maintained that Titanifrone gave "music and the human voice a quality of reality which the Movietone and the Vitaphone and other talking pictures have lacked." He claimed that it could be used equally effectively to enhance the sound quality of radio, the phonograph, and the talkies.[52]

The McDonnell Process.   An ingenious but curiously retrogressive system described in some detail in *Film Daily Yearbook* for 1927.

> At a time when talking pictures were seen as an imminent reality, or in late August [1927] to be approximate, the U. S. Patent Office awarded rights to George P. McDonnell of St. Louis on a system of synchronizing the voice to movement on the screen. The in-

ventor's method of achieving this coordination is by providing every frame of film with a film strip containing cues for concealed orators or actors, who recite the appropriate lines to suit the action. . . . The words on the film strip are projected through . . . [a] slit [at the top of the main screen] and reflected on a [second, smaller] screen back of the main screen. An orator is positioned between the two screens and repeats the words as they appear, consonant with the action.[53]

Cinephone. Last, but far from least, there was Cinephone, a system developed by R. R. Halpenny and William Garity and promoted by Patrick A. Powers, onetime distributor for Universal Pictures. It was based on De Forest's Phonofilm system, was relatively inexpensive to install, and provided fine tone quality. But its primary importance was that it was the system Walt Disney was to use in making *his* transition to sound. It was to play a major role in establishing his reputation and in building his studio into the world's main producer of animated cartoons. And more than any single factor it was to lead directly to the acceptance of Mickey Mouse as one of the cinema's few universal and presumably immortal character creations.

In *Harrison's Reports* for October 27, 1928, P. S. Harrison presented his conclusions and made several generalizations about sound-on-disk and sound-on-film after sampling all the current, publicly demonstrated sound systems. He found that sound-on-disk systems possessed up to seven serious disadvantages. First, they could not record sounds below 120 cycles or above 3,500 cycles, whereas sound-on-film systems could record sound as low as 60 cycles and provided satisfactory results as high as 5,000 cycles. Harrison concluded that there was "a loss in the disk system[s] of as much as one full octave in the bass note end of the musical scale and one octave in the high note end." He maintained that disk systems could not satisfactorily record orchestral music and that recorded sounds of shooting came out of the loudspeakers sounding like wind puffs.

The second disadvantage of sound-on-disk, according to Harrison, arose from the obvious fact that the inner grooves of the disks were of smaller circumference than the outer ones. This produced an unequal tone quality that became progressively worse as the needle approached the center of the record. Harrison maintained that the inner grooves did not record as many overtones as the outer grooves. The third shortcoming of the disk systems was the likelihood of the needle's jumping and entering another groove—thus creating a loss of synchronization. Harrison observed: "I have been reliably informed that while *The Jazz Singer* was shown in this city [New York], the operator one evening had to change fifteen records. The needle either jumped or broke the wall of the groove and entered another groove while it was on the spot of the record."

The fourth problem was caused by the movement of the pickup arm. As it moved during the playing of the record it inevitably changed its angle in relation to the disk, and, according to Harrison, that was detrimental to the sound quality. Fifth, the disks lasted only a short time and had to be replaced after five or six uses. The sixth limitation mentioned by Harrison was that the "solution" of using blank strips of film to preserve synchronization when part of the movie was torn or otherwise damaged was not working too well. "If the film is patched in several places and the part cut off is not put back from new stock, the action and words are thrown out of synchronism. This will necessitate replacing of prints, making the cost of film to the smaller exhibitor almost prohibitive." Finally, Harrison noted that disks were likely to break in transit and that mixups in shipments could lead to the wrong disks being sent with the films.

Turning to sound-on-film, Harrison divided the systems into those using variable density sound tracks and those using variable width (or area) sound tracks. In the former, used in Movietone, the sound track moved along the film in bands of varying density; in the latter, used in Photophone, the sound track moved along the film in a wavy shape. Harrison noted that the sound quality was adversely affected (there was ground noise) when there was any defect in the emulsion of films with variable density sound tracks. Ground noise had been evident in almost every Fox Movietone sound film he had experienced. However, ground noise seldom if ever occurred in films with variable width sound tracks because their variations of sound did not depend on "shadings" of the emulsion. Harrison concluded that the variable density system of sound recording "if not dropped, is going to cost the producers millions of dollars a year in retakes and in discarded old prints. . . . The producers should adopt the Photophone system because it gives the best results." He added with prophetic accuracy, that "even though the Warners are just now ahead of every other talking picture producer, the disk system cannot endure; it is wrong in principle."

Regardless of who was going to be proved right or wrong, in principle or in practice, every company that could afford to climb onto the sound bandwagon was feverishly engaged in the production of sound pictures. A roundup of the studios in 1928 would have looked like this:

ﾍﾍﾍ

FOX

The Fox Film Corporation, having got into the act the previous year (1927), was busily grinding out Movietone Newsreels. The first one had been presented at the sumptuous Roxy in New York, on October 28, 1927. Its subjects included: Niagara Falls, the Army-Yale football game, the Romance of the Iron Horse, the New York Rodeo, King George V of Great Britain, David Lloyd George, the Crown Prince of Sweden, and Marshal Foch. Starting early in December 1927, a special production unit—with Edward Percy Howard as editor-in-chief, Hal Stone as news editor, and Thomas Chalmers as director—began issuing a new Movietone Newsreel each week. *Moving Picture World* noted: "A fleet of high powered automobile trucks, each equipped with complete Movietone apparatus, is being used for gathering of news subjects to make up the weekly reel. . . . Cameramen and trucks will be stationed in central locations throughout the world."[54] It was the beginning of an era of motion-picture journalism that would culminate, in the thirties, with *The March of Time* series. Following a Fox press release that Movietone Newsreel would henceforth be a "permanent institution," offers of contracts for immediate installation of Movietone apparatus poured into the offices of the Fox Film Corporation.

Early Movietone subjects included glimpses—in sight and sound—of Conan-Doyle, Calvin Coolidge, Al Smith (being nominated at the Democratic convention of 1928), the King of Spain, and Dame Clara Butt (singing "Rule Britannia" at an Empire Day celebration). During April, considerable publicity was given in Europe to the German premiere of Movietone at the American Embassy in Berlin. Movietones of Ambassador Jacob Schurman and the German foreign minister, Gustav Stresemann, were shown to a large audience of diplomats and celebrities.[55] Among the many news events covered by Movietone in its first year were the English Derby, the Republican convention in Kansas City, the Harvard-Yale boat crews at New London, and King George V speaking at the opening of the Tyne Bridge.

Aside from the newsreels there were also numerous Movietone shorts presenting a wide variety of artists in concert performances or vaudeville sketches. Modeled on the immensely successful Vitaphone shorts (which were still being released with breathtaking frequency), they proved to be invaluable as a means of testing and developing the effectiveness of the sound system. The originator of these shorts was Fox's general manager, Winfield Sheehan, who, in the fall of 1927, ordered one of the newsreel crews to begin production on a hastily prepared soundproof stage in Hollywood. Among the first shorts were a talkie, *Napoleon's Barber* (based on a playlet by Arthur Caesar and directed by John Ford), and what was probably the first dialogue movie to be filmed outside a studio, a little sketch entitled *The Family Picnic.* Other memorable shorts included Robert Benchley's amusing "lecture" *The Sex Life of the Polyp,* Lionel Atwill in a playlet entitled *The White-Faced Fool,* and Mischa Levitzki playing Liszt's Sixth Hungarian Rhapsody, all released in 1928. An even more notable Movietone was to be made in 1929, when the Fox cameramen filmed George Gershwin at the piano during a rehearsal of his show *Strike Up the Band.* They were to capture, for posterity, a few delightful moments of the composer exchanging small talk with the show's dance director and playing "Hangin' Around with You," "Strike Up the Band," and "Mademoiselle in New Rochelle."

However, none of the newsreels and shorts excited more public interest than the Movietone of Bernard Shaw, which was premiered at the Globe Theatre, New York, on June 25, 1928. Shaw, who had received the Nobel Prize three years earlier, was generally considered in the United States to be the greatest twentieth-century writer and the most important dramatist since Shakespeare. He had received countless offers to visit the U. S., but had persistently refused to cross the Atlantic. His refusals, frequently spiced with salty anti-American observations, only served to inflame the desire of Americans to see and hear him— in person. The first of his two brief visits to America would not occur until 1933. So the Movietone, filmed in the garden of Shaw's house in England, was the next best thing. It gave an attractive foretaste of what America could expect.

The Movietone opens with the seventy-two-year-old author, dressed in his customary Norfolk jacket and plus fours, emerging from behind a bush and wandering along the garden path towards the camera. Instantly making himself at home with talking pictures, he assumes the pose of suddenly noticing his off-screen audience. After introducing himself in his gentle brogue, Shaw casually rambles through a few anecdotes and delivers an amusing impersonation of Mussolini (probably a parody of the Movietone film of the dictator). Then, pulling out his watch, he declares that he is a notoriously busy man and it is time to take his leave. Shaw says nothing profound or memorably witty, but comes across as a sprightly, puckish personality, radiating considerable charm and using his voice more effectively, perhaps, than anyone hitherto recorded by either Vitaphone or Movietone. (He was also undoubtedly assisted by the exceptionally good quality of the sound recording.) There are good reasons for believing that this particular Movietone was directed by Shaw himself; if so, it was certainly an anticipation of the kind of skillful stage-managing of his own public appearances that he would demonstrate to the American press in 1933.

The regular inclusion of Movietones in film-programming was to play as important a role as Vitaphone in establishing sound cinema as a familiar and expected part of moviegoing experience. By the end of 1928, big-city audiences were enjoying two or more Vitaphone or Movietone shorts with every Warner or Fox program, and more and more frequently, programs would offer a mixture of Vitaphones and Movietones. Many of the critics—and probably a large number of nonprofessional moviegoers—preferred the sound newsreels and shorts to the synchronized features that were trickling out of the studios in 1928. They frequently had good reason. Where sound was concerned, art still had everything to learn from actuality.

Understandably, after Warner Bros., the Fox Film Corporation was the major producer of sound features during 1928. Fox released no fewer than fifteen sound movies that year, all either part-talkies or silent pictures to which synchronized scores and sound effects had been added. In retrospect, the earliest releases are of particular interest since they provided the initial experiences of sound cinema to three film makers who were to become distinguished directors during the sound era.

Four Sons (premiered February 13, 1928 at the Gaiety Theatre, New York), was directed by John Ford and starred Francis X. Bushman, George Meeker, and Margaret Mann. It was a sentimental drama about a widow who lost three of her four sons in World War I. The picture had a synchronized score, sound effects, and a song, "Little Mother" by Erno Rapee and Lew Pollack. The *New York Times* noted that the "Movietone accompaniment to this production was not always as melodious as one might hope for. The inclusion of a Movietone song is not especially appealing in this instance. . . ."[56]

Ford's second "sound picture," *Mother Machree* (March 5, 1928 at the Globe Theatre, New York), was a society melodrama flavored with a touch of old Ireland characteristic of the director who would one day make *The Quiet Man*. It starred Victor McLaglen (another anticipation of the later Ford), Belle Bennett, and Philippe De Lacy. Again, there was no spoken dialogue —but a synchronized score by S. L. Rothafel and Erno Rapee, sound effects, and, of course, the song, "Mother Machree." Unfortunately, the feature aroused less critical interest than the supporting program of Movietone shorts, which included songs by Beatrice Lillie and Gertrude Lawrence.

Fox's third sound feature for 1928 was *Fazil* (June 4 at the Gaiety), directed by Howard Hawks and starring Charles Farrell, Greta Nissen, and Mae Busch. *Fazil* was a fanciful romantic tragedy about the love of a French girl and an Arabian prince. Rothafel and Rapee provided the synchronized score; there was no spoken dialogue.

Next came *The Red Dance* (June 25, 1928, at the Globe), directed by Raoul Walsh and starring Dolores Del Rio, Charles Farrell, and Dorothy Revier. The picture was an interesting contribution to the vogue of features about the Russian Revolution, but was unfortunately eclipsed by critical and public interest in the Shaw Movietone film, with which it was billed. Rothafel and Rapee also provided the score for this, Walsh's first "sound" movie.

Fox's other sound features for 1928 in order of release were as follows:

Street Angel. A part-talkie that again teamed Janet Gaynor and Charles Farrell in what turned out to be a less successful picture than *Seventh Heaven*. It was the story of a Neapolitan waif who poses for a portrait of the Madonna and eventually wins the artist who paints it. Directed by Frank Borzage (who had made *Seventh Heaven*), it introduced a hit song, "Angela Mia" by Erno Rapee.

The Air Circus. A part-talkie about an aviator with acrophobia. Directed by Howard Hawks and starring Louise Dresser and Arthur Lake.

The River Pirate. Another part-talkie. A melodrama directed by William K. Howard and starring Victor McLaglen, Lois Moran, and Donald Crisp.

Plastered in Paris. A war comedy with sound effects and music. Directed by Benjamin Stoloff and starring Sammy Cohen, Jack Pennick, and Lola Salvi.

Mother Knows Best. A part-talkie with music by Erno Rapee. It concerned a talented girl dominated by her overly ambitious mother. Directed by John Blystone and starring Madge Bellamy, Louise Dresser, and Barry Norton.

Me, Gangster. A crime melodrama with sound effects and music. Directed by Raoul Walsh and starring Don Terry and June Collyer, it used the curious device of insert titles that were supposed to be in the handwriting of the gangster-hero—a rather late original twist to the practice of silent-film titling.

Dry Martini. A comedy drama with a musical score by Erno Rapee and S. L. Rothafel. Directed by Harry D'Arrast and starring Mary Astor and Matt Moore.

Riley the Cop. A comedy drama with sound effects and music. Directed by John Ford and starring Louise Fazenda, Farrell MacDonald, David Rollins, and Billy Bevan.

Blindfold. A melodrama with sound effects and music. Directed by Charles Klein and starring George O'Brien and Lois Moran.

Prep and Pep. A comedy drama with sound effects and music. Directed by David Butler and starring Nancy Drexel and David Rollins.

Fox's final sound release for 1928 gave the clearest indication to date that the future of talking pictures lay with sound-on-film and not with sound-on-disk. Where Vitaphone production remained confined to the controlled acoustics of the studio, Movietone could be used with almost equal effectiveness in the studio and outdoors. As we noted in the previous chapter, the flexibility of Fox's system had been demonstrated in 1927 when Movietone engineers had taken their apparatus outdoors to film cadets parading at West Point. Now, in the fall of 1928, Movietone was used far more ambitiously to make the first outdoor feature: Fox's talkie, *In Old Arizona,* which premiered at the Los Angeles Criterion on December 25, 1928.*

In Old Arizona was based on O. Henry's short story "The Caballero's Way." Directed by Raoul Walsh and Irving Cummings (the latter took over when Walsh suffered an eye injury), it starred Warner Baxter (as the Cisco Kid), Edmund Lowe, and Dorothy Burgess. In shooting the picture, Walsh and Cummings took Movietone on location to Zion National Park, Cedar City (Utah), the Mojave Desert, and the San Fernando Mission in California. The sound quality of *In Old Arizona* impressed audiences and reviewers alike. Throughout the film *natural* sound contributed to the sense of distance (receding and approaching noises such as the gallop of horses' hoofs), the creation of moods (the distant peal of mission bells at a highly dramatic moment), the building of tension (the relentless ticking

---

* Several pages of commentary on the production of *In Old Arizona* appear in *Each Man in His Time* (New York: Farrar, Straus & Giroux, 1974), Raoul Walsh's autobiography.

of a clock), and the creation of humor (the hee-haw of a jackass and the hero's loud lip-smacking on downing a drink). Effective use was also made of the contrast of accents—particularly the colorful broken English of Warner Baxter grinding against the blunt "gringo" dialect of Edmund Lowe as Sergeant Dunn. *In Old Arizona* was perhaps the first feature film of which it could truly be said that the sound track was as naturalistic as the visuals. Its intelligent, creative use of sound did much to make it one of the best adventure movies of the year.

FIRST NATIONAL

First National released nine sound movies during 1928, the year in which it lost its independence and became a subsidiary of Warner Bros. *Ladies' Night in a Turkish Bath* (a part-talkie evidently using Movietone), directed by Eddie Cline, and *The Goodbye Kiss* (a Mack Sennett comedy released through First National and supplied with a Vitaphone music score and sound effects) were premiered in April and June, respectively. First National was acquired by Warner Bros. in the late summer of 1928. Inevitably, it was now committed to using Vitaphone. During the remainder of the year, it released six more sound features: one part-talkie, the rest with synchronized music.

The first and most prestigious of these productions was the World War I romance *Lilac Time,* directed by George Fitzmaurice and starring Colleen Moore and Gary Cooper. The film's theme song, "Jeanine, I Dream of Lilac Time" (by L. Wolfe Gilbert), quickly became one of the first song hits of the sound era.

Vitaphone was not used for *Lilac Time.* The picture had already been shot and was being synchronized when Warner Bros. took over First National. Colleen Moore maintains in her autobiography, *Silent Star,* that the music and effects for the movie were provided by "sound on a film played from another projector. Properly synchronized, the sound and action would match."[57] Ms. Moore is clearly referring to the Gaumont system promoted by British Acoustic. However, it could not have been used for *Lilac Time*. British Acoustic sound was first publicly demonstrated—in London—a month *after* the New York premiere of Colleen Moore's film. It was used then only to supply sound accompaniments for a program of short films. The system does not seem to have been used in conjunction with a feature-length picture until the making of the British movie *High Treason* (directed by Maurice Elvey), which premiered in October 1929. Music and sound effects heard in synchronization with *Lilac Time* were, in fact, supplied by the Firnatone process. As the *New York Times* noted on April 19, 1928, *Lilac Time* was the first feature picture to use Firnatone, and First National had temporarily affiliated with ERPI and the Victor Talking Machine Co. for this specific purpose. While *Lilac Time* was still in production, Clifford B. Hanley, president of First National, revealed that his company had no plans for the future use of Firnatone. Certainly no "photoplays . . . in which characters speak all their lines" were being contemplated by First National. Then the company was acquired by Warner Bros., and it was suddenly involved in the production of Vitaphone features.

Though none of First National's remaining sound features for 1928 were to prove as popular as *Lilac Time,* they all fared at least adequately at the box office. Only one had recorded dialogue. First came *The Night Watch,* directed by a little-known Hungarian named Alexander Korda, who, in the thirties, would do more than anyone to vitalize the British film industry. *The Night Watch,* a war drama, starred Billie Dove and Paul Lukas. Then came the comedy *Show Girl,* directed by Alfred Santell and starring Alice White, Donald Reed, Richard Tucker, and James Finlayson. The next release was a circus drama, *The Barker,* directed by George Fitzmaurice and starring Milton Sills, Betty Compson, and Douglas Fairbanks, Jr. This film was First National's only part-talkie of 1928. Unfortunately, its erratically placed and usually irrelevant dialogues served only as distractions from Fitzmaurice's skilful direction and the performances of a talented cast. The studio wound up its first year of sound with two unusual films, *The Haunted House,* a comedy drama directed by Benjamin Christensen (famed Swedish director of *Haxen* [*Witchcraft Through the Ages*], 1921), and John Dillon's *Scarlet Seas,* a raw but well-acted melodrama about the love of a shipwrecked sailor (Richard Barthelmess) for a dockside prostitute (Betty Compson).

~~~~~~

FILM BOOKING OFFICES

Early in 1928, RCA acquired the theater chains of B. F. Keith and Orpheum and the film production company FBO (Film Booking Offices). They were merged to form a new company known as RKO (Radio-Keith-Orpheum). From the standpoint of sound movies, the acquisition and merger meant that RKO could immediately avail itself of the RCA Photophone (sound-on-film) system, equipment, and personnel. However, the initial productions for which Photophone was used were films being completed at the time of the take-over of FBO, and they were released as part-talkies, still under the FBO logo.

First came *The Perfect Crime,* based on Israel Zangwill's *The Big Bow Mystery.* Directed by Bert Glennon and photographed by James Wong Howe, the picture starred Clive Brook, Irene Rich, and Tully Marshall. It turned out to be an exercise in the ludicrous, a "jabberwocky of inane incidents" that could not be saved even by its exceptional cast. "What it is all about," wrote the *New York Times* critic, "can be called only an open question. A guess at the solution, however, would be that F. B. O. had a mystery story, and in an effort to keep up with the times had synchronized it. The synchronization is faulty in many places, and several vocal selections are added in curious out-of-the-way scenes."[58] FBO's next, and somewhat better, effort was a Joe E. Brown vehicle, *Hit of the Show,* directed by Ralph Ince. It had originally been made as a silent feature and was released in that form in July 1928; it was re-released in September of the same year with the addition of a couple of songs ("You're in Love and I'm in Love" and "Waitin' for Katie") and brief dialogue passages. FBO's remaining part-talkies for 1928 were the crime picture *Gang War,* directed by Bert Glennon; *The Circus Kid* (another Joe E. Brown picture), also directed by George B. Seitz; and *Blockade,* a pirate story, directed by George Seitz and starring Anna Q. Nilsson and Wallace MacDonald.

PATHE EXCHANGE, RKO-PATHE, AND TIFFANY-STAHL

Like FBO, Pathe Exchange, RKO-Pathe, and Tiffany Stahl Productions tentatively tried out Photophone. Pathe Exchange released only three sound movies in 1928: two melodramas— *Marked Money* (directed by Spencer Gordon Bennett) and *Captain Swagger* (directed by Edward H. Griffith)—and a comedy-drama, *Show Folks* (directed by Paul Stein). All these films were first released with synchronized music and sound effects; in 1929, they were re-released with the addition of brief dialogue passages. RKO-Pathe's one and only sound movie of 1928 was Christy Cabanne's *Annapolis,* starring Johnny Mack Brown and Jeannette Loff. Provided with music and sound effects but no recorded dialogue, the film nevertheless made a minor hit with its song "My Annapolis and You." Tiffany-Stahl's two Photophone features were visually impressive and used synchronized music and sound effects in a relatively restrained manner. *The Toilers,* directed by Reginald Barker, costarred Douglas Fairbanks, Jr., and Jobyna Ralston in the story of a mine disaster; *The Cavalier,* directed by Irving Willat, starred Richard Talmadge as El Caballero, the Zorro-like hero of an adventure-melodrama set in Spain and old California. Hugo Riesenfeld provided the score.

GOTHAM

Towards the end of 1928, a minor film company, Gotham Productions, released through the Lumas Film Corporation its one and only sound film of the year, the part-talkie *The River,* directed by Joseph Henabery and starring Lionel Barrymore, Jacqueline Logan, and Sheldon Lewis. This rough-and-tumble melodrama of a saloonkeeper and a bar-girl was the first American production to use the Bristolphone disk system.

Universal, Paramount, Columbia, MGM, and United Artists were, as we have seen, contracted to use Movietone.

www

UNIVERSAL

Universal entered the sound era by re-releasing, with synchronized scores and sound effects, two of its most prestigious silent features of 1927: Harry Pollard's version of *Uncle Tom's Cabin* and Paul Leni's *The Man Who Laughs*. *Uncle Tom's Cabin*, with music by Hugo Riesenfeld, starred James Lowe, Virginia Grey, and George Siegmann. Ironically, Siegmann, who had played the villainous mulatto, Silas Lynch, in *The Birth of a Nation* (1915), was cast as Simon Legree, the sadistic white slave-owner in Universal's treatment of Harriet Beecher Stowe's novel. Leni's film was dominated by Conrad Veidt's sensitive performance as the grotesquely grinning Gwynplaine. The plot, based on a story by Victor Hugo, was adorned by a sentimental melody, "When Love Comes Stealing," by Walter Hirsch, Lew Pollack, and Erno Rapee. Music and sound effects were also contributed to one of Universal's silent Westerns, *Greased Lightning,* directed by Ray Taylor.

Universal's first part-talkie, perhaps the best of the year, was Paul Fejos's charming picture, *Lonesome,* a Coney Island romance sensitively acted by Glenn Tryon and Barbara Kent. Its delightful score was enriched by some evocatively used sound effects: the noises of the big city; the sounds of the subway, trolley cars, skyscraper elevators, factory machinery, roller coasters, and carousels; the peal of thunder; and the slap of naked feet on a sandy beach. The first dialogue passage, coming twenty or thirty minutes into the picture, was reserved for the moment when Glenn Tryon, sunbathing on the overcrowded seashore, suddenly notices Barbara Kent and leans over to introduce himself. The spoken words are a surprise but not a distraction. The unexpected intrusion of audible dialogue heightens the dramatic impact of Boy's first meeting with Girl.

Lonesome was followed by the same studio's first all-talkie: A. B. Heath's *Melody of Love,* whose plot resembled that of King Vidor's *The Big Parade* (1926), just as the story of *Lonesome* resembled the Coney Island sequence of Vidor's *The Crowd* (1928). Heath's picture (also called *Madelon*) was a rush job—synchronized in less than a week, and the results, for the unfortunate audience, were far from pleasant. Universal's final sound production of the year was another part-talkie, William Beaudine's comedy drama, *Give and Take,* with music by Joseph Cherniavsky. The *New York Times* reviewer found this effort no better than *Melody of Love.* "In the talking passages the players [they included Jean Hersholt and George Sidney] appear to be reacting rather than conversing. There are many spots where the long silences cause one to feel that the people in the story are waiting for the sound wizard to unlock their tongues."[59]

PARAMOUNT

Paramount got off to an awkward start with Fred Newmeyer's *Warming Up,* a baseball comedy—starring Richard Dix and Jean Arthur—whose sound effects were out of synchronization. Its next offering was *Loves of an Actress,* a love story set in the Napoleonic era, directed by Rowland Lee and starring Pola Negri and Nils Asther. For this film Paramount rather curiously obtained permission to use Vitaphone. It was a one-shot deal; thereafter the studio decisively reverted to Movietone, using that system, during 1928, for three of its most memorable films of the transitional period: *The Patriot, Beggars of Life,* and *The Wedding March.*

Ernst Lubitsch's *The Patriot* gave Emil Jannings one of his finest roles, that of Czar Paul I, son of Catherine the Great. Widely acclaimed for its direction and visual qualities as well as for its exceptional performances (by Lewis Stone and Florence Vidor as well as Jannings), the film was nevertheless considered by many critics to have been weakened by the addition of sound. In his book *The Lubitsch Touch,* Herman G. Weinberg notes, "*The Patriot* . . . was not only given a synchronized score but had sound effects grafted onto it, and occasional voices at climactic moments, such as Jannings's cry, 'Pahlen! Pahlen!' calling for his best friend when he realizes an attempt is being made to assassinate him. . . . Originally, all voice sounds were assigned to subtitles and Lubitsch was not responsible for the added sound."[60]

Paramount's next sound film was *The Sawdust Paradise*, directed by Luther Reed. It was followed by the studio's second major offering, *Beggars of Life*, William Wellman's remarkably prophetic drama of Depression America. The leading players, Louise Brooks, Richard Arlen, and Wallace Beery, turned in powerful performances as a trio of freight-car–hopping tramps. Like *The Patriot*, the film's synchronized score and sound effects were considered by contemporary critics to be more of a handicap than a virtue. That was also true of Paramount's third major venture into sound—Erich von Stroheim's butchered masterpiece, *The Wedding March*, starring Zasu Pitts and George Fawcett—which was provided not only with a synchronized score (by J. S. Zamecnik) but also with color sequences by Technicolor! Paramount concluded its first year of sound with *Variety*, a part-talkie directed by Frank Tuttle and starring Buddy Rogers; *Manhattan Cocktail*, a melodrama (with a synchronized score) directed by Dorothy Arzner;[61] and *Interference*, the studio's first all-talkie.

Interference was about a war veteran who lives incognito, in London, after being reported killed in action. A former girlfriend discovers that he is still alive and begins to blackmail his wife, who has remarried. The hero kills the blackmailer and gives himself up to the police, knowing that he will die of an incurable heart disease before he can be tried and executed. Two directors worked on the picture: Lothar Mendes was responsible for the purely visual scenes, while Roy J. Pomeroy directed the dialogue scenes. The distinguished cast was headed by William Powell, Evelyn Brent, Clive Brook, and Doris Kenyon. Clive Brook's recollections of *Interference* offer a vivid impression of an actor's experience in an early sound studio:

> I found that the microphone is more difficult to face than the most hardened audience. . . . So impressive is the stillness of the stage where audible pictures are born that I could fancy myself delivering a monologue to a group of unanswering ghosts. I was conscious of a metallic little instrument hanging like a sword of Damocles over my head. . . . My voice sounded unfamiliar to my ears, for it seemed to pass away into nothingness as it left my lips. Every word was oddly muffled: there was no echo, no resonance. Instead of an audience to carry me along on this 'first night' ap-

pearance, two ominous, tank-like objects were focused on me. Faces peered at me from the darkness inside these caverns. I caught the reflection of camera lenses in the plate-glass windows that form the front walls of the 'tanks.' Cameras were grinding, but the sound of their mechanisms had been silenced. Not even the familiar splutter of the Klieg lights could be heard, for they had been supplanted by huge banks of incandescent lamps. . . . It seemed strange not to receive the customary signal to begin the scene. . . . Now the director cannot even tell us when to start. . . . We must watch a monitor man, who waves his hand for us to begin. . . . It is only natural that these sudden changes should affect us. . . . We are forced to acquire a new technique. No longer can we express ourselves solely in pantomime; neither can we turn back to the technique of the stage. The microphone is a new and severe master. . . . I found myself starting off in the declamatory fashion of the stage. I was not thinking in terms of microphone sensitivity or the tremendous amplification of the apparatus . . . . Then, when I had finished . . . technicians turned on the record they had made. I heard a deep and strange voice come booming out of the loud-speakers. . . . It was not, I told myself, the voice of Clive Brook. It alternately faded into nothing-ness and then rang out in a thunderous crescendo. Pomeroy smiled at me.

"Was that my voice?" I asked.

"Yes, but you couldn't recognize it, could you?"

". . . Try it again," he said, "and speak just as you would in a small room at home. . . . Don't think of anyone in the gallery. The gallery doesn't exist here."

[Again Brook faced the microphone.]

. . . Soon I heard the voice in the loudspeakers again. This time it was unmistakably my own. . . . Although it was not loud, somehow it seemed to fill every corner of the huge room. . . . I had learned my first lesson in microphone recording.[62]

At its premiere, *Interference* was preceded by a filmed address by theater impresario Daniel Frohman, welcoming talking pictures as a technological advance that would make it possible to show great drama to audiences in the smallest towns as well as in the largest cities. It was the first notable olive branch extended to the new medium by the world of legitimate theatre. And it was not a moment too soon. For as *Interference* unrolled, it became clear to critics and public alike that sound cinema was on the threshold of becoming a real challenge to live theater. The bugs were being rapidly shaken out of the machine. As recently as 1972, William K. Everson dismissed *Interference* as "typical . . . one of the talkiest and most static of all early sound films."[63] But from the perspective of 1929, Mordaunt Hall singled it out as a turning point in the evolution of the talkie. This film, he wrote, "is in many respects so remarkable that it may change the opinion of countless skeptics concerning talking photoplays. The vocal reproductions are extraordinarily fine and the incidental sounds have been registered with consummate intelligence . . . as a specimen in the strides made by the talking picture, it is something to create no little wonderment."[64]

COLUMBIA

Columbia released only two sound features in 1928. Alan Crosland and Bess Meredyth, having quit Warner Bros. and moved over to Columbia, were to make that studio's first sound picture. One might have expected these two veterans to proceed by turning out their first all-talkie, but Columbia was not yet equipped for anything so ambitious. The film they did make was *The Scarlet Lady,* a lurid melodrama of the Russian Revolution of 1917 (an intensely popular subject for Hollywood movies in the late twenties). Its stars were Warner Oland (who had also joined the exodus from Warner Bros.) and Lya De Putti. The use of sound was restricted to a synchronized score, a few sound effects and a song, "My Heart Belongs to You," by Lou Herscher. However, *The Scarlet Lady* gave Crosland his first experience of working with sound-on-film.

Columbia's other sound effort was *Submarine,* which Irving Willatt was originally assigned to direct. But Willatt walked off the set after only a couple of reels had been shot. He refused to take any nonsense from Columbia's boss, Harry Cohn. Willatt was promptly replaced by a young man named Frank Capra, who was more diplomatic and also had a thicker hide than his predecessor. *Submarine,* which starred Ralph Graves and Jack Holt, was a turning point in Capra's career—his first success as a director after shaking off his association with silent comedian Harry Langdon. According to Capra, the picture also helped to revive the sinking fortunes of the studio. "Columbia's earnings rose from $.81 per share in 1927 to $1.27 in 1928—Harry Cohn's personal stock soared into the higher brackets. He took—and deserved—all credit for the success of his hunch to change directors. It consolidated his 'one-man rule' over his partners."[65] Little if any credit for this triumph can be attributed to *Submarine*'s poorly synchronized sound effects. But the public seems to have enjoyed the picture in spite of its sound track (there was no dialogue). Indeed, it was a success even in theaters that were not yet wired for sound. To all intents and purposes, Columbia was still making silent movies in 1928.

METRO-GOLDWYN-MAYER

MGM's first sound picture was, possibly, *The Baby Cyclone,* directed by Edward Sutherland, based on a George M. Cohan play and starring Lew Cody and Aileen Pringle. The film was originally made—and perhaps shown—as a silent comedy, but music and sound effects were added later. It is not clear when the sound version was released.

The film actually publicized as MGM's first sound feature was W. S. Van Dyke's *White Shadows of the South Seas,* starring Monte Blue, Raquel Torres, and Robert Anderson. The film was generally well received, but there were objections to the poor amplification and often unintelligent use of sound in what was supposed to be a part-talkie. The *New York Times* generously described it as "average" in comparison with sound pictures from other studios. The reviewer continued, "The theme song is pretty, but when shouts and wailings are introduced the effects become bathetic. Mr. Blue, trying to attract attention, once calls 'Hello,' but not being much above a whisper, the result is a bit ridiculous. A group of male voices heard every now and then is also unfortunate."[66] *Our Dancing Daughters,* which came next, was directed by Harry Beaumont and starred Joan Crawford, Johnny Mack Brown, and Nils Asther. It was essentially a silent movie, despite its title, but was originally released with Movietone sound effects and a score. One jaded reviewer irritably dismissed this strident drama of flappers and the Jazz Age as a movie with "several love songs, stentorian cheering, and, at the end, a chorus of shrieks." *Our Dancing Daughters* was followed by King Vidor's *Show People,* a scintillating satire on Hollywood that gained nothing in particular from its sound effects and music. Its main attractions were outstanding comedy performances by Marion Davies and William Haines, and a galaxy of cameo appearances by such notables as Charlie Chaplin, Douglas Fairbanks, John Gilbert, Mae Murray, and Elinor Glyn.

In mid-November 1928, MGM released a particularly interesting program of sound films. It opened with several amusing "sketches" demonstrating the range of Movietone and the audible talents of some of the studio's stock players, including Joan Crawford, John Gilbert, Ernest Torrence, and George K. Arthur. These "shorts" were followed by a part-talkie, *Alias Jimmy Valentine,* a rather noisy crime melodrama, directed by Jack Conway and starring Lionel Barrymore and William Haines. As with *The Lion and the Mouse* earlier in the year, Barrymore again demonstrated an instinctive sensitivity to the limitations and potentialities of the microphone. His dialogue was delivered in a clearer and more natural fashion than anyone else's in the picture. Last came *Masks of the Devil,* a drama of old Vienna based on a story by Jakob Wassermann. It was directed by the veteran Swedish director, Victor Seastrom, and commendable performances were turned in by John Gilbert and Alma Rubens. But there was no recorded dialogue and nothing particularly memorable about the recorded music or sound effects. It was the last of MGM's adventures in sound for 1928 —a demonstration of initial efforts that were almost as unenterprising as Columbia's.

UNITED ARTISTS

At this period, United Artists was operating mainly as a distributing organization for the productions of smaller, independent film producers. Thus three of the four sound films released in 1928 under the studio's logo were actually independent productions—though UA provided the facilities for synchronization by Movietone. The first of these independent features was *Two Lovers,* a Sam Goldwyn production directed by Fred Niblo. An historical romance set in seventeenth-century Flanders, it starred Ronald Colman, Vilma Banky, Paul Lukas, and Eugenie Besserer. (Eugenie Besserer had even less to say in this picture than in *The Jazz Singer,* for there was no recorded dialogue.) Originally premiered in March 1928, before United Artists had access to Movietone sound, the picture was first released in silent form, then re-released with recorded music and sound effects. UA's major sound feature of the year was *The Battle of the Sexes,* which D. W. Griffith directed for the Art Cinema Corporation. The film was based on a story by Daniel Carson Goodman and starred Phyllis Haver, Jean Hersholt, and Belle Bennett. In her monograph on Griffith, Iris Barry noted, "A synchronous music track [the music was by R. Schildkret] and a theme song sung by Phyllis Haver were added to this essentially silent film, and it is as a silent film that it survives today. It was typical of this period of Griffith's career that he had little to do with the synchronized score, and that when he heard it he didn't like it."[67] UA's only nonindependent sound release for 1928 was *The Woman Disputed,* based on Guy de Maupassant's story "Boule de Suif" and directed by Henry King and Sam Taylor. The picture starred Norma Talmadge and Gilbert Roland and boasted a song with the absurd title "Woman Disputed I Love You." Like all of UA's sound films before 1929, this film had no recorded dialogue. Finally, in December, the studio released *Revenge,* an Edwin Carewe production directed by Carewe and starring Dolores Del Rio and James Marcus. The score for this exotic gypsy melodrama was provided by Hugo Riesenfeld.

WALT DISNEY

Thus far we have glanced at the output of every studio in Hollywood except the smallest. But the smallest was, in fact, the most creative and was to make the most significant contribution to sound cinema since Vitaphone.

Before 1928, Walt Disney was merely one of many struggling producers of animated cartoons. The capital assets of his modest studio had never amounted to more than about $30,000. His attempts to popularize two cartoon series—the *Alice* films (combining a real little girl with animated figures) and the *Oswald the Rabbit* films—paled beside the successes of his leading competitors: Max Fleischer (*Out of the Inkwell* series), Pat Sullivan (*Felix the Cat* series), and Paul Terry (*Aesop's Fables* and *Farmer Al Falfa* series). So, when, some time in 1927, a new cartoon character, Mickey Mouse (originally named Mortimer Mouse), began to take shape on the drawing boards, Disney had no reason to suspect that he had arrived at the turning point of his career.

Mickey (and Minnie) Mouse were supposed to make their debuts in a silent cartoon entitled *Plane Crazy*. But while it was being made, Hollywood was rocked by the spectacular public response to *The Jazz Singer*. Disney went on to complete *Plane Crazy* and a second—also silent—Mickey Mouse picture, *Gallopin' Gaucho;* but he did not release them when he saw that the big studios were rushing into sound. Early in 1928, he decided to join the revolution by making a synchronized Mickey Mouse film. That was, as Christopher Finch remarks,

> perhaps the most important decision that Disney ever made. He wanted Mickey Mouse to have real impact, and he saw that the future lay with sound. What he had in mind was a cartoon in which music, effects, and action would all be synchronized. Max and Dave Fleischer had already produced a cartoon which used a Lee De Forest sound track, but the track had been unsynchronized and the experiment had had little impact on the industry. Disney's plan was for something far more radical.[68]

It was to be realized with *Steamboat Willie* (1928), the cartoon in which Mickey and Minnie actually made their first public appearance.

Curiously, it was Disney's relative insignificance in the industry that enabled and also encouraged him to take the leap into sound. Richard Schickel observes that Walt and his brother and partner Roy Disney

> were in somewhat the same position as the nearly bankrupt Warner Brothers had been: they had nothing to lose by experimenting with sound; their investment in unreleased product was negligible; they had no investment in actors whose vocal qualities might not be suitable to the microphone, and in the animated cartoon they had a medium ideally adapted to sound. . . . The

animation was shot silently as always, and sound was added later. This meant that . . . [Disney's] little films retained their ability to move while all about them were losing theirs. Just as important was the control he could exercise over the relationship between pictures and sound. They could be perfectly integrated simply by matching the musical rhythm to the rhythm of the drawn characters' movements.[69]

With *Steamboat Willie* Disney was to contribute one of the cinema's first truly creative treatments of sound. In making the film he was assisted by his brother Roy, Ub Iwerks, Wilfred Jackson, Les Clark, and a handful of other Disney employees. Iwerks was in charge of the actual drawing for the film's storyboard and separate cartoon cells. Jackson, who could play the harmonica, was required to improvise the music—a medley of popular songs including "Auld Lang Syne," "Yankee Doodle," "Dixie," and "Turkey in the Straw." His performance was augmented by the sounds of cowbells, whistles, a washboard, and an ocarina. "The picture was plotted to the tick of a metronome, which set rhythms for both Jackson . . . and Iwerks, who got from the metronome a sense of the rhythms he would have to use in his animations."[70] Les Clark would later recall,

> we worked with an exposure sheet on which every line was a single frame of action. We could break down the sound effects so that every eight frames we'd have an accent, or every sixteen frames, or every twelve frames. [Sound film runs through the projector at twenty-four frames a second.] And on that twelfth drawing, say, we'd accent whatever was happening—a hit on the head or a footstep or whatever it would be, to synchronize to the sound effect or the music.[71]

The tempo of the music was one beat to every twelve frames of film. The work-print was marked so that a flash of light showed up on the screen at those regular intervals; the accents were indicated by a bouncing ball. To achieve precise synchronization, to arrive at exact conformity of visual and aural rhythms, the conductor of the music simply had to time his beat to the flashes and be guided by the accenting of the bouncing ball. (The method was a primitive anticipation of techniques of audio-visual montage that would be employed by Eisenstein and Prokofiev in making *Alexander Nevsky,* 1938.)

Disney eventually got his score down on paper. Now came the problem of getting it recorded. Who would do the job for him? He approached RCA, but the technicians in charge of Photophone were not interested in the assignment—partly, perhaps, as Schickel suggests, because they considered the precise synchronization that he wanted to be either impossible or not worth their efforts. When he got the same reaction from Western Electric, he was forced to turn to one of the less-known sound systems. Pat Powers was eager to promote his Cinephone system, so he readily agreed to undertake the recording for *Steamboat Willie*. Carl Edouwards, conductor at the Capital Theater in New York, was hired to provide an orchestra and conduct the two recording sessions. The first, in which thirty-five musicians were used, was a disaster because Edouwards and his orchestra insisted that they knew better than Disney and ignored the marked beats and accents. At the second session the orchestra was reduced to seventeen, and Disney managed to persuade Edouwards to conduct the score as he had originally been asked to. Disney wrote his brother Roy,

> I finally got him to see it my way (he thinks he thought of the idea). The fact is that he just saw what I have been telling him for the last two weeks. . . . They are very clever in their line—but want too much beauty and too many Symphonic effects. . . . They think comedy music is low brow. . . . Believe me, I have had a tough fight getting them to come down to our level. . . . I feel positive we have everything worked out perfect now.[72]

Disney's idea of perfection at this period is perhaps best represented by the "Turkey in the Straw" sequence of *Steamboat Willie*. Here the humor is created out of a grotesque mistreatment of domestic and farm animals which "produce" the synchronized music and sound effects. Mickey Mouse supplies the music of "Turkey in the Straw" by tweaking a cow's udders and playing on her teeth as if they were a xylophone, and by plucking a cat's tail as if it were a guitar string. Minnie accompanies him by churning away at a goat's tail as if it were a hurdy-gurdy. The synchronized sound is absolutely integral to the total effect of this bizarre sequence.

Steamboat Willie was soon ready for distribution, but at this stage, Disney discovered that finding a distributor was even more of a problem than getting his little picture synchronized. Wearily, he hawked his film around New York. No one in the movie business showed the slightest interest in it until, at last, Harry Reichenbach, manager of the Colony Theatre, saw the cartoon at a special screening and offered Disney the chance of a two-week run. Disney asked for and received $1,000 for this exclusive presentation, which began on September 18, 1928—the day on which *The Singing Fool* was also premiered. Reichenbach had been a press agent and knew how to get the maximum newspaper publicity for his shows. Skillful promotion combined with considerable press coverage and growing public interest in the unique little film led to its being booked at the highly prestigious Roxy Theatre when it had concluded its run at the Colony. Distributors now began to approach Disney with demands for more synchronized Mickey Mouse cartoons. At this juncture, Pat Powers reappeared and offered what Disney considered the best deal available at the time: He would retain all rights to his films and Powers would receive 10 percent of the gross profits for arranging the distribution of Disney cartoons on a states' rights basis. If Disney had had to make a deal with one of the big studios (which at that time controlled most of the theaters), it would have been much less favorable and he would almost certainly have lost his independence. He could now afford to turn back to his creative work.

By the end of 1929, he had supplied *Plane Crazy* and *Gallopin' Gaucho,* his first two (silent) Mickey Mouse cartoons, with synchronized scores, and had made a fourth Mickey Mouse picture, *The Opry House.* These films, together with *Steamboat Willie,* were the basis of Disney's successful career, and they rapidly established Mickey Mouse as an international celebrity. Mickey did not appear in Disney's *The Skeleton Dance* (1929), but the film was as well received as the earlier sound cartoons and launched the celebrated series of *Silly Symphonies.* In that same year, Mickey challenged his only considerable cinematic rival of the sound era by starring in a cartoon called *The Jazz Fool*—to which Jolson could have no reply. Everyone was delighted to see Mickey masquerading as a man, but nobody was interested in seeing Jolson playing a mouse.

CHAPTER SEVEN

THE END OF
THE BEGINNING

Sounds and sweet airs, that give delight,
                                and hurt not.
Sometimes a thousand twangling instruments
Will hum about mine ears; and sometimes voices. . . .
SHAKESPEARE, *The Tempest*

In the shadows let me come and sing to you
Let me dream a song that I can bring to you. . . .
WARREN and DUBIN, *"The Shadow Waltz"*

We didn't need dialogue; we had *faces* then. . . . I'm still big;
it's the pictures that got smaller. . . .
GLORIA SWANSON AS NORMA DESMOND in *Sunset Boulevard*

1929: a year of sound and fury, signifying that the silent cinema
was doomed.[1]

Sound poured out of the studios in an ever-increasing cascade
of talkies, part-talkies and souped-up silents. The major contribution to the torrent was the combined feature production
of Warner Bros. and First National, a total of 67 sound pictures.
In the same year, Paramount pulled into second place, out-
stripping Fox by releasing 49 sound features to the latter's 47.
This achievement was remarkable in view of the fire that destroyed Paramount's newly constructed $400,000 sound stage

at the beginning of 1929.* In July, Winfield Sheehan, Fox's general manager, estimated that Hollywood had already invested more than $50 million in the transformation to sound and that it would take up to ten years for the investment to start paying off. But he also noted that movie theaters were doing 30 percent more business than in 1928 and that studio heads expected to do even better business in 1930. In fact, during the first years of the Depression, the film industry turned out to be one of the few oases of prosperity.

But there was fury as well as sound. It was expressed in a crescendo of objections—particularly from critics, theater managers, and a growing army of unemployed theater musicians.

Theater critics objected that Hollywood was robbing Broadway of its talent in order to make canned versions of stage productions. Movie critics objected that talkies were destroying the art of film. Some "sophisticates," who had never had anything good to say about Film, suddenly discovered that silent cinema was High Art and thereupon rushed to a spirited defense of the Tenth Muse, who was being wantonly throttled by those Philistines in Hollywood.

Theater managers were divided between those, like J. J. Shubert, who maintained that talking pictures posed no threat to legitimate theater at its best, and those involved with stock companies who suddenly found their profits dwindling as talkies began invading the suburbs and the provinces. In June 1929, twenty out of twenty-two theater managers at the annual convention of the Theatrical Stock Managers' Association complained that talking pictures were destroying business for their companies in the U. S. A *New York Times* editorial offered them cold comfort by observing that while "Talking pictures can never completely take the place of real people on a real stage . . . in their imitation of actual plays and musical shows the talkies are taking the essence of Broadway to every hamlet in the land."

The plight of many musicians was far worse than anything yet experienced by the theater managers. In August 1931, the

* See Appendix B for a detailed listing of Hollywood sound productions for 1929.

Monthly Labor Review of the U. S. Bureau of Labor Statistics revealed staggering information about the rise of unemployment among musicians as a result of technological changes in the film industry. In 1928 some 20,000 musicians had been employed by movie theaters across the country. *Monthly Labor Review* estimated that

> during the two years which marked the rapid growth of the sound picture, 9,885 musicians, or about 50 per cent of the total number of musicians employed in theaters were displaced. These figures, for the country as a whole, seem to be corroborated by the figures taken from [the American Federation of Musicians] Local No.802, the organization of musicians in New York City. In 1928 there were 3,200 musicians employed in theaters in that city. In 1931 only 1,500 musicians were thus employed, showing a loss of 1,700 or nearly 53 per cent of the total number.[2]

All these setbacks, it will be realized, exactly coincided with the first years of the Depression. The effects, in terms of human misery, can only be guessed at now, though one or two examples furnished by *Monthly Labor Review* are worth recalling in relation to the euphoria that prevailed at Warner Bros. and Fox after their initial triumphs with sound movies:

> *Case No. 14* has had a few miscellaneous engagements for playing, but no permanent job. He is compelled to live off savings which, according to his statement, may not last through the winter. He is 56 years old and has two sons, both musicians. One son is married and has a job, but the younger son still depends on the support of the parents. He is very discouraged about the future, particularly since he knows no other trade; he is trying to get at least a temporary job with a local symphony orchestra, but is not very hopeful.
>
> *Case No. 17* was a pianist in a small theater, averaging about $40 a week. He has been without a job since October, 1930; has taken the civil-service examination as translator, and is hoping to get a job soon. He is absolutely without means except for the little income that his wife brings in by occasional sewing in private homes; of late she too has been without work. The family lacks proper means of subsistence, and at times does not know where the food for the next day will come from; it may be a case for charity.[3]

Stunned, confused and angered, the musicians attempted to counteract the threat of sound movies by petitioning the studios, organizing public demonstrations, and placing pickets outside movie theaters. Joseph Weber, president of the American Federation of Musicians tried unsuccessfully to calm the rank and file by assuring his fellow members that their hardships would only be temporary, that within a year or so the industry would "adjust itself back to the human element." By April 1929 the *New York Times* was insisting that the crisis was already over, that musicians had every reason to be optimistic. The movie industry, it editorialized, had recently spent over $20 million in building new sound studios. "This looks like business, and not bad business for the musicians. The old silent studios carried from two to four musicians. Now they have two or more orchestras on hand for every studio. . . ."

But the crisis was not over. It was getting worse. The *Times's* "solution" was based on ignorance of the number of unemployed musicians and the relatively few that could be absorbed by the new demands of the sound studios. In May 1929, as a test case for union members in the 30,000 movie theaters in the U. S., the San Francisco musicians' union filed suit against Allied Amusements Industries, Inc., to restrain that organization's theaters from using sound projection apparatus without also employing organists and/or orchestras. The suit got the musicians nowhere. Like all their battles against Hollywood's new technology, it was doomed from the outset. Hordes of foreign-born musicians packed up and returned to Europe, where they expected to find that the impact of talkies was negligible. But French musicians were already up in arms about the threat that sound films were beginning to pose to their profession. They were even more incensed at the influx of musicians fleeing from America and swelling the ranks of the unemployed in France. In Britain, where a comparable situation existed, the Variety Artists' Federation issued the following appeal to the public:

> You should at the very least refrain from patronizing any place of amusement where an all-talker program has been introduced and where the management has ruthlessly discharged their mu-

sicians, artists and stage staff and substituted canned entertainment.[4]

By contrast with the theater musicians, composers—if they
had any talent at all—suddenly found themselves riding the
crest of the wave. In 1929 it looked as if Tin Pan Alley was
moving to Hollywood. Every studio was making musicals, and
theme songs were in constant demand for picture after picture
following the phenomenal popularity of such ditties as "Sonny
Boy," "Charmaine," and "Lilac Time." At the end of 1929,
George and Ira Gershwin accepted a $100,000 contract from
Fox to write the music and lyrics of their first sound picture.
The movie was *Delicious* (1931), directed by David Butler and
starring Janet Gaynor and Charles Farrell. The Gershwins
supplied four of their less-memorable numbers including the
title song, and George ventured into writing incidental film
music by scoring accompaniments for a dream sequence (music
for voice and orchestra) and for a montage of the sights and
sounds of a great city (orchestral background music). Most of
the music written for the montage sequence was not actually
used for the film, but it was later to become the basis for the
composer's *Second Rhapsody for Piano and Orchestra* (1932).[5]
Aside from the Gershwins, handsome contracts also lured Irving
Berlin, Harold Arlen, Jerome Kern, Jimmy McHugh, Harry
Warren, Vincent Youmans, Nacio Herb Brown, Harry Ruby,
Buddy DeSylva, and a host of other song writers to the movie
capital. As commentator John Flinn noted, talent scouts were
being sent to "every cabaret in New York and to every night
club in a mad search for song writers and lyricists."[6]

If the composers were doing well, stage hands and projectionists weren't doing too badly either. While the musicians
were wringing their hands in helpless desperation, Frank Gill-
more, acting president of Equity, and William F. Canavan,
president of the International Alliance of Theatrical Stage Employees, smugly announced that talkies had not created any unemployment problems for actors and stagehands. And *Monthly
Labor Review* for August 1931 noted that the talkies had
actually increased employment opportunities among motion
picture projectionists.

In the majority of theaters operating under an agreement with the motion picture machine operators' union, the place of every man, assisted by a boy helper, formerly employed to operate one silent-picture machine is now taken by two licensed men operating a sound-picture machine. The introduction of sound in the moving-picture theaters has thus theoretically doubled the chances for employment among the projectionists. . . . Membership of the International Alliance of Theatrical Stage Employees and Moving Picture Machine Operators shows an increase from 24,342 in 1926 to approximately 32,000 in 1931. . . . Unfortunately, however, the additional men employed as machine operators did not come from the ranks of the displaced musicians, and the situation among musicians is not improved by the greater demand for motion picture operators. Although the unions of musicians and operators have an agreement to cooperate in the case of strikes or other emergencies, there exists no understanding by which the increased demands for labor in the booth of the theatre could be filled from the ranks of labor released from the pit.[7]

Added to the cries and protests of the musicians were those of deaf moviegoers, for whom silent cinema had been a major source of entertainment. They were now suddenly confronted with movies with no insert titles but with spoken dialogue, music, and sound effects that they could not hear. Hard-of-hearing clubs throughout America appealed to the movie studios to continue making silent films—or at least to provide readable captions or subtitles for the talkies. But the studios were also getting enthusiastic and appreciative letters from the blind, who had got nothing out of silent movies but now found that they could go to the cinema and enjoy listening to musicals or to the dialogue of film dramas.

Movie patrons who were neither blind nor deaf complained about the intrusion of external noises (passing traffic, etc.), echoes from auditoria walls, and the uneven quality of sound in various parts of the theaters. From some seats the talkie dialogue was barely audible, while in others persons in the audience were in danger of losing their hearing from the excessive volume. These problems were not to be successfully overcome until the early thirties—when movie theaters were soundproofed and "multi-cellular high frequency horn loudspeakers" were introduced. Through the latter, as Dennis Sharp has noted, "It . . . [became] possible . . . to focus and unify the sound and beam it to various parts of the auditorium."[8] These developments were to affect radically the design of movie theaters from 1930 onwards.[9] But meanwhile, in 1929, there were widespread objections to the talkies for developing public insensitivity to sound in general and to music in particular.

Rosa Ponselle, famed soprano of the Metropolitan Opera Company, denounced sound movies as a cacophony—"something between a hacksaw and Edison's first phonograph. *Faust* and *Aida*," she maintained, "would sound like a mammy song" if they were made into sound pictures. The *New York Times*, echoing some of the current criticism of the sound quality of talkies, editorialized with tongue-in-cheek:

> One of the troubles which the sound films have had is that the voices of men sound almost exactly alike. Audiences have had real difficulty in deciding which of the characters in a scene is speaking, and wry necks have resulted from the swift turnings of the cervical vertebrae to ascertain the face from which the voice is coming. Some of the finest modulations ever acquired by actors in drawing-room comedy come off the film sounding like a cascade of mush. This has become one of the super-industrial problems of America.

More serious industrial problems were brewing in Europe. During March 1929, representatives of the major film companies (and related organizations) of Germany, France, and Britain, having spent several months denouncing America's virtual monopoly of the sound film market in Europe, met in Berlin to decide a common strategy against the growing transatlantic threat. Within a short time they revealed a merger of their interests in a $100 million trust that controlled more than 400 patents in the field of sound recording. They simultaneously announced that they were planning an extensive program of European coproductions. The companies involved were Siemens-Halske, General Electric of Germany, German and Foreign Tobis (representing Tri-Ergon), Kuechenmeister and Messter, and British and French Photophone.

The merger permitted the British and French companies to use Tri-Ergon patents, specifically those that were basic to the

Movietone system. General Electric undertook to manufacture, install, and service sound equipment for all the companies involved. Related developments further helped to bring the European and American systems into compatibility. The German firms of A. E. G., Siemens, and Telefunken, in conjunction with a Dr. Koenemann, had formed the Klangfilm Corporation, to promote research into the problems of sound film. Klangfilm was soon to merge with Tobis, which owned the rights to Tri-Ergon and now had access to Oskar Messter's patents and to Ultraphone, a sound system controlled by Kuechenmeister. The British journal *Wireless World* noted in April 1929:

> The "Tobis" group set themselves the task of combining the different processes belonging to them, and have produced a single-unit system, which is notable for the fact that the films conform to the international standards of size and perforation, so that standard film can be used in making it, with the consequence that the cinema proprietor is able to use standard projectors or to make use of speaking films of other makes. There are only a few unimportant alterations to be made to a standard projector to enable it to be used at will for silent or speaking films.[10]

A major objection of the European concerns was that American companies had adopted the restrictive practice of allowing only their own films to be shown with the sound systems that they controlled. Their practice was soon to be declared illegal by courts in all the European countries concerned, but in the interim it served to confirm the charges of American monopoly and to polarize the European and American film industries.

The Federation of British Industries followed up the European merger by immediately proclaiming that it would do everything possible to combat the American talkie monopoly. A month later, in April 1928, British Instructional Films Ltd. announced its own merger with Tobis-Klangfilm of Germany for the purpose of coproducing films in England and in order "to create a solid Anglo-European front against American sound film producers." About the same time, the great UFA organization of Germany revealed that it would enter large-scale competition with American film production by going over entirely to the making of sound movies. (In doing so, it would first use a magnetic sound-on-film recording system based on a 1913 German patent of Dr. Stille.) Meanwhile, oblivious of or indifferent to the imminent industrial war, J. E. Otterson, president of ERPI, proudly informed the press that 100 European movie theaters had already been supplied with Western Electric sound systems and that his company expected to equip at least 900 more before the end of the year.*

An amusing glimpse of ERPI and Western Electric engaged at this period in both promotion of sound movies and public enlightenment as to how they work, survives in the form of an animated sound cartoon, *Finding His Voice,* directed by F. Lyle Goldman and Max Fleischer. The story credit was given to "W. E. Erpi." It tells how a poor little strip of silent movie, muffled and unable to express himself except through visual titles (which, rather curiously, appear at the top of the screen), is brought up to date with the aid of an all-talking, all-singing jolly strip of talkie and his friend Dr. Western. Complaining that he has been out of work for a long time, the silent movie asks his audible pal, "Where did you get your voice?" Talkie assures him that he'll never get a job unless he learns how to use his voice. Whereupon he takes his silent partner along to the office of Dr. Western—"Film Surgeon: Voices Lifted." The good doctor obligingly takes the two movies on a swift tour of the inner workings of his sound-on-film system, at the end of which, the silent movie has learned how to find his voice and is able to join his fellow film in singing a duet.

By mid-1929 almost every capital city in Europe had had its first experience of sound movies. In most instances that meant yet another premiere of *The Jazz Singer.*

In the Soviet Union, where inventor Professor Shorin claimed to have developed a successful Russian sound system, there was serious talk of reneging on a deal for importing talkie apparatus from the West and ordering mass production of Shorin's equipment. A few months earlier, in the August 5, 1928 issue of the journal *Zhizn Iskusstva,* Eisenstein, Pudovkin, and G. V. Alexandrov made what was to become an historical statement plead-

* An elaborate diagram showing the use of various sound systems by American and European studios appears in *Business Week,* September 17, 1930, p.22.

ing for the contrapuntal use of sound, for nonsynchronization with the visual image rather than sound recording on a naturalistic level. The statement, later to be included as an appendix to Eisenstein's *Film Form,* prophetically warned against the upsurge of photographed theater in place of true cinematic art.

In the Orient two theaters in Tokyo and one in Shanghai had been wired for sound by mid-1929. The premiere presentation was, of course, *The Jazz Singer,* in China retitled "Song of Pious Son."[11] By the end of the year American sound movies were also showing in six other Japanese cities, and in Bombay, Calcutta, Manila, Singapore, and Batavia, and plans were afoot to begin production of Japanese-language talkies in the Nikkatsu and Schojiki studios near Kyoto.

Back in Hollywood the coming of sound undoubtedly created panic among many established stars of the silent screen. Did they have the right kind of voices? Could they adapt or would they be replaced by a horde of new stars from legitimate theater? Among silent stars without stage experience an elocution teacher suddenly became much more of a necessity than a swimming pool or a new Rolls-Royce. (Mrs. Patrick Campbell was imported to coach Norma Shearer; Gloria Swanson's teacher was Laura Hope Crews; while Constance Collier was hired to improve the diction of Colleen Moore.) "It was natural," observed William DeMille, "that as the coming of sound cast some actors into outer darkness, it raised others into the light. Even as certain voices destroyed the glamor of a personality, others gave power and character which the silent screen could not convey."[12]

But there is little truth to the persistent myth that all or even most of the careers of silent stars were eclipsed as soon as they spoke from the screen. In fact, there were those—like Richard Barthelmess and Wallace Beery—who took the transition in stride, and others—like Joan Crawford, Evelyn Brent, Ronald Colman, and Gary Cooper—whose popularity actually increased as they entered the sound era. The careers of Betty Compson, Bebe Daniels, Bessie Love, Myrna Loy, Jean Arthur, Carole Lombard, Conrad Nagel, and William Powell—all either supporting players or stars whose appeal had begun to wane—improved spectacularly with the arrival of talkies.[13]

Those stars whose careers were adversely affected by the coming of sound fell into four main categories. First there were those—like John Gilbert—whose voices failed to measure up to the expectations raised by their silent-screen personalities. Gilbert, one of the "great lovers" of the silent-film period, turned out to have a rather slight, undistinguished voice instead of the strong, masculine tones expected by his fans. The preview audience at his first talkie, *His Glorious Night* (1929), greeted his most serious utterances with derisive laughter. The effect on Gilbert's self-esteem was disastrous. Therafter, his career began a slow decline from which he never recovered. A second group —mainly women—were those whose voices were adequate but whose silent-screen images or acting styles increasingly failed to conform to the changing demands of sound cinema. Among them were Clara Bow, Mary Pickford, and Colleen Moore, all of whom retired from the screen in the early thirties after making easy and initially successful transitions to talkies. A third category consisted of silent comedians who were eclipsed by the rise of gag comedy typified by the Marx Brothers and Mae West or by the popularity of screwball comedies like *It Happened One Night, Bombshell,* and *Bringing Up Baby.* This group included Buster Keaton, Harold Lloyd, and Harry Langdon. Only Chaplin survived the transition without making any concessions to sound or suffering any decline in his reputation.

Finally, certain foreign stars established in Hollywood movies were adversely affected by the coming of talkies. "The whole problem of foreigners in sound films appeared to be this," writes Julian Fox on the transitional period 1929–33. "Mexicans—yes; Swedes—yes; Germans—occasionally; French—providing they happened to be Maurice Chevalier or the totally unaccented Claudette Colbert, yes. But Slavs? Very definitely 'no.' "[14] In other words Latins like Dolores Del Rio and Lupe Velez, Scandinavians like Garbo (and to a lesser extent Nils Asther), and Germans like Marlene Dietrich (but not Emil Jannings, whose accent was incomprehensible to many Americans) either remained or became popular in the thirties, while "Slavs" like Vilma Banky and Pola Negri were definitely "out."

But stars of the theater were definitely "in." Ironically, as the talkie *Broadway Melody of 1929* sang of the lights that were gay on the Great White Way, many of the leading luminaries of Broadway were heading West for their debuts in talking pictures. In fact, the lights became dimmer that year than at any time since World War I. Some of Broadway's brightest stars departed, never to return, and some theaters that managed to survive the increasing competition from the talkies would be forced to close in the wake of the financial cataclysm that hit Wall Street in October 1929.

The theatrical invasion of Hollywood was headed by Jeanne Eagels, sensational star of the Broadway production of *Rain.* Her talkie debut was in another Somerset Maugham opus, *The Letter* (1929), in which she costarred with Reginald Owen and Herbert Marshall, and for which she received an Academy Award nomination as Best Actress. (The Oscar went to Mary Pickford for her role as Norma Besant, in her first talkie, *Coquette.*) Ruth Chatterton, who had graced memorable stage productions of *Daddy Long Legs* and *Mary Rose,* began her very active talkie career with *Sins of the Fathers* (1929). She, too, was nominated for an Oscar for her performance in *Madame X,* another 1929 talkie.

In the same year, Hollywood productions were enriched by such theatrical talent as Sophie Tucker in *Honky Tonk* (in which she sang two of her best-known numbers: "He's a Good Man to Have Around" and "I'm the Last of the Red-Hot Mammas"), Beatrice Lillie in *Show of Shows,* Gertrude Lawrence in *The Battle of Paris* (in which she sang four songs by Cole Porter), George Arliss in *Disraeli* (Arliss had appeared in a silent version in 1921), Rudy Vallee in *The Vagabond Lover,* Basil Rathbone in *The Last of Mrs. Cheyney* (he had acted in silent films with Helen Chadwick, Mae Murray, and Gloria Swanson), and Paul Muni in *The Valiant* (for which he received an Oscar nomination; but the award went to Warner Baxter for his performance as the Cisco Kid in *In Old Arizona*), and Walter Huston in *Gentlemen of the Press.*

Ziegfeld stars Marilyn Miller, Fanny Brice, Helen Morgan, Ina Claire, Eddie Cantor, Will Rogers, and Harry Richman all appeared in their first talkies between 1928 and 1930, while many of the girls that Ziegfeld shows had glorified left the chorus line and headed for stardom via the silver screen. This particular contingent was led by Ruby Keeler and Barbara Stanwyck.

Ziegfeld himself made appearances in Universal's *Show Boat* and in Paramount's part-color movie spectacular *Glorifying the American Girl*. Not even *his* most star-studded stage productions were able to match the galaxies that appeared in Warner Bros.' *The Show of Shows* (1929), MGM's *Hollywood Revue of 1929*, and *Paramount on Parade* (1930). If opulence and stars were all that were needed, the talkies would have rendered vaudeville extinct within three years of *The Jazz Singer*.[15]

Relatively few of the big theatrical stars imported by Hollywood in the first years of the talkies were to survive in movies beyond the mid-thirties. But a hardier breed of theatrical performer followed the invasion of the big Broadway talent. From this less-publicized group of actors were to come Hollywood's most enduring stars.

The unsinkable Bette Davis began her Broadway career in 1929 in Martin Flavin's comedy *Broken Dishes*. A year later, after two stage flops, she was signed up by Universal for her first picture, *Bad Sister,* in which one of the supporting actors was Humphrey Bogart. During the twenties, Bogey played a romantic juvenile in a succession of Broadway plays in which he often walked on wearing flannels and sneakers and carrying a tennis racquet. His first movie appearance was in 1930 in a Vitaphone short (they had reached no.960 by this time!) in which he costarred with Ziegfeld singer Ruth Etting and Joan Blondell. Unimpressive performances in ten features and an ignominious retreat from Hollywood back to legitimate theater were to occupy him until his triumphal return as Duke Mantee in the screen version of *The Petrified Forest* (1936). Edward G. Robinson, by contrast, had had an impressive stage career in the twenties, receiving critical acclaim for performances in plays by Ibsen, Shaw, and Pirandello, and also thrilling theater audiences with his portrayal of a Capone-like gangster in Bartlett Cormack's play *The Racket* (1927), an anticipation of his unforgettable performance in *Little Caesar* (1931). In Robinson's one silent film, *The Bright Shawl* (1923), he had played the supporting role of a Spanish grandee. But in his first talkie, *The Hole in the Wall* (1930), which was also the first talkie of his costar, Claudette Colbert, he played the lead, and his performance in the role of Tony Garotta established him as the

Italian-American gangster type. The ever-versatile James Cagney, an expert hoofer in the vaudeville of the twenties, co-starred with Joan Blondell in Marie Baumer's drama, *Penny Arcade*. Al Jolson bought the rights to the play and sold them to Warner Bros. on condition that Cagney and Blondell repeated their performances for the screen adaptation. *Penny Arcade*, retitled *Sinner's Holiday* (1930), brought Cagney and Blondell to Hollywood. A year and three features later, Cagney starred in *The Public Enemy*. The rest is movie history.[16]

Few screenwriters of the silent period made successful transitions into the sound era. Notable exceptions were Frances Marion, Anita Loos, Bess Meredyth, C. Gardner Sullivan, Jules Furthman, and Ernest Vajda. Frances Marion had written scenarios for Mary Pickford (e.g., *Pollyanna*, 1920) and adapted Fannie Hurst's *Humoresque* (1920) for the first of two versions of that story to be directed by Frank Borzage. Her first screenplay of the sound period was the pace-making prison melodrama, *The Big House* (1930). Anita Loos, whose earliest scripts were for D. W. Griffith in 1913, entered the sound era with the screenplay for his disastrous final film, *The Struggle* (1931), but continued with such commercial successes as *San Francisco* (directed by W. S. Van Dyke, 1936), *Riffraff* (directed by J. Walter Rubin, 1935), and *The Women* (directed by George Cukor, 1939). Her perennially popular novel, *Gentlemen Prefer Blondes*, was filmed in 1928 (screenplay by Loos and her husband, John Emerson) and again in 1953, as a vehicle for Marilyn Monroe (screenplay) by Charles Lederer). C. Gardner Sullivan wrote such sermonizing melodramas as *Hairpins* (directed by Fred Niblo, 1920), *The Soul of the Beast*, and *Human Wreckage* (both directed by John Griffith Wray, 1923), and also the screenplays for Cecil B. De Mille's talkie epics, *The Buccaneer* (1938), *Union Pacific* (1939), and *North West Mounted Police* (1940).

Jules Furthman began screenwriting in 1918, under the pseudonym of Stephen Fox. Among the several dozen of his scripts filmed in the silent years were *Hotel Imperial* (directed by Mauritz Stiller, 1927), *The Way of All Flesh* (directed by Victor Fleming, 1927), and *The Docks of New York* (directed by Josef von Sternberg, 1928). His screenplays of the sound period included more films by von Sternberg (*Morocco,* 1930; *Shanghai Express,* 1932; and *The Shanghai Gesture,* 1941) and Victor Fleming (*Common Clay* and *Renegades,* both 1930, and *Bombshell,* 1933), as well as films directed by Raoul Walsh (*The Yellow Ticket,* 1931), Tay Garnett (*China Seas,* 1935), Frank Lloyd (*Mutiny on the Bounty,* 1935), and Howard Hughes (*The Outlaw,* 1943). Among his later scripts was one for Howard Hawks's *Rio Bravo* (1959). The handful of other screenwriters who survived the silent period included Julien Josephson, Edmund Goulding, Sonya Levien, Harvey Thew, and Grover Jones.

At the end of the twenties Hollywood became a mecca for writers who had never written a screenplay but were experienced in writing dramatic dialogue. They did much to make the first two or three years of the talkies sound like filmed theater as well as look like it. They were to be followed, however, by a generation of screenwriters who understood that cinematic dialogue requires an idiom of its own. The screenplays of Norman Krasna, Ben Hecht, Walter Reisch, Gene Markey, Donald Ogden Stewart, Joseph L. Mankiewicz, Charles Lederer, Dudley Nichols, Robert E. Sherwood, Kubec Glasmon, Francis Faragoh, Morrie Ryskind, and Nunnally Johnson—all of whom wrote their first Hollywood scripts between 1929 and 1934—were full of brief, vivid scenes and characters who spoke a language that was concise, racy, and dynamic, echoing the ceaseless, teeming vitality of America's burgeoning cities.

Many genres of the silent cinema declined in popularity or disappeared altogether with the coming of sound. But gangster and mystery/detective melodramas got a new lease on life. They offered superabundant opportunities for talk and noise, for stretches of dialogue in which police and detectives, gangsters and other villains sometimes strained the patience of audiences with long-winded explanations or self-revelations; for interminable courtroom scenes; for the sounds of machine guns, exploding bombs, screeching cars, police sirens, and whistles; high-pitched screams of threatened heroines and low-pitched growls of man-hunting bloodhounds. Also, two new genres, the musical (established with the Jolson pictures) and the gag comedy (strongly boosted by the Marx Brothers' first film, *The*

Cocoanuts, 1929), began to vie in popular appeal with the gangster melodrama.

The year before Cagney took to toting guns through a long succession of movies, Alan Crosland was back at Warner Bros. directing *On with the Show,* the first "audible prismatic feature film"—sound movie in two-tone Technicolor. Several studios, including Warner Bros., also released other sound movies containing color *sequences.*

With the 1928 film *In Old Arizona* (directed by Raoul Walsh), Fox had tried the experiment of making a feature in the great outdoors. MGM, not to be outdone, encouraged director Sam Wood to take his Movietone apparatus into city streets, where he found that he was able to record dialogue for his feature *So This Is College?* quite audibly above the din of heavy traffic. These films convincingly demonstrated that—at least when Movietone was being used—talkies did not have to be made exclusively in the insulated confines of sound studios. The camera could be liberated from its booth, and the actor could again become mobile. More spectacularly than the experiments of Walsh and Wood, director W. S. Van Dyke announced that he was having tons of sound equipment crated and shipped abroad to make a talkie in the jungles of Africa! This film was to be his very successful *Trader Horn* (1931).

The Fox Company, impressed with the technological "perfection" of their sound system as well as by the soaring profits from their sound movies, announced in March 1929 that their studio would be going over entirely to the production of musical and dialogue pictures. Columbia released a similar statement a few days later. The other studios held back, but one by one in the next few months they capitulated to the inevitable, declaring that they too were in the business of making talkies, talkies, and only talkies.

Fox's general manager, Winfield Sheehan, was placed at the head of a new $10 million sound studio complex, to be called Fox Hills. When completed, it was stated, the plant would cover 180 acres and incorporate 25 sound stages. It was a whole continent, a billion dollars, and half a century away from where it had all started: in Edison's laboratory in West Orange.

The spreading ripples of motion picture sound technology

and the widespread acceptance of the talkies as an institution that had arrived to stay were evident in three unrelated news items appearing in 1929. In the spring the *New York Times* noted that the White House had been wired for talkies. An editorial commented, "If any stubborn persons have resisted the overwhelming invitation of the talkies, they may as well give up now. The President and Mrs. Hoover have accepted the innovation." In October the same paper published a glossary of more than 100 terms used by motion picture sound engineers, many of which had gained currency outside the studios. They included such "new" words as *dubbing, flutter, boom, mixer, movieola,* and *camera blimp.* But the major news event that showed unequivocally that the sound era had "arrived" was Hollywood's own approval of the talkies: for it was a talkie, *Broadway Melody,* that received the Academy Award for Best Picture of 1929, while Oscars for the Best Actor and Actress went to performers who had also appeared in sound features.

And so, for better or worse, sound had married image: the talkies had been born, and Hollywood had legitimized the birth. What next? "I think," wrote D. W. Griffith in 1929, "that the talking picture, when it is made into a rhythmic and cogent whole, will be an eighth art, a combination and synthesis of all the arts, and hence will be more flexible and useful to the complex twentieth century."[17] It took fifty years from the invention of the phonograph to the birth of the talkies. It has taken considerably less than half a century to prove Griffith's prophecy correct.

SPECTRUM OF OPINION, 1928–29

Talkies, squeakies, moanies, songies, squawkies. . . . But whatever you call them, I'm absolutely serious in what I have to say about them. Just give them ten years to develop and you're going to see the greatest artistic medium the world has known. Just think: you can get all the movement, the swing, the rhythm and the drive of the best of the old silent pictures into them. There you have your appeal to the eye. And added to this you have the human voice. And music, the one perfect art. You can combine the features of the picture, the opera, the legitimate theatre. As for the picture part of it, it will be superior to the painter's art, for it will be alive. . . .

   D. W. GRIFFITH, *film director*

To wish the movies to be articulate is about as sensible as wishing the drama to be silent. The movies are designed for pantomime, nothing more. . . . If the Vitaphone were to stick to words of one syllable, the movies might use it to some advantage. . . . But the moment it went in for words of two or, on gala occasions, three, Mr. Adolph Zukor would have to sell his twelve Rolls-Royces and 82-carat diamond suspender buckles, learn English, and go back to work.

   GEORGE JEAN NATHAN, *drama critic and editor*

As rapidly as theatres throughout the country are being fitted for the audible films, it is preposterous to suppose that the time will ever come when all houses, the length and breadth of the United States, will be so equipped. . . . An occasional audible picture will suffice for some audiences whose steady and uninterrupted patronage will continue to be accorded to the silent picture.

   ALBERT WARNER *of Warner Bros.*

I believe in the future of talking films because the day of the director is over and that of the author and playwright arrived. . . . I believe that through the help of audible pictures, English will become the universal language.

SAMUEL GOLDWYN, *film producer*

The nicest thing about film so far was that it kept its mouth shut. It would have been terrible if one had accompanied with words the stupidities which were played. That was the only reason I did not permit the filming of my plays, because their greatest strength was their dialogue. . . . The mere fact that the importance of words in the film is recognized will pave the way for writers because ultimately one will be able to distinguish between the good and the bad text. That will secure for the films gifted playwrights the same as it does the stage, although both are different in character.

BERNARD SHAW, *dramatist*

With the word mechanically engraved on the film, the cinema—which is the dumb expression of images and the language of appearances—achieves the result of destroying itself in order to become a mechanical copy of the theatre—a copy which can only be bad. . . .

LUIGI PIRANDELLO, *dramatist*

The talking picture will . . . in its perfection accomplish the making of the audience a party to the dramatic conflict. . . . In the audible picture . . . there is no line of demarcation between the characters and the audiences such as is inevitably formed by the footlights of the stage, nor is there the spectre of unreality, or uninterrupted action, such as the titles of a silent picture. . . . It is the enormous dynamics of the screen, as compared with the confines of the stage, which should . . . enable audiences to participate in the doings of the characters. Nor is the achievement of this objective a lowly goal for which to strive. For an hour where dreams come true is worth years of strife in the present mad scramble for wealth; nothing could be closer to the pursuit of happiness than the fantasy produced by a few thousand feet of realistic bits of photography.

PAUL FEJOS, *film director*

There have been enough sound and talking pictures to give every fan the opportunity of judging for himself. They are a distinct advance over the silent picture and have created a new class of theatre-goers, whose interest in the play interpreted by flesh-and-blood actors has been revived.

J. J. SHUBERT, *theatre manager and producer*

I am still Max Reinhardt, but if I signed a talkie contract I should no more be myself. I admit that at Hollywood I enjoyed the talkies, but for me they miss the greatest sensation of the legitimate theatre: . . . the mystic link between the audience and the people on the stage. . . .

　　MAX REINHARDT, *stage director and producer*

Personally, I am convinced that films should be seen and not heard. The business of the film is to depict action, not to reproduce sound. It is not that one is opposed to something which is new, for the film itself is new and we would not be without it. But the spoken word, mechanically introduced, is not proper to the film medium, and tends to destroy the illusion which the film is trying to build up. . . . There is something monstrous about a speaking film. . . .

　　ERNEST BETTS, *film critic*

The future of the talkie is one of the most entertaining speculations; roughly there are three paths:

1　The talkie may develop as a separate medium, having hardly anything to do with the movie except that it uses the same mechanism for entirely different purposes;
2　It may create a sort of hybrid with itself and the movie as the components in variable proportions;
3　The movie may incorporate the talkie, or vice versa, creating an entirely new form—cinephonics, perhaps—in which the principles of the movie will not be abandoned.

　　GILBERT SELDES, *critic of popular culture*

The future certainly belongs to the talking films and Germans, who are the best actors in the world, will and must take the leadership in this respect.

　　EMIL JANNINGS, *film actor*

INTERVIEWER: What do you think about the future of talking pictures?
EDISON: Without great improvements people will tire of them. Talking is no substitute for [the] good acting that we have had in the silent pictures.

　　THOMAS ALVA EDISON, *inventor*

The life of the theatre is a matter of centuries; that of the talkie a few months. The former has been the struggle of an art to assert itself, in spite of poverty, persecution and contumely, until it has won worthy acceptance in the world. The latter has been the sudden revelation of a scientific discovery emerging from a glut of gold which attempts to do the same thing.

SACHA GUITRY, *actor and dramatist*

The latest and most frightful creation-saving device for the production of standardized amusement. . . .

ALDOUS HUXLEY, *novelist*

Only a contrapuntal use of sound in relation to the visual montage piece will afford a new potentiality of montage development and perfection. . . . Such a method for constructing the sound-film will not confine it to a national market, as must happen with the photographing of plays, but will give a greater possibility than ever before for the circulation throughout the world of a filmically expressed idea.

S. M. EISENSTEIN, V. I. PUDOVKIN, G. V. ALEXANDROV, *film directors*

Scientifically the invention is fascinating. It belongs with the other mechanical marvels of the age, with the aeroplane, the automobile, and the telephone. But artistically it is about as exciting as a vacuum cleaner. It makes no contribution to beauty.

F. T. PATTERSON, *screenwriter*

The talking picture is apparently doomed to grope blindly for several years before it reaches anything that may properly be described as an original form of drama. That it will reach this goal eventually does not seem to me in the least doubtful. . . . So far its greatest successes have been scored in a field which does not quite come under the definition of "talking." Pictures like *The Singing Fool* or *My Man* are really "song pictures." The fact, however, that they succeed in conveying their appeal to the audience is vastly significant. Lacking as they are in color and depth, they still capture something of the personality of the artist.

ALEXANDER BAKSHY, *critic*

To realize the greatest possibilities of characterization of sound in talkies, a loud sound shaking the talkie theatre to its foundation and a trifling sound as of dripping water are both necessary.

YASUSHI OGINO, *critic*

To the director, the most interesting possibility of the talking, or synchronized, picture is that of presenting a complex situation, such as that of hearing the voice of one actor and seeing the face of another. The reaction of the person addressed is frequently of more importance than the person speaking. Take this one very simple illustration. A man goes to the telephone and picks up the receiver. A voice on the other end says, "I'm sorry, but your wife and child have just been killed." We hear the voice without seeing the speaker. What we do see is the husband to whom this tragic news has been brought. That, to the director, would be something worth while. It has real dramatic interest. You can feel the grip of it; and out of this simple little illustration may come a thousand variations.

MONTA BELL, *film director*

As I see it, the talking picture is much more than a violent temporary rival of the theatre. It is a wealthy cousin that intends to rule the roost, however urbanely.

BASIL DEAN, *theatre producer*

Talkies may internationalize motion pictures if American and European actors become linguists. Otherwise the film industry will become more strictly nationalized than it has ever been.

ADOLPHE MENJOU, *actor*

APPENDIX **B**

HOLLYWOOD SOUND FEATURE FILMS

PRODUCED IN 1929

Abbreviations:
- (T) *all-talking film*
- (P) *part-talkie*
- (S) *synchronized sound film, usually only sound effects and/or music*
- D *director*
- Ls *leading stars*

WARNER BROS.

All productions used Vitaphone

The Aviator D: Roy Del Ruth (T)
　　Ls: Edward Everett Horton, Patsy Ruth Miller

Conquest D: Roy Del Ruth (T)
　　Ls: H. B. Warner, Monte Blue, Lois Warner, Tully Marshall

The Desert Song D: Roy Del Ruth (T) Some sequences in Technicolor.
　　Ls: John Boles, Carlotta King, Louise Fazenda, Myrna Loy, John Miljan

Evidence D: John G. Adolfi (T)
　　Ls: Pauline Frederick, Conway Tearle, Lowell Sherman, Myrna Loy

Fancy Baggage   D: John G. Adolfi   (P)
Ls: Myrna Loy, George Fawcett, Audrey Ferris

From Headquarters   D: Howard Bretherton   (P)
Ls: Henry B. Walthall, Monte Blue, Guinn Williams

Frozen River   D: F. Harmon Weight   (P)
Ls: Rin-Tin-Tin, Davey Lee, Josef Swickard

The Gamblers   D: Michael Curtiz   (T)
Ls: H. B. Warner, Lois Wilson, Jason Robards

General Crack   D: Alan Crosland   (T) Some sequences in Technicolor.
Ls: John Barrymore, Philippe De Lacy, Lowell Sherman, Hobart Bosworth

The Glad Rag Doll   D: Michael Curtiz   (T)
Ls: Dolores Costello, Ralph Graves, Audrey Ferris

Gold Diggers of Broadway   D: Roy Del Ruth   (T) In Technicolor.
Ls: Lilyan Tashman, Nancy Welford, Conway Tearle
Songs included "Tiptoe through the Tulips," "Painting the Clouds with Sunshine."

Greyhound Limited   D: Howard Bretherton   (P)
Ls: Monte Blue, Grant Withers, Edna Murphy

Hardboiled Rose   D: F. Harmon Weight   (P)
Ls: Myrna Loy, John Miljan, William Collier, Jr.

Hearts in Exile   D: Michael Curtiz   (T)
Ls: Dolores Costello, Grant Withers, James Kirkwood

Honky Tonk   D: Lloyd Bacon   (T)
Ls: Sophie Tucker, Audrey Ferris, Lila Lee
Songs included "He's a Good Man to Have Around," "I'm the Last of the Red-Hot Mammas."

The Hottentot   D: Roy Del Ruth   (T)
Ls: Edward Everett Horton, Patsy Ruth Miller

In the Headlines   D: John G. Adolfi   (T)
Ls: Grant Withers, Marion Nixon

Is Everybody Happy?   D: Archie Mayo   (T)
Ls: Ted Lewis, Alice Day
Songs included "Tiger Rag," "St. Louis Blues."

Kid Gloves   D: Ray Enright   (P)
Ls: Lois Wilson, Conrad Nagel

The Little Wildcat   D: Ray Enright   (P)
Ls: Robert Edeson, Audrey Ferris, George Fawcett, James Murray

The Madonna of Avenue A   D: Michael Curtiz   (P)
Ls: Dolores Costello, Grant Withers, Louise Dresser

The Million Dollar Collar   D: D. Ross Lederman   (P)
Ls: Rin-Tin-Tin, Evelyn Pierce, Matty Kemp

No Defense   D: Lloyd Bacon   (P)
Ls: May McAvoy, Monte Blue, Kathryn Carver

Noah's Ark   D: Michael Curtiz   (S)
Ls: Dolores Costello, Noah Beery, George O'Brien, Myrna Loy, Louise Fazenda

On with the Show   D: Alan Crosland   (P) "Prismatic" color film
Ls: Betty Compson, Ethel Waters, Joe E. Brown, Louise Fazenda, Wheeler Oakman, Arthur Lake
Songs included "Am I Blue?"

One Stolen Night   D: R. Scott Dunlap   (P)
Ls: Betty Bronson, Mitchell Lewis, William Collier, Jr.

Queen of the Night Clubs   D: Bryan Foy   (T)
Ls: Texas Guinan, Lila Lee, Eddie Foy, Jr., John Davidson, George Raft

The Royal Box   D: Bryan Foy   (T)
Ls: Alexander Moissi, Camilla Horn, Lew Hearn

The Sap   D: Archie Mayo
Ls: Edward Everett Horton, Alan Hale, Patsy Ruth Miller, Franklin Pangborn

Say It with Songs   D: Lloyd Bacon   (T)
Ls: Al Jolson, Davey Lee, Marion Nixon.
Songs included "One Sweet Kiss," "Back in Your Own Backyard."

The Show of Shows   D: John G. Adolfi   (T) Technicolor
Ls: Frank Fay, H. B. Warner, Hobart Bosworth, Marion Nixon, Myrna Loy, Patsy Ruth Miller, Ben Turpin, Lupino Lane, Noah Beery, Tully Marshall, Carmel Myers, Lloyd

Hamilton, Douglas Fairbanks, Jr., Bull Montana, John Barrymore, Richard Barthelmess, Sally Blane, Dolores Costello, Betty Compson, Helene Costello, Beatrice Lillie, Monte Blue, Loretta Young, Rin-Tin-Tin, etc., etc.
Songs included "You Were Meant for Me," "Rock-A-Bye Your Baby with a Dixie Melody."

Skin Deep   D: Ray Enright   (T)
> Ls: Monte Blue, Betty Compson, Davey Lee, Tully Marshall

Sonny Boy   D: Archie Mayo   (P)
> Ls: Davey Lee, Betty Bronson, Edward Everett Horton

Stark Mad   D: Lloyd Bacon   (T)
> Ls: H. B. Warner, Henry B. Walthall, Louise Fazenda, Jacqueline Logan, John Miljan

Stolen Kisses   D: Ray Enright   (P)
> Ls: May McAvoy, Hallam Cooley

Tiger Rose   D: Sidney A. Franklin   (T)
> Ls: Lenore Ulric, Forrest Stanley, André de Peranger

The Time, the Place and the Girl   D: Howard Bretherton   (T)
> Ls: Betty Compson, Grant Withers
> Songs included "Doin' the Raccoon," "I Wonder Who's Kissing Her Now."

FIRST NATIONAL
All productions used Vitaphone

Broadway Babies   D: Mervyn LeRoy   (P)
> Ls: Alice White, Charles Delaney

Careers   D: John Francis Dillon   (P)
> Ls: Billie Dove, Noah Beery, Carmel Myers, Antonio Moreno

The Careless Age   D: John Griffith Wray   (T)
> Ls: Carmel Myers, Douglas Fairbanks, Jr., Loretta Young

Children of the Ritz   D: John Francis Dillon   (S)
> Ls: Jack Mulhall, Dorothy Mackail

Dark Streets   D: Frank Lloyd   (T)
> Ls: Jack Mulhall, Lila Lee

The Divine Lady   D: Frank Lloyd   (S)
Ls: Corinne Griffith, Victor Varconi, H. B. Warner, Marie Dressler, Montague Love

Drag   D: Frank Lloyd   (T)
Ls: Richard Barthelmess, Lucien Littlefield

Fast Life   D: John Francis Dillon   (T)
Ls: Loretta Young, Douglas Fairbanks, Jr., Chester Morris

Footlights and Fools   D: William A. Seiter   (T)   Some sequences in Technicolor.
Ls: Fredric March, Colleen Moore

The Forward Pass   D: Eddie Cline   (T)
Ls: Loretta Young, Douglas Fairbanks, Jr.

The Girl from Woolworth's   D: William Beaudine   (T)
Ls: Alice White, Charles Delaney, Wheeler Oakman

The Girl in the Glass Cage   D: Ralph Dawson   (P)
Ls: Loretta Young, Ralph Lewis, Carroll Nye

Hard to Get   D: William Beaudine   (T)
Ls: Dorothy Mackail, James Finlayson, Louise Fazenda

Her Private Life   D: Alexander Korda   (T)
Ls: Billie Dove, Walter Pidgeon, Roland Young, Montague Love, Zasu Pitts, Thelma Todd

His Captive Woman   D: George Fitzmaurice   (P)
Ls: Milton Sills, Dorothy Mackail

The House of Horror   D: Benjamin Christensen   (P)
Ls: Louise Fazenda, James Ford, Chester Conklin, Dale Fuller

Isle of Lost Ships   D: Irvin Willat   (T)
Ls: Jason Robards, Virginia Valli

The Man and the Moment   D: George Fitzmaurice   (P)
Ls: Rod La Rocque, Billie Dove

A Most Immoral Lady   D: John Griffith Wray   (T)
Ls: Walter Pidgeon, Sidney Blackmer, Leatrice Joy, Montagu Love, Robert Edeson

Naughty Baby   D: Mervyn LeRoy   (S)
Ls: Jack Mulhall, Alice White, Thelma Todd

Prisoners   D: William A. Seiter   (P)
    Ls: Corinne Griffith, Ian Keith, Bela Lugosi
    Walter Morosco Production distributed by First National.

Sally   D: Alfred E. Green   (T)
    Ls: Colleen Moore, Leon Errol, Lloyd Hughes

Saturday's Children   D: Gregory La Cava   (P)
    Ls: Grant Withers, Corinne Griffith
    Walter Morosco Production distributed by First National.

Seven Footprints to Satan   D: Benjamin Christensen   (P)
    Ls: Sheldon Lewis, Thelma Todd

Smiling Irish Eyes   D: William A. Seiter   (T)
    Ls: Colleen Moore, James Hall, Robert Homans
    Songs included "Smiling Irish Eyes."

The Squall   D: Alexander Korda   (T)
    Ls: Myrna Loy, Richard Tucker, Alice Joyce, Loretta Young, Zasu Pitts

Twin Beds   D: Alfred Santell   (T)
    Ls: Patsy Ruth Miller, Jack Mulhall, Zasu Pitts

Two Weeks Off   D: William Beaudine   (P)
    Ls: Jack Mulhall, Dorothy Mackail, Gertrude Astor

Weary River   D: Frank Lloyd   (P)
    Ls: Richard Barthelmess, Betty Compson

Young Nowheres   D: Frank Lloyd   (T)
    Ls: Richard Barthelmess, Marion Nixon

FOX FILM CORPORATION
All productions used Movietone

Behind That Curtain   D: Irving Cummings   (T)
    Ls: Warner Baxter, Lois Moran, Boris Karloff

Big Time   D: Kenneth Hawks   (T)
    Ls: Lee Tracy, Mae Clark, Daphne Pollard, Stepin Fetchit, John Ford (playing himself)

Black Magic   D: George B. Seitz   (S)
    Ls: Henry B. Walthall, Josephine Dunn, Earle Fox, John Holland

Blue Skies   D: Alfred L. Werker   (S)
Ls: Helen Twelvetrees, Frank Albertson, Claude King

Captain Lash   D: John Blystone   (S)
Ls: Victor McLaglen, Claire Windsor, Clyde Cook

Chasing through Europe   D: David Butler   (P)
Ls: Sue Carol, Nick Stuart

Christina   D: William K. Howard   (P)
Ls: Janet Gaynor, Charles Morton

The Cockeyed World   D: Raoul Walsh   (T)
Ls: Victor McLaglen, Lily Damita, Edmund Lowe

The Exalted Flapper   D: James Tinling   (S)
Ls: Barry Norton, Sue Carol, Irene Rich, Stuart Erwin

The Far Call   D: Allan Dwan   (S)
Ls: Leila Hyams, Charles Morton, Arthur Stone, Randolph Scott

Four Devils   D: F. W. Murnau   (P)
Ls: Farrell MacDonald, Claire McDowell, Janet Gaynor

Fox Movietone Follies of 1929   D: David Butler   (T)
Ls: Lola Lane, John Breeden, Dixie Lee

Frozen Justice   D: Allan Dwan   (T)
Ls: Louis Wolheim, Robert Frazer, Lenore Ulric

Fugitives   D: William Beaudine   (S)
Ls: Don Terry, Madge Bellamy, Arthur Stone

The Ghost Talks   D: Lewis Seiler   (T)
Ls: Helen Twelvetrees, Stepin Fetchit, Carmel Myers

The Girl from Havana   D: Benjamin Stoloff   (T)
Ls: Lola Lane, Paul Page

Girls Gone Wild   D: Lewis Seiler   (S)
Ls: Sue Carol, Nick Stuart, Hedda Hopper

Hearts in Dixie   D: Paul Sloane   (T)
Ls: Clarence Muse, Eugene Jackson, Stepin Fetchit

Homesick   D: Henry Lehrman   (S)
Ls: Sammy Cohen, Marjorie Beebe, Henry Armetta

Hot for Paris   D: Raoul Walsh   (T)
Ls: Victor McLaglen, El Brendel, Fifi D'Orsay

Joy Street   D: Raymond Cannon   (S)
 Ls: Lois Moran, Nick Stuart

Love, Live and Laugh   D: William K. Howard   (T)
 Ls: George Jessel, Lila Lee

Making the Grade   D: Alfred E. Green   (P)
 Ls: Lois Moran, Edmund Lowe

Masked Emotions   D: David Butler   (S)
 Ls: George O'Brien, Nora Lane

Masquerade   D: Russell J. Birdwell   (T)
 Ls: Leila Hyams, Alan Birmingham, Clyde Cook

Nix on Dames   D: Donald Gallaher   (T)
 Ls: Mae Clark, Robert Ames, William Harrigan

Not Quite Decent   D: Irving Cummings   (P)
 Ls: Louise Dresser, Allan Lane, June Collyer

The One Woman Idea   D: Berthold Viertel   (S)
 Ls: Rod La Rocque, Marceline Day

Pleasure Crazed   D: Donald Gallaher   (T)
 Ls: Dorothy Burgess, Marguerite Churchill, Kenneth Mac-
 Kenna

Protection   D: Benjamin Stoloff   (S)
 Ls: Dorothy Burgess, Robert Elliott, Paul Page

Red Wine   D: Raymond Cannon   (S)
 Ls: Conrad Nagel, June Collyer, Arthur Stone

Romance of the Rio Grande   D: Alfred Santell   (T)
 Ls: Warner Baxter, Mary Duncan, Antonio Moreno

Romance of the Underworld   D: Irving Cummings   (S)
 Ls: Mary Astor, Ben Bard, John Boles

Salute   D: John Ford   (T)
 Ls: Helen Chandler, George O'Brien, Frank Albertson

Seven Faces   D: Berthold Viertel   (T)
 Ls: Paul Muni, Marguerite Churchill, Gustav von Seyffer-
 titz, Eugenie Besserer

The Sin Sister   D: Charles Klein   (S)
 Ls: Nancy Carroll, Josephine Dunn, Lawrence Gray

The Sky Hawk   D: John G. Blystone   (T)
Ls: Helen Chandler, John Garrick, Billy Bevan

A Song of Kentucky   D: Lewis Seiler   (T)
Ls: Lois Moran, Joseph Wagstaff

South Sea Rose   D: Allan Dwan   (T)
Ls: Charles Bickford, Lenore Ulric

Strong Boy   D: John Ford   (S)
Ls: Victor McLaglen, Leatrice Joy, Slim Summerville, Clyde Cook

Sunny Side Up   D: David Butler   (T)
Ls: Charles Farrell, Janet Gaynor, El Brendel

They Had to See Paris   D: Frank Borzage   (T)
Ls: Will Rogers, Irene Rich

Thru Different Eyes   D: John G. Blystone   (T)
Ls: Warner Baxter, Edmund Lowe, Mary Duncan

The Valiant   D: William K. Howard   (P)
Ls: Paul Muni, Johnny Mack Brown

Why Leave Home?   D: Raymond Cannon   (T)
Ls: Dixie Lee, Nick Stuart, Sue Carol, Walter Catlett, Ilka Chase

Words and Music   D: James Tinling   (T)
Ls: Lois Moran, Helen Twelvetrees, David Percy, Ward Bond
Songs included "Too Wonderful for Words."

PARAMOUNT–FAMOUS PLAYERS–LASKY
All productions used Movietone

Applause   D: Rouben Mamoulian   (T)
Ls: Helen Morgan, Fuller Mellish, Jr., Joan Peers
Songs included "What Wouldn't I Do for that Man?"

The Battle of Paris   D: Robert Florey   (T)
Ls: Gertrude Lawrence, Charles Ruggles, Arthur Treacher

Betrayal   D: Lewis Milestone   (S)
Ls: Emile Jannings, Gary Cooper, Esther Ralston

The Canary Murder Case   D: Malcolm St. Clair
Ls: William Powell, Louise Brooks, Jean Arthur

The Carnation Kid   D: E. Mason Hopper   (P)
Ls: Francis Lee, Douglas McLean
Christie Film Company production distributed by Paramount.

Chinatown Nights   D: William Wellman   (T)
Ls: Wallace Beery, Florence Vidor, Warner Oland, Jack Oakie

Close Harmony   D: John Cromwell   (T)
Ls: Nancy Carroll, "Buddy" Rogers, Jack Oakie

The Cocoanuts   D: Joseph Santley and Robert Florey   (T)
Ls: The Marx Brothers, Margaret Dumont

The Dance of Life   D: John Cromwell   (T)   Some sequences in Technicolor.
Ls: Nancy Carroll, Hal Skelly, Dorothy Revier

Dangerous Curves   D: Lothar Mendes   (T)
Ls: Richard Arlen, Clara Bow, Kay Francis

A Dangerous Woman   D: Rowland V. Lee   (T)
Ls: Clive Brook, Baclanova, Neil Hamilton, Clyde Cook

Darkened Rooms   D: Louis Gasnier   (T)
Ls: Evelyn Brent, Neil Hamilton, Doris Hill

Divorce Made Easy   D: Walter Graham   (T)
Ls: Marie Prevost, Douglas McLean, Johnny Arthur
Christie Film Company production distributed by Paramount.

The Doctor's Secret   D: William C. DeMille   (T)
Ls: Ruth Chatterton, H. B. Warner, John Loder, Nancy Price

The Dummy   D: Robert Milton   (T)
Ls: Fredric March, Ruth Chatterton, Jack Oakie, Zasu Pitts, John Cromwell, Richard Tucker, Eugene Pallette

Fashions in Love   D: Victor Schertzinger   (T)
Ls: Adolphe Menjou, Fay Compton, Miriam Seegar, John Miljan

Four Feathers   D: Merian C. Cooper, Ernst B. Schoedsack, Lothar
    Mendes   (S)
    Ls: Richard Arlen, Fay Wray, Clive Brook, William Powell,
    Noah Beery

Gentlemen of the Press   D: Millard Webb   (T)
    Ls: Walter Huston, Charles Ruggles, Katherine Francis

Glorifying the American Girl   D: Millard Webb   (T)   Techni-
    color scenes.
    Ls: Eddie Cantor, Helen Morgan, Rudy Vallee, Flo Ziegfeld,
    Otto Kahn, Ring Lardner, Adolph Zukor, Mayor Jimmy
    Walker, Texas Guinan, Johnny Weissmuller
    Songs included "Blue Skies," "I'm Just a Vagabond Lover."

The Greene Murder Case   D: Frank Tuttle   (T)
    Ls: William Powell, Florence Eldridge, Jean Arthur, Eugene
    Pallette

Halfway to Heaven   D: George Abbott   (T)
    Ls: "Buddy" Rogers, Paul Lukas, Jean Arthur

Illusion   D: Lothar Mendes   (T)
    Ls: "Buddy" Rogers, Nancy Carroll, Kay Francis, Eugenie
    Besserer, Regis Toomey

Innocents of Paris   D: Richard Wallace   (T)
    Ls: Maurice Chevalier, Sylvia Beecher, George Fawcett
    Songs included "Louise," "Wait Till You See My Chérie."

Jealousy   D: Jean De Limur   (T)
    Ls: Jeanne Eagels, Fredric March, Henry Daniell

The Kibitzer   D: Edward Sloman   (T)
    Ls: Harry Green, Neil Hamilton, Mary Brian

The Lady Lies   D: Hobart Henley   (T)
    Ls: Walter Huston, Claudette Colbert, Charles Ruggles

The Letter   D: Jean De Limur   (T)
    Ls: Jeanne Eagels, O. P. Heggie, Reginald Owen, Herbert
    Marshall

The Love Doctor   D: Melville Brown   (T)
    Ls: Richard Dix, June Collyer

The Love Parade   D: Ernst Lubitsch   (T)
    Ls: Maurice Chevalier, Jeannette MacDonald, Lupino Lane,
    Eugene Pallette, Ben Turpin
    Songs included "Dream Lover," "My Love Parade."

The Man I Love D: William Wellman   (T)
Ls: Richard Arlen, Jack Oakie, Mary Brian

Men Are Like That D: Frank Tuttle   (T)
Ls: Hal Skelly, Doris Hill

Nothing but the Truth D: Victor Schertzinger   (T)
Ls: Richard Dix, Berton Churchill, Ned Sparks, Helen Kane

Pointed Heels D: Edward Sutherland   (T)   Some sequences in Technicolor.
Ls: Fay Wray, Helen Kane, William Powell, Phillips Holmes, Eugene Pallette

The Rainbow Man D: Fred Newmeyer   (T)
Ls: Eddie Dowling, Frankie Darrow, Marion Nixon, George Hayes
Sono-Art production distributed by Paramount.

Redskin D: Victor Schertzinger   (S)   Some sequences in Technicolor.
Ls: Tully Marshall, Richard Dix, Gladys Belmont

The Return of Sherlock Holmes D: Basil Dean   (T)
Ls: Clive Brook, Betty Lawford, Phillips Holmes

River of Romance D: Richard Wallace   (T)
Ls: "Buddy" Rogers, June Collyer, Mary Brian, Wallace Beery, Henry B. Walthall

The Saturday Night Kid D: Edward Sutherland   (T)
Ls: Clara Bow, James Hall, Jean Arthur, Edna May Oliver, Jean Harlow

The Shopworn Angel D: Richard Wallace   (P)
Ls: Gary Cooper, Nancy Carroll, Paul Lukas, Roscoe Karns

The Studio Murder Mystery D: Frank Tuttle   (T)
Ls: Neil Hamilton, Fredric March, Doris Hill, Warner Oland, Florence Eldridge, Chester Conklin, Eugene Pallette

Sweetie D: Frank Tuttle   (T)
Ls: Helen Kane, Jack Oakie, Nancy Carroll, Stuart Erwin
Songs included "Sweeter than Sweet."

Thunderbolt D: Josef von Sternberg   (T)
Ls: George Bancroft, Richard Arlen, Fay Wray, Tully Marshall

The Virginian   D: Victor Fleming   (T)
      Ls: Gary Cooper, Walter Huston, Richard Arlen, Mary Brian

Welcome Danger   D: Clyde Bruckman   (T)
      Ls: Harold Lloyd, Barbara Kent

The Wheel of Life   D: Victor Schertzinger   (T)
      Ls: Richard Dix, Esther Ralston, O. P. Heggie

Why Bring That Up?   D: George Abbott   (T)
      Ls: Evelyn Brent, Charles E. Mack, Harry Green

The Wild Party   D: Dorothy Arzner   (T)
      Ls: Clara Bow, Fredric March, Joyce Compton, Jack Oakie

The Wolf of Wall Street   D: Rowland V. Lee   (T)
      Ls: George Bancroft, Paul Lukas, Nancy Carroll, Baclanova

Wolf Song   D: Victor Fleming   (S)
      Ls: Gary Cooper, Lupe Velez, Louis Wolheim

UNIVERSAL
All productions used Movietone.

Barnum Was Right   D: Del Lord   (T)
      Ls: Glenn Tryon, Merna Kennedy, Otis Harlan

Broadway   D: Paul Fejos   (T)   Some sequences in Technicolor.
      Ls: Evelyn Brent, Merna Kennedy, Glenn Tryon

Clear the Decks   D: Joseph E. Henabery   (P)
      Ls: Reginald Denny, Olive Hasbrouck, Lucien Littlefield

The Cohens and the Kellys in Atlantic City   D: W. J. Craft   (P)
      Ls: George Sidney, Mack Swain, Vera Gordon

College Love   D: Nat Ross (T)
      Ls: George Lewis, Eddie Phillips

Come Across   D: Ray Taylor   (P)
      Ls: Lina Basquette, Flora Finch, Reed Howes

The Drake Case   D: Edward Laemmle   (T)
      Ls: Gladys Brockwell, Robert Frazer, Forrest Stanley

The Girl on the Barge   D: Edward Sloman   (P)
      Ls: Jean Hersholt, Sally O'Neill, Malcolm McGregor

Girl Overboard   D: Wesley Ruggles   (P)
Ls: Mary Philbin, Fred Mackaye, Otis Harlan

Hell's Heroes   D: William Wyler   (T)
Ls: Charles Bickford, Raymond Hatton, Maria Alba

His Lucky Day   D: Eddie Cline   (P)
Ls: Reginald Denny, Otis Harlan, Lorayne Du Val

Hold Your Man   D: Emmett J. Flynn   (T)
Ls: Laura La Plante, Eugene Borden, Walter Kolk

It Can Be Done   D: Fred Newmeyer   (P)
Ls: Glenn Tryon, Sue Carol

The Last Performance   D: Paul Fejos   (P)
Ls: Mary Philbin, Conrad Veidt

The Last Warning   D: Paul Leni   (P)
Ls: Montague Love, Laura La Plante, John Boles, Mack Swain

The Love Trap   D: William Wyler   (P)
Ls: Neil Hamilton, Laura La Plante

Melody Lane   D: Robert F. Hill   (T)
Ls: Josephine Dunn, Eddie Leonard, George E. Stone

Modern Love   D: Arch Heath   (P)
Ls: Charley Chase, Jean Hersholt, Kathryn Crawford

Red Hot Speed   D: Joseph E. Henabery   (P)
Ls: Reginald Denny, Alice Day, Charles Byer

Shanghai Lady   D. John S. Robertson   (T)
Ls: Mary Nolan, James Murray, Wheeler Oakman

The Shannons of Broadway   D: Emmett J. Flynn   (T)
Ls: James Gleason, Mary Philbin, Lucille Webster, Walter Brennan, Slim Summerville

Show Boat   D: Harry Pollard   (P)
Ls: Otis Harlan, Helen Morgan, Carl Laemmle, Flo Ziegfeld, Joseph Schildkraut, Alma Rubens, Stepin Fetchit
Songs included "Ol' Man River," "Look Down That Lonesome Road."

Skinner Steps Out   D: W. J. Craft   (T)
Ls: Glenn Tryon, Merna Kennedy

Tonight at Twelve   D: Harry A. Pollard   (T)
    Ls: Robert Ellis, Madge Bellamy, Margaret Livingston

The Wagon Master   D: Harry J. Brown   (P)
    Ls: Ken Maynard, Edith Roberts
    Ken Maynard production distributed by Universal.

METRO-GOLDWYN-MAYER
All productions except one used Movietone

The Bellamy Trial   D: Monta Bell   (P)
    Ls: Leatrice Joy, Betty Bronson, Margaret Livingston

The Bridge of San Luis Rey   D: Charles Brabin   (P)
    Ls: Lila Damita, Ernest Torrence, Henry B. Walthall

Broadway Melody   D: Harry Beaumont   (T)   Some sequences in
    Technicolor.
    Ls: Charles King, Bessie Love, Anita Page
    Songs included "Broadway Melody," "You Were Meant for
    Me," "Wedding of the Painted Doll," "Give My Regards to
    Broadway."

Desert Nights   D: William Nigh   (S)
    Ls: John Gilbert, Mary Nolan, Ernest Torrence

Devil-May-Care   D: Sidney Franklin   (T)
    Ls: Ramon Novarro, Marion Harris, John Miljan, Dorothy
    Jordan
    Songs included "Madame Pompadour," "Why Waste Your
    Charms."

The Duke Steps Out   D: James Cruze   (P)
    Ls: William Haines, Joan Crawford, Delmer Daves
    Songs included "Just You."

Dynamite   D: Cecil B. DeMille   (T)
    Ls: Conrad Nagel, Joel McCrea, Charles Bickford, Robert
    Edeson

The Flying Fleet   D: George Hill   (S)
    Ls: Ramon Novarro, Ralph Novarro, Anita Page

The Great Power   D: Joe Rock   (P, Bristolphone)
    Ls: Minna Gombell, Herschel Mayall
    Franklin Warner production distributed by MGM.

Hallelujah!   D: King Vidor   (T)
  Ls: Daniel L. Haynes, Nina Mae McKinney
  Songs included "Swanee Shuffle," "Waiting at the End of the Road."

His Glorious Night   D: Lionel Barrymore   (T)
  Ls: John Gilbert, Nance O'Neil, Catherine Dale Owen

The Hollywood Revue of 1929   D: Charles Reisner   (T)   Some sequences in Technicolor.
  Ls: Conrad Nagel, John Gilbert, Joan Crawford, Norma Shearer, Lionel Barrymore, Bessie Love, Stan Laurel and Oliver Hardy, Marion Davies, Nils Asther, William Haines, Buster Keaton, Marie Dressler, Charles King, Jack Benny, Polly Moran, etc.
  Songs included "You Were Meant for Me," "Strike Up the Band."

It's a Great Life   D: Sam Wood   (T)   Some sequences in Technicolor.
  Ls: The Duncan Sisters, Laurence Gray
  Songs included "Smile, smile, smile."

The Kiss   D: Jacques Feyder   (S)
  Ls: Greta Garbo, Conrad Nagel, Lew Ayres

A Lady of Chance   D: Robert Z. Leonard   (P)
  Ls: Norma Shearer, Johnny Mack Brown, Lowell Sherman

The Last of Mrs. Cheyney   D: Sidney Franklin   (P)
  Ls: Basil Rathbone, Norma Shearer, Hedda Hopper

Madame X   D: Lionel Barrymore   (T)
  Ls: Ruth Chatterton, Lewis Stone, Sidney Toler, Eugenie Besserer

A Man's Man   D: James Cruze   (S)
  Ls: William Haines, Josephine Dunn, Mae Busch, Greta Garbo, John Gilbert

Marianne   D: Robert Z. Leonard   (T)
  Ls: Marion Davies, George Baxter, Robert Edeson
  Songs included "Hang on to Me."

The Mysterious Island   D: Lucien Hubbard, Maurice Tourneur, Benjamin Christensen   (P)   Filmed in Technicolor.
  Ls: Lionel Barrymore, Montagu Love, Jane Daly, Gibson Gowland

The Pagan   D: W. S. Van Dyke   (S)
> Ls: Ramon Novarro, Donald Crisp, Renée Adorée

The Road Show   [*Retitled* Chasing Rainbows]   D: Charles F. Reisner   (T)   Some sequences in Technicolor.
> Ls: Charles King, Bessie Love, Jack Benny, George K. Arthur, Marie Dressler
> Songs included "I Got a Feeling for You."

So This Is College?   D: Sam Wood   (T)
> Ls: Elliott Nugent, Robert Montgomery, Sally Starr, Polly Moran

The Thirteenth Chair   D: Tod Browning   (T)
> Ls: Conrad Nagel, Leila Hyams, Margaret Wycherley, Bela Lugosi

Tide of Empire   D: Allan Dwan   (S)
> Ls: Renée Adorée, George Fawcett
> Cosmopolitan production distributed by MGM.

The Trail of '98   D: Clarence Brown   (S)
> Ls: Dolores Del Rio, Ralph Forbes, Harry Carey, Tully Marshall

The Trial of Mary Dugan   D: Bayard Veiller   (T)
> Ls: Norma Shearer, H. B. Warner, Lewis Stone, Lilyan Tashman

Voice of the City   D: Willard Mack   (T)
> Ls: Willard Mack, Robert Ames, Sylvia Field, John Miljan

The Unholy Night   D: Lionel Barrymore   (T)
> Ls: Ernest Torrence, Roland Young, Boris Karloff, Polly Moran, John Miljan, John Loder, Richard Tucker

UNITED ARTISTS
All productions used Movietone

Alibi   D: Roland West   (T)
> Ls: Chester Morris, Mae Busch, Harry Stubbs
> Feature production distributed by UA.

Bulldog Drummond   D: F. Richard Jones   (T)
> Ls: Ronald Colman, Lilyan Tashman, John Bennett, Montagu Love
> Samuel Goldwyn production distributed by UA.

Condemned   D: Wesley Ruggles   (T)
 Ls: Ronald Colman, Louis Wolheim, Dudley Digges, Ann
 Harding
 Samuel Goldwyn production distributed by UA.

Coquette   D: Sam Taylor   (T)
 Ls: Mary Pickford, Johnny Mack Brown
 Pickford Corporation production distributed by UA.

Eternal Love   D: Ernst Lubitsch   (S)
 Ls: John Barrymore, Victor Varconi, Camilla Horn
 Feature production distributed by UA.

Evangeline   D: Edwin Carewe   (S)
 Ls: Dolores Del Rio, Alec G. Francis, Roland Drew
 Edwin Carewe production distributed by UA.

The Iron Mask   D: Allan Dwan   (P)
 Ls: Belle Bennett, Dorothy Revier, Vera Lewis, Rolfe Sedan
 Elton Corporation production distributed by UA.

Lady of the Pavements   D: D. W. Griffith   (P)
 Ls: Lupe Velez, William Boyd, Jetta Goudal, Henry
 Armetta
 Song: "Where Is the Song of Songs for Me?"
 Art Cinema Corporation production distributed by UA.

The Rescue   D: Herbert Brenon   (S)
 Ls: Ronald Colman, Lily Damita, John Davidson
 Samuel Goldwyn production distributed by UA.

She Goes to War   D: Henry King   (P)
 Ls: Eleanor Boardman, John Holland, Al St. John, Alma
 Rubens
 Inspiration Pictures production distributed by UA.

The Taming of the Shrew   D: Sam Taylor   (T)
 Ls: Mary Pickford, Douglas Fairbanks, Clyde Cook
 Pickford-Elton production distributed by UA.

This Is Heaven   D: Alfred Santell   (P)
 Ls: Vilma Banky, James Hall, Richard Tucker
 Samuel Goldwyn production distributed by UA.

Three Live Ghosts   D: Thornton Freeland   (T)
 Ls: Beryl Mercer, Hilda Vaughn, Joan Bennett, Robert
 Montgomery, Nancy Price
 Joseph M. Schenck production distributed by UA.

The Trespasser   D: Edmund Golding   (T)
Ls: Gloria Swanson, Robert Ames, H. B. Walthall
Gloria production distributed by UA.

COLUMBIA
All productions used Movietone

Acquitted   D: Frank R. Strayer   (T)
Ls: Lloyd Hughes, Margaret Livingston, Sam Hardy

The Bachelor Girl   D: Richard Thorpe   (P)
Ls: William Collier, Jacqueline Logan, Thelma Todd

Broadway Scandals   D: George Archainbaud   (T)
Ls: Carmel Myers, Sally O'Neil, Jack Egan
Songs included "Kickin' the Blues Away."

The College Coquette   D: George Archainbaud   (T)
Ls: William Collier, Ruth Taylor, Jobyna Ralston

The Donovan Affair   D: Frank Capra   (T)
Ls: Jack Holt, Agnes Ayres, Dorothy Revier

The Fall of Eve   D: Frank R. Strayer   (T)
Ls: Patsy Ruth Miller, Ford Sterling

Father and Son   D: Erle C. Kenton   (P)
Ls: Jack Holt, Dorothy Revier, Wheeler Oakman

Flight   D: Frank Capra   (T)
Ls: Jack Holt, Ralph Graves, Lila Lee

The Flying Marine   D: Albert Rogell   (P)
Ls: Ben Lyon, Jason Robards, Shirley Mason

Hurricane   D: Ralph Ince   (T)
Ls: Johnny Mack Brown, Hobart Bosworth, Leila Hyams

Light Fingers   D: Joseph Henabery   (P)
Ls: Dorothy Revier, Ian Keith

The Song of Love   D: Erle C. Kenton   (T)
Ls: Belle Baker, Ralph Graves
Song: "I'm Somebody's Baby Now."
Edward Small production distributed by Columbia Pictures.

The Younger Generation   D: Frank Capra   (T)
Ls: Jean Hersholt, Lina Basquette, Ricardo Cortez

RKO PATHE EXCHANGE
All productions used Photophone

The Awful Truth   D: Marshall Neilan   (T)
    Ls: Ina Claire, Henry Daniell, Paul Harvey

Big News   D: Gregory La Cava   (T)
    Ls: Robert Armstrong, Carole Lombard

Dance Hall   D: Melville Brown   (T)
    Ls: Olive Borden, Arthur Lake

The Delightful Rogue   D: Lynn Shores   (T)
    Ls: Rod La Rocque, Rita La Roy

The Flying Fool   D: Tay Garnett   (T)
    Ls: William Boyd, Marie Prevost
    Song: "If I Had My Way."

Geraldine   D: Melville Brown   (P)
    Ls: Eddie Quillan, Marion Nixon

Girl of the Port   D: Bert Glennon   (T)
    Ls: Sally O'Neil, Reginald Sharland

The Godless Girl   D: Cecil B. DeMille   (P)
    Ls: Lina Basquette, Marie Prevost, Noah Beery, Eddie
    Quillan

Half Marriage   D: William J. Cowen   (T)
    Ls: Olive Borden, Morgan Farley, Ken Murray
    Song: "After the Clouds Roll By."

Her Private Affair   D: Paul Stein   (P)
    Ls: Ann Harding, John Loder, Harry Bannister, Kay
    Hammond

High Voltage   D: Howard Higgin   (T)
    Ls: Owen Moore, William Boud, Carole Lombard, Billy
    Bevan

Jazz Heaven   D: Melville Brown   (T)
    Ls: Johnny Mack Brown, Sally O'Neil

Leathernecking   D: Eddie Cline   (P)
    Ls: Irene Dunne, Lilyan Tashman, Eddie Foy, Jr., Louise
    Fazenda, Ned Sparks

Night Parade   D: Malcolm St. Clair   (T)
Ls: Hugh Trevor, Lloyd Ingraham

The Office Scandal   D: Paul L. Stein   (P)
Ls: Phyllis Haver, Raymond Hatton, Leslie Fenton, Margaret Livingston

Paris Bound   D: Edward H. Griffith   (T)
Ls: Ann Harding, Fredric March, Leslie Fenton, Ilka Chase

Red Hot Rhythm   D: Leo McCarey   (T)   Some sequences in Technicolor.
Ls: Alan Hale, Kathryn Crawford, Josephine Dunn, Ilka Chase

Rio Rita   D: Luther Reed   (T)   Some sequences in Technicolor.
Ls: Bebe Daniels, John Boles, Don Alvarado
Songs included "Rio Rita," "You're Always in My Arms (But Only in My Dreams)."

Sailor's Holiday   D: Fred Newmeyer   (T)
Ls: Alan Hale, Sally Eilers, Marry Carr

Sal of Singapore   D: Howard Higgin   (P)
Ls: Phyllis Haver, Alan Hale, Noble Johnson

Seven Keys to Baldpate   D: Reginald Barker   (T)
Ls: Richard Dix, Miriam Seegar, Margaret Livingston

Side Street   D: Malcolm St. Clair   (T)
Ls: Owen Moore, Tom Moore, Mildred Harris

The Sophomore   D: Leo McCarey   (T)
Ls: Eddie Quillan, Sally O'Neil

The Spieler   D: Tay Garnett   (P)
Ls: Alan Hale, Renée Adorée, Clyde Cook
Ralph Block production distributed by Pathe Exchange.

Square Shoulders   D: E. Mason Hopper   (P)
Ls: Louis Wolheim, Anita Louise

Street Girl   D: Wesley Ruggles   (T)
Ls: Betty Compson, Ned Sparks, John Harron, Jack Oakie

Syncopation   D: Bert Glennon   (T)
Ls: Barbara Bennett, Ian Hunter, Bobby Watson
Songs included "Mine Alone."

Tanned Legs   D: Marshall Neilan   (T)
 Ls: June Clyde, Arthur Lake, Sally Blane

This Thing Called Love   D: Paul Stein   (T)   Some Technicolor scenes.
 Ls: Edmund Lowe, Constance Bennett, Zasu Pitts, Roscoe Karns, Stuart Erwin

The Vagabond Lover   D: Marshall Neilan   (T)
 Ls: Rudy Vallee, Sally Blane, Marie Dressler
 Songs included "Piccolo Pete."

The Very Idea   D: Richard Rosson   (T)
 Ls: Sally Blane, Allen Kearns, Jeanne De Bard

FBO (Film Booking Offices)
All productions used Photophone

Idaho Red   D: Robert De Lacey   (S)
 Ls: Tom Tyler, Frankie Darro, Patricia Caron

Love in the Desert   D: George Melford   (P)
 Ls: Noah Beery, Clive Borden, Hugh Trevor

Taxi 13   D: Marshall Neilan   (P)
 Ls: Chester Conklin, Ethel Wales

TIFFANY-STAHL PRODUCTIONS
All productions used Photophone

Lucky Boy   D: Norman Taurog   (P)
 Ls: George Jessel, Richard Tucker
 Songs included "My Mother's Eyes," "Lucky Boy."

Midstream   D: James Flood   (P)
 Ls: Ricardo Cortez, Montagu Lord, Claire Windsor

Mister Antonio   D: James Flood   (T)
 Ls: Leo Carillo, Frank Reicher, Virginia Valli

Molly and Me   D: Albert Ray   (P)
 Ls: Joe E. Brown, Belle Bennett

New Orleans   D: Reginald Barker   (P)
 Ls: Ricardo Cortez, Alma Bennett, William Collier, Jr.

The Voice Within   D: George Archainbaud   (P)
Ls: Walter Pidgeon, Eve Southern, Montagu Love

Woman to Woman   D: Victor Saville   (T)
Ls: Betty Compson, George Barraud

TREM CARR PRODUCTIONS
Used various sound systems

Bride of the Desert   D: Duke Worne   (T, Filmtone)
Ls: LeRoy Mason, Alice Calhoun
Distributed by Rayart Pictures.

Handcuffed   D: Duke Worne   (T, sound system not known)
Ls: Wheeler Oakman, Virginia Brown Faire, Dean Jagger
Distributed by Rayart Pictures.

The Phantom in the House   D: Phil Rosen   (T)
Ls: Ricardo Cortez, Henry B. Walthall, Nancy Welford
Distributed by Continental Talking Pictures.

Should a Girl Marry?   D: Scott Pembroke   (P, Filmtone)
Ls: Helen Foster, Donald Keith, Andy Clyde
Distributed by Rayart Pictures.

TRINITY PICTURES
Sound systems not known

Broken Hearted   D: Frank S. Mattison   (P)
Ls: Agnes Ayres, Eddie Brownell

Bye-Bye Buddy   D: Frank S. Mattison   (P)
Ls: Agnes Ayres, Buddy Shaw
A Hercules film.

SONO-ART–WORLD WIDE PRODUCTIONS
Sound systems not known

The Great Gabbo   D: James Cruze   (T)   Some sequences in
color.
Ls: Erich von Stroheim, Betty Compson

The Talk of Hollywood   D: Mark Sandrich   (T)
    Ls: Nat Carr, Renée Adorée, Hope Sutherland
    A Prudence Picture.

MISCELLANEOUS STUDIOS AND COMPANIES
Various sound systems used

Bachelor's Club   D: Noel Mason   (S, Photophone)
    Ls: Richard Talmadge, Edna Murphy, Barbara Worth
    Parthenon Pictures production.

Dark Skies   D: Harry S. Webb   (T, Telefilm)
    Ls: Evelyn Brent, Shirley Mason, Wallace MacDonald
    Biltmore production.

The House of Secrets   D: Edmund Lawrence   (T)
    Ls: Marcia Manning, Joseph Striker
    Chesterfield Motion Pictures Corporation production.

In Old California   D: Burton King   (T, Photophone)
    Ls: Henry B. Walthall, Helen Ferguson
    Audible Pictures production.

The Invaders   D: J. P. McGowan   (S, sound system not known)
    Ls: Bob Steele, Edna Aslin
    Big Productions Film Corporation production.

Linda   D: Mrs. Wallace Reid   (S, Vitaphone)
    Ls: Warner Baxter, Noah Beery, Helen Foster
    Mrs. Wallace Reid production.

Midnight Daddies   D: Mack Sennett   (T, Photophone)
    Ls: Andy Clyde, Rosemary Theby
    Mack Sennett production.

Overland Bound   D: Leo Maloney   (T, Telefilm)
    Ls: Leo Maloney, Jack Perrin, Allene Ray
    Presidio production.

Sea Fury   D: George Melford   (P, sound system not known)
    Ls: Mildred Harris, James Hallet
    Tom White production distributed by H. H. Rosenfield.

Sex Madness   D: not known   (S, sound system not known)
    Ls: Jack Richardson, Corliss Palmer
    Circle Film Company production distributed by Public Welfare Pictures.

Strange Cargo   D: Benjamin Glazer   (T, Photophone)
    Ls: Lee Patrick, June Nash
    Pathe Cargo production.

Unmasked   D: Edgar Lewis   (T, De Forest Phonofilm)
    Ls: Robert Warwick, Milton Krims, Sam Ash, Susan Conroy
    Weiss Brothers Artclass picture.

SOUND-ON-DISK PATENTS, 1897–1927

Detailed descriptions of many of the patents listed below will be found in the issues of *Film Daily,* February 24, 1929 through July 26, 1929.

Year	Inventor and patent number
1897	G. W. Brown US 576,542
1898	A. Baron Fr. 276,628
1899	L. A. Berthon, C. F. Dussaud, G. F. Jaubert Ger. 104,475
1900	A. Baron US 656,762
1901	L. Gaumont & Cie. Fr. 328,613
1902	L. Gaumont Fr. 328,145
1903	O. Messter Ger. 145,780
1904	L. Gaumont Fr. 752,394 F. Schaefer US 762,948
1905	O. Messter Gr. Br. 405
1906	O. Messter Gr. Br. 2,157 W. C. Fairweather Gr. Br. 26,440 A. J. Boult Gr. Br. 26,552 H. Joly US 839,152
1907	G. Pomarede Fr. 375,057 O. de Faria Fr. 375,869 L. Gaumont Fr. 378,146

L. Gaumont   Fr. 7,121 (additional)

L-N. LaFay   Fr. 379,351

H. Hantz   Fr. 380,777

A. Kolzow   Ger. 182,413

T. A. Edison   US 1,182,897

1908   A. Duskes   Fr. 381,655

C. De Proszynski   Gr. Br. 22,415

1909   R. Roupnel, H-P. Loiseleur, J. Pappalardo   Fr. 399,612

M. Hellman   Ger. 205,887

P. Effing   Ger. 214,401

G. Mendel   Ger. 214,402

J. Greenbaum   Gr. Br. 7,426

A. L. Davis   Gr. Br. 15,140

J. Greenbaum   Gr. Br. 16,611

O. Messter   Gr. Br. 16,728

F. A. Thomassin   Gr. Br. 27,717

J. Greenbaum   US 923,511

J. G. Meredith   US 925,933

J. C. S. Rousselot   US 928,070

P. Seiler   US 939, 337

F. E. Thormeyer   US 941,211

P. Pierini   US 941,891

L. S. Stiles   US 1,308,875

1910   E. P. Latrait   Fr. 412,107

Duskes Kinematographen und Filmen-Fabriken   G.mb.H
    Ger. 219,576

Deutsche Bioscop   Ger. 222,958

W. G. Barker   Gr. Br. 8,838

C. M. Hepworth   Ger. 223,153

G. P. McDonnell   US 945,976

W. M. Davison   US 958,731

1911   J. Lupo   Fr. 420,020

M. Couadeon   Fr. 421,795

W. E. Lake   Br. 9,622

Deutsches Motoscop und Biograph G.mb.H.   Ger. 234,937

F. E. Thormeyer   US 989,207

F. E. A. Mathelot & H. G. Gentilhomme   US 993,610

1912   C. G. Williams   Fr. 438,935

F. Hildebrand   Fr. 438,937

R. Philippe   Gr. Br. 13,701
H. Portier, G. Schaible & F. Darragon   Gr. Br. 19,593
F. Donisthorpe   Gr. Br. 24,091
J. Greenbaum   US 1,027,248
A. D. Adamopoulos   US 1,031,315
F. E. Thormeyer   US 1,049,171

1913   R. Philippe   Fr. 16,318 (additional)
E. Nitsche & A. Knieper   Fr. 458,718
I. Kitsee   Gr. Br. 10,519
D. Higham   US 1,054,203
H. T. Crapo   US 1,080,265
E. H. Amet   US 1,065,576
L. Gaumont   US 1,074,943
H. T. Crapo   US 1,080,265

1914   G. W. Ford   Fr. 467,153
E. Costanti   Fr. 471,712
C. Pasteur   Ger. 272,873
L. Cerebotanion   Ger. 275,759
Talking M. P. Co. Inc. of Syracuse, N. Y.   Ger. 277,297
C. Pasteur   Gr. Br. 22,459
W. E. Partridge   Gr. Br. 25,206
I. Kitsee   US 1,083,498

1915   L. Pineschi   Ger. 282,537
T. Graf   Ger. 282,895
L. H. Bonnard   Gr. Br. 15,683
E. H. Amet   US 1,162,433

1916   E. Gasch, E. R. von Mertens, F. Oprendek   Ger. 294,558
R. A. Whitehead   US 1,179,591
T. A. Edison   US 1,182,897
G. P. McDonnell   US 1,184,704
J. B. Olinger   US 1,186,494
E. E. Norton   US 1,190,943
L. Janssens   US 1,210,323

1917   F. W. Matthewson   US 1,210,665
I. Kitsee   US 1,213,883
H. Hess   US 1,222,626
D. Higham   US 1,226,883
W. H. Bristol   US 1,234,127
A. Luciano   US 1,239,800

1918   D. O. Royster   US 1,252,304
       C. W. Ebeling   US 1,254,487
       H. W. Rogers   US 1,255, 822
       C. J. Coleman   US 1,275,227

1919   O. E. Kellum   US 1,292,798
       O. E. Kellum   US 1,294,672
       E. S. Hopkins, Jr.   US 1,302,367
       L. S. Stiles   US 1,308,875
       C. J. Coleman   US 1,312,103
       L. O. Kozar   US 1,314,081

1920   J. F. Osborn   US 1,328,189
       A. Cortella   US 1,331,049
       J. G. Saltzmann   US 1,341,933
       R. H. Hatfield   US 1,352,126
       J. G. Harris   US 1,354,742
       L. O. Kozar   US 1,362,876

1921   F. E. Mosley   Gr. Br. 166,850
       F. E. Mosley   Gr. Br. 168,831
       W. H. Bristol   US 1,396,401

1922   H. A. Johnson   Gr. Br. 174,762
       A. T. M. Johnson   Gr. Br. 183,763
       F. von Madaler   US 1,408,620
       F. von Madaler   US 1,408,621
       W. P. Stunz & L. R. Gilbert   US 1,418,180

1923   E. Zeppieri   Gr. Br. 191,059
       W. H. Bristol   US 1,452,063
       W. H. Bristol   US 1,464,329

1924   A. Stowers & L. de Hymel   US 1,494,514

1925   L. O. Kozar   US 1,522,132
       W. M. Clark   US 1,523,173
       N. H. Holland   US 1,528,424

1927   S. Brown   Gr. Br. 264,046
       M. Hoffman   US 1,648,480

PATENTS FOR MAJOR SOUND-ON-FILM
DEVELOPMENTS THROUGH 1927

Year	Inventor and patent number

1900   V. Poulsen: Magnetic wire recording   US 661,619

1905   V. Poulsen: Magnetic wire recording   US 789,336

1906   J. Ballance: Groove-on-film system   US 823,022
Lee De Forest: Diode Audion with B battery   US 836,070
V. Poulsen: Magnetic wire recording   US 873,078
V. Poulsen: Magnetic wire recording   US 873,083

1907   Lee De Forest: Audion with external electrodes   US 841,386
Lee De Forest: Audion Amplifier   US 841,387
R. T. Haines, J. S. Pletts, and Eugene Lauste: Sound and picture recorded on single film   Gr. Br. 18,057

1923   E. E. Ries: Single film sound-system   US 1,473,976

1924   Lee De Forest: Sound-on-film system   US 1,489,314

1925-26 H. Vogt, J. Massolle, and J. Engl: Tri-Ergon system   US 1,512,681; 1,534,148; 1,555,301; 1,557,678; 1,558,032; 1,566,413; 1,590,185; 1,597,323; 1,608,261; 1,628,377; 1,634,201; 1,713,726 (the flywheel patent); 1,756,681; 1,825,598.

1927   Lee De Forest: Equipment for talking films   US 1,653,155
T. W. Case: Aeo-Light   US 1,816,825.

PATENT APPEAL DOCKET: *LEE DE FOREST* v. *TRI-ERGON*

**United States Court of Customs and Patent Appeals
Patent Appeal Docket No. 2749**

Interference No. 53103. Subject Matter: Recording Sounds.

**Lee De Forest, Appellant,
vs. Hans Vogt, Joseph Massolle and Josef Engl.**

To the U. S. Court of Customs and Patent Appeals:

Your petitioner, Lee De Forest, of New York, in the County of New York and State of New York, respectfully represents:

That he is the original and first inventor of certain new and useful improvements in Recording Sounds.

That on the 16th day of July, 1921, in the manner prescribed by law, he presented his application to the Patent Office, praying that a patent be issued to him for the said invention; and that a patent was issued to him on April 8, 1924, bearing No. 1489314.

That thereafter, to wit, on the 10th day of November, 1925, an interference proceeding was instituted and declared between his said Letters Patent No. 1489314, and a pending application of Hans Vogt, Joseph Massolle and Josef Engl, Serial No. 547860, filed March 29, 1922, for a similar invention.

That the subject matter of said interference, as set forth in the official declaration, was as follows:

"Count 1. The method of producing talking moving pictures on the same film which comprises photographing simultaneously upon separate films the picture and the sound, and photographing the sound record on an unexposed portion of the picture film.

"Count 2. The method of producing talking moving pictures on

304

the same film which comprises photographing simultaneously upon separate films the picture and the sound, and photographing the sound record on an unexposed portion of the picture film between the marginal edge and the sprocket perforations thereof."

That thereafter, to wit, on the 14th day of July, 1928, the case having been submitted upon the preliminary statements and evidence presented by the parties thereto, the Examiner of Interferences rendered a decision awarding priority of invention to Hans Vogt, Joseph Massolle and Josef Engl.

That pursuant to the statutes and the rules of practice in the Patent Office in such case made and provided, Lee De Forest appealed from the said adverse decision of the Examiner of Interferences to the Board of Appeals, and, the case having been argued and submitted to said Board, a decision was rendered by said Board on the 7th day of January, 1930, affirming the decision of the Examiner of Interferences.

That on the 24th day of February, 1930, your petitioner, pursuant to sections 4912 and 4913, Revised Statutes of the United States, gave notice to the Commissioner of Patents of his appeal to this honorable court from the decision of the Board of Appeals awarding priority of invention to said Hans Vogt, Joseph Massolle and Josef Engl, as aforesaid, and filed with him, in writing specific reasons of appeal.

That the Commissioner of Patents has furnished your petitioner a certified transcript of the record and proceedings relating to said interference case, including the notice and reasons of appeal, which transcript is filed herewith and is to be deemed and taken as a part hereof.

Wherefore your petitioner prays that his said appeal may be heard upon and for the reasons assigned therefor to the Commissioner, as aforesaid, and that said appeal may be determined and the decision of the Board of Appeals be revised and reversed, that justice may be done in the premises.

LEE DE FOREST,
By SAMUEL E. DARBY, JR.,
His Attorney.

Washington, D. C., April 9, 1930.

Indorsed: United States Court of Customs and Patent Appeals. Filed Apr. 9, 1930. Arthur B. Shelton, Clerk.

390.

Department of Commerce, United States Patent Office.

To all persons to whom these presents shall come, Greeting:

This is to certify that the annexed is a true copy from the records of this office of Certain Papers, including Printed Testimony as used before the Office, in the matter of Interference Number 53,103, De Forest vs. Vogt, Massolle and Engl, Subject Matter: Recording Sounds; said Papers being the Record for the United States Court of Customs and Patent Appeals.

In testimony whereof I have hereunto set my hand and caused the seal of the Patent Office to be affixed, at the City of Washington, this second day of April, in the year of our Lord, one thousand nine hundred and thirty, and of the Independence of the United States of America the one hundred and fifty-fourth.

[Seal Patent Office, United States of America.]

THOMAS E. ROBERTSON,
Commissioner of Patents.

Attest:

D. E. WILSON,
Chief of Division.

Application of HANS VOGT, JOSEPH MASSOLLE and JOSEF ENGL, Filed March 29, 1922. Serial No. 547860. Process for Producing Combined Sound Picture Films.

To all whom it may concern:

Be it known that we, Hans Vogt, Joseph Massolle and Josef Engl, citizens of the German Republic, and residents respectively, the first of Berlin-Wilmersdorf, the second and third of Berlin-Grunewald, Germany, have invented a new and improved Process for Producing Combined Sound Picture Films of which the following is a full, clear and exact description:

In the production of speaking films [it] is of great advantage especially from the point of view of use, to arrange the sound sequence and the picture sequence upon one and the same material separate (film).

In this procedure, however, there frequently occur in consequence of the changing lighting conditions in the cinematographing process, changes in the degree of light and the bromide of silver layer, and this causes the picture sequence to be either overlighted or underlighted.

As the same film, however, bears close to the picture sequence the continuously normally lighted sound sequence, these differences cannot be removed in the case of combined negatives by developing, weakening, strengthening and so forth. They can only be removed by subjecting the underlighted or the overlighted negative places to separate corresponding treatment.

Technically, this treatment is practically impossible so long as the two sequences are photographed upon the same film.

According to the present invention the difficulty is overcome by either employing entirely separate films for the production of the negatives or films which are connected during the photographing, but which are separated from one another before the developing.

The synchronism is assured in both cases by the perforations and by corresponding marks. The production of the positive films can take place by copying the two negative films preferably consecutively upon the same positive films.

One can however, also unite previously the two negative films longitudinally together, and then copy this so united negative in the usual manner.

We claim:

1. Process for the production of combined sound and picture films, in which the sound sequence and picture sequence positives are copied upon single film, characterized by the feature that the respective negatives have been developed separately.

2. Process for the production of combined sound and picture films according to claim 1, characterized by the feature that the photographing of the sound sequence and of the picture sequence takes place on separate films.

3. Process for the production of combined sound and picture films as set forth in claim 1, characterized by the feature that the photographing of the sound sequence and of the picture sequence takes place upon a single film and subsequently divided.

4. Process for the production of combined sound and picture films as set forth in claim 1 to 3, characterised by the feature that the negatives after development are re-united.

HANS VOGT,
JOSEPH MASSOLLE,
JOSEF ENGL.

Witnesses:
BRUNO LEARWENKA,
JOHN W. BULKLEY.

Amendment, April 1, 1925

Hon. Commissioner of Patents.

Sir:

In response to Patent Office action of January 26, 1925, please amend the above entitled application as follows:

* * * * * *

3. The method of producing talking moving pictures on the same film which comprises photographing simultaneously upon separate films the picture and the sound, and photographing the sound record on an unexposed portion of the picture film.

4. The method of producing talking moving pictures on the same film which comprises photographing simultaneously upon separate films the picture and the sound, and photographing the sound record on an unexposed portion of the picture film between the marginal edge and the sprocket perforations thereof.

* * * * * *

Respectfully submitted,

HANS VOGT,

JOSEPH MASSOLLE and

JOSEF ENGL.

By WARD, CROSBY and SMITH,

Their Attorneys.

4. The Honorable Examiner of Interferences erred in ruling that the testimony of De Forest as to the date[s] when he made the entries in his note book are not corroborated by Garity.

5. The Honorable Examiner of Interferences erred in ruling that the testimony of De Forest and Senner taken together did not establish a conception of the invention before April 14, 1921, the foreign filing date of Engl, Massolle and Vogt.

6. The Honorable Examiner of Interferences erred in holding that De Forest was not diligent between the dates of April 14, 1921 and July 16, 1921, the filing date of his application.

7. The Honorable Examiner of Interferences erred in ruling that the work De Forest was doing between April 14, 1921, and July 16, 1921, should not be credited as activity to show diligence in reducing to practice the invention of this interference.

The appeal fee of $25.00 is enclosed herewith.

An oral hearing is requested.

Respectfully,   DARBY & DARBY,

Attorneys for De Forest.

Dated: New York, N. Y., July 17, 1928.

Decision of Board of Appeals, January 7, 1930.

This is an appeal by De Forest from the decision of the Examiner of Interferences awarding priority of invention to Engl, Massolle and Vogt, the senior party, upon all the counts which read as follows:

1. The method of producing talking moving pictures on the same film which comprises photographing simultaneously upon separate films the picture and the sound, and photographing the sound record on an unexpected portion of the picture film.

2. The method of producing talking moving pictures on the same film which comprises photographing simultaneously upon separate films the picture and the sound, and photographing the sound record on an unexposed portion of the picture film between the marginal edge and the sprocket perforations thereof.

The counts are claims 1 and 3 of the patent No. 1,489,314 of De Forest and the interference was originally declared with De Forest as the senior party but upon motion, Vogt et al., by a decision dated April 13, 1926, were given the benefit of their German application date of April 14, 1921, and made the senior party.

The Examiner of Interferences points out that Vogt et al. copied the two counts from the De Forest patent but they were rejected by the Primary Examiner. The rejection was reversed by the Board of Examiners-in-Chief, and in their opinion they mentioned the word "simultaneously" occurring in both claims as distinguishing them from the Greenfelder patent cited against them. He therefore emphasized in his decision the word "simultaneously" as an essential limitation in the claims. He held that the testimony submitted by De Forest fails to prove that he had conceived this feature of *simultaneously* photographing the picture and the sound prior to his filing date.

For proof of conception De Forest relied primarily upon his note book No. 2, De Forest Exhibit 1, in which, under date of December 28, 1920, is an entry which reads:

Developed this last 10 minutes until wholly fogged. This would be too long for cine picture. Hence will probably need to make two negatives (picture and sound) and print on same pos.

A second entry under date of Jan. 18, 1921, reads:

Developed 11 minutes (very cold day) (longer development is best for sound film but not for picture. Hence will probably use 2 films.)

These notes clearly indicate that as the sound and picture films require a different degree or time of development, it would be necessary to use two films and develop them separately. The Examiner of Interferences held that there was nothing in these notes to indicate that the sound and picture films were to be photographed "simultaneously" as required by the counts.

De Forest, in his brief, contends that the object of the invention is to synchronize the sounds with the movement of the lips of a person in the picture and that it is at once apparent that the picture and sound must be recorded simultaneously. He further points out that on the motion to shift the burden of proof, the Law Examiner gave to Engl et al. the benefit of the filing date of his German application and if it be held that De Forest's testimony fails to support the issues, it is equally true that the German application of Engl et al. fails in the same respect.

In the German application we find the following:

According to the invention this difficulty is obviated in that for the making of the negatives either entirely separate films are provided or those which although still united during the recording are, however, detached from each other before the developing. Synchronism in both cases is insured by perforation and by suitable marks.

In our opinion the statements that the films are still united during the recording indicates that the record is made simultaneously on both films and this is further borne out by the statement that, when separated for development purposes, the synchronization is insured by perforations and suitable marks so that they can be reconnected with proper registration. The same disclosure is found in the U. S. application of Engl et al.

As to the De Forest testimony, it appears that the reason why two films were to be used was that different degrees of development were necessary for the sound and picture negatives and it might seem obvious that the original idea which rendered this change necessary was that the sound and pictures were supposed to be photographed simultaneously. At this time only sound had been photographed in the laboratory which may be the reason why nothing was said in the notes as to simultaneous photography of the sound and picture. While the simultaneous exposure of the sound and picture negatives would seem to be the most obvious procedure, the brief of Engl et al. points out that other methods were known prior to De Forest's alleged conception, (see Engl et al. brief, pages 24 and 25,) and appear to be disclosed in the patent to Greenfelder, No. 1,254,684, which was cited in the application of Engl et al., and the burden was on De Forest, as the junior party, to prove his case. Furthermore, he must rely for corroboration upon his witnesses Garity and Senner. Garity has no way of fixing the dates when the entries were made in the note books and these dates are fixed only by De Forest's own testimony. Garity merely knows that he saw the note books between December, 1920, and prior to De Forest's trip to Germany the last of July, 1921, and that, at some time, De Forest discussed the subject matter of the notes with him. Senner can fix no date except with relation to the purchase of a camera from him on February 18, 1921, and thinks that De Forest, within a week or ten days thereafter, brought some films to him for development which films contained both sound and picture records which were of unequal exposure. De Forest suggested that it would be best to use separate negatives while he discouraged this method and suggested the use of light of different intensity in making the records. This disclosure does not mention "simultaneous" exposure and the time between about March 1 and April 14, 1921, when Engl et al. entered the field is so short that a person testifying six or seven years after the event could hardly fix the time with sufficient definiteness. De Forest says (X Q. 74) that it was several weeks after he got the camera before he had the necessary attachment placed on same for recording sound on the same film with the picture. We must, therefore, agree with the Examiner of Interferences that De Forest has failed to establish conception of the invention in issue prior to the constructive reduction to practice of the senior party.

Even if De Forest were given a conception as of January 1, 1921, the date set up in his preliminary statement, he would have to prove diligence from just prior to April 14, 1921, when Engl et al. entered the field, up to his filing date of July 16, 1921. There is no testimony which clearly establishes any work done on the invention in issue from January 1, 1921, up to April 14, 1921, and De Forest seeks to rely upon his work on the general subject of talking moving pictures. This work was the subject of the other interference No. 51,947, and the present invention relates to entirely different subject matter. His note books show that he had already obtained good results in making sound records and after obtaining the moving picture camera on February 18, 1921, he could have coupled the two cameras without great difficulty and reduced the invention to practice, but on page 13 of his record (Q. 25) he admits that he had not attempted to actually use the invention of the interference prior to filing his application on July 16, 1921. This is also verified by the testimony of Garity on page 41, Q. 20, page 47, X Q. 52, and page 48, X Q. 55.

De Forest has failed to prove conception prior to his filing date and even if he had he has not established the diligence required of him.

The decision of the Examiner of Interferences is affirmed.

> WM. A. KINNAN,
> *First Assistant Commissioner,*
> FRANK C. SKINNER,
> > *Examiner-in-Chief,*
> G. R. IDE,
> > *Examiner-in-Chief.*
> > *Board of Appeals.*

Notice of Appeal to Court of Appeals, February 24, 1930.

And now comes Lee De Forest, by Darby & Darby, his attorneys, and gives notice to the Commissioner of Patents of his appeal to the United States Court of Customs and Patent Appeals from the decision of the Board of Appeals rendered on or about January 7, 1930, awarding priority of invention to Vogt, Massolle and Engl in the above entitled case, and assigns as his reason for the appeal the following:

1. The Board of Appeals erred in awarding priority of invention to Vogt et al.

2. The Board of Appeals erred in failing to award priority of invention to Lee De Forest.

3. The Board of Appeals erred in holding in effect that Lee De Forest failed to prove conception prior to his filing date.

4. The Board of Appeals erred in holding in effect that De Forest had not established diligence.

5. The Board of Appeals erred in holding that De Forest was required to establish diligence.

> LEE DE FOREST,
> By DARBY & DARBY,
> *His Attorneys.*

Dated: New York, N. Y., February 21, 1930.

Indorsed: United States Court of Customs and Patent Appeals. Filed Apr. 9, 1930. Arthur B. Shelton, Clerk.

One. The Invention of the Phonograph

1 John Cain, *Talking Machines* (London: Methuen, 1961), p.14.
2 Count du Moncel, *The Telephone, the Microphone and the Phonograph* (New York: Harper & Brothers, 1879), p.235.
3 Cain, pp.15–16.
4 The French text of the document by Cros is to be found in Charles Cros, *Oeuvres Complets* (Paris: J-J. Pauvert, 1964), pp.523–524. See also the commentary on pp.626–627. A translation of the Cros document is included as a long footnote in the Count du Moncel's book see n.2 above), p.236. For a fuller account of Cros and the Paléophone, see Louis Forestier, *Charles Cros: L'homme et l'oeuvre* (Paris: Lettres Modernes, Minard, 1969), pp.155–165.
5 V. K. Chew, *Talking Machines 1877–1914* (London: Her Majesty's Stationery Office, 1967), p.5.
6 Frank Lewis Dyer, Thomas Commerford Martin, and William Henry Meadowcroft, *Edison: His Life and Inventions*, 2 vols. (New York and London: Harper & Brothers, 1929), vol. 1, pp.207–208.
7 Chew, p.2. The writer provides a sketch of the proposed telephone repeater.
8 Ibid., p.3.
9 Gordon Hendricks, *The Edison Motion Picture Myth* (Berkeley and Los Angeles: University of California Press, 1961), p.2. (Hereinafter referred to as Hendricks, *Myth*.)
10 André Bazin, "The Myth of Total Cinema," in *What is Cinema?* (Berkeley and Los Angeles: University of California Press, 1967), p.21.
11 *Nature,* January 24, 1878, p.242.
12 Martin Quigley, Jr., *Magic Shadows* (Washington, D.C.: Georgetown University Press, 1948), pp.140–141.
13 Chew, pp.10–12.
14 See Dyer, et al., vol.II, pp.992–994, for a detailed list of patents for this period of Edison's career.
15 See Chew, pp.14–24; and C. A. Schicke, *Revolution in Sound* (Boston: Little, Brown, 1974), pp.16–38.
16 W. K. L. Dickson, "A Brief History of the Kinetograph, the Kinetoscope and the Kineto-phonograph," originally published in *Journal of the Society of Motion Picture and Television Engineers,* December 1933; reprinted in Raymond Fielding, ed., *A Technological History of Motion Pictures and Television* (Berkeley and Los Angeles: University

of California Press, 1967), pp.9–10. (Hereinafter referred to as Dickson, "Brief History." Page references are to the 1967 reprint.)

17 W. K. L. and Antonia Dickson, *History of the Kinetograph, Kinetoscope and Kinetophonograph* (New York: Albert Bunn, 1895). The edition used here is the facsimile reprint by Arno Press and the *New York Times,* 1970, in which Edison's letter appears on p.[4.]. (Hereinafter referred to as Dicksons, *Kinetograph.*)

18 Hendricks, *Myth,* p.10.

19 Quoted, ibid., p.12. See also the reprint, Eadweard Muybridge, *Animals in Motion,* edited by Lewis S. Brown (New York: Dover Books, 1970, p.16).

20 Hendricks, *Myth,* p.12.

21 Ibid., p.11.

22 Gordon Hendricks, *The Kinetoscope* (New York: The Beginnings of the American Film, 1966), p.118.

23 D. B. Thomas, *The Origins of the Motion Picture* (London: Her Majesty's Stationery Office, 1964), p.17.

24 Terry Ramsaye, *A Million and One Nights,* reprint ed. (New York: Simon and Schuster, 1964), p.36.

25 See Muybridge, *Animals in Motion.*

26 Both were optical devices utilizing the principle of persistence of vision. The Zoetrope was a rotating drum lined with pictures showing separate phases of an action or movement; the pictures were viewed through vertical slits along the side of drum. The Zoöpraxiscope, invented by Muybridge, was a more complex device for projecting successive photographs so that they could be viewed by an audience. Illustrations of both devices may be seen in C. W. Ceram, *Archaeology of the Cinema* (New York: Harcourt Brace and Co., n.d.).

27 Dicksons, *Kinetograph,* p.6.

28 Quigley, p.134.

29 Dickson, "Brief History," p.13. See also Dicksons, *Kinetograph,* p.19.

30 Hendricks, *Myth,* p.8on.

31 Ibid.

32 Ibid, p.80.

33 Ibid, p.81.

34 Raymond Spottiswoode, ed., *The Focal Encylopedia of Film and Television Techniques* (New York: Hastings House, 1969), p.318.

35 Hendricks, *Myth,* p.163.

36 Ibid., p.141.

37 See *Science,* July 1893; Hendricks, *Myth,* chap. 15; and Hendricks, *The Kinetoscope,* p.41.

38 Hendricks, *The Kinetoscope,* p.41.

39 Ibid., p.37.

40 Ibid., p.23.

41 See *Electrical World,* June 16, 1894, pp.799–801.

42 Ibid., p.125.

43   Quigley, p.144.

44   G. Demeny, "Les Photographies Parlantes," *La Nature* (Paris), pt.1, pp.311–315. See also Kenneth Macgowan, *Behind the Screen* (New York: Delacorte Press, 1965), p.276.

45   Quigley, p.146.

46   Ray Allister, *Friese-Greene: Close-Up of an Inventor* (London: Marsland Publications, 1948), p.53.

47   Ibid., pp.54–55.

48   Ramsaye, p.95.

49   Ibid., pp.98–99.

50   On the Lumière program, see Georges Sadoul, *Louis Lumière,* Cinéma d'Aujourd'hui series, no.29 (Paris: Editions Seghers, 1964).

51   Quigley, p.58.

Two. The Application of the Phonograph

1   See George Donald Pasquella, "An Investigation in the Use of Sound in American Motion Picture Exhibition, 1908–1919" (dissertation, University of Iowa, 1968), p.59.

2   Much valuable information on the creation and use of sound effects during the so-called silent period is contained in chap. IV, ibid., to which the foregoing paragraph is indebted.

3   H. F. Hoffman, "Drums and Taps," *Moving Picture World,* July 23, 1910, p.185.

4   "Sound Effects: Good, Bad and Indifferent," *Moving Picture World,* October 2, 1909, p.441.

5   W. Stephen Bush, "When Effects are Unnecessary Noises," *Moving Picture World,* September 9, 1911, p.690.

6   Terry Ramsaye, *A Million and One Nights,* reprint ed. (New York: Simon and Schuster, 1964), pp.75, 312–14.

7   *Moving Picture World,* October 2, 1909, p.441.

8   Clyde Martin, "Working the Sound Effects," *Moving Picture World,* September 23, 1911, p.873.

9   According to Roger Manvell and John Huntley, *The Technique of Film Music* (London and New York: Focal Press, 1957), p.17.

10   George W. Beynon, *Musical Presentation of Motion Pictures* (New York and Boston: G. Schirmer, 1921), pp.5–6.

11   Ibid., pp.4–5.

12   *Moving Picture World,* July 23, 1910, p.184.

13   Pasquella, p.25.

14   Ibid., p.11.

15   Beynon, p.6. See further: John W. Landon, "Long Live the Mighty Wurlitzer," *Journal of Popular Film* II, no.1 (Winter 1973), pp.3–13; Reginald Foort, *The Cinema Organ,* 2d ed. (New York: The Vestal Press, 1970).

16   Pasquella, p.16.
17   Good examples of cue sheets are to be found in Charles Hofmann's *Sounds for Silents* (New York: DBS Publications, 1970) and in Manvell and Huntley. Max Winkler claims to have invented the cue sheets: see James L. Limbacher, *Film Music from Violins to Video* (Metuchen, N. J.: Scarecrow Press, 1974), pp.15–24.
18   Pasquella, p.11.
19   *The Birth of a Nation* score is analyzed and discussed at length in Seymour Stern, "Griffith:I The Birth of a Nation," *Film Culture* (special Griffith issue), Spring-Summer, 1965, pp.114–132. A. Nicolas Vardac, *Stage to Screen* (New York: Benjamin Blom, 1968), p.209, reprints the titles of the pastiche selection for Griffith's *Judith of Bethulia* (1913) and the specific cues.
20   Manvell and Huntley, pp.17–18.
21   Joseph L. Anderson and Donald Richie, *The Japanese Film* (New York: Grove Press, 1959), pp.24–25.
22   W. Stephen Bush, "The Added Attraction: Article 11," *Moving Picture World*, November 25, 1911.
23   "The Baroness Blanc Talks About Talking Pictures," *Moving Picture World*, January 28, 1911, p.186.
24   Carl Herbert, "The Truth About Talking Pictures," *Moving Picture World*, March 20, 1909, p.327.
25   Pasquella, pp.58–59. A picture of a theater advertising Humanuva Talking Pictures ("Uncle Tom's Cabin in Talking Pictures") appears in Ben M. Hall, *The Best Remaining Seats* (New York: Bramhall House, 1961), p.243.
26   On these three methods see further David Sherill Hulfish, *Motion Picture Work* (Chicago: American Technical Society, 1915), pt.I, pp.245–255.
27   *Times* (London), May 11, 1912.
28   See further, Frederick A. Talbot, *Moving Pictures* (Philadelphia: J. B. Lippincott, 1912), p.186.
29   See *Film Daily*, February 24 through July 26, 1929.
30   The accounts of the French inventors and their work are based mainly on information in G.-Michael Coissac, *Histoire du Cinématographe* (Paris: Editions du 'Cinéopse,' 1925), pp.328–337; Georges Sadoul, *Histoire Générale du Cinéma* (Paris: Editions Denöel, 1948), II, pp.100–118; Rene Jeanne and Charles Ford, *Histoire Encyclopédique du Cinéma* (Paris: R. Laffont, 1958), IV, pp.13–23; and Jacques Deslandes and Jacques Richard, *Histoire Comparée du Cinéma* (Paris, Tournai: Casterman, 1968), II, pp.59–79.
31   Coissac, p.328.
32   See Sadoul, p.485.
33   Ibid., p.266.
34   Jeanne and Ford, p.15.
35   Ibid., p.16.

36 Quoted by Sadoul, p.112.

37 *Le Figaro,* Paris, September 9, 1900.

38 Quoted by Deslandes and Richard, p.69.

39 Quoted by Sadoul, p.114.

40 Ibid., p.114. On the recovery of the films and cylinders, see also H. Cossira, "La Resurrection des Premiers Films Parlants de 1900," *L'Illustration,* Paris, April 1, 1933, p.395.

41 Quoted in Marcel Lapierre, ed., *Anthologie du Cinéma* (Paris: Bibliothèque du Cinéma, 1946), p.217.

42 Talbot, pp.184–185.

43 See further, *Moving Picture World,* March 28, 1908, p.263; *Scientific American,* June 14, 1913, p.539.

44 *Times* (London), May 11, 1912; *Scientific American,* June 14, 1913, p.539.

45 *Times* (London), June 24, 1922.

46 Quoted in Lapierre, p.218.

47 On early sound films in Germany, see in addition to Messter's book, Roger Manvell and Heinrich Fraenkel, *The German Cinema* (New York: Praeger, 1971), pp.1–7 (from which much of my factual material on German sound-on-disk is derived); and Rudolf Oertel, *Filmspiegel: Ein Brevier aus der Welt des Films* (Vienna: W. Frick, 1943), pp.169–195.

48 Jeanne and Ford, pp.20–21.

49 Ray Allister, *Friese-Greene: Close-Up of an Inventor* (London: Marsland Publications, 1948), p.53.

50 Ibid., pp.53–54.

51 Garry Alligham, *The Romance of the Talkies* (London: Claude Stacey, 1929), p.14.

52 Rachel Low, *The History of the British Film 1906–1914* (London: Allen and Unwin, 1949), p.265.

53 Alligham, p.15.

54 See Low, pp.265–266 for more details.

55 Ibid., p.266.

56 *Times* (London), February 9, 1920.

57 *Moving Picture World,* April 25, 1908, pp.369–370.

58 See further, ibid., January 16, 1909.

59 On Valiquet's Photophone, see *Scientific American,* April 25, 1908, p.292; on Greenbaum's Synchroscope, see John Drinkwater, *The Life and Adventures of Carl Laemmle* (New York: G. P. Putnam's Sons, 1931), pp.166–167; on the Vitagraph device, see announcement in *Moving Picture World,* December 19, 1908, p.498; on Cinephone in the U. S., see ibid., March 13, 1909, p.299; on Orlando Kellum's Talking Picture Company, see Albert Marples, "Combining the Phonograph and the Camera," *Scientific American,* September 17, 1914, p.208; and Louis J. Stellman, "He Makes the Movies Talk," *Sunset Magazine,* August 1925, p.52. On talking and singing pictures generally in the

U. S. c.1913-14, see Robert Grau, *Theatre of Science* (New York and London: Broadway Publishing Co., 1914), pp.348-357.

60   Robert Grau, "The 'Talking' Picture and the Drama," *Scientific American,* August 12, 1911, p.155.

61   Isaac F. Marcosson, "The Coming of the Talking Picture," *Munsey's Magazine,* March 1913, pp.957-958.

62   Eddie O'Connor, "When the Movies Married the Phonograph," *Equity,* May 1929, p.30.

63   Ibid., p.15.

64   Ibid., p.16.

65   Marcosson, pp.959-960. On Edison and the 1913 Kinetophone, see also Robert Grau, "Talking Pictures a Reality," *Lippincott's Magazine,* August 1913, pp.191-194; "Moving and Talking Pictures," *Scientific American,* January 18, 1913, pp.64, 78.

66   Iris Barry, *D. W. Griffith: American Film Master* (New York: Museum of Modern Art, 1965), pp.67, 81. See also the *Times* (London), March 4, 1920, for a note on a 1920 American "talkie" starring Sir Harry Lauder.

67   *Times* (London), June 6, 1921.

Three: Sound-on-Film: Fritts to De Forest

1   *Moving Picture World,* March 26, 1927, pp.343-345.

2   *Film Daily,* August 28, 1929.

3   See further the *Times* (London), October 13, 1923.

4   Earl Thiesen, "The History of Sound Pictures," *International Photographer,* April 1933, p.2.

5   See further "Films that Talk," *Literary Digest,* December 3, 1921, pp. 20-21; A. O. Rankine, "Speaking Films," *Nature,* October 27, 1921, p.276.

6   *Moving Picture World,* March 26, 1927, pp.343-345; Garry Alligham, *The Romance of the Talkies* (London: Claude Stacey, 1929), p.13.

7   Ernst Rühmer, *Wireless Telephony in Theory and Practice* (London: Crosby Lockwood and Son, 1908), pp.20, 31.

8   See Merritt Crawford, "Eugene Augustin Lauste, Father of the Sound Film—A Recognition," *International Photographer Bulletin,* August 1929, pp.3, 13, 18; also the same author's "Pioneer Experiments of Eugene Lauste in Recording Sound," in Raymond Fielding, ed., *A Technological History of Motion Pictures and Television* (Berkeley and Los Angeles: University of California Press, 1967), pp.71-75.

9   On Ries see Lee De Forest, "Pioneering in Talking Pictures," *American Cinematographer,* April 1941, pp.164, 201-202.

10   *Kinematograph Year Book* (London, 1915), p.37, as quoted by Rachel Low, *The History of the British Film 1906-1914* (London: Allen and Unwin, 1949), p.267.

11   *Scientific American,* January 1923, p.19.

12 Main sources of information on Tykociner are John B. McCullough, "Joseph T. Tykociner: Pioneer in Sound Recording" and Joseph E. Aiken, "Technical Notes and Reminiscences on the Presentation of Tykociner's Sound Picture Contributions," both in Fielding; and R. A. Kingery, R. D. Berg, and E. H. Schillinger, *Men and Ideas in Engineering* (Urbana: University of Illinois Press, 1967). Tykociner's date of birth is given as 1867 in Kingery et al. and 1877 in McCullough.

13 Kingery et al., p.23.

14 Ibid., p.24.

15 Ibid., p.26.

16 Joseph E. Aiken, in Fielding, p.222.

17 Ibid.

18 Kingery et al., pp.19–20.

19 Ibid., p.21.

20 Quoted, ibid., p.30.

21 "Mr. Hoxie's Talking Film," *Literary Digest,* December 9, 1927, p.26; "Pictures that Talk," *Scientific American,* January 1923, pp.19, 71.

22 Fielding, p.183.

23 *Times* (London), September 28, 1921.

24 Ibid., February 19, 1921 and September 28, 1921.

25 Facts on Tri-Ergon derived from René Jeanne and Charles Ford, *Histoire Encyclopédique du Cinéma* (Paris: R. Laffont, 1958), IV, p.21.

26 The Fox story is told in elaborate detail up to 1932 in *Upton Sinclair Presents William Fox* (Los Angeles: Sinclair Press, 1933); the story is completed in less detail in Glendon Allvine, *The Greatest Fox of Them All* (New York: Lyle Stuart, 1969).

27 Lee De Forest, *Father of Radio: The Autobiography of Lee De Forest* (Chicago: Wilcox and Follett, 1950), p.359.

28 Quoted in "Dr. De Forest's Talking Film," *Literary Digest,* September 16, 1922, pp.28–29.

29 The account here is based on the more detailed description in Lee De Forest, "When Light Speaks," *Scientific American,* August 1923, p.94.

30 Maurice H. Zouary, "The New History of Motion Picture Sound, Part II," *I. A. T. S. E. Official Bulletin,* Summer 1970, p.27.

31 *Father of Radio,* p.361.

32 Ibid., pp.365–366.

33 Quoted in Georgette Carneal, *A Conqueror of Space: An Authorized Biography of the Life and Work of Lee De Forest* (New York: Horace Liveright, 1930), pp.283, 284.

34 Quoted, ibid., p.283.

35 See further, *Father of Radio,* p.370.

36 Ibid.

37 Ibid., p.371.

38 Carneal, p.285.

39 *Spectator* (London), June 7, 1924, p.915.

40 *Times* (London), November 29, 1924.

41 *Father of Radio,* p.387.

42 Lee De Forest, "Pioneering in Talking Pictures," *American Cinematographer,* April 1941, p.201.

43 Ibid.

44 *Father of Radio,* pp.388–389.

45 Carneal, p.286.

46 As in his *American Cinematographer* article, see n.42.

47 *Father of Radio,* p.389.

48 Ibid., p.388.

49 De Forest, "Pioneering in Talking Pictures," p.201.

50 Zouary, p.27.

51 E. S. Gregg, *Shadow of Sound* (New York: Vantage Press, 1968), p.14.

52 See Fielding, p.78.

53 Carneal, p.288.

54 Ibid., pp.288–289.

Four: The Voice of Vitaphone

1 Edward W. Kellogg, "History of Sound Motion Pictures," in Raymond Fielding, ed., *A Technological History of Motion Pictures and Television* (Berkeley and Los Angeles: University of California Press, 1967), p.179.

2 Ibid., p.180.

3 "Development of Talking Films," *Film Daily Yearbook of Motion Pictures, 1927* (New York, 1928), p.184.

4 Fitzhugh Green, *The Film Finds Its Tongue* (New York and London: G. P. Putnam's Sons, 1929), p.163.

5 "Development of Talking Films," p.184.

6 E. S. Gregg, *Shadow of Sound* (New York: Vantage Press, 1968), p.14.

7 Jack L. Warner, *My First Hundred Years in Hollywood* (New York: Random House, 1965), p.166.

8 Gregg, p.15.

9 Ibid., p.46.

10 Warner, p.167.

11 Green, p.49.

12 Joseph P. Kennedy, *The Story of the Films* (Chicago and New York: A. W. Shaw Co., 1927), p.319.

13 Green, p.50.

14 Ibid., p.53.

15 Frederick Thrasher, *Okay for Sound* (New York: Duell, Sloan and Pearce, 1946), p.46.

16 Ibid., pp.68–69.

17 Ibid., p.69. See also still from the film, p.69.

18 Kennedy, p.319.

19 Thrasher, p.46.

20 Green, p.158.

21 Ibid., pp.166–167.

22 Ibid., pp.166–167. Green does not discuss methods for dealing with undesired sound effects created by actors' costumes—the rustle of silk, the slither of satin, the click-click of necklaces, the squeak of shoes—which were often amplified and distorted in early sound recording systems. For a discussion of how H. M. K. Smith, costume director of Paramount-Famous-Lasky, dealt with this problem at his studio during 1928, see *New York Times,* September 9, 1928, IX, p.5. Smith observed, "The scenario of the future will contain a carefully prepared sound score in which the sound made by garments and jewels will have a definite place." The clothes and jewels problem is amusingly satirized in the film *Singin' in the Rain* (1952).

23 B. Brown, *Talking Pictures* (London: Sir Isaac Pitman and Sons, 1933), p.46.

24 Harold B. Franklin, *Sound Motion Pictures* (Garden City, N. Y.: Doubleday, Doran and Co., 1929), pp.45–46.

25 Quoted by Colby Harriman in "The Vitaphone as a Presentation Feature," *Moving Picture World,* August 28, 1926, p.555.

26 *Moving Picture World,* August 14, 1926, p.1.

27 Ibid.

28 Kennedy, p.323.

29 Ibid., p.330–331.

30 *Kinematograph Weekly* (London), July 15, 1926, p.32.

31 Will H. Hays, *See and Hear* (New York: Motion Picture Producers and Distributors of America, 1929), pp.48–49.

32 Abel Green and Joe Laurie, Jr., *Show Biz from Vaude to Video* (New York: Henry Holt, 1951), p.265.

33 *New York Times,* August 7, 1926.

34 *Moving Picture World,* August 14, 1926, p.7.

35 Paul Rotha and Richard Griffith, *The Film Till Now* (London: Spring Books, 1967), p.429.

36 "The Vitaphone: An Appraisal," *Moving Picture World,* August 14, 1926, p.7.

37 Kennedy, p.332.

38 *Moving Picture World,* August 14, 1926, p.7.

39 *New York Times,* August 7, 1926.

40 *Moving Picture World,* August 14, 1926, p.7.

41 James Agate, the eminent theater critic of the London *Times* did not see the Martinelli film until October 1928, but he immediately reacted to it as a development of great significance:

> This seems to me to solve the difficulties of opera in this country [England]. There is no reason why Middlesbrough, Peebles and Rochdale should not, if they want them, have their performances of *The Ring*. Visually operas performed in this way will be very nearly as good as, and sometimes better than, the real thing. The

last time I heard *Salomé* at Covent Garden I paid eighteen shillings for a seat in the gallery *from which I could not see one-fourth of the stage*, whereas at the Piccadilly Theatre I saw the whole of Signor Martinelli. Here let me suggest that the performance on the Vita-phone was better than any flesh-and-blood performance which any small town is ever likely to get—if indeed it gets any operatic per-formance at all. Here also is the place to say that as accompaniment to the silent picture the Vitaphone, while immeasurably inferior to orchestras such as those at the Tivoli, the Marble Arch Pavilion, and the best provincial houses, is certainly a great deal better than the small, inefficient, picture-palace band. [James Agate, *Around Cinemas* (London: Home and Van Thal, 1946), p.27.]

42 Both scores have been recorded: Lavagnino's on United Artists disk UAL 4031; Previn's on MGM disk S 3993. A few bars of the *Don Juan* theme music are recorded as the opening selection on side one of *Fifty Years of Film* (Warner Bros. Record 3XX 2737.).

43 The "love" theme was turned into a song entitled "Don Juan," which was published as part of the promotional campaign for the film. The sheet music indicates that the lyrics were by Harry Lee and the music by William Axt. It also states that the song was originally sung by Anna Case and was the "theme song" of the Warner Bros. film. How-ever, there is no evidence that Anna Case (or anyone else) sang it in the program or in a live performance at the premiere—let alone in *Don Juan* itself. The lyrics are hardly relevant to the story of Juan and Adriana:

> Don Juan—when the vows are all broken
> Will you leave no token
> Of the love that is flame now?
> Don Juan—when the flames are but embers
> In the dark love remembers—
> Love remembers but you. . . .

44 *New York Times,* November 13, 1923.

Five. "You Ain't Heard Nothin' Yet!"

1 Abel Green and Joe Laurie, Jr., *Show Biz from Vaude to Video* (New York: Henry Holt, 1951), p.265.

2 *New York Times,* October 8, 1926.

3 *Moving Picture World,* November 29, 1926.

4 *New York Times,* October 8, 1926.

5 Ibid.

6 *Moving Picture World,* October 9, 1926.

7 *New York Times,* February 4, 1927.

8 Ibid.

9 Fitzhugh Green, *The Film Finds Its Tongue* (New York and London: G. P. Putnam's Sons, 1929), pp.79–81.

10 *Moving Picture World,* February 19, 1927.

11 Ibid., January 8, 1927.

12 Quoted in Joseph P. Kennedy, *The Story of the Films* (Chicago and New York: A. W. Shaw Co., 1927), p.333.

13 *Moving Picture World,* January 8, 1927.

14 Green, p.78.

15 Rachel Low, *The History of the British Film 1918–1929* (London: Allen and Unwin, 1971), p.202.

16 *Moving Picture World,* January 29, 1927.

17 Ibid., March 12, 1927.

18 Ibid.

19 Ibid., December 24, 1927.

20 Ibid., March 26, 1927.

21 Gertrude Jobes, *Motion Picture Empire* (Hamden Conn.: Archon Books, 1966), p.263.

22 *Moving Picture World,* May 21, 1927.

23 Green, p.215.

24 Ibid., p.186.

25 *Moving Picture World,* June 4, 1927.

26 Green, p.186.

27 Ibid., p.187.

28 *Moving Picture World,* June 4, 1927.

29 Green, p.189.

30 *Moving Picture World,* October 8, 1927.

31 *New York Times,* June 22, 1927.

32 Green, pp.195–198.

33 Frederick Thrasher, *Okay for Sound* (New York: Duell, Sloan and Pearce, 1946), p.69.

34 Alexander Walker, *Stardom* (New York: Stein and Day, 1970), p.220.

35 Ibid.

36 See further, Michael Freedland, *Jolson* (New York: Stein and Day, 1972), p.72; Dave Jay, *Jolsonography* (Washington, D. C.: Big Time Press, n.d.), passim.

37 D. W. Griffith, "The Movies 100 Years from Now," reprinted in Harry M. Geduld, *Film Makers on Film Making* (Bloomington: Indiana University Press, 1967).

38 *Moving Picture World,* June 4, 1927.

39 Pearl Sieben, *The Immortal Jolson* (New York: Frederick Fell, 1962), p.118.

40 Walker, pp.20–21.

41 Freedland, pp.114–115.

42 Leo Guild, *Zanuck: Hollywood's Last Tycoon* (Los Angeles: Holloway House, 1970), pp.40–41.

43 Quoted in Hal C. Herman, *How I Broke into the Movies* (Hollywood, Cal.: privately published, 1930).

44 *Moving Picture World,* May 28, 1927.

45   Ibid., August 20, 1927.

46   Green, pp.206–207.

47   *Moving Picture World*, October 1, 1927.

48   The first disk to be released was a recording of the song "Mother O'Mine" (Brunswick 3719), which went on sale concurrently with the film's premiere. The next phonograph recordings, "My Mammy" (Brunswick 3912) and "Dirty Hands, Dirty Face" (Brunswick 3790), were not released until the fall of 1928.

49   Harry Jolson and Alban Emley, *Mistah Jolson* (Hollywood, Cal.: House-Warven, 1951), p.180.

50   The essay is included in Aldous Huxley, *Do What You Will* (New York: Harper and Row, 1929).

51   Walker, pp.221–222.

52   Robert E. Sherwood, in *The Silent Drama*, October 27, 1927, p.24.

53   Lewis Jacobs, *The Rise of the American Film* (New York: Teachers College Press, 1967), p.298.

54   Paul Rotha and Richard Griffith, *Film Till Now* (London: Spring Books, 1967), p.429.

55   David Robinson, *The History of World Cinema* (New York: Stein and Day, 1973), p.163.

56   Gerald Mast, *A Short History of the Movies* (Indianapolis: Pegasus, 1971), p.229.

57   Sherwood, p.24.

58   See, for example, the copy of the screenplay in the archives of the British Film Institute. None of the other copies examined showed additional directions for the use of Vitaphone.

59   Alexander Walker, after noting James Agate's contemporary impression of Eugenie Besserer's mumbling as an illusion that was "perfect and unmannered," comments:

> Eugenie Besserer was simply poorly recorded and her few, probably improvised interpolations into the middle of Al's spiel would in any case lack the sock-it-over impact of the vaudeville man's technique. But the effect she makes is indisputably more naturalistic; and this was the hardest lesson that the silent stars had to master when they took to sound. So long as the voice took priority in a performance, the naturalness of the acting was bound to suffer. [*Stardom*, p.223.]

The present writer does *not* find Eugenie Besserer "indisputably more naturalistic" than Jolson. It is the latter who seems naturalistic; Besserer comes across as bewildered—even embarrassed—at finding herself little more than a puppet in a scene in which Jolson is perfectly at ease because he is, in effect, creating it in spite of her.

60   Walker, p.221.

61   *New York Herald Tribune*, October 7, 1927.

62   *Moving Picture World*, October 22, 1927.

63 *Los Angeles Times,* December 19, 1933 (italics mine, H. M. G.).

64 *Today's Cinema,* January 24, 1935.

65 By ironic coincidence, William Demarest, who appeared in a very minor role in *The Jazz Singer,* was given one of the more important roles in *The Jolson Story*—that of Steve Martin, the vaudevillian who first "discovers" the boy Jolson and later becomes his business manager.

66 Green and Laurie, p.263.

67 *New York Times,* January 14, 1953.

Six: *Lights of New York* and Sounds of Hollywood

1 The statistics are from E. I. Sponable, "Historical Development of Sound Films," *Journal of the Society of Motion Picture Engineers,* April 1947, pp.275–303; May 1947, pp.407–422.

2 Fitzhugh Green, *The Film Finds Its Tongue* (New York and London, G. P. Putnam's Sons, 1929), pp.189, 199, 213–214.

3 *New York Times,* March 15, 1927.

4 Green, p.214.

5 *New York Times,* April 27, 1928.

6 William C. DeMille, *Hollywood Saga* (New York: E. P. Dutton, 1939), pp.268–270.

7 *New York Times,* June 16, 1928.

8 Mel Gussow, *Don't Say Yes until I Finish Talking* (New York: Pocket Books, 1972), p.42.

9 Lewis Jacobs, *The Rise of the American Film* (New York: Harcourt, Brace and Co., 1939), p.435. Jacobs continues: "The pacing of the scenes also was unduly slow because of the adjustment that had to be made in the speed of the camera. . . ." See further pp.435–436.

10 Clara Bow, the phenomenally popular "It" girl, was among the silent screen stars who felt seriously constrained by the new impositions of the sound studio. Adolph Zukor notes that "the unrestrained vitality which had been her greatest asset now was a curious handicap. . . . Clara was too restless. She would be all over the set, and then, realizing that the microphone was not picking up her voice, would sometimes stand and curse it." Adolph Zukor, *The Public Is Never Wrong* (New York: G. P. Putnam's Sons, 1953), p.255.

11 As Darryl F. Zanuck was later to recall, "Microphones had to be hidden. Every telephone had a microphone in it. We hid them in the chandeliers. We would hang microphones on the wall, the same color as the wall. The cameramen went out of their minds trying to keep the microphones out of the picture." Quoted in Gussow, pp.41–42.

12 *New York Times,* July 9, 1928.

13 *Exhibitors' Herald and Moving Picture World,* July 21, 1928, p. 22.

14 Ibid., July 14, 1928, p.14.

15 Ibid., July 14, 1928, p.19.

16 *New York Times,* July 9, 1928.

17 Stephen Louis Karpf, *The Gangster Film* (New York: Arno Press, 1973), pp.39–40.
18 *New York Times,* August 16, 1928.
19 Ibid.
20 Rachel Low, *The History of the British Film 1918–1929* (London: Allen and Unwin, 1971), p.203.
21 *New York Times,* September 20, 1928.
22 Ibid.
23 Harry Jolson and Alban Emley, *Mistah Jolson* (Hollywood, Cal.: House-Warven, 1951), pp.180–181.
24 *Harrison's Reports* (New York) X, no.3, October 27, 1928.
25 *New York Times,* December 3, 1928.
26 Charles Higham, *Ziegfeld* (Chicago: Henry Regnery Co., 1972), pp.144–145.
27 Gertrude Jobes, *Motion Picture Empire* (Hamden, Conn.: Archon Books, 1966), p.275.
28 See further, I. Witmark and I. Goldberg, *From Ragtime to Swingtime* (New York: Lee Furnam, Inc., 1939), p.426; and Jack Burton, *The Blue Book of Hollywood Musicals* (New York: Century House, 1953), p.11. On general links between Tin Pan Alley and Hollywood see Ian Whitcomb, *After the Ball* (Baltimore, Md.: Penguin Books, 1974), pp.117–123.
29 E. S. Gregg, *Shadow of Sound* (New York: Vantage Press, 1968), pp. 39–40.
30 Jobes, p.267.
31 Gregg, p.41.
32 *New York Times,* May 16, 1928.
33 Ibid., July 8, 1928, III, p.1.
34 Ibid., December 5, 1928.
35 Ibid., August 5, 1928, VII, p.4.
36 Ibid., May 5, 1928.
37 Ibid., July 29, 1928, VII, p.3.
38 Ibid., July 29, 1928, VII, p.4.
39 Ibid., August 5, 1928, VII, p.4.
40 Ibid., August 22, 1928.
41 Ibid., July 8, 1928, VIII, p.2.
42 Ibid., October 21, 1928, IX, p.6.
43 Harold B. Franklin, *Sound Motion Pictures* (Garden City, N. Y.: Doubleday, Doran & Co., 1929), pp.47–57.
44 Raymond Fielding, ed., *A Technological History of Motion Pictures and Television* (Berkeley and Los Angeles: University of California Press, 1967), p.184.
45 Maurice H. Zouary, *I. A. T. S. E. Official Bulletin,* Fall 1970, p.34.
46 Edward W. Kellogg, "The History of Sound Motion Pictures," *Journal of the Society of Motion Picture and Television Engineers,* July 1955.
47 *Exhibitors' Herald and Moving Picture World,* July 14, 1928, p.32.

48 Ibid.

49 *New York Times*, May 15, 1928.

50 *Film Daily Yearbook of Motion Pictures, 1927*, p.814.

51 *Exhibitors' Herald and Moving Picture World*, July 14, 1928, p.32.

52 *New York Times*, October 4, 1928.

53 *Film Daily Yearbook of Motion Pictures, 1927* (New York, 1928), p.814.

54 *Exhibitors' Herald and Motion Picture World*, December 3, 1927.

55 *New York Times*, April 9, 1928.

56 Ibid., February 14, 1928, p.27.

57 Colleen Moore, *Silent Star* (Garden City, N. Y.: Doubleday, 1968), p.186.

58 *New York Times*, August 6, 1928.

59 Ibid., December 27, 1928.

60 Herman G. Weinberg, *The Lubitsch Touch* (New York: E. P. Dutton, 1968), p.320.

61 According to Marjorie Rosen (presumably basing her claim on information received from Dorothy Arzner herself), it was Arzner who "improvised the first moving microphone by insisting that sound technicians at Paramount attach a mike to a fishing pole balanced on a ladder and thus follow Clara Bow about the sound stages in *The Wild Party* [1929]." M. Rosen, *Popcorn Venus* (New York: Coward, McCann and Geoghegan, 1973), p.377.

62 *New York Times*, November 11, 1928, X, p.6.

63 William K. Everson, *The Detective in Film* (Secaucus, N. J.: The Citadel Press, 1972), pp.52–53.

64 *New York Times*, November 17, 1928.

65 Frank Capra, *The Name above the Title* (New York: The Macmillan Co., 1971), p.99.

66 *New York Times*, August 1, 1928.

67 Iris Barry, *D. W. Griffith: American Film Master* (New York: Museum of Modern Art, 1965), p.81.

68 Christopher Finch, *The Art of Walt Disney* (New York: Harry N. Abrams, 1973), pp.50, 53.

69 Richard Schickel, *The Disney Version* (New York: Avon Books, 1969), pp. 96–97.

70 Ibid., p.57.

71 Quoted by Finch, p.57.

72 Ibid., p.58.

Seven. The End of the Beginning

1 Except where otherwise indicated, factual material appearing in this chapter is based on *New York Times* news items and feature articles published during 1929.

2 *Monthly Labor Review*, U. S. Bureau of Labor Statistics, August 1931, p.262.

3   Ibid., November 1931, p.1017.

4   *New York Times,* July 28, 1929, III, p.4.

5   See further David Ewen, *George Gershwin: His Journey to Greatness* (Englewood Cliffs, N. J.: Prentice-Hall, 1971), pp.178–180. The Gershwin songs in *Delicious* were "Delishious," "Bla-Bla-Bla," "Somebody from Somewhere," and "Katinkitschka."

6   *New York Times,* June 9, 1929, VIII, p.6.

7   *Monthly Labor Review,* August 1931, p.263.

8   Dennis Sharp, *The Picture Palace* (New York and Washington: Frederick A. Praeger, 1969), p.102.

9   See Sharp, pp.104–148, for an account of developments in moviehouse design during the first years of the sound period.

10   "Talking Films no.3: Tri-Ergon Single-Unit Process," *Wireless World* (London), April 10, 1929, pp.376–378.

11   According to Jay Leyda in *Dianying Electric Shadows: An Account of Films and the Film Audience in China* (Cambridge: MIT Press, 1972), p.64n.

12   William C. DeMille, *Hollywood Saga* (New York: E. P. Dutton, 1939), p.287. DeMille's book contains the best brief account of the effects of the sound revolution on Hollywood.

13   The information about the stellar upheaval is based on Arthur Knight, "All Singing! All Talking! All Laughing!" *Theatre Arts,* September 1949, pp.33–40; and Julian Fox, "Casualties of Sound," *Films and Filming,* October 1972, pp. 34–40, November 1972, pp.32–40.

14   Fox, p.40.

15   Much of the material in this paragraph is based on information in David Shipman, *The Great Movie Stars—The Golden Years* (New York: Crown Publishers, Inc., 1970).

16   See further: Gene Ringold, *The Films of Bette Davis* (New York: Citadel Press, 1971); Clifford McCarty, *Bogey* (New York: Cadillac Publishing Co., 1965); James Robert Parish and Alan H. Marill, *The Cinema of Edward G. Robinson* (South Brunswick and New York: A. S. Barnes, 1972); Edward G. Robinson and Leonard Spigelglass, *All My Yesterdays* (New York: Hawthorn Books, Inc., 1973); Homer Dickens, *The Films of James Cagney* (Secaucus, N. J.: Citadel Press, 1972); Ron Offen, *Cagney* (Chicago: Henry Regnery Co., 1972).

17   "Griffith Turns Prophet," *New York Times* interview, January 27, 1929.